BIT BY BIT

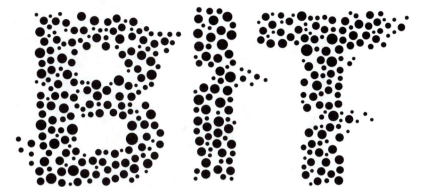

SOCIAL RESEARCH

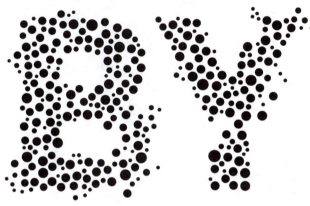

in the DIGITAL AGE

· MATTHEW J. SALGANIK ·

PRINCETON UNIVERSITY PRESS
PRINCETON & OXFORD

Requests for permission to reproduce material from this
work should be sent to Permissions, Princeton University Press

Published by Princeton University Press,
41 William Street, Princeton, New Jersey 08540
In the United Kingdom: Princeton University Press,
6 Oxford Street, Woodstock, Oxfordshire OX20 1TR

press.princeton.edu

Cover design by Amanda Weiss

First paperback printing, 2019
Paperback ISBN 978-0-691-19610-7
Cloth ISBN 978-0-691-15864-8

Library of Congress Control Number: 2017935851

British Library Cataloging-in-Publication Data is available

This book has been composed in Minion Pro and DIN Pro

Printed on acid-free paper. ∞

Typeset by Nova Techset Pvt Ltd, Bangalore, India
Printed in the United States of America

To Amanda

SUMMARY OF CONTENTS

CONTENTS

CHAPTER 5 • **CREATING MASS COLLABORATION**   231

CHAPTER 6 • **ETHICS** 281

CHAPTER 7 • **THE FUTURE** 355

PREFACE

This book began in 2005 in a basement at Columbia University. At the time, I was a graduate student, and I was running an online experiment that would eventually become my dissertation. I'll tell you all about the scientific parts of that experiment in chapter 4, but now I'm going to tell you about something that's not in my dissertation or in any of my papers. And it's something that fundamentally changed how I think about research. One morning, when I came into my basement office, I discovered that overnight about 100 people from Brazil had participated in my experiment. This simple experience had a profound effect on me. At that time, I had friends who were running traditional lab experiments, and I knew how hard they had to work to recruit, supervise, and pay people to participate in these experiments; if they could run 10 people in a single day, that was good progress. However, with my online experiment, 100 people participated *while I was sleeping*. Doing your research while you are sleeping might sound too good to be true, but it isn't. Changes in technology—specifically the transition from the analog age to the digital age—mean that we can now collect and analyze social data in new ways. This book is about doing social research in these new ways.

This book is for social scientists who want to do more data science, data scientists who want to do more social science, and anyone interested in the hybrid of these two fields. Given who this book is for, it should go without saying that it is not just for students and professors. Although I currently work at a university (Princeton), I've also worked in government (at the US Census Bureau) and in the tech industry (at Microsoft Research), so I know that there is a lot of exciting research happening outside of universities. So if you think of what you are doing as social research, then this book is for you, no matter where you work or what kind of techniques you currently use.

As you might have noticed already, the tone of this book is a bit different from that of many other academic books. That's intentional. This book emerged from a graduate seminar on computational social science that I have taught at Princeton in the Department of Sociology since 2007, and

I'd like it to capture some of the energy and excitement from that seminar. In particular, I want this book to have three characteristics: I want it to be helpful, future-oriented, and optimistic.

Helpful: My goal is to write a book that is helpful for you. Therefore, I'm going to write in an open, informal, and example-driven style. That's because the most important thing that I want to convey is a certain way of thinking about social research. And my experience suggests that the best way to convey this way of thinking is informally and with lots of examples. Also, at the end of each chapter, I have a section called "What to read next" that will help you transition into more detailed and technical readings on many of the topics that I introduce. In the end, I hope this book will help you both do research and evaluate the research of others.

Future-oriented: I hope that this book will help you to do social research using the digital systems that exist today *and* those that will be created in the future. I started doing this kind of research in 2004, and since then I've seen many changes, and I'm sure that over the course of your career you will see many changes too. The trick to staying relevant in the face of change is *abstraction*. For example, this is not going to be a book that teaches you exactly how to use the Twitter API as it exists today; instead, it is going to teach you how to learn from big data sources (chapter 2). This is not going to be a book that gives you step-by-step instructions for running experiments on Amazon Mechanical Turk; instead, it is going to teach you how to design and interpret experiments that rely on digital age infrastructure (chapter 4). Through the use of abstraction, I hope this will be a timeless book on a timely topic.

Optimistic: The two communities that this book engages—social scientists and data scientists—have very different backgrounds and interests. In addition to these science-related differences, which I talk about in the book, I've also noticed that these two communities have different styles. Data scientists are generally excited; they tend to see the glass as half full. Social scientists, on the other hand, are generally more critical; they tend to see the glass as half empty. In this book, I'm going to adopt the optimistic tone of a data scientist. So, when I present examples, I'm going to tell you what I love about these examples. And when I do point out problems with the examples—and I will do that because no research is perfect—I'm going to try to point out these problems in a way that is positive and optimistic. I'm not going to be critical for the sake of being critical—I'm going to be critical so that I can help you create better research.

We are still in the early days of social research in the digital age, but I've seen some misunderstandings that are so common that it makes sense for me to address them here, in the preface. From data scientists, I've seen two common misunderstandings. The first is thinking that more data automatically solves problems. However, for social research, that has not been my experience. In fact, for social research, better data—as opposed to more data—seems to be more helpful. The second misunderstanding that I've seen from data scientists is thinking that social science is just a bunch of fancy talk wrapped around common sense. Of course, as a social scientist—more specifically as a sociologist—I don't agree with that. Smart people have been working hard to understand human behavior for a long time, and it seems unwise to ignore the wisdom that has accumulated from this effort. My hope is that this book will offer you some of that wisdom in a way that is easy to understand.

From social scientists, I've also seen two common misunderstandings. First, I've seen some people write off the entire idea of social research using the tools of the digital age because of a few bad papers. If you're reading this book, you've probably already read a bunch of papers that use social media data in ways that are banal or wrong (or both). I have too. However, it would be a serious mistake to conclude from these examples that all digital-age social research is bad. In fact, you've probably also read a bunch of papers that use survey data in ways that are banal or wrong, but you don't write off all research using surveys. That's because you know that there is great research done with survey data, and in this book I'm going to show you that there is also great research done with the tools of the digital age.

The second common misunderstanding that I've seen from social scientists is to confuse the present with the future. When we assess social research in the digital age—the research that I'm going to describe—it's important that we ask two distinct questions: "How well does this style of research work right now?" and "How well will this style of research work in the future?" Researchers are trained to answer the first question, but for this book I think the second question is more important. That is, even though social research in the digital age has not yet produced massive, paradigm-changing intellectual contributions, the rate of improvement in digital-age research is incredibly rapid. It is this rate of change—more than the current level—that makes digital-age research so exciting to me.

Even though that last paragraph might seem to offer you potential riches at some unspecified time in the future, my goal is not to sell you on any particular type of research. I don't personally own shares in Twitter, Facebook, Google, Microsoft, Apple, or any other tech company (although, for the sake of full disclosure, I should mention that I have worked at, or received research funding from, Microsoft, Google, and Facebook). Throughout the book, therefore, my goal is to remain a credible narrator, telling you about all the exciting new stuff that is possible, while guiding you away from a few traps that I've seen others fall into (and occasionally fallen into myself).

The intersection of social science and data science is sometimes called computational social science. Some consider this to be a technical field, but this will not be a technical book in the traditional sense. For example, there are no equations in the main text. I chose to write the book this way because I wanted to provide a comprehensive view of social research in the digital age, including big data sources, surveys, experiments, mass collaboration, and ethics. It turned out to be impossible to cover all these topics and provide technical details about each one. Instead, pointers to more technical material are given in the "What to read next" section at the end of each chapter. In other words, this book is not designed to teach you how to do any specific calculation; rather, it is designed to change the way that you think about social research.

How to use this book in a course

As I said earlier, this book emerged in part from a graduate seminar on computational social science that I've been teaching since 2007 at Princeton. Since you might be thinking about using this book to teach a course, I thought that it might be helpful for me to explain how it grew out of my course and how I imagine it being used in other courses.

For several years, I taught my course without a book; I'd just assign a collection of articles. While students were able to learn from these articles, the articles alone were not leading to the conceptual changes that I was hoping to create. So I would spend most of the time in class providing perspective, context, and advice in order to help the students see the big picture. This book is my attempt to write down all that perspective, context, and advice in a way that has no prerequisites—in terms of either social science or data science.

In a semester-long course, I would recommend pairing this book with a variety of additional readings. For example, such a course might spend two weeks on experiments, and you could pair chapter 4 with readings on topics such as the role of pre-treatment information in the design and analysis of experiments; statistical and computational issues raised by large-scale A/B tests at companies; design of experiments specifically focused on mechanisms; and practical, scientific, and ethical issues related to using participants from online labor markets, such as Amazon Mechanical Turk. It could also be paired with readings and activities related to programming. The appropriate choice between these many pairings depends on the students in your course (e.g., undergraduate, master's, or PhD), their backgrounds, and their goals.

A semester-length course could also include weekly problem sets. Each chapter has a variety of activities that are labeled by degree of difficulty: easy (🌗), medium (🌗), hard (🌒), and very hard (🌑). Also, I've labeled each problem by the skills that it requires: math (🔢), coding (📟), and data collection (🧊). Finally, I've labeled a few of the activities that are my personal favorites (♥). I hope that within this diverse collection of activities, you'll find some that are appropriate for your students.

In order to help people using this book in courses, I've started a collection of teaching materials such as syllabuses, slides, recommended pairings for each chapter, and solutions to some activities. You can find these materials— and contribute to them—at http://www.bitbybitbook.com.

BIT BY BIT

CHAPTER 1

INTRODUCTION

1.1 An ink blot

In the summer of 2009, mobile phones were ringing all across Rwanda. In addition to the millions of calls from family, friends, and business associates, about 1,000 Rwandans received a call from Joshua Blumenstock and his colleagues. These researchers were studying wealth and poverty by conducting a survey of a random sample of people from a database of 1.5 million customers of Rwanda's largest mobile phone provider. Blumenstock and colleagues asked the randomly selected people if they wanted to participate in a survey, explained the nature of the research to them, and then asked a series of questions about their demographic, social, and economic characteristics.

Everything I have said so far makes this sound like a traditional social science survey. But what comes next is not traditional—at least not yet. In addition to the survey data, Blumenstock and colleagues also had the complete call records for all 1.5 million people. Combining these two sources of data, they used the survey data to train a machine learning model to predict a person's wealth based on their call records. Next, they used this model to estimate the wealth of all 1.5 million customers in the database. They also estimated the places of residence of all 1.5 million customers using the geographic information embedded in the call records. Putting all of this together—the estimated wealth and the estimated place of residence—they were able to produce high-resolution maps of the geographic distribution of wealth in Rwanda. In particular, they could produce an estimated wealth for each of Rwanda's 2,148 cells, the smallest administrative unit in the country.

It was impossible to validate these estimates because nobody had ever produced estimates for such small geographic areas in Rwanda. But when Blumenstock and colleagues aggregated their estimates to Rwanda's thirty districts, they found that these estimates were very similar to those from the

Demographic and Health Survey, which is widely considered to be the gold standard of surveys in developing countries. Although these two approaches produced similar estimates in this case, the approach of Blumenstock and colleagues was about ten times faster and fifty times cheaper than the traditional Demographic and Health Surveys. These dramatically faster and cheaper estimates create new possibilities for researchers, governments, and companies (Blumenstock, Cadamuro, and On 2015).

This study is kind of like a Rorschach inkblot test: what people see depends on their background. Many *social scientists* see a new measurement tool that can be used to test theories about economic development. Many *data scientists* see a cool new machine learning problem. Many *business people* see a powerful approach for unlocking value in the big data that they have already collected. Many *privacy advocates* see a scary reminder that we live in a time of mass surveillance. And finally, many *policy makers* see a way that new technology can help create a better world. In fact, this study is all of those things, and because it has this mix of characteristics, I see it as a window into the future of social research.

1.2   Welcome to the digital age

> The digital age is everywhere, it's growing, and it changes what is possible for researchers.

The central premise of this book is that the digital age creates new opportunities for social research. Researchers can now observe behavior, ask questions, run experiments, and collaborate in ways that were simply impossible in the recent past. Along with these new opportunities come new risks: researchers can now harm people in ways that were impossible in the recent past. The source of these opportunities and risks is the transition from the analog age to the digital age. This transition has not happened all at once—like a light switch turning on—and, in fact, it is not yet complete. However, we've seen enough by now to know that something big is going on.

One way to notice this transition is to look for changes in your daily life. Many things in your life that used to be analog are now digital. Maybe you used to use a camera with film, but now you use a digital camera (which is probably part of your smart phone). Maybe you used to read a physical newspaper, but now you read an online newspaper. Maybe you used to pay for things with cash, but now you pay with a credit card. In each case, the change from analog to digital means that more data about you are being captured and stored digitally.

In fact, when looked at in aggregate, the effects of the transition are astonishing. The amount of information in the world is rapidly increasing, and more of that information is stored digitally, which facilitates analysis, transmission, and merging (figure 1.1). All of this digital information has come to be called "big data." In addition to this explosion of digital data, there is a parallel growth in our access to computing power (figure 1.1). These trends—increasing amounts of digital data and increasing use of computing—are likely to continue for the foreseeable future.

For the purposes of social research, I think the most important feature of the digital age is *computers everywhere*. Beginning as room-sized machines that were available only to governments and big companies, computers have been shrinking in size and increasing in ubiquity. Each decade since the 1980s has seen a new kind of computing emerge: personal computers, laptops, smart phones, and now embedded processors in the "Internet of Things" (i.e., computers inside of devices such as cars, watches, and thermostats) (Waldrop 2016). Increasingly, these ubiquitous computers do more than just calculate: they also sense, store, and transmit information.

For researchers, the implications of the presence of computers everywhere are easiest to see online, an environment that is fully measured and amenable to experimentation. For example, an online store can easily collect incredibly precise data about the shopping patterns of millions of customers. Further, it can easily randomize groups of customers to receive different shopping experiences. This ability to randomize on top of tracking means that online stores can constantly run randomized controlled experiments. In fact, if you've ever bought anything from an online store, your behavior has been tracked and you've almost certainly been a participant in an experiment, whether you knew it or not.

This fully measured, fully randomizable world is not just happening online; it is increasingly happening everywhere. Physical stores already collect extremely detailed purchase data, and they are developing infrastructure to monitor customers' shopping behavior and mix experimentation into routine business practice. The "Internet of Things" means that behavior in the physical world will increasingly be captured by digital sensors. In other

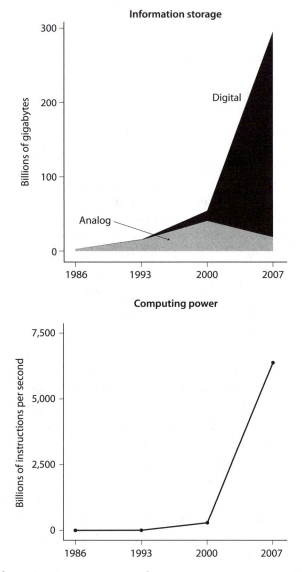

Figure 1.1: Information storage capacity and computing power are increasing dramatically. Further, information storage is now almost exclusively digital. These changes create incredible opportunities for social researchers. Adapted from Hilbert and López (2011), figures 2 and 5.

words, when you think about social research in the digital age, you should not just think *online*, you should think *everywhere*.

In addition to enabling the measurement of behavior and randomization of treatments, the digital age has also created new ways for people to communicate. These new forms of communication allow researchers to run innovative surveys and to create mass collaboration with their colleagues and the general public.

A skeptic might point out that none of these capabilities are really new. That is, in the past, there have been other major advances in people's abilities to communicate (e.g., the telegraph (Gleick 2011)), and computers have been getting faster at roughly the same rate since the 1960s (Waldrop 2016). But what this skeptic is missing is that at a certain point more of the same becomes something different (Halevy, Norvig, and Pereira 2009). Here's an analogy that I like. If you can capture an image of a horse, then you have a photograph. And if you can capture 24 images of a horse per second, then you have a movie. Of course, a movie is just a bunch of photos, but only a die-hard skeptic would claim that photos and movies are the same.

Researchers are in the process of making a change akin to the transition from photography to cinematography. This change, however, does not mean that everything we have learned in the past should be ignored. Just as the principles of photography inform those of cinematography, the principles of social research that have been developed over the past 100 years will inform the social research taking place over the next 100 years. But the change also means that we should not just keep doing the same thing. Rather, we must combine the approaches of the past with the capabilities of the present and future. For example, the research of Joshua Blumenstock and colleagues was a mixture of traditional survey research with what some might call data science. Both of these ingredients were necessary: neither the survey responses nor the call records by themselves were enough to produce high-resolution estimates of poverty. More generally, social researchers will need to combine ideas from social science and data science in order to take advantage of the opportunities of the digital age: neither approach alone will be enough.

1.3 Research design

Research design is about connecting questions and answers.

This book is written for two audiences that have a lot to learn from each other. On the one hand, it is for social scientists who have training and experience studying social behavior, but who are less familiar with the opportunities created by the digital age. On the other hand, it is for another group of researchers who are very comfortable using the tools of the digital age, but who are new to studying social behavior. This second group resists an easy name, but I will call them data scientists. These data scientists—who often have training in fields such as computer science, statistics, information science, engineering, and physics—have been some of the earliest adopters of digital-age social research, in part because they have access to the necessary data and computational skills. This book attempts to bring these two communities together to produce something richer and more interesting than either community could produce individually.

The best way to create this powerful hybrid is not to focus on abstract social theory or fancy machine learning. The best place to start is research design. If you think of social research as the process of asking and answering questions about human behavior, then research design is the connective tissue; research design links questions and answers. Getting this connection right is the key to producing convincing research. This book will focus on four approaches that you have seen—and maybe used—in the past: observing behavior, asking questions, running experiments, and collaborating with others. What is new, however, is that the digital age provides us with different opportunities for collecting and analyzing data. These new opportunities require us to modernize—but not replace—these classic approaches.

1.4   Themes of this book

> Two themes in the book are (1) mixing readymades and custommades and (2) ethics.

Two themes run throughout this book, and I'd like to highlight them now so that you notice them as they come up over and over again. The first can be illustrated by an analogy that compares two greats: Marcel Duchamp and Michelangelo. Duchamp is mostly known for his readymades, such as *Fountain*, where he took ordinary objects and repurposed them as art. Michelangelo, on the other hand, didn't repurpose. When he wanted to

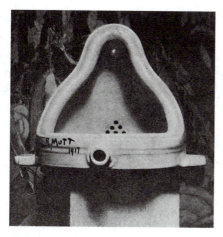

Readymade   Custommade

Figure 1.2: *Fountain* by Marcel Duchamp and *David* by Michelangelo. *Fountain* is an example of a readymade, where an artist sees something that already exists in the world and then creatively repurposes it for art. *David* is an example of art that was intentionally created; it is a custommade. Social research in the digital age will involve both readymades and custommades. Photograph of *Fountain* by Alfred Stieglitz, 1917 (Source: *The Blind Man*, no. 2/Wikimedia Commons). Photograph of *David* by Jörg Bittner Unna, 2008 (Source: Galleria dell'Accademia, Florence/Wikimedia Commons).

create a statue of David, he didn't look for a piece of marble that kind of looked like David: he spent three years laboring to create his masterpiece. *David* is not a readymade; it is a custommade (figure 1.2).

These two styles—readymades and custommades—roughly map onto styles that can be employed for social research in the digital age. As you will see, some of the examples in this book involve clever repurposing of big data sources that were originally created by companies and governments. In other examples, however, a researcher started with a specific question and then used the tools of the digital age to create the data needed to answer that question. When done well, both of these styles can be incredibly powerful. Therefore, social research in the digital age will involve both readymades and custommades; it will involve both Duchamps and Michelangelos.

If you generally use readymade data, I hope that this book will show you the value of custommade data. And likewise, if you generally use custommade data, I hope that this book will show you the value of readymade data. Finally, and most importantly, I hope that this book will show you the value of combining these two styles. For example, Joshua Blumenstock and colleagues were part Duchamp and part Michelangelo: they repurposed the call records (a readymade), and they created their own survey data (a custommade). This blending of readymades and custommades is a pattern that you'll see throughout this book; it tends to require ideas from both social science and data science, and it often leads to the most exciting research.

A second theme that runs through this book is ethics. I'll show you how researchers can use the capabilities of the digital age to conduct exciting and important research. And I'll show you how researchers who take advantage of these opportunities will confront difficult ethical decisions. Chapter 6 will be entirely devoted to ethics, but I integrate ethics into the other chapters as well because, in the digital age, ethics will become an increasingly integral part of research design.

The work of Blumenstock and colleagues is again illustrative. Having access to the granular call records from 1.5 million people creates wonderful opportunities for research, but it also creates opportunities for harm. For example, Jonathan Mayer and colleagues (2016) have shown that even "anonymized" call records (i.e., data without names and addresses) can be combined with publicly available information in order to identify specific people in the data and to infer sensitive information about them, such as certain health information. To be clear, Blumenstock and colleagues did not attempt to identify specific people and infer sensitive information about them, but this possibility meant that it was difficult for them to acquire the call data, and it forced them to take extensive safeguards while conducting their research.

Beyond the details of the call records, there is a fundamental tension that runs through a lot of social research in the digital age. Researchers—often in collaboration with companies and governments—have increasing power over the lives of participants. By power, I mean the ability to do things to people without their consent or even awareness. For example, researchers can now observe the behavior of millions of people, and, as I'll describe later, researchers can also enroll millions of people in massive experiments. Further, all of this can happen without the consent or awareness of the people involved. As the power of researchers is increasing, there has not been an equivalent increase in clarity about how that power should be used. In fact, researchers must decide how to exercise their power based on inconsistent and overlapping rules, laws, and norms. This combination of powerful capabilities and vague guidelines can force even well-meaning researchers to grapple with difficult decisions.

If you generally focus on how digital-age social research creates new opportunities, I hope that this book will show you that these opportunities also create new risks. And likewise, if you generally focus on these risks, I hope that this book will help you see the opportunities—opportunities that may require certain risks. Finally, and most importantly, I hope that this book will help everyone to responsibly balance the risks and opportunities created by digital-age social research. With an increase in power, there must also come an increase in responsibility.

1.5   Outline of this book

This book progresses through four broad research designs: observing behavior, asking questions, running experiments, and creating mass collaboration. Each of these approaches requires a different relationship between researchers and participants, and each enables us to learn different things. That is, if we ask people questions, we can learn things that we could not learn merely by observing behavior. Likewise, if we run experiments, we can learn things that we could not learn merely by observing behavior and asking questions. Finally, if we collaborate with participants, we can learn things that we could not learn by observing them, asking them questions, or enrolling them in experiments. These four approaches were all used in some form fifty years ago, and I'm confident that they will all still be used in some form fifty years from now. After devoting one chapter to each approach, including the ethical issues raised by that approach, I'll devote a full chapter to ethics. As mentioned in the preface, I'm going to keep the main text of the chapters as clean as possible, and each of them will conclude with a section called "What to read next" that includes important bibliographic information and pointers to more detailed material.

Looking ahead, in chapter 2 ("Observing behavior"), I'll describe what and how researchers can learn from observing people's behavior. In particular, I'll focus on big data sources created by companies and governments. Abstracting away from the details of any specific source, I'll describe 10 common features of the big data sources and how these impact researchers' ability to use these data sources for research. Then, I'll illustrate three research strategies that can be used to successfully learn from big data sources.

In chapter 3 ("Asking questions"), I'll begin by showing what researchers can learn by moving beyond preexisting big data. In particular, I'll show that by asking people questions, researchers can learn things that they can't easily learn by just observing behavior. In order to organize the opportunities created by the digital age, I'll review the traditional total survey error framework. Then, I'll show how the digital age enables new approaches to both sampling and interviewing. Finally, I'll describe two strategies for combining survey data and big data sources.

In chapter 4 ("Running experiments"), I'll begin by showing what researchers can learn when they move beyond observing behavior and asking survey questions. In particular, I'll show how randomized controlled experiments—where the researcher intervenes in the world in a very specific way—enable researchers to learn about causal relationships. I'll compare the kinds of experiments that we could do in the past with the kinds that we can do now. With that background, I'll describe the trade-offs involved in the two main strategies for conducting digital experiments. Finally, I'll conclude with some design advice about how you can take advantage of the real power of digital experiments, and I'll describe some of the responsibilities that come with that power.

In chapter 5 ("Creating mass collaboration"), I'll show how researchers can create mass collaborations—such as crowdsourcing and citizen science—in order to do social research. By describing successful mass collaboration projects and by providing a few key organizing principles, I hope to convince you of two things: first, that mass collaboration can be harnessed for social research, and, second, that researchers who use mass collaboration will be able to solve problems that had previously seemed impossible.

In chapter 6 ("Ethics"), I'll argue that researchers have rapidly increasing power over participants and that these capabilities are changing faster than our norms, rules, and laws. This combination of increasing power and lack of agreement about how that power should be used leaves well-meaning researchers in a difficult situation. To address this problem, I'll argue that researchers should adopt a *principles-based* approach. That is, researchers should evaluate their research through existing rules—which I'll take as given—and through more general ethical principles. I'll describe four established principles and two ethical frameworks that can help guide researchers' decisions. Finally, I'll explain some specific ethical challenges that I expect will confront researchers in the future, and I'll offer practical tips for working in an area with unsettled ethics.

Finally, in chapter 7 ("The future"), I'll review the themes that run through the book, and then use them to speculate about themes that will be important in the future.

Social research in the digital age will combine what we have done in the past with the very different capabilities of the future. Thus, social research will be shaped by both social scientists and data scientists. Each group has something to contribute, and each has something to learn.

What to read next

- **An ink blot (section 1.1)**

  For a more detailed description of the project of Blumenstock and colleagues, see chapter 3 of this book.

- **Welcome to the digital age (section 1.2)**

  Gleick (2011) provides a historical overview of changes in humanity's ability to collect, store, transmit, and process information.

  For an introduction to the digital age that focuses on potential harms, such as privacy violations, see Abelson, Ledeen, and Lewis (2008) and Mayer-Schönberger (2009). For an introduction to the digital age that focuses on research opportunities, see Mayer-Schönberger and Cukier (2013).

  For more about firms mixing experimentation into routine practice, see Manzi (2012), and for more about firms tracking behavior in the physical world, see Levy and Baracas (2017).

  Digital-age systems can be both instruments and objects of study. For example, you might want to use social media to measure public opinion or you might want to understand the impact of social media on public opinion. In one case, the digital system serves as an instrument that helps you do new measurement. In the other case, the digital system is the object of study. For more on this distinction, see Sandvig and Hargittai (2015).

- **Research design (section 1.3)**

  For more on research design in the social sciences, see Singleton and Straits (2009), King, Keohane, and Verba (1994), and Khan and Fisher (2013).

  Donoho (2015) describes data science as the activities of people learning from data, and offers a history of data science, tracing the intellectual origins of the field to scholars such as Tukey, Cleveland, Chambers, and Breiman.

For a series of first-person reports about conducting social research in the digital age, see Hargittai and Sandvig (2015).

- **Themes of this book (section 1.4)**

For more about mixing readymade and custommade data, see Groves (2011).

For more about failure of "anonymization," see chapter 6 of this book. The same general technique that Blumenstock and colleagues used to infer people's wealth can also be used to infer potentially sensitive personal attributes, including sexual orientation, ethnicity, religious and political views, and use of addictive substances; see Kosinski, Stillwell, and Graepel (2013).

CHAPTER 2
OBSERVING BEHAVIOR

2.1   Introduction

In the analog age, collecting data about behavior—who does what, and when—was expensive and therefore relatively rare. Now, in the digital age, the behaviors of billions of people are recorded, stored, and analyzable. For example, every time you click on a website, make a call on your mobile phone, or pay for something with your credit card, a digital record of your behavior is created and stored by a business. Because these types of data are a by-product of people's everyday actions, they are often called *digital traces*. In addition to these traces held by businesses, there are also large amounts of incredibly rich data held by governments. Together, these business and government records are often called *big data*.

The ever-rising flood of big data means that we have moved from a world where behavioral data was scarce to one where it is plentiful. A first step to learning from big data is realizing that it is part of a broader category of data that has been used for social research for many years: *observational data*. Roughly, observational data is any data that results from observing a social system without intervening in some way. A crude way to think about it is that observational data is everything that does not involve talking with people (e.g., surveys, the topic of chapter 3) or changing people's environments (e.g., experiments, the topic of chapter 4). Thus, in addition to business and government records, observational data also includes things like the text of newspaper articles and satellite photos.

This chapter has three parts. First, in section 2.2, I describe big data sources in more detail and clarify a fundamental difference between them and the data that have typically been used for social research in the past. Then, in section 2.3, I describe 10 common characteristics of big data sources. Understanding these characteristics enables you to quickly recognize the strengths and weaknesses of existing sources and will help you harness the new sources that will be available in the future. Finally, in section 2.4, I describe three main research strategies that you can use to learn from observational data: counting things, forecasting things, and approximating an experiment.

2.2 Big data

Big data are created and collected by companies and governments for purposes other than research. Using this data for research therefore requires repurposing.

The first way that many people encounter social research in the digital age is through what is often called *big data*. Despite the widespread use of this term, there is no consensus about what big data even is. However, one of the most common definitions of big data focuses on the "3 Vs": Volume, Variety, and Velocity. Roughly, there is a lot of data, in a variety of formats, and it is being created constantly. Some fans of big data also add other "Vs," such as Veracity and Value, whereas some critics add "Vs" such as Vague and Vacuous. Rather than the "3 Vs" (or the "5 Vs" or the "7 Vs"), for the purposes of social research, I think a better place to start is the "5 Ws": Who, What, Where, When, and Why. In fact, I think that many of the challenges and opportunities created by big data sources follow from just one "W": Why.

In the analog age, most of the data that were used for social research were created for the purpose of doing research. In the digital age, however, huge amounts of data are being created by companies and governments for purposes other than research, such as providing services, generating profit, and administering laws. Creative people, however, have realized that you can *repurpose* this corporate and government data for research. Thinking back to the art analogy in chapter 1, just as Duchamp repurposed a found object to create art, scientists can now repurpose found data to create research.

While there are undoubtedly huge opportunities for repurposing, using data that were not created for the purposes of research also presents new challenges. Compare, for example, a social media service, such as Twitter, with a traditional public opinion survey, such as the General Social Survey.

Twitter's main goals are to provide a service to its users and to make a profit. The General Social Survey, on the other hand, is focused on creating general-purpose data for social research, particularly for public opinion research. This difference in goals means that the data created by Twitter and that created by the General Social Survey have different properties, even though both can be used for studying public opinion. Twitter operates at a scale and speed that the General Social Survey cannot match, but, unlike the General Social Survey, Twitter does not carefully sample users and does not work hard to maintain comparability over time. Because these two data sources are so different, it does not make sense to say that the General Social Survey is better than Twitter, or vice versa. If you want hourly measures of global mood (e.g., Golder and Macy (2011)), Twitter is the best choice. On the other hand, if you want to understand long-term changes in the polarization of attitudes in the United States (e.g., DiMaggio, Evans, and Bryson (1996)), then the General Social Survey is best. More generally, rather than trying to argue that big data sources are better or worse than other types of data, this chapter will try to clarify for which kinds of research questions big data sources have attractive properties and for which kinds of questions they might not be ideal.

When thinking about big data sources, many researchers immediately focus on online data created and collected by companies, such as search engine logs and social media posts. However, this narrow focus leaves out two other important sources of big data. First, increasingly, corporate big data sources come from digital devices in the physical world. For example, in this chapter, I'll tell you about a study that repurposed supermarket check-out data to study how a worker's productivity is impacted by the productivity of her peers (Mas and Moretti 2009). Then, in later chapters, I'll tell you about researchers who used call records from mobile phones (Blumenstock, Cadamuro, and On 2015) and billing data created by electric utilities (Allcott 2015). As these examples illustrate, corporate big data sources are about more than just online behavior.

The second important source of big data missed by a narrow focus on online behavior is data created by governments. These government data, which researchers call *government administrative records*, include things such as tax records, school records, and vital statistics records (e.g., registries of births and deaths). Governments have been creating these kinds of data for, in some cases, hundreds of years, and social scientists have been exploiting them for nearly as long as there have been social scientists. What has changed, however, is digitization, which has made it dramatically easier for governments to collect, transmit, store, and analyze data. For example, in this chapter, I'll tell you about a study that repurposed data from New York City government's digital taxi meters in order to address a fundamental debate in labor economics (Farber 2015). Then, in later chapters, I'll tell you about how government-collected voting records were used in a survey (Ansolabehere and Hersh 2012) and an experiment (Bond et al. 2012).

I think the idea of repurposing is fundamental to learning from big data sources, and so, before talking more specifically about the properties of big data sources (section 2.3) and how these can be used in research (section 2.4), I'd like to offer two pieces of general advice about repurposing. First, it can be tempting to think about the contrast that I've set up as being between "found" data and "designed" data. That's close, but it's not quite right. Even though, from the perspective of researchers, big data sources are "found," they don't just fall from the sky. Instead, data sources that are "found" by researchers are designed by someone for some purpose. Because "found" data are designed by someone, I always recommend that you try to understand as much as possible about the people and processes that created your data. Second, when you are repurposing data, it is often extremely helpful to imagine the ideal dataset for your problem and then compare that ideal dataset with the one that you are using. If you didn't collect your data yourself, there are likely to be important differences between what you want and what you have. Noticing these differences will help clarify what you can and cannot learn from the data you have, and it might suggest new data that you should collect.

In my experience, social scientists and data scientists tend to approach re-purposing very differently. Social scientists, who are accustomed to working with data designed for research, are typically quick to point out the problems with repurposed data, while ignoring its strengths. On the other hand, data scientists are typically quick to point out the benefits of repurposed data, while ignoring its weaknesses. Naturally, the best approach is a hybrid. That is, researchers need to understand the characteristics of big data sources—both good and bad—and then figure out how to learn from them. And, that is the plan for the remainder of this chapter. In the next section, I will describe 10 common characteristics of big data sources. Then, in the following section, I will describe three research approaches that can work well with such data.

2.3 Ten common characteristics of big data

Big data sources tend to have a number of characteristics in common; some are generally good for social research and some are generally bad.

Even though each big data source is distinct, it is helpful to notice that there are certain characteristics that tend to occur over and over again. Therefore, rather than taking a platform-by-platform approach (e.g., here's what you need to know about Twitter, here's what you need to know about Google search data, etc.), I'm going to describe 10 general characteristics of big data sources. Stepping back from the details of each particular system and looking at these general characteristics enables researchers to quickly learn about existing data sources and have a firm set of ideas to apply to the data sources that will be created in the future.

Even though the desired characteristics of a data source depend on the research goal, I find it helpful to crudely group the 10 characteristics into two broad categories:

- generally helpful for research: big, always-on, and nonreactive
- generally problematic for research: incomplete, inaccessible, nonrepresentative, drifting, algorithmically confounded, dirty, and sensitive

As I'm describing these characteristics, you'll notice that they often arise because big data sources were not created for the purpose of research.

2.3.1 Big

Large datasets are a means to an end; they are not an end in themselves.

The most widely discussed feature of big data sources is that they are BIG. Many papers, for example, start by discussing—and sometimes bragging—about how much data they analyzed. For example, a paper published in

Science studying word-use trends in the Google Books corpus included the following (Michel et al. 2011):

> "[Our] corpus contains over 500 billion words, in English (361 billion), French (45 billion), Spanish (45 billion), German (37 billion), Chinese (13 billion), Russian (35 billion), and Hebrew (2 billion). The oldest works were published in the 1500s. The early decades are represented by only a few books per year, comprising several hundred thousand words. By 1800, the corpus grows to 98 million words per year; by 1900, 1.8 billion; and by 2000, 11 billion. The corpus cannot be read by a human. If you tried to read only English-language entries from the year 2000 alone, at the reasonable pace of 200 words/min, without interruptions for food or sleep, it would take 80 years. The sequence of letters is 1000 times longer than the human genome: If you wrote it out in a straight line, it would reach to the Moon and back 10 times over."

The scale of this data is undoubtedly impressive, and we are all fortunate that the Google Books team has released these data to the public (in fact, some of the activities at the end of this chapter make use of this data). However, whenever you see something like this, you should ask: Is that all that data really doing anything? Could they have done the same research if the data could reach to the Moon and back only once? What if the data could only reach to the top of Mount Everest or the top of the Eiffel Tower?

In this case, their research does, in fact, have some findings that require a huge corpus of words over a long time period. For example, one thing they explore is the evolution of grammar, particularly changes in the rate of irregular verb conjugation. Since some irregular verbs are quite rare, a large amount of data is needed to detect changes over time. Too often, however, researchers seem to treat the size of big data source as an end—"look how much data I can crunch"—rather than a means to some more important scientific objective.

In my experience, the study of rare events is one of the three specific scientific ends that large datasets tend to enable. The second is the study of heterogeneity, as can be illustrated by a study by Raj Chetty and colleagues (2014) on social mobility in the United States. In the past, many researchers have studied social mobility by comparing the life outcomes of parents and

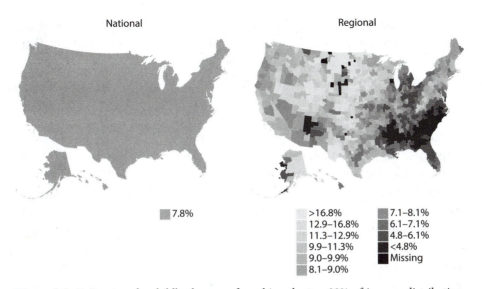

National

Regional

7.8%

>16.8%	7.1–8.1%
12.9–16.8%	6.1–7.1%
11.3–12.9%	4.8–6.1%
9.9–11.3%	<4.8%
9.0–9.9%	Missing
8.1–9.0%	

Figure 2.1: Estimates of a child's chances of reaching the top 20% of income distribution given parents in the bottom 20% (Chetty et al. 2014). The regional-level estimates, which show heterogeneity, naturally lead to interesting and important questions that do not arise from a single national-level estimate. These regional-level estimates were made possible in part because the researchers were using a large big data source: the tax records of 40 million people. Created from data available at http://www.equality-of-opportunity.org/.

children. A consistent finding from this literature is that advantaged parents tend to have advantaged children, but the strength of this relationship varies over time and across countries (Hout and DiPrete 2006). More recently, however, Chetty and colleagues were able to use the tax records from 40 million people to estimate the heterogeneity in intergenerational mobility across regions in the United States (figure 2.1). They found, for example, that the probability that a child reaches the top quintile of the national income distribution starting from a family in the bottom quintile is about 13% in San Jose, California, but only about 4% in Charlotte, North Carolina. If you look at figure 2.1 for a moment, you might begin to wonder why intergenerational mobility is higher in some places than others. Chetty and colleagues had exactly the same question, and they found that that high-mobility areas have less residential segregation, less income inequality, better primary schools, greater social capital, and greater family stability. Of course, these correlations alone do not show that these factors cause higher mobility, but they do suggest possible mechanisms that can be explored in further work, which is exactly what Chetty and colleagues have done in subsequent work. Notice how the size of the data was really important in this project. If Chetty and colleagues had used the tax records of 40 thousand people rather than 40 million, they would not have been able to estimate regional heterogeneity, and they never would have been able to do subsequent research to try to identify the mechanisms that create this variation.

Finally, in addition to studying rare events and studying heterogeneity, large datasets also enable researchers to detect small differences. In fact, much of the focus on big data in industry is about these small differences: reliably detecting the difference between 1% and 1.1% click-through rates on an ad can translate into millions of dollars in extra revenue. In some scientific settings, however, such small differences might not be particular important, even if they are statistically significant (Prentice and Miller 1992). But, in some policy settings, they can become important when viewed in aggregate. For example, if there are two public health interventions and one is slightly more effective than the other, then picking the more effective intervention could end up saving thousands of additional lives.

Although bigness is generally a good property when used correctly, I've noticed that it can sometimes lead to a conceptual error. For some reason, bigness seems to lead researchers to ignore how their data was generated. While bigness does reduce the need to worry about random error, it actually *increases* the need to worry about systematic errors, the kinds of errors that I'll describe below that arise from biases in how data are created. For example, in a project I'll describe later in this chapter, researchers used messages generated on September 11, 2001 to produce a high-resolution emotional timeline of the reaction to the terrorist attack (Back, Küfner, and Egloff 2010). Because the researchers had a large number of messages, they didn't really need to worry about whether the patterns they observed—increasing anger over the course of the day—could be explained by random variation. There was so much data and the pattern was so clear that all the statistical statistical tests suggested that this was a real pattern. But these statistical tests were ignorant of how the data was created. In fact, it turned out that many of the patterns were attributable to a single bot that generated more and more meaningless messages throughout the day. Removing this one bot completely destroyed some of the key findings in the paper (Pury 2011; Back, Küfner, and Egloff 2011). Quite simply, researchers who don't think about systematic error face the risk of using their large datasets to get a precise estimate of an unimportant quantity, such as the emotional content of meaningless messages produced by an automated bot.

In conclusion, big datasets are not an end in themselves, but they can enable certain kinds of research, including the study of rare events, the estimation of heterogeneity, and the detection of small differences. Big datasets also seem to lead some researchers to ignore how their data was created, which can lead them to get a precise estimate of an unimportant quantity.

2.3.2 Always-on

Always-on big data enables the study of unexpected events and real-time measurement.

Many big data systems are *always-on*; they are constantly collecting data. This always-on characteristic provides researchers with longitudinal data (i.e., data over time). Being always-on has two important implications for research.

First, always-on data collection enables researchers to study unexpected events in ways that would not otherwise be possible. For example, researchers interested in studying the Occupy Gezi protests in Turkey in the summer of 2013 would typically focus on the behavior of protesters during the event. Ceren Budak and Duncan Watts (2015) were able to do more by using the always-on nature of Twitter to study protesters who used Twitter before, during, and after the event. And they were able to create a comparison group of nonparticipants before, during, and after the event (figure 2.2). In total, their *ex-post panel* included the tweets of 30,000 people over two years. By augmenting the commonly used data from the protests with this other information, Budak and Watts were able to learn much more: they were able to estimate what kinds of people were more likely to participate in the Gezi protests and to estimate the changes in attitudes of participants and nonparticipants, both in the short term (comparing pre-Gezi with during Gezi) and in the long term (comparing pre-Gezi with post-Gezi).

A skeptic might point out that some of these estimates could have been made without always-on data collection sources (e.g., long-term estimates of attitude change), and that is correct, although such a data collection for 30,000 people would have been quite expensive. Even given an unlimited

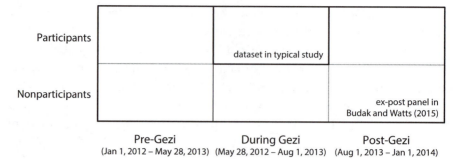

	Pre-Gezi (Jan 1, 2012 – May 28, 2013)	During Gezi (May 28, 2012 – Aug 1, 2013)	Post-Gezi (Aug 1, 2013 – Jan 1, 2014)
Participants		dataset in typical study	
Nonparticipants			ex-post panel in Budak and Watts (2015)

Figure 2.2: Design used by Budak and Watts (2015) to study the Occupy Gezi protests in Turkey in the summer of 2013. By using the always-on nature of Twitter, the researchers created what they called an *ex-post panel* that included about 30,000 people over two years. In contrast to a typical study that focused on participants during the protests, the ex-post panel adds (1) data from participants before and after the event and (2) data from nonparticipants before, during, and after the event. This enriched data structure enabled Budak and Watts to estimate what kinds of people were more likely to participate in the Gezi protests and to estimate the changes in attitudes of participants and nonparticipants, both in the short term (comparing pre-Gezi with during Gezi) and in the long term (comparing pre-Gezi with post-Gezi).

budget, however, I can't think of any other method that essentially allows researchers to *travel back in time* and directly observe participants' behavior in the past. The closest alternative would be to collect retrospective reports of behavior, but these would be of limited granularity and questionable accuracy. Table 2.1 provides other examples of studies that use an always-on data source to study an unexpected event.

In addition to studying unexpected events, always-on big data systems also enable researchers to produce real-time estimates, which can be important in settings where policy makers—in government or industry—want to respond based on situational awareness. For example, social media data can be used to guide emergency response to natural disasters (Castillo 2016), and a variety of different big data sources can be used produce real-time estimates of economic activity (Choi and Varian 2012).

In conclusion, always-on data systems enable researchers to study unexpected events and provide real-time information to policy makers. I do not, however, think that always-on data systems are well suited for tracking changes over very long periods of time. That is because many big data systems are constantly changing—a process that I'll call *drift* later in the chapter (section 2.3.7).

Table 2.1: Studies of Unexpected Events Using Always-On Big Data Sources

Unexpected event	Always-on data source	References
Occupy Gezi movement in Turkey	Twitter	Budak and Watts (2015)
Umbrella protests in Hong Kong	Weibo	Zhang (2016)
Shootings of police in New York City	Stop-and-frisk reports	Legewie (2016)
Person joining ISIS	Twitter	Magdy, Darwish, and Weber (2016)
September 11, 2001 attack	livejournal.com	Cohn, Mehl, and Pennebaker (2004)
September 11, 2001 attack	Pager messages	Back, Küfner, and Egloff (2010), Pury (2011), Back, Küfner, and Egloff (2011)

2.3.3 Nonreactive

> Measurement in big data sources is much less likely to change behavior.

One challenge of social research is that people can change their behavior when they know that they are being observed by researchers. Social scientists generally call this *reactivity* (Webb et al. 1966). For example, people can be more generous in laboratory studies than field studies because in the former they are very aware that they are being observed (Levitt and List 2007a). One aspect of big data that many researchers find promising is that participants are generally not aware that their data are being captured or they have become so accustomed to this data collection that it no longer changes their behavior. Because participants are *nonreactive*, therefore, many sources of big data can be used to study behavior that has not been amenable to accurate measurement previously. For example, Stephens-Davidowitz (2014) used the prevalence of racist terms in search engine queries to measure racial animus in different regions of the United States. The nonreactive and big (see section 2.3.1) nature of the search data enabled measurements that would be difficult using other methods, such as surveys.

Nonreactivity, however, does not ensure that these data are somehow a direct reflection of people's behavior or attitudes. For example, as one respondent in an interview-based study said, "It's not that I don't have problems, I'm just not putting them on Facebook" (Newman et al. 2011). In other words, even though some big data sources are nonreactive, they are not always free of social desirability bias, the tendency for people to want to present themselves in the best possible way. Further, as I'll describe later in the chapter, the behavior captured in big data sources is sometimes impacted by the goals of platform owners, an issue I'll call *algorithmic confounding*. Finally, although nonreactivity is advantageous for research, tracking people's behavior without their consent and awareness raises ethical concerns that I'll describe in chapter 6.

The three properties that I just described—big, always-on, and nonreactive—are generally, but not always, advantageous for social research. Next, I'll turn to the seven properties of big data sources—incomplete, inaccessible, nonrepresentative, drifting, algorithmically confounded, dirty, and sensitive—that generally, but not always, create problems for research.

2.3.4 Incomplete

No matter how big your big data, it probably doesn't have the information you want.

Most big data sources are *incomplete*, in the sense that they don't have the information that you will want for your research. This is a common feature of data that were created for purposes other than research. Many social scientists have already had the experience of dealing with incompleteness, such as an existing survey that didn't ask the question that was needed. Unfortunately, the problems of incompleteness tend to be more extreme in big data. In my experience, big data tends to be missing three types of information useful for social research: demographic information about participants, behavior on other platforms, and data to operationalize theoretical constructs.

Of the three kinds of incompleteness, the problem of incomplete data to operationalize theoretical constructs is the hardest to solve. And in my experience, it is often accidentally overlooked. Roughly, *theoretical constructs* are abstract ideas that social scientists study, and *operationalizing* a theoretical construct means proposing some way to capture that construct with observable data. Unfortunately, this simple-sounding process often turns out to be quite difficult. For example, let's imagine trying to empirically test the apparently simple claim that people who are more intelligent earn more money. In order to test this claim, you would need to measure "intelligence." But what is intelligence? Gardner (2011) argued that there are actually eight different forms of intelligence. And are there procedures that could accurately measure any of these forms of intelligence? Despite enormous amounts of work by psychologists, these questions still don't have unambiguous answers.

Thus, even a relatively simple claim—people who are more intelligent earn more money—can be hard to assess empirically because it can be hard to operationalize theoretical constructs in data. Other examples of theoretical constructs that are important but hard to operationalize include "norms," "social capital," and "democracy." Social scientists call the match between theoretical constructs and data *construct validity* (Cronbach and Meehl 1955). As this short list of constructs suggests, construct validity is a problem that social scientists have struggled with for a very long time. But in my experience, the problems of construct validity are even greater when working with data that were not created for the purposes of research (Lazer 2015).

When you are assessing a research result, one quick and useful way to assess construct validity is to take the result, which is usually expressed in terms of constructs, and re-express it in terms of the data used. For example, consider two hypothetical studies that claim to show that people who are more intelligent earn more money. In the first study, the researcher found that people who score well on the Raven Progressive Matrices Test—a well-studied test of analytic intelligence (Carpenter, Just, and Shell 1990)—have higher reported incomes on their tax returns. In the second study, the researcher found that people on Twitter who used longer words are more likely to mention luxury brands. In both cases, these researchers could claim that they have shown that people who are more intelligent earn more money. However, in the first study the theoretical constructs are well operationalized by the data, while in the second they are not. Further, as this example illustrates, more data does not automatically solve problems with construct validity. You should doubt the results of the second study whether it involved a million tweets, a billion tweets, or a trillion tweets. For researchers not

Table 2.2: Examples of Digital Traces That Were Used to Operationalize Theoretical Constructs

Data source	Theoretical construct	References
Email logs from a university (metadata only)	Social relationships	Kossinets and Watts (2006), Kossinets and Watts (2009), De Choudhury et al. (2010)
Social media posts on Weibo	Civic engagement	Zhang (2016)
Email logs from a firm (metadata and complete text)	Cultural fit in an organization	Srivastava et al. (2017)

familiar with the idea of construct validity, table 2.2 provides some examples of studies that have operationalized theoretical constructs using digital trace data.

Although the problem of incomplete data for capturing theoretical constructs is pretty hard to solve, there are common solutions to the other common types of incompleteness: incomplete demographic information and incomplete information on behavior on other platforms. The first solution is to actually collect the data you need; I'll tell you about that in chapter 3 when I talk about surveys. The second main solution is to do what data scientists call *user-attribute inference* and social scientists call *imputation*. In this approach, researchers use the information that they have on some people to infer attributes of other people. A third possible solution is to combine multiple data sources. This process is sometimes called *record linkage.* My favorite metaphor for this process was written by Dunn (1946) in the very first paragraph of the very first paper ever written on record linkage:

> "Each person in the world creates a Book of Life. This Book starts with birth and ends with death. Its pages are made up of records of the principal events in life. Record linkage is the name given to the process of assembling the pages of this book into a volume."

When Dunn wrote that passage, he was imagining that the Book of Life could include major life events like birth, marriage, divorce, and death. However, now that so much information about people is recorded, the Book of Life could be an incredibly detailed portrait, if those different pages (i.e., our digital traces) can be bound together. This Book of Life could be a great resource for researchers. But it could also be called a *database of ruin* (Ohm 2010), which could be used for all kinds of unethical purposes, as I'll describe in chapter 6 (Ethics).

2.3.5 Inaccessible

Data held by companies and governments are difficult for researchers to access.

In May 2014, the US National Security Agency opened a data center in rural Utah with an awkward name, the Intelligence Community Comprehensive National Cybersecurity Initiative Data Center. However, this data center, which has come to be known as the Utah Data Center, is reported to have astounding capabilities. One report alleges that it is able to store and process all forms of communication including "the complete contents of private emails, cell phone calls, and Google searches, as well as all sorts of personal data trails—parking receipts, travel itineraries, bookstore purchases, and other digital 'pocket litter'" (Bamford 2012). In addition to raising concerns about the sensitive nature of much of the information captured in big data, which will be described further below, the Utah Data Center is an extreme example of a rich data source that is inaccessible to researchers. More generally, many sources of big data that would be useful are controlled and restricted by governments (e.g., tax data and educational data) or companies (e.g., queries to search engines and phone call meta-data). Therefore, even though these data sources exist, they are useless for the purposes of social research because they are inaccessible.

In my experience, many researchers based at universities misunderstand the source of this inaccessibility. These data are inaccessible not because people at companies and governments are stupid, lazy, or uncaring. Rather, there are serious legal, business, and ethical barriers that prevent data access. For example, some terms-of-service agreements for websites only allow data to be used by employees or to improve the service. So certain forms of data sharing could expose companies to legitimate lawsuits from customers. There are also substantial business risks to companies involved in sharing data. Try to imagine how the public would respond if personal search data accidentally leaked out from Google as part of a university research project.

Such a data breach, if extreme, might even be an existential risk for the company. So Google—and most large companies—are very risk-averse about sharing data with researchers.

In fact, almost everyone who is in a position to provide access to large amounts of data knows the story of Abdur Chowdhury. In 2006, when he was the head of research at AOL, he intentionally released to the research community what he thought were anonymized search queries from 650,000 AOL users. As far as I can tell, Chowdhury and the researchers at AOL had good intentions, and they thought that they had anonymized the data. But they were wrong. It was quickly discovered that the data were not as anonymous as the researchers thought, and reporters from the *New York Times* were able to identify someone in the dataset with ease (Barbaro and Zeller 2006). Once these problems were discovered, Chowdhury removed the data from AOL's website, but it was too late. The data had been reposted on other websites, and it will probably still be available when you are reading this book. Ultimately, Chowdhury was fired, and AOL's chief technology officer resigned (Hafner 2006). As this example shows, the benefits for specific individuals inside of companies to facilitate data access are pretty small, and the worst-case scenario is terrible.

Researchers can, however, sometimes gain access to data that is inaccessible to the general public. Some governments have procedures that researchers can follow to apply for access, and, as the examples later in this chapter show, researchers can occasionally gain access to corporate data. For example, Einav et al. (2015) partnered with a researcher at eBay to study online auctions. I'll talk more about the research that came from this collaboration later in the chapter, but I mention it now because it had all four of the ingredients that I see in successful partnerships: researcher interest, researcher capability, company interest, and company capability. I've seen many potential collaborations fail because either the researcher or the partner—be it a company or government—lacked one of these ingredients.

Even if you are able to develop a partnership with a business or to gain access to restricted government data, however, there are some downsides for you. First, you will probably not be able to share your data with other researchers, which means that other researchers will not be able to verify and extend your results. Second, the questions that you can ask may be limited; companies are unlikely to allow research that could make them look bad. Finally, these partnerships can create at least the appearance of a conflict of interest, where people might think that your results were influenced by your partnerships. All of these downsides can be addressed, but it is important to be clear that working with data that is not accessible to everyone has both upsides and downsides.

In summary, lots of big data are inaccessible to researchers. There are serious legal, business, and ethical barriers that prevent data access, and these barriers will not go away as technology improves, because they are not technical barriers. Some national governments have established procedures for enabling data access for some datasets, but the process is especially ad hoc at the state and local levels. Also, in some cases, researchers can partner with companies to obtain data access, but this can create a variety of problems for researchers and companies.

2.3.6 Nonrepresentative

Nonrepresentative data are bad for out-of-sample generalizations, but can be quite useful for within-sample comparisons.

Some social scientists are accustomed to working with data that comes from a probabilistic random sample from a well-defined population, such as all adults in a particular country. This kind of data is called *representative* data because the sample "represents" the larger population. Many researchers prize representative data, and, to some, representative data is synonymous with rigorous science whereas nonrepresentative data is synonymous with sloppiness. At the most extreme, some skeptics seem to believe that nothing can be learned from nonrepresentative data. If true, this would seem to severely limit what can be learned from big data sources because many of them are nonrepresentative. Fortunately, these skeptics are only partially right. There are certain research goals for which nonrepresentative data is clearly not well suited, but there are others for which it might actually be quite useful.

To understand this distinction, let's consider a scientific classic: John Snow's study of the 1853–54 cholera outbreak in London. At the time, many doctors believed that cholera was caused by "bad air," but Snow believed that it was an infectious disease, perhaps spread by sewage-laced drinking water. To test this idea, Snow took advantage of what we might now call a natural experiment. He compared the cholera rates of households served by two different water companies: Lambeth and Southwark & Vauxhall. These companies served similar households, but they differed in one important way: in 1849—a few years before the epidemic began—Lambeth moved its intake point upstream from the main sewage discharge in London, whereas Southwark & Vauxhall left their intake pipe downstream from the sewage discharge. When Snow compared the death rates from cholera in households served by the two companies, he found that customers of Southwark & Vauxhall—the company that was providing customers sewage-tainted water—were 10 times more likely to die from cholera. This result provides strong scientific evidence for Snow's argument about the cause of cholera, even though it is not based on a representative sample of people in London.

The data from these two companies, however, would not be ideal for answering a different question: what was the prevalence of cholera in London during the outbreak? For that second question, which is also important, it would be much better to have a representative sample of people from London.

As Snow's work illustrates, there are some scientific questions for which nonrepresentative data can be quite effective, and there are others for which it is not well suited. One crude way to distinguish these two kinds of questions is that some questions are about within-sample comparisons and some are about out-of-sample generalizations. This distinction can be further illustrated by another classic study in epidemiology: the British Doctors Study, which played an important role in demonstrating that smoking causes cancer. In this study, Richard Doll and A. Bradford Hill followed approximately 25,000 male doctors for several years and compared their death rates based on the amount that they smoked when the study began. Doll and Hill (1954) found a strong exposure–response relationship: the more heavily people smoked, the more likely they were to die from lung cancer. Of course, it would be unwise to estimate the prevalence of lung cancer among all British people based on this group of male doctors, but the within-sample comparison still provides evidence that smoking causes lung cancer.

Now that I've illustrated the difference between within-sample comparisons and out-of-sample generalizations, two caveats are in order. First, there are naturally questions about the extent to which a relationship that holds within a sample of male British doctors will also hold within a sample of female British doctors or male British factory workers or female German factory workers or many other groups. These questions are interesting and important, but they are different from questions about the extent to which we can generalize from a sample to a population. Notice, for example, that you probably suspect that the relationship between smoking and cancer that was found in male British doctors will probably be similar in these other groups. Your ability to do this extrapolation does not come from the fact that male British doctors are a probabilistic random sample from any population; rather, it comes from an understanding of the mechanism that links smoking and cancer. Thus, the generalization from a sample to the population from which it is drawn is a largely a statistical issue, but questions about the *transportability* of pattern found in one group to another group is largely a nonstatistical issue (Pearl and Bareinboim 2014; Pearl 2015).

At this point, a skeptic might point out that most social patterns are probably less transportable across groups than the relationship between smoking and cancer. And I agree. The extent to which we should expect patterns to be transportable is ultimately a scientific question that has to be decided based on theory and evidence. It should not automatically be assumed that patterns will be transportable, but nor should be it assumed that they won't be transportable. These somewhat abstract questions about transportability will be familiar to you if you have followed the debates about how much researchers can learn about human behavior by studying undergraduate students (Sears 1986, Henrich, Heine, and Norenzayan (2010b)). Despite these debates, however, it would be unreasonable to say that researchers can't learn anything from studying undergraduate students.

The second caveat is that most researchers with nonrepresentative data are not as careful as Snow or Doll and Hill. So, to illustrate what can go wrong when researchers try to make an out-of-sample generalization from nonrepresentative data, I'd like to tell you about a study of the 2009 German parliamentary election by Andranik Tumasjan and colleagues (2010). By analyzing more than 100,000 tweets, they found that the proportion of tweets mentioning a political party matched the proportion of votes that party received in the parliamentary election (figure 2.3). In other words, it appeared that Twitter data, which was essentially free, could replace traditional public opinion surveys, which are expensive because of their emphasis on representative data.

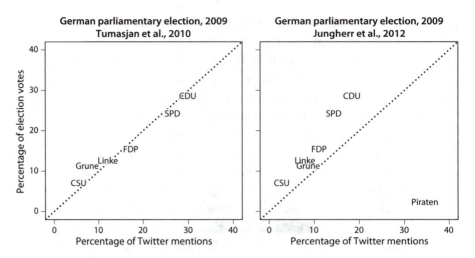

Figure 2.3: Twitter mentions appear to predict the results of the 2009 German election (Tumasjan et al. 2010), but this result depends on excluding the party with the most mentions: the Pirate Party (Jungherr, Jürgens, and Schoen 2012). See Tumasjan et al. (2012) for an argument in favor of excluding the Pirate Party. Adapted from Tumasjan et al. (2010), table 4, and Jungherr, Jürgens, and Schoen (2012), table 2.

Given what you probably already know about Twitter, you should immediately be skeptical of this result. Germans on Twitter in 2009 were not a probabilistic random sample of German voters, and supporters of some parties might tweet about politics much more often than supporters of other parties. Thus, it seems surprising that all of the possible biases that you could imagine would somehow cancel out so that this data would be directly reflective of German voters. In fact, the results in Tumasjan et al. (2010) turned out to be too good to be true. A follow-up paper by Andreas Jungherr, Pascal Jürgens, and Harald Schoen (2012) pointed out that the original analysis had excluded the political party that had received the most mentions on Twitter: the Pirate Party, a small party that fights government regulation of the Internet. When the Pirate Party was included in the analysis, Twitter mentions becomes a terrible predictor of election results (figure 2.3). As this example illustrates, using nonrepresentative big data sources to do out-of-sample generalizations can go very wrong. Also, you should notice that the fact that there were 100,000 tweets was basically irrelevant: lots of nonrepresentative data is still nonrepresentative, a theme that I'll return to in chapter 3 when I discuss surveys.

To conclude, many big data sources are not representative samples from some well-defined population. For questions that require generalizing results from the sample to the population from which it was drawn, this is a serious problem. But for questions about within-sample comparisons, nonrepresentative data can be powerful, so long as researchers are clear about the characteristics of their sample and support claims about transportability with theoretical or empirical evidence. In fact, my hope is that big data sources will enable researchers to make more within-sample comparisons in many nonrepresentative groups, and my guess is that estimates from many different groups will do more to advance social research than a single estimate from a probabilistic random sample.

2.3.7 Drifting

Population drift, usage drift, and system drift make it hard to use big data sources to study long-term trends.

One of the great advantages of many big data sources is that they collect data over time. Social scientists call this kind of over-time data *longitudinal data*. And, naturally, longitudinal data are very important for studying change. In order to reliably measure change, however, the measurement system itself must be stable. In the words of sociologist Otis Dudley Duncan, "if you want to measure change, don't change the measure" (Fischer 2011).

Unfortunately, many big data systems—especially business systems—are changing all the time, a process that I'll call *drift.* In particular, these systems change in three main ways: *population drift* (change in who is using them), *behavioral drift* (change in how people are using them), and *system drift* (change in the system itself). The three sources of drift mean that any pattern in a big data source could be caused by an important change in the world, or it could be caused by some form of drift.

The first source of drift—population drift—is caused by changes in who is using the system, and these changes can happen on both short and long timescales. For example, during the US Presidential election of 2012 the proportion of tweets about politics that were written by women fluctuated from day to day (Diaz et al. 2016). Thus, what might appear to be a change in the mood of the Twitter-verse might actually just be a change in who is talking at any moment. In addition to these short-term fluctuations, there has also been a long-term trend of certain demographic groups adopting and abandoning Twitter.

In addition to changes in who is using a system, there are also changes in how the system is used, which I call behavioral drift. For example, during the 2013 Occupy Gezi protests in Turkey, protesters changed their use of hashtags as the protest evolved. Here's how Zeynep Tufekci (2014) described the behavioral drift, which she was able to detect because she was observing behavior on Twitter and in person:

> "What had happened was that as soon as the protest became the dominant story, large numbers of people … stopped using the hashtags except to draw attention to a new phenomenon … While the protests continued, and even intensified, the hashtags died down. Interviews revealed two reasons for this. First, once everyone knew the topic, the hashtag was at once superfluous and wasteful on the character-limited Twitter platform. Second, hashtags were seen only as useful for attracting attention to a particular topic, not for talking about it."

Thus, researchers who were studying the protests by analyzing tweets with protest-related hashtags would have a distorted sense of what was happening because of this behavioral drift. For example, they might believe that the discussion of the protest decreased long before it actually decreased.

The third kind of drift is system drift. In this case, it is not the people changing or their behavior changing, but the system itself changing. For example, over time, Facebook has increased the limit on the length of status updates. Thus, any longitudinal study of status updates will be vulnerable to artifacts caused by this change. System drift is closely related to a problem called algorithmic confounding, which I'll cover in section 2.3.8.

To conclude, many big data sources are drifting because of changes in who is using them, in how they are being used, and in how the systems work. These sources of change are sometimes interesting research questions, but these changes complicate the ability of big data sources to track long-term changes over time.

2.3.8 Algorithmically confounded

Behavior in big data systems is not natural; it is driven by the engineering goals of the systems.

Although many big data sources are nonreactive because people are not aware their data are being recorded (section 2.3.3), researchers should not consider behavior in these online systems to be "naturally occurring." In reality, the digital systems that record behavior are highly engineered to induce specific behaviors such as clicking on ads or posting content. The ways that the goals of system designers can introduce patterns into data is called *algorithmic confounding*. Algorithmic confounding is relatively unknown to social scientists, but it is a major concern among careful data scientists. And, unlike some of the other problems with digital traces, algorithmic confounding is largely invisible.

A relatively simple example of algorithmic confounding is the fact that on Facebook there are an anomalously high number of users with approximately 20 friends, as was discovered by Johan Ugander and colleagues (2011). Scientists analyzing this data without any understanding of how Facebook works could doubtless generate many stories about how 20 is some kind of magical social number. Fortunately, Ugander and his colleagues had a substantial understanding of the process that generated the data, and they knew that Facebook encouraged people with few connections on Facebook to make more friends until they reached 20 friends. Although Ugander and colleagues don't say this in their paper, this policy was presumably created by Facebook in order to encourage new users to become more active. Without knowing about the existence of this policy, however, it is easy to draw the wrong conclusion from the data. In other words, the surprisingly high number of people with about 20 friends tells us more about Facebook than about human behavior.

In this previous example, algorithmic confounding produced a quirky result that a careful researcher might detect and investigate further. However, there is an even trickier version of algorithmic confounding that occurs when designers of online systems are aware of social theories and then bake these theories into the working of their systems. Social scientists call this *performativity*: when a theory changes the world in such a way that it bring the world more into line with the theory. In the case of performative algorithmic confounding, the confounded nature of the data is likely invisible.

One example of a pattern created by performativity is transitivity in online social networks. In the 1970s and 1980s, researchers repeatedly found that if you are friends with both Alice and Bob, then Alice and Bob are more likely to be friends with each other than if they were two randomly chosen people. This very same pattern was found in the social graph on Facebook (Ugander et al. 2011). Thus, one might conclude that patterns of friendship on Facebook replicate patterns of offline friendships, at least in terms of transitivity. However, the magnitude of transitivity in the Facebook social graph is partially driven by algorithmic confounding. That is, data scientists at Facebook knew of the empirical and theoretical research about transitivity and then baked it into how Facebook works. Facebook has a "People You May Know" feature that suggests new friends, and one way that Facebook decides who to suggest to you is transitivity. That is, Facebook is more likely to suggest that you become friends with the friends of your friends. This feature thus has the effect of increasing transitivity in the Facebook social graph; in other words, the theory of transitivity brings the world into line with the predictions of the theory (Zignani et al. 2014; Healy 2015). Thus, when big data sources appear to reproduce predictions of social theory, we must be sure that the theory itself was not baked into how the system worked.

Rather than thinking of big data sources as observing people in a natural setting, a more apt metaphor is observing people in a casino. Casinos are highly engineered environments designed to induce certain behaviors, and a researcher would never expect behavior in a casino to provide an unfettered window into human behavior. Of course, you could learn something about human behavior by studying people in casinos, but if you ignored the fact that the data was being created in a casino, you might draw some bad conclusions.

Unfortunately, dealing with algorithmic confounding is particularly difficult because many features of online systems are proprietary, poorly documented, and constantly changing. For example, as I'll explain later in this chapter, algorithmic confounding was one possible explanation for the gradual breakdown of Google Flu Trends (section 2.4.2), but this claim was hard to assess because the inner workings of Google's search algorithm are proprietary. The dynamic nature of algorithmic confounding is one form of system drift. Algorithmic confounding means that we should be cautious about any claim regarding human behavior that comes from a single digital system, no matter how big.

2.3.9 Dirty

Big data sources can be loaded with junk and spam.

Some researchers believe that big data sources, especially online sources, are pristine because they are collected automatically. In fact, people who have worked with big data sources know that they are frequently *dirty.* That is, they frequently include data that do not reflect real actions of interest to researchers. Most social scientists are already familiar with the process of cleaning large-scale social survey data, but cleaning big data sources seems to be more difficult. I think the ultimate source of this difficulty is that many of these big data sources were never intended to be used for research, and so they are not collected, stored, and documented in a way that facilitates data cleaning.

The dangers of dirty digital trace data are illustrated by Back and colleagues' (2010) study of the emotional response to the attacks of September 11, 2001, which I briefly mentioned earlier in the chapter. Researchers typically study the response to tragic events using retrospective data collected over months or even years. But, Back and colleagues found an always-on source of digital traces—the timestamped, automatically recorded messages from 85,000 American pagers—and this enabled them to study emotional response on a much finer timescale. They created a minute-by-minute emotional timeline of September 11 by coding the emotional content of the pager messages by the percentage of words related to (1) sadness (e.g., "crying" and "grief"), (2) anxiety (e.g., "worried" and "fearful"), and (3) anger (e.g., "hate" and "critical"). They found that sadness and anxiety fluctuated throughout the day without a strong pattern, but that there was a striking increase in anger throughout the day. This research seems to be a wonderful illustration of the power of always-on data sources: if traditional data sources had been used, it would have been impossible to obtain such a high-resolution timeline of the immediate response to an unexpected event.

Just one year later, however, Cynthia Pury (2011) looked at the data more carefully. She discovered that a large number of the supposedly angry messages were generated by a single pager and they were all identical. Here's

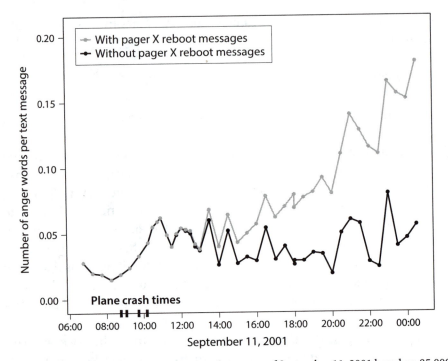

Figure 2.4: Estimated trends in anger over the course of September 11, 2001 based on 85,000 American pagers (Back, Küfner, and Egloff 2010; Pury 2011; Back, Küfner, and Egloff 2011). Originally, Back, Küfner, and Egloff (2010) reported a pattern of increasing anger throughout the day. However, most of these apparently angry messages were generated by a single pager that repeatedly sent out the following message: "Reboot NT machine [name] in cabinet [name] at [location]:CRITICAL:[date and time]". With this message removed, the apparent increase in anger disappears (Pury 2011; Back, Küfner, and Egloff 2011). Adapted from Pury (2011), figure 1b.

what those supposedly angry messages said:

> "Reboot NT machine [name] in cabinet [name] at [location]: CRITI-CAL:[date and time]"

These messages were labeled angry because they included the word "CRITICAL," which may generally indicate anger but in this case does not. Removing the messages generated by this single automated pager completely eliminates the apparent increase in anger over the course of the day (figure 2.4). In other words, the main result in Back, Küfner, and Egloff (2010) was an artifact of one pager. As this example illustrates, relatively simple analysis of relatively complex and messy data has the potential to go seriously wrong.

While dirty data that is created unintentionally—such as that from one noisy pager—can be detected by a reasonably careful researcher, there are also some online systems that attract intentional spammers. These spammers actively generate fake data, and—often motivated by profit—work very hard to keep their spamming concealed. For example, political activity on Twitter seems to include at least some reasonably sophisticated spam, whereby some political causes are intentionally made to look more popular than they actually are (Ratkiewicz et al. 2011). Unfortunately, removing this intentional spam can be quite difficult.

Of course what is considered dirty data can depend, in part, on the research question. For example, many edits to Wikipedia are created by automated bots (Geiger 2014). If you are interested in the ecology of Wikipedia, then these bot-created edits are important. But if you are interested in how humans contribute to Wikipedia, then the bot-created edits should be excluded.

There is no single statistical technique or approach that can ensure that you have sufficiently cleaned your dirty data. In the end, I think the best way to avoid being fooled by dirty data is to understand as much as possible about how your data were created.

2.3.10 Sensitive

> Some of the information that companies and governments have is sensitive.

Health insurance companies have detailed information about the medical care received by their customers. This information could be used for important research about health, but if it became public, it could potentially lead to emotional harm (e.g., embarrassment) or economic harm (e.g., loss of employment). Many other big data sources also have information that is sensitive, which is part of the reason why they are often inaccessible.

Unfortunately, it turns out to be quite tricky to decide what information is actually sensitive (Ohm, 2015), as was illustrated by the Netflix Prize. As I will describe in chapter 5, in 2006, Netflix released 100 million movie ratings provided by almost 500,000 members and had an open call where people from all over the world submitted algorithms that could improve Netflix's ability to recommend movies. Before releasing the data, Netflix removed any obvious personally identifying information, such as names. But, just two weeks after the data was released Arvind Narayanan and Vitaly Shmatikov (2008) showed that it was possible to learn about specific people's movie ratings using a trick that I'll show you in chapter 6. Even though an attacker could discover a person's movie ratings, there still doesn't seem to be anything sensitive here. While that might be true in general, for at least some of the 500,000 people in the dataset, movie ratings were sensitive. In fact, in response to the release and re-identification of the data, a closeted lesbian woman joined a class-action suit against Netflix. Here's how the problem was expressed in this lawsuit (Singel 2009):

> "[M]ovie and rating data contains information of a ... highly personal and sensitive nature. The member's movie data exposes a Netflix member's personal interest and/or struggles with various highly personal issues, including sexuality, mental illness, recovery from alcoholism, and victimization from incest, physical abuse, domestic violence, adultery, and rape."

This example shows that there can be information that some people consider sensitive inside of what might appear to be a benign database. Further, it shows that a main defense that researchers employ to protect sensitive data—de-identification—can fail in surprising ways. These two ideas are developed in greater detail in chapter 6.

The final thing to keep in mind about sensitive data is that collecting it without people's consent raises ethical questions, even if no specific harm is caused. Much like watching someone taking a shower without their consent might be considered a violation of that person's privacy, collecting sensitive information—and remember how hard it can be to decide what is sensitive—without consent creates potential privacy concerns. I'll return to questions about privacy in chapter 6.

In conclusion, big data sources, such as government and business administrative records, are generally not created for the purpose of social research. The big data sources of today, and likely tomorrow, tend to have 10 characteristics. Many of the properties that are generally considered to be good for research—big, always-on, and nonreactive—come from the fact in the digital age companies and governments are able to collect data at a scale that was not possible previously. And many of the properties that are generally considered to be bad for research—incomplete, inaccessible, nonrepresentative, drifting, algorithmically confounded, inaccessible, dirty, and sensitive—come from the fact that these data were not collected by researchers for researchers. So far, I've talked about government and business data together, but there are some differences between the two. In my experience, government data tends to be less nonrepresentative, less algorithmically confounded, and less drifting. One the other hand, business administrative records tend to be more always-on. Understanding these 10 general characteristics is a helpful first step toward learning from big data sources. And now we turn to research strategies we can use with this data.

2.4 Research strategies

Given these 10 characteristics of big data sources and the inherent limitations of even perfectly observed data, I see three main strategies for learning from big data sources: counting things, forecasting things, and approximating experiments. I'll describe each of these approaches—which could be called "research strategies" or "research recipes"—and I'll illustrate them with examples. These strategies are neither mutually exclusive nor exhaustive.

2.4.1 Counting things

Simple counting can be interesting if you combine a good question with good data.

Although it is couched in sophisticated-sounding language, lots of social research is really just counting things. In the age of big data, researchers can count more than ever, but that does not mean that they should just start counting haphazardly. Instead, researchers should ask: What things are worth counting? This may seem like an entirely subjective matter, but there are some general patterns.

Often students motivate their counting research by saying: I'm going to count something that no-one has ever counted before. For example, a student might say that many people have studied migrants and many people have studied twins, but nobody has studied migrant twins. In my experience, this strategy, which I call *motivation by absence*, does not usually lead to good research.

Instead of motivating by absence, I think a better strategy is to look for research questions that are *important* or *interesting* (or ideally both). Both of these terms a bit hard to define, but one way to think about important research is that it has some measurable impact or feeds into an important decision by policy makers. For example, measuring the rate of unemployment is important because it is an indicator of the economy that drives policy decisions. Generally, I think that researchers have a pretty good sense of what is important. So, in the rest of this section, I'm going to provide two examples where I think counting is interesting. In each case, the researchers were not counting haphazardly; rather, they were counting in very particular settings that revealed important insights into more general ideas about how social systems work. In other words, a lot of what makes these particular counting exercises interesting is not the data itself, it comes from these more general ideas.

One example of the simple power of counting comes from Henry Farber's (2015) study of the behavior of New York City taxi drivers. Although this group might not sound inherently interesting, it is a *strategic research site* for testing two competing theories in labor economics. For the purposes of Farber's research, there are two important features about the work environment of taxi drivers: (1) their hourly wage fluctuates from day to day, based in part on factors like the weather, and (2) the number of hours they work can fluctuate each day based on their decisions. These features lead to an interesting question about the relationship between hourly wages and hours worked. Neoclassical models in economics predict that taxi drivers will work more on days where they have higher hourly wages. Alternatively, models from behavioral economics predict exactly the opposite. If drivers set a particular income target—say $100 per day—and work until that target is met, then drivers will end up working fewer hours on days that they are earning more. For example, if you were a target earner, you might end up working four hours on a good day ($25 per hour) and five hours on a bad day ($20 per hour). So, do drivers work more hours on days with higher hourly wages (as predicted by the neoclassical models) or more hours on days with lower hourly wages (as predicted by behavioral economic models)?

To answer this question, Farber obtained data on every taxi trip taken by New York City cabs from 2009 to 2013, data that are now publicly available.

These data—which were collected by electronic meters that the city requires taxis to use—include information about each trip: start time, start location, end time, end location, fare, and tip (if the tip was paid with a credit card). Using this taxi meter data, Farber found that most drivers work more on days when wages are higher, consistent with the neoclassical theory.

In addition to this main finding, Farber was able to use the size of the data for a better understanding of heterogeneity and dynamics. He found that, over time, newer drivers gradually learn to work more hours on high-wage days (e.g., they learn to behave as the neoclassical model predicts). And new drivers who behave more like target earners are more likely to quit being taxi drivers. Both of these more subtle findings, which help explain the observed behavior of current drivers, were only possible because of the size of the dataset. They were impossible to detect in earlier studies that used paper trip sheets from a small number of taxi drivers over a short period of time (Camerer et al. 1997).

Farber's study was close to a best-case scenario for a study using a big data source because the data that were collected by the city were pretty close to the data that Farber would have collected (one difference is that Farber would have wanted data on total wages—fares plus tips—but the city data only included tips paid by credit card). However, the data alone were not enough. The key to Farber's research was bringing an interesting question to the data, a question that has larger implications beyond just this specific setting.

A second example of counting things comes from research by Gary King, Jennifer Pan, and Molly Roberts (2013) on online censorship by the Chinese government. In this case, however, the researchers had to collect their own big data and they had to deal with the fact that their data was incomplete.

King and colleagues were motivated by the fact that social media posts in China are censored by an enormous state apparatus that is thought to include tens of thousands of people. Researchers and citizens, however, have little sense of how these censors decide what content should be deleted. Scholars of China actually have conflicting expectations about which kinds of posts are most likely to get deleted. Some think that censors focus on posts that are critical of the state, while others think that they focus on posts that encourage collective behavior, such as protests. Figuring out which of these expectations is correct has implications for how researchers understand China and other authoritarian governments that engage in censorship. Therefore, King and colleagues wanted to compare posts that were published and subsequently deleted with posts that were published and never deleted.

Collecting these posts involved the amazing engineering feat of crawling more than 1,000 Chinese social media websites—each with different page layouts—finding relevant posts, and then revisiting these posts to see which were subsequently deleted. In addition to the normal engineering problems associated with large scale web-crawling, this project had the added challenge that it needed to be extremely fast because many censored posts are taken down in less than 24 hours. In other words, a slow crawler would miss lots of posts that were censored. Further, the crawlers had to do all this data collection while evading detection lest the social media websites block access or otherwise change their policies in response to the study.

By the time that this massive engineering task had been completed, King and colleagues had obtained about 11 million posts on 85 different prespecified topics, each with an assumed level of sensitivity. For example, a topic of high sensitivity is Ai Weiwei, the dissident artist; a topic of middle sensitivity is appreciation and devaluation of the Chinese currency; and a topic of low sensitivity is the World Cup. Of these 11 million posts, about 2 million had been censored. Somewhat surprisingly, King and colleagues found that posts on highly sensitive topics were censored only slightly more often than posts on middle- and low-sensitivity topics. In other words, Chinese censors are about as likely to censor a post that mentions Ai Weiwei as a post that mentions the World Cup. These findings do not support the idea that the government censors all posts on sensitive topics.

This simple calculation of censorship rate by topic could be misleading, however. For example, the government might censor posts that are supportive of Ai Weiwei, but leave posts that are critical of him. In order to distinguish between posts more carefully, the researchers needed to measure the *sentiment* of each post. Unfortunately, despite much work, fully automated methods of sentiment detection using pre-existing dictionaries are still not very good in many situations (think back to the problems creating an emotional timeline of September 11, 2001 described in section 2.3.9). Therefore, King and colleagues needed a way to label their 11 million social media posts as to whether they were (1) critical of the state, (2) supportive of the state, or (3) irrelevant or factual reports about the events. This sounds

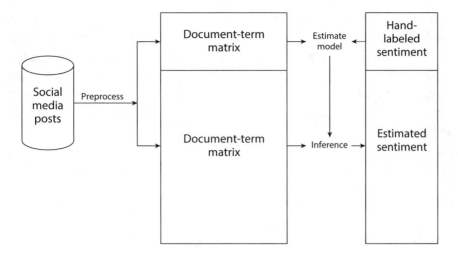

Figure 2.5: Simplified schematic of the procedure used by King, Pan, and Roberts (2013) to estimate the sentiment of 11 million Chinese social media posts. First, in a *preprocessing* step, they converted the social media posts into a *document–term matrix* (see Grimmer and Stewart (2013) for more information). Second, they hand-coded the sentiment of a small sample of posts. Third, they trained a supervised learning model to classify the sentiment of posts. Fourth, they used the supervised learning model to estimate the sentiment of all the posts. See King, Pan, and Roberts (2013), appendix B for a more detailed description.

like a massive job, but they solved it using a powerful trick that is common in data science but relatively rare in social science: *supervised learning*; see figure 2.5.

First, in a step typically called *preprocessing*, they converted the social media posts into a *document–term matrix*, where there was one row for each document and one column that recorded whether the post contained a specific word (e.g., protest or traffic). Next, a group of research assistants hand-labeled the sentiment of a sample of posts. Then, they used this hand-labeled data to create a machine learning model that could infer the sentiment of a post based on its characteristics. Finally, they used this model to estimate the sentiments of all 11 million posts.

Thus, rather than manually reading and labeling 11 million posts—which would be logistically impossible—King and colleagues manually labeled a small number of posts and then used supervised learning to estimate the sentiment of all the posts. After completing this analysis, they were able to conclude that, somewhat surprisingly, the probability of a post being deleted was unrelated to whether it was critical of the state or supportive of the state.

In the end, King and colleagues discovered that only three types of posts were regularly censored: pornography, criticism of censors, and those that had collective action potential (i.e., the possibility of leading to large-scale protests). By observing a huge number of posts that were deleted and posts that were not deleted, King and colleagues were able to learn how the censors work just by watching and counting. Further, foreshadowing a theme that will occur throughout this book, the supervised learning approach that they used—hand-labeling some outcomes and then building a machine learning model to label the rest—turns out to be very common in social research in the digital age. You will see pictures very similar to figure 2.5 in chapters 3 (Asking questions) and 5 (Creating mass collaboration); this is one of the few ideas that appears in multiple chapters.

These examples—the working behavior of taxi drivers in New York and the social media censorship behavior of the Chinese government—show that relatively simple counting of big data sources can, in some situations, lead to interesting and important research. In both cases, however, the researchers had to bring interesting questions to the big data source; the data by itself was not enough.

2.4.2 Forecasting and nowcasting

Predicting the future is hard, but predicting the present is easier.

The second main strategy researchers can use with observational data is *forecasting*. Making guesses about the future is notoriously difficult, and, perhaps for that reason, forecasting is not currently a large part of social research (although it is a small and important part of demography, economics, epidemiology, and political science). Here, however, I'd like to focus on a special kind of forecasting called *nowcasting*—a term derived from combining "now" and "forecasting." Rather than predicting the future, nowcasting attempts to use ideas from forecasting to measure the current state of the world: it attempts to "predict the present" (Choi and Varian 2012). Nowcasting has the potential to be especially useful to governments and companies that require timely and accurate measures of the world.

One setting where the need for timely and accurate measurement is very clear is epidemiology. Consider the case of influenza ("the flu"). Each year, seasonal influenza epidemics cause millions of illnesses and hundreds of thousands of deaths around the world. Further, each year, there is a possibility that a novel form of influenza could emerge that would kill millions. The 1918 influenza outbreak, for example, is estimated to have killed between 50 and 100 million people (Morens and Fauci 2007). Because of the need to track and potentially respond to influenza outbreaks, governments around the world have created influenza surveillance systems. For example, the US Centers for Disease Control and Prevention (CDC) regularly and systematically collect information from carefully selected doctors around the country. Although this system produces high-quality data, it has a reporting lag. That is, because of the time it takes for the data arriving from doctors to be cleaned, processed, and published, the CDC system releases estimates of how much flu there was two weeks ago. But, when handling an emerging epidemic, public health officials don't want to know how much influenza there was two weeks ago; they want to know how much influenza there is right now.

At the same time that the CDC is collecting data to track influenza, Google is also collecting data about influenza prevalence, although in a quite different form. People from around the world are constantly sending queries to Google, and some of these queries—such as "flu remedies" and "flu symptoms"—might indicate that the person making the query has the flu. But, using these search queries to estimate flu prevalence is tricky: not everyone who has the flu makes a flu-related search, and not every flu-related search is from someone who has the flu.

Jeremy Ginsberg and a team of colleagues (2009), some at Google and some at CDC, had the important and clever idea to combine these two data sources. Roughly, through a kind of statistical alchemy, the researchers combined the fast and inaccurate search data with the slow and accurate CDC data in order to produce fast and accurate measurements of influenza prevalence. Another way to think about it is that they used the search data to speed up the CDC data.

More specifically, using data from 2003 to 2007, Ginsberg and colleagues estimated the relationship between the prevalence of influenza in the CDC data and the search volume for 50 million distinct terms. From this process, which was completely data-driven and did not require specialized medical knowledge, the researchers found a set of 45 different queries that seemed to be most predictive of the CDC flu prevalence data. Then, using the relationships that they learned from the 2003–2007 data, Ginsberg and colleagues tested their model during the 2007–2008 influenza season. They found that their procedures could indeed make useful and accurate nowcasts (figure 2.6). These results were published in *Nature* and received adoring press coverage. This project—which was called Google Flu Trends—became an often-repeated parable about the power of big data to change the world.

However, this apparent success story eventually turned into an embarrassment. Over time, researchers discovered two important limitations that make Google Flu Trends less impressive than it initially appeared. First, the performance of Google Flu Trends was actually not much better than that of a simple model that estimates the amount of flu based on a linear extrapolation from the two most recent measurements of flu prevalence (Goel et al. 2010). And, over some time periods, Google Flu Trends was actually worse than this simple approach (Lazer et al. 2014). In other words, Google Flu Trends with all its data, machine learning, and powerful computing did not dramatically outperform a simple and easier-to-understand heuristic. This suggests that when evaluating any forecast or nowcast, it is important to compare against a baseline.

The second important caveat about Google Flu Trends is that its ability to predict the CDC flu data was prone to short-term failure and long-term decay because of *drift* and *algorithmic confounding*. For example, during the 2009 Swine Flu outbreak, Google Flu Trends dramatically overestimated the amount of influenza, probably because people tend to change their search behavior in response to widespread fear of a global pandemic (Cook et al. 2011; Olson et al. 2013). In addition to these short-term problems, the performance of Google Flu Trends gradually decayed over time. Diagnosing the reasons for this long-term decay are difficult because the Google search algorithms are proprietary, but it appears that in 2011 Google began suggesting related search terms when people search for flu symptoms like "fever" and "cough" (it also seem that this feature is no longer active). Adding this feature is a totally reasonable thing to do if you are running a search engine, but this algorithmic change had the effect of generating more health-related searches, which caused Google Flu Trends to overestimate flu prevalence (Lazer et al. 2014).

These two caveats complicate future nowcasting efforts, but they do not doom them. In fact, by using more careful methods, Lazer et al. (2014) and Yang, Santillana, and Kou (2015) were able to avoid these two problems.

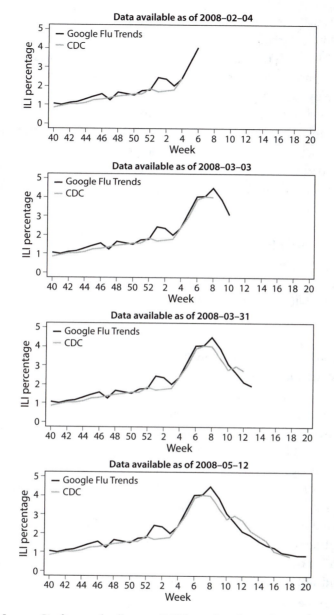

Figure 2.6: Jeremy Ginsberg and colleagues (2009) combined Google search data with CDC data to create Google Flu Trends, which could nowcast the rate of influenza-like illness (ILI). Results in this figure are for the mid-Atlantic region of the United States in the 2007–2008 influenza season. Although it was initially very promising, the performance of Google Flu Trends decayed over time (Cook et al. 2011; Olson et al. 2013; Lazer et al. 2014). Adapted from Ginsberg et al. (2009), figure 3.

Going forward, I expect that nowcasting studies that combine big data sources with researcher-collected data will enable companies and governments to create more timely and more accurate estimates by essentially speeding up any measurement that is made repeatedly over time with some lag. Nowcasting projects such as Google Flu Trends also show what can happen if big data sources are combined with more traditional data that were created for the purposes of research. Thinking back to the art analogy of chapter 1, nowcasting has the potential to combine Duchamp-style readymades with Michelangelo-style custommades to provide decision makers with more timely and more accurate measurements of the present and predictions of the near future.

2.4.3 Approximating experiments

> We can approximate experiments that we can't do. Two approaches that especially benefit from the digital age are natural experiments and matching.

Some important scientific and policy questions are causal. For example, what is the effect of a job training program on wages? A researcher attempting to answer this question might compare the earnings of people who signed up for training with those that didn't. But how much of any difference in wages between these groups is because of the training and how much is because of preexisting differences between the people that sign up and those that don't? This is a difficult question, and it is one that doesn't automatically go away with more data. In other words, the concern about possible preexisting differences arises no matter how many workers are in your data.

In many situations, the strongest way to estimate the causal effect of some treatment, such as job training, is to run a randomized controlled experiment where a researcher randomly delivers the treatment to some people and not others. I'll devote all of chapter 4 to experiments, so here I'm going to focus on two strategies that can be used with non-experimental data. The first strategy depends on looking for something happening in the world that randomly (or nearly randomly) assigns the treatment to some people and not others. The second strategy depends on statistically adjusting non-experimental data in an attempt to account for preexisting differences between those who did and did not receive the treatment.

A skeptic might claim that both of these strategies should be avoided because they require strong assumptions, assumptions that are difficult to assess and that, in practice, are often violated. While I am sympathetic to this claim, I think it goes a bit too far. It is certainly true that it is difficult to reliably make causal estimates from non-experimental data, but I don't think that means that we should never try. In particular, non-experimental approaches can be helpful if logistical constraints prevent you from conducting an experiment or if ethical constraints mean that you do not want to run an experiment. Further, non-experimental approaches can be helpful if you want to take advantage of data that already exist in order to design a randomized controlled experiment.

Before proceeding, it is also worth noting that making causal estimates is one of the most complex topics in social research, and one that can lead to intense and emotional debate. In what follows, I will provide an optimistic description of each approach in order to build intuition about it, then I will describe some of the challenges that arise when using that approach. Further details about each approach are available in the materials at the end of this chapter. If you plan to use either of these approaches in your own research, I highly recommend reading one of the many excellent books on causal inference (Imbens and Rubin 2015; Pearl 2009; Morgan and Winship 2014).

One approach to making causal estimates from non-experimental data is to look for an event that has randomly assigned a treatment to some people and not to others. These situations are called *natural experiments*. One of the clearest examples of a natural experiment comes from the research of Joshua Angrist (1990) measuring the effect of military service on earnings. During the war in Vietnam, the United States increased the size of its armed forces through a draft. In order to decide which citizens would be called into service, the US government held a lottery. Every birth date was written on a piece of paper, and, as shown in figure 2.7, these pieces of paper were selected one at a time in order to determine the order in which young men would be called to serve (young women were not subject to the draft). Based on the results, men born on September 14 were called first, men born on April 24 were called second, and so on. Ultimately, in this lottery, men born on 195 different days were drafted, while men born on 171 days were not.

Although it might not be immediately apparent, a draft lottery has a critical similarity to a randomized controlled experiment: in both situations,

Figure 2.7: Congressman Alexander Pirnie (R-NY) drawing the first capsule for the Selective Service draft on December 1, 1969. Joshua Angrist (1990) combined the draft lottery with earnings data from the Social Security Administration to estimate the effect of military service on earnings. This is an example of research using a natural experiment. (Source: U.S. Selective Service System (1969)/Wikimedia Commons).

participants are randomly assigned to receive a treatment. In order to study the effect of this randomized treatment, Angrist took advantage of an always-on big data system: the US Social Security Administration, which collects information on virtually every American's earnings from employment. By combining the information about who was randomly selected in the draft lottery with the earnings data that were collected in governmental administrative records, Angrist concluded that the earnings of veterans were about 15% less than the earnings of comparable non-veterans.

As this example illustrates, sometimes social, political, or natural forces create experiments that can be leveraged by researchers, and sometimes the effects of those experiments are captured in always-on big data sources. This research strategy can be summarized as follows:

random (or as if random) variation + always-on data = natural experiment

To illustrate this strategy in the digital age, let's consider a study by Alexandre Mas and Enrico Moretti (2009) that tried to estimate the effect of working with productive colleagues on a worker's productivity. Before seeing the results, it is worth pointing out that there are conflicting expectations that you might have. On the one hand, you might expect that working with productive colleagues would lead a worker to increase her productivity because of peer pressure. Or, on the other hand, you might expect that having hard-working peers might lead a worker to slack off because the work will be done by her peers anyway. The clearest way to study peer effects on productivity would be a randomized controlled experiment where workers are randomly assigned to shifts with workers of different productivity levels and then the resulting productivity is measured for everyone. Researchers, however, do not control the schedule of workers in any real business, and so Mas and Moretti had to rely on a natural experiment involving cashiers at a supermarket.

In this particular supermarket, because of the way that scheduling was done and the way that shifts overlapped, each cashier had different co-workers at different times of day. Further, in this particular supermarket, the assignment of cashiers was unrelated to the productivity of their peers or how busy the store was. In other words, even though the scheduling of cashiers was not determined by a lottery, it was as if workers were sometimes randomly assigned to work with high (or low) productivity peers. Fortunately, this supermarket also had a digital-age checkout system that tracked the items that each cashier was scanning at all times. From this checkout log data, Mas and Moretti were able to create a precise, individual, and always-on measure of productivity: the number of items scanned per second. Combining these two things—the naturally occurring variation in peer productivity and the always-on measure of productivity—Mas and Moretti estimated that if a cashier was assigned co-workers who were 10% more productive than average, her productivity would increase by 1.5%. Further, they used the size and richness of their dataset to explore two important issues: the *heterogeneity* of this effect (For which kinds of workers is the effect larger?) and the *mechanisms* behind the effect (Why does having high-productivity peers lead to higher productivity?). We will return to these two important issues—heterogeneity of treatment effects and mechanisms—in chapter 4 when we discuss experiments in more detail.

Generalizing from these two studies, table 2.3 summarizes other studies that have this same structure: using an always-on data source to measure the effect of some random variation. In practice, researchers use two different strategies for finding natural experiments, both of which can be fruitful. Some researchers start with an always-on data source and look for random events in the world; others start with a random event in the world and look for data sources that capture its impact.

Table 2.3: Examples of Natural Experiments Using Big Data Sources

Substantive focus	Source of natural experiment	Always-on data source	Reference
Peer effects on productivity	Scheduling process	Checkout data	Mas and Moretti (2009)
Friendship formation	Hurricanes	Facebook	Phan and Airoldi (2015)
Spread of emotions	Rain	Facebook	Coviello et al. (2014)
Peer-to-peer economic transfers	Earthquake	Mobile money data	Blumenstock, Fafchamps, and Eagle (2011)
Personal consumption behavior	2013 US government shutdown	Personal finance data	Baker and Yannelis (2015)
Economic impact of recommender systems	Various	Browsing data at Amazon	Sharma, Hofman, and Watts (2015)
Effect of stress on unborn babies	2006 Israel–Hezbollah war	Birth records	Torche and Shwed (2015)
Reading behavior on Wikipedia	Snowden revelations	Wikipedia logs	Penney (2016)
Peer effects on exercise	Weather	Fitness trackers	Aral and Nicolaides (2017)

In the discussion so far about natural experiments, I've left out an important point: going from what nature has provided to what you want can sometimes be quite tricky. Let's return to the Vietnam draft example. In this case, Angrist was interested in estimating the effect of military service on earnings. Unfortunately, military service was not randomly assigned; rather, it was being drafted that was randomly assigned. However, not everyone who was drafted served (there were a variety of exemptions), and not everyone who served was drafted (people could volunteer to serve). Because being drafted was randomly assigned, a researcher can estimate the effect of being drafted for all men in the draft. But Angrist didn't want to know the effect of being drafted; he wanted to know the effect of serving in the military. To make this estimate, however, additional assumptions and complications are required. First, researchers need to assume that the only way that being drafted impacted earnings is through military service, an assumption called the *exclusion restriction*. This assumption could be wrong if, for example, men who were drafted stayed in school longer in order to avoid serving or if employers were less likely to hire men who were drafted. In general, the exclusion restriction is a critical assumption, and it is usually hard to verify. Even if the exclusion restriction is correct, it is still impossible to estimate the effect of service on all men. Instead, it turns out that researchers can only estimate the effect on a specific subset of men called compliers (men who would serve when drafted, but would not serve when not drafted) (Angrist, Imbens, and Rubin 1996). Compliers, however, were not the original population of interest. Notice that these problems arise even in the relatively clean case of the draft lottery. A further set of complications arise when the treatment is not assigned by a physical lottery. For example, in Mas and Moretti's study of cashiers, additional questions arise about the assumption that the assignment of peers is essentially random. If this assumption were strongly violated, it could bias their estimates. To conclude, natural experiments can be a powerful strategy for making causal estimates from non-experimental data, and big data sources increase our ability to capitalize on natural experiments when they occur. However, it will probably require great care—and sometimes strong assumptions—to go from what nature has provided to the estimate that you want.

The second strategy I'd like to tell you about for making causal estimates from non-experimental data depends on statistically adjusting non-experimental data in an attempt to account for preexisting differences between those who did and did not receive the treatment. There are many such adjustment approaches, but I'll focus on one called *matching*. In matching, the researcher looks through non-experimental data to create pairs of people who are similar except that one has received the treatment and one has not. In the process of matching, researchers are actually also *pruning*, that is, discarding cases where there is no obvious match. Thus, this method would be more accurately called matching-and-pruning, but I'll stick with the traditional term: matching.

One example of the power of matching strategies with massive non-experimental data sources comes from research on consumer behavior by Liran Einav and colleagues (2015). They were interested in auctions taking place on eBay, and in describing their work, I'll focus on the effect of auction starting price on auction outcomes, such as the sale price or the probability of a sale.

The most naive way to estimate the effect of starting price on sale price would be to simply calculate the final price for auctions with different starting prices. This approach would be fine if you wanted to predict the sale price given the starting price. But if your question concerns the effect of the starting price, then this approach will not work, because it is not based on a fair comparison: auctions with lower starting prices might be quite different from those with higher starting prices (e.g., they might be for different types of goods or include different types of sellers).

If you are already aware of the problems that can arise when making causal estimates from non-experimental data, you might skip the naive approach and consider running a field experiment where you would sell a specific item—say, a golf club—with a fixed set of auction parameters— say, free shipping and auction open for two weeks—but with randomly assigned starting prices. By comparing the resulting market outcomes, this field experiment would offer a very clear measurement of the effect of starting price on sale price. But this measurement would only apply to one particular product and set of auction parameters. The results might be different, for example, for different types of products. Without a strong theory, it is difficult to extrapolate from this single experiment to the full range of possible experiments that could have been run. Further, field experiments are sufficiently expensive that it would be infeasible to run every variation that you might want to try.

In contrast to the naive and the experimental approaches, Einav and colleagues took a third approach: matching. The main trick in their strategy is to discover things similar to field experiments that have already happened on eBay. For example, figure 2.8 shows some of the 31 listings for exactly the same golf club—a Taylormade Burner 09 Driver—being sold by exactly the same seller—"budgetgolfer." However, these 31 listings have slightly different characteristics, such as different starting prices, end dates, and shipping fees. In other words, it is as if "budgetgolfer" is running experiments for the researchers.

These listings of the Taylormade Burner 09 Driver being sold by "budgetgolfer" are one example of a matched set of listings, where the exact same item is being sold by the exact same seller, but each time with slightly

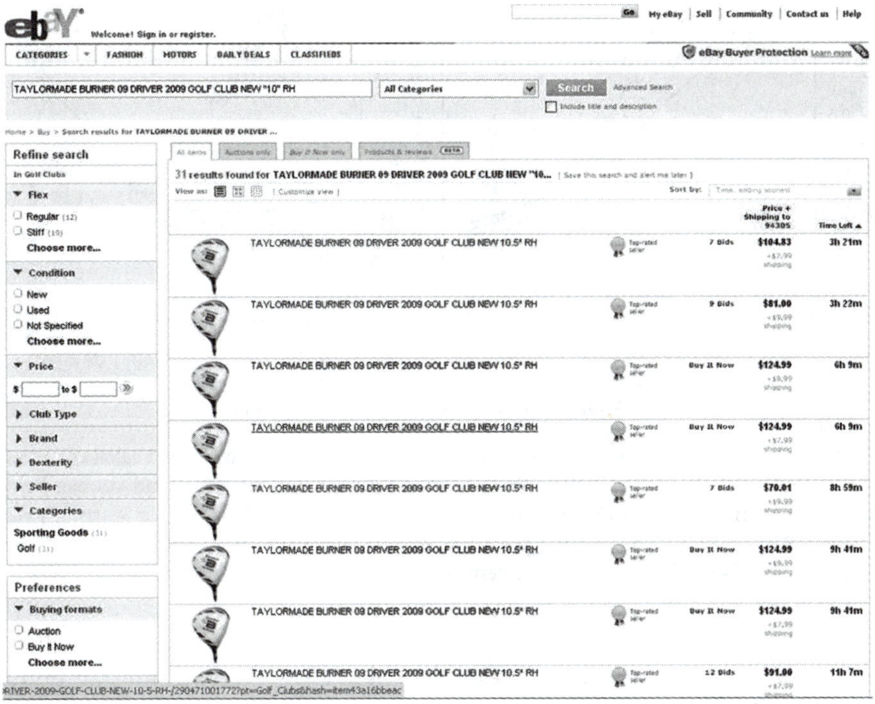

Figure 2.8: An example of a matched set. This is the exact same golf club (a Taylormade Burner 09 Driver) being sold by the exact same person ("budgetgolfer"), but some of these sales were performed under different conditions (e.g., different starting prices). Reproduced courtesy of the American Economic Association from Einav et al. (2015), figure 1b.

different characteristics. Within the massive logs of eBay there are literally hundreds of thousands of matched sets involving millions of listings. Thus, rather than comparing the final price for all auctions with a given starting price, Einav and colleagues compared within matched sets. In order to combine results from the comparisons within these hundreds of thousands of matched sets, Einav and colleagues re-expressed the starting price and final price in terms of the reference value of each item (e.g., its average sale price). For example, if the Taylormade Burner 09 Driver had a reference value of $100 (based on its sales), then a starting price of $10 would be expressed as 0.1 and a final price of $120 as 1.2.

Recall that Einav and colleagues were interested in the effect of start price on auction outcomes. First, they used linear regression to estimate

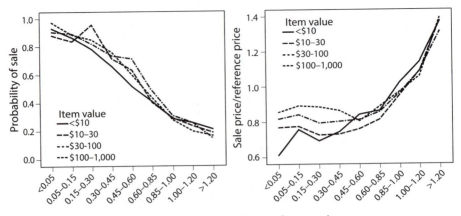

Ratio of auction start price to reference value

Figure 2.9: Relationship between auction starting price and probability of a sale (a) and sale price (b). There is roughly a linear relationship between starting price and probability of sale, but a nonlinear relationship between starting price and sale price; for starting prices between 0.05 and 0.85, the starting price has very little impact on sale price. In both cases, the relationships are basically independent of item value. Adapted from Einav et al. (2015), figures 4a and 4b.

that higher starting prices decrease the probability of a sale, and that higher starting prices increase the final sale price (conditional on a sale occurring). By themselves, these estimates—which describe a linear relationship and are averaged over all products—are not all that interesting. Then, Einav and colleagues used the massive size of their data to create a variety of more subtle estimates. For example, by estimating the effect separately for a variety of different starting prices, they found that the relationship between starting price and sale price is nonlinear (figure 2.9). In particular, for starting prices between 0.05 and 0.85, the starting price has very little impact on sale price, a finding that was completely missed by their first analysis. Further, rather than averaging over all items, Einav and colleagues estimated the impact of starting price for 23 different categories of items (e.g., pet supplies, electronics, and sports memorabilia) (figure 2.10). These estimates show that for more distinctive items—such as memorabilia—starting price has a smaller effect on the probability of a sale and a larger effect on the final sale price. Further, for more commodified items—such as DVDs—the starting price has almost no impact on the final price. In other words, an average that combines results from 23 different categories of items hides important differences between these items.

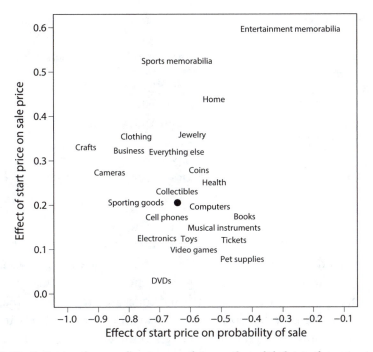

Figure 2.10: Estimates from each category of items; the solid dot is the estimate for all categories pooled together (Einav et al., 2015). These estimates show that for more distinctive items—such as memorabilia—the starting price has a smaller effect on the probability of a sale (*x*-axis) and a larger effect on the final sale price (*y*-axis). Adapted from Einav et al. (2015), figure 8.

Even if you are not particularly interested in auctions on eBay, you have to admire the way that figures 2.9 and 2.10 offer a richer understanding of eBay than simple estimates that describe a linear relationship and combine many different categories of items. Further, although it would be scientifically possible to generate these estimates with field experiments, the cost would make such experiments essentially impossible.

As with natural experiments, there are a number of ways that matching can lead to bad estimates. I think the biggest concern with matching estimates is that they can be biased by things that were not used in the matching. For example, in their main results, Einav and colleagues did exact matching on four characteristics: seller ID number, item category, item title, and subtitle. If the items were different in ways that were not used for matching, then this could create an unfair comparison. For example, if "budgetgolfer" lowered

Table 2.4: Examples of Studies That Use Matching to Find Comparisons Within Big Data Sources

Substantive focus	Big data source	Reference
Effect of shootings on police violence	Stop-and-frisk records	Legewie (2016)
Effect of September 11, 2001 on families and neighbors	Voting records and donation records	Hersh (2013)
Social contagion	Communication and product adoption data	Aral, Muchnik, and Sundararajan (2009)

prices for the Taylormade Burner 09 Driver in the winter (when golf clubs are less popular), then it could appear that lower starting prices lead to lower final prices, when in fact this would be an artifact of seasonal variation in demand. One approach to addressing this concern is trying many different kinds of matching. For example, Einav and colleagues repeated their analysis while varying the time window used for matching (matched sets included items on sale within one year, within one month, and contemporaneously). Fortunately, they found similar results for all time windows. A further concern with matching arises from interpretation. Estimates from matching apply only to matched data: they do not apply to the cases that could not be matched. For example, by limiting their research to items that had multiple listings, Einav and colleagues are focusing on professional and semiprofessional sellers. Thus, when interpreting these comparisons we must remember that they only apply to this subset of eBay.

Matching is a powerful strategy for finding fair comparisons in non-experimental data. To many social scientists, matching feels second-best to experiments, but that is a belief that can be revised, slightly. Matching in massive data might be better than a small number of field experiments when (1) heterogeneity in effects is important and (2) the important variables needed for matching have been measured. Table 2.4 provides some other examples of how matching can be used with big data sources.

In conclusion, estimating causal effects from non-experimental data is difficult, but approaches such as natural experiments and statistical adjustments (e.g., matching) can be used. In some situations, these approaches can go badly wrong, but when deployed carefully, these approaches can be a useful complement to the experimental approach that I describe in chapter 4.

Further, these two approaches seem especially likely to benefit from the growth of always-on, big data systems.

2.5 Conclusion

Big data sources are everywhere, but using them for social research can be tricky. In my experience, there is something like a "no free lunch" rule for data: if you don't put in a lot of work collecting it, then you are probably going to have to put in a lot of work thinking about it and analyzing it.

The big data sources of today—and likely tomorrow—will tend to have 10 characteristics. Three of these are generally (but not always) helpful for research: big, always-on, and nonreactive. Seven are generally (but not always) problematic for research: incomplete, inaccessible, nonrepresentative, drifting, algorithmically confounded, dirty, and sensitive. Many of these characteristics ultimately arise because big data sources were not created for the purpose of social research.

Based on the ideas in this chapter, I think that there are three main ways that big data sources will be most valuable for social research. First, they can enable researchers to decide between competing theoretical predictions. Examples of this kind of work include Farber (2015) (New York Taxi drivers) and King, Pan, and Roberts (2013) (censorship in China). Second, big data sources can enable improved measurement for policy through nowcasting. An example of this kind of work is Ginsberg et al. (2009) (Google Flu Trends). Finally, big data sources can help researchers make causal estimates without running experiments. Examples of this kind of work are Mas and Moretti (2009) (peer effects on productivity) and Einav et al. (2015) (effect of starting price on auctions at eBay). Each of these approaches, however, tends to require researchers to bring a lot to the data, such as the definition of a quantity that is important to estimate or two theories that make competing predictions. Thus, I think the best way to think about what big data sources can do is that they can help researchers who can ask interesting and important questions.

Before concluding, I think that it is worth considering that big data sources may have an important effect on the relationship between data and theory. So far, this chapter has taken the approach of theory-driven empirical research. But big data sources also enable researchers to do *empirically driven theorizing*. That is, through the careful accumulation of empirical facts, patterns, and puzzles, researchers can build new theories. This alternative, data-first approach to theory is not new, and it was most forcefully articulated by Barney Glaser and Anselm Strauss (1967) with their call for *grounded theory*. This data-first approach, however, does not imply "the end of theory," as has been claimed in some of the journalism around research in the digital age (Anderson 2008). Rather, as the data environment changes, we should expect a rebalancing in the relationship between data and theory. In a world where data collection was expensive, it made sense to collect only the data that theories suggest will be the most useful. But in a world where enormous amounts of data are already available for free, it makes sense to also try a data-first approach (Goldberg 2015).

As I have shown in this chapter, researchers can learn a lot by watching people. In the next three chapters, I'll describe how we can learn more and different things if we tailor our data collection and interact with people more directly by asking them questions (chapter 3), running experiments (chapter 4), and even involving them in the research process directly (chapter 5).

Mathematical notes

In this appendix, I will summarize some ideas about making causal inference from non-experimental data in a slightly more mathematical form. There are two main approaches: the causal graph framework, most associated with Judea Pearl and colleagues, and the potential outcomes framework, most associated with Donald Rubin and colleagues. I will introduce the potential outcomes framework because it is more closely connected to the ideas in the mathematical notes at the end of chapter 3 and 4. For more on the causal graphs framework, I recommend Pearl, Glymour, and Jewell (2016) (introductory) and Pearl (2009) (advanced). For a book-length treatment of causal inference that combines the potential outcomes framework and the causal graph framework, I recommend Morgan and Winship (2014).

The goal of this appendix is to help you get comfortable with the notation and style of the potential outcomes tradition so that you can transition to some of the more technical material written on this topic. First, I'll describe the potential outcomes framework. Then, I'll use it to further discuss natural experiments like the one by Angrist (1990) on the effect of military service on earnings. This appendix draws heavily on Imbens and Rubin (2015).

Potential outcomes framework

The potential outcomes framework has three main elements: *units*, *treatments*, and *potential outcomes*. In order to illustrate these elements, let's consider a stylized version of the question addressed in Angrist (1990): What is the effect of military service on earnings? In this case, we can define the *units* to be people eligible for the 1970 draft in the United States, and we can index these people by $i = 1, \ldots, N$. The *treatments* in this case can be "serving in the military" or "not serving in the military." I'll call these the treatment and control conditions, I'll write $W_i = 1$ if person i is in the treatment condition and $W_i = 0$ if person i is in the control condition. Finally, the *potential outcomes* are bit more conceptually difficult because they involve "potential" outcomes; things that could have happened. For each person eligible for the 1970 draft, we can imagine the amount that they would have earned in 1978 if they served in the military, which I will call $Y_i(1)$, and the amount that they would have earned in 1978 if they did not serve in the military, which I will call $Y_i(0)$. In the potential outcomes framework, $Y_i(1)$ and $Y_i(0)$ are considered fixed quantities, while W_i is a random variable.

The choice of units, treatments, and outcomes is critical because it defines what can—and cannot—be learned from the study. The choice of units—people eligible for the 1970 draft—does not include women, and so, without additional assumptions, this study will not tell us anything about the effect of military service on women. Decisions about how to define treatments and outcomes are important as well. For example, should the study be focused on serving in the military or experiencing combat? Should the outcome of interest be earnings or job satisfaction? Ultimately, the choice of units, treatments, and outcomes should be driven by the scientific and policy goals of the study.

Given the choices of units, treatments, and potential outcomes, the causal effect of the treatment on person i, τ_i, is

$$\tau_i = Y_i(1) - Y_i(0) \tag{2.1}$$

In other words, we compare how much person i would have earned after serving to how much person i would have earned without serving. To me, eq. 2.1 is the clearest way to define a causal effect, and although extremely simple, this framework turns out to generalizable in many important and interesting ways (Imbens and Rubin 2015).

Table 2.5: Table of Potential Outcomes

Person	Earnings in treatment condition	Earning in control condition	Treatment effect
1	$Y_1(1)$	$Y_1(0)$	τ_1
2	$Y_2(1)$	$Y_2(0)$	τ_2
$\vdots$	$\vdots$	$\vdots$	$\vdots$
N	$Y_N(1)$	$Y_N(0)$	τ_N
Mean	$\bar{Y}(1)$	$\bar{Y}(0)$	$\bar{\tau}$

When using the potential outcomes framework, I often find it helpful to write out a table showing the potential outcomes and the treatment effects for all units (table 2.5). If you are not able to imagine a table like this for your study, then you might need to be more precise in your definitions of your units, treatments, and potential outcomes.

When defining the causal effect in this way, however, we run into a problem. In almost all cases, we don't get to observe both potential outcomes. That is, a specific person either served or did not serve. Therefore, we observe one of the potential outcomes—$Y_i(1)$ or $Y_i(0)$—but not both. The inability to observe both potential outcomes is such a major problem that Holland (1986) called it the *Fundamental Problem of Causal Inference.*

Fortunately, when we are doing research, we don't just have one person; rather, we have many people, and this offers a way around the Fundamental Problem of Causal Inference. Rather than attempting to estimate the individual-level treatment effect, we can estimate the *average treatment effect* for all units:

$$\text{ATE} = \bar{\tau} = \frac{1}{N} \sum_{i=1}^{N} \tau_i \qquad (2.2)$$

This equation is still expressed in terms of the τ_i, which are unobservable, but with some algebra (eq. 2.8 of Gerber and Green (2012)), we get

$$\text{ATE} = \frac{1}{N} \sum_{i=1}^{N} Y_i(1) - \frac{1}{N} \sum_{i=1}^{N} Y_i(0) \qquad (2.3)$$

This shows that if we can estimate the population average outcome under treatment ($N^{-1} \sum_{i=1}^{N} Y_i(1)$) and the population average outcome under

Table 2.6: Table of Observable Data

Person	Earnings in treatment condition	Earnings in control condition	Treatment effect
1	?	$Y_1(0)$	?
2	$Y_2(1)$	?	?
⋮	⋮	⋮	⋮
N	$Y_N(1)$	?	?
Mean	?	?	?

control $N^{-1} \sum_{i=1}^{N} Y_i(0)$, then we can estimate the average treatment effect, even without estimating the treatment effect for any particular person.

Now that I've defined our estimand—the thing we are trying to estimate—I'll turn to how we can actually estimate it with data. And here we run directly into the problem that we only observe one of the potential outcomes for each person; we see either $Y_i(0)$ or $Y_i(1)$ (table 2.6). We could estimate the average treatment effect by comparing the income of people that served to the earnings of people that did not serve:

$$\widehat{\text{ATE}} = \underbrace{\frac{1}{N_t} \sum_{i:W_i=1} Y_i(1)}_{\text{average earnings, treatment}} - \underbrace{\frac{1}{N_c} \sum_{i:W_i=0} Y_i(0)}_{\text{average earnings, control}} \qquad (2.4)$$

where N_t and N_c are the numbers of people in the treatment and control conditions. This approach will work well if the treatment assignment is independent of potential outcomes, a condition sometimes called *ignorability*. Unfortunately, in the absence of an experiment, ignorability is not often satisfied, which means that the estimator in eq. 2.4 is not likely to produce good estimate. One way to think about it is that in the absence of random assignment of treatment, eq 2.4 is not comparing like with like: it is comparing the earnings of different kinds of people. Or, expressed slightly differently, without random assignment of treatment, the treatment allocation is probably related to potential outcomes.

In chapter 4, I'll describe how randomized controlled experiments can help researchers make causal estimates, and here I'll describe how researchers can take advantage of natural experiments, such as the draft lottery.

Table 2.7: Four Types of People

Type	Service if drafted	Service if not drafted
Compliers	Yes, $W_i(Z_i = 1) = 1$	No, $W_i(Z_i = 0) = 0$
Never-takers	No, $W_i(Z_i = 1) = 0$	No, $W_i(Z_i = 0) = 0$
Defiers	No, $W_i(Z_i = 1) = 0$	Yes, $W_i(Z_i = 0) = 1$
Always-takers	Yes, $W_i(Z_i = 1) = 1$	Yes, $W_i(Z_i = 0) = 1$

Natural experiments

One approach to making causal estimates without running an experiment is to look for something happening in the world that has randomly assigned a treatment for you. This approach is called *natural experiments*. In many situations, unfortunately, nature does not randomly deliver the treatment that you want to the population of interest. But sometimes nature randomly delivers a related treatment. In particular, I'll consider the case where there is some secondary treatment that encourages people to receive the primary treatment. For example, the draft could be considered a randomly assigned secondary treatment that encouraged some people to take the primary treatment, which was serving in the military. This design is sometimes called an *encouragement design*. And the analysis method that I'll describe to handle this situation is sometimes called *instrumental variables*. In this setting, with some assumptions, researchers can use the encouragement to learn about the effect of the primary treatment for a particular subset of units.

In order to handle the two different treatments—the encouragement and the primary treatment—we need some new notation. Suppose that some people are randomly drafted ($Z_i = 1$) or not drafted ($Z_i = 0$); in this situation, Z_i is sometimes called an *instrument*.

Among those who were drafted, some served ($Z_i = 1$, $W_i = 1$) and some did not ($Z_i = 1$, $W_i = 0$). Likewise, among those that were not drafted, some served ($Z_i = 0$, $W_i = 1$) and some did not ($Z_i = 0$, $W_i = 0$). The potential outcomes for each person can now be expanded to show their status for both the encouragement and the treatment. For example, let $Y(1, W_i(1))$ be the earnings of person i if he was drafted, where $W_i(1)$ is his service status if drafted. Further, we can split the population into four groups: compliers, never-takers, defiers, and always-takers (table 2.7).

Before we discuss estimating the effect of the treatment (i.e., military service), we can define two effects of the encouragement (i.e., being drafted). First, we can define the effect of the encouragement on the primary treatment. Second, we can define the effect of the encouragement on the outcome. It will turn out that these two effects can be combined to provide an estimate of the effect of the treatment on a specific group of people.

First, the effect of the encouragement on treatment can be defined for person i as

$$\text{ITT}_{W,i} = W_i(1) - W_i(0) \tag{2.5}$$

Further, this quantity can be defined over the entire population as

$$\text{ITT}_W = \frac{1}{N} \sum_{i=1}^{N} [W_i(1) - W_i(0)] \tag{2.6}$$

Finally, we can estimate ITT_W using data:

$$\widehat{\text{ITT}_W} = \bar{W}_1^{\text{obs}} - \bar{W}_0^{\text{obs}} \tag{2.7}$$

where $\bar{W}_1^{\text{obs}}$ is the observed rate of treatment for those who were encouraged and $\bar{W}_0^{\text{obs}}$ is the observed rate of treatment for those who were not encouraged. ITT_W is also sometimes called the *uptake rate*.

Next, the effect of the encouragement on the outcome can be defined for person i as

$$\text{ITT}_{Y,i} = Y_i(1, W_i(1)) - Y_i(0, W_i(0)) \tag{2.8}$$

Further, this quantity can be defined over the entire population as

$$\text{ITT}_Y = \frac{1}{N} \sum_{i=1}^{N} [Y_i(1, W_i(1)) - Y_i(0, W_i(0))] \tag{2.9}$$

Finally, we can estimate ITT_Y using data:

$$\widehat{\text{ITT}_Y} = \bar{Y}_1^{\text{obs}} - \bar{Y}_0^{\text{obs}} \tag{2.10}$$

where $\bar{Y}_1^{\text{obs}}$ is the observed outcome (e.g., income) for those who were encouraged (e.g., drafted) and $\bar{Y}_0^{\text{obs}}$ is the observed outcome for those who were not encouraged.

Finally, we turn our attention to the effect of interest: the effect of the primary treatment (e.g., military service) on the outcome (e.g., earnings).

Unfortunately, it turns out that one cannot, in general, estimate the effect of treatment on all units. However, with some assumptions, researchers can estimate the effect of treatment on compliers (i.e., people who will serve if drafted and people who will not serve if not drafted; table 2.7). I'll call this estimate the *complier average causal effect* (CACE) (which is also sometimes called the *local average treatment effect*, LATE):

$$\text{CACE} = \frac{1}{N_{\text{co}}} \sum_{i:G_i=\text{co}} [Y(1, W_i(1)) - Y(0, W_i(0))] \tag{2.11}$$

where G_i denotes the group of person i (see table 2.7) and N_{co} is the number of compliers. In other words, eq. 2.11 compares the earnings of compliers who are drafted, $Y_i(1, W_i(1))$, and not drafted, $Y_i(0, W_i(0))$. The estimand in eq. 2.11 seems hard to estimate from observed data because it is not possible to identify compliers using only observed data (to know if someone is a complier, you would need to observe whether he served when drafted and whether he served when not drafted).

It turns out—somewhat surprisingly—that if there are any compliers, then, provided one makes three additional assumptions, it is possible to estimate CACE from observed data. First, one has to assume that the assignment of the encouragement is random. In the case of the draft lottery, this is reasonable. However, in some settings where natural experiments do not rely on physical randomization, this assumption may be more problematic. Second, one has to assume that their are no defiers (this assumption is also sometimes called the monotonicity assumption). In the context of the draft, it seems reasonable to assume that there are very few people who will not serve if drafted and will serve if not drafted. Third, and finally, comes the most important assumption, which is called the *exclusion restriction*. Under the exclusion restriction, one has to assume that all of the effect of the encouragement is passed through the treatment itself. In other words, one has to assume that there is no direct effect of encouragement on outcomes. In the case of the draft lottery, for example, one needs to assume that draft status has no effect on earnings other than through military service (figure 2.11). The exclusion restriction could be violated if, for example, people who were drafted spent more time in school in order to avoid service or if employers were less likely to hire people who were drafted.

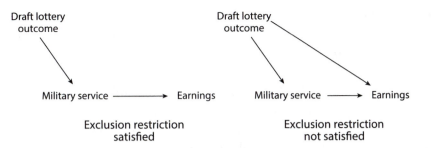

Draft lottery outcome → Military service → Earnings

Exclusion restriction satisfied

Draft lottery outcome → Military service → Earnings

Exclusion restriction not satisfied

Figure 2.11: The exclusion restriction requires that the encouragement (draft lottery) has an effect on the outcome (earnings) only through the treatment (military service). The exclusion restriction could be violated if, for example, people who were drafted spent more time in school in order to avoid service and that this increased time in school led to higher earnings.

If these three conditions (random assignment to treatment, no defiers, and the exclusion restriction) are met, then

$$\mathrm{CACE} = \frac{\mathrm{ITT}_Y}{\mathrm{ITT}_W} \tag{2.12}$$

so we can estimate CACE:

$$\widehat{\mathrm{CACE}} = \frac{\widehat{\mathrm{ITT}_Y}}{\widehat{\mathrm{ITT}_W}} \tag{2.13}$$

One way to think about CACE is that it is the difference in outcomes between those who were encouraged and those not encouraged, inflated by the uptake rate.

There are two important caveats to keep in mind. First, the exclusion restriction is a strong assumption, and it needs to be justified on a case-by-case basis, which frequently requires subject-area expertise. The exclusion restriction cannot be justified with randomization of the encouragement. Second, a common practical challenge with instrumental variable analysis comes when the encouragement has little effect on the uptake of treatment (when ITT_W is small). This is called a *weak instrument*, and it leads to a variety of problems (Imbens and Rosenbaum 2005; Murray 2006). One way to think about the problem with weak instruments is that $\widehat{\mathrm{CACE}}$ can be sensitive to small biases in $\widehat{\mathrm{ITT}_Y}$—potentially due to violations of the exclusion restriction—because these biases get magnified by a small $\widehat{\mathrm{ITT}_W}$

(see eq. 2.13). Roughly, if the treatment that nature assigns doesn't have a big impact on the treatment you care about, then you are going to have a hard time learning about the treatment you care about.

See chapters 23 and 24 of Imbens and Rubin (2015) for a more formal version of this discussion. The traditional econometric approach to instrumental variables is typically expressed in terms of estimating equations, not potential outcomes. For an introduction from this other perspective, see Angrist and Pischke (2009), and for a comparison between the two approaches, see section 24.6 of Imbens and Rubin (2015). An alternative, slightly less formal presentation of the instrumental variables approach is also provided in chapter 6 of Gerber and Green (2012). For more on the exclusion restriction, see Jones (2015). Aronow and Carnegie (2013) describe an additional set of assumptions that can be used to estimate ATE rather than CATE. For a more general introduction to natural experiments—one that goes beyond just the instrumental variables approach to also include designs such as regression discontinuity—see Dunning (2012).

What to read next

- **Introduction (section 2.1)**

  One kind of observing that is not included in this chapter is ethnography. For more on ethnography in digital spaces, see Boellstorff et al. (2012), and for more on ethnography in mixed digital and physical spaces, see Lane (2016).

- **Big data (section 2.2)**

  There is no single consensus definition of "big data," but many definitions seem to focus on the "3 Vs": volume, variety, and velocity (e.g., Japec et al. (2015)). See De Mauro et al. (2015) for a review of definitions.

  My inclusion of government administrative data in the category of big data is a bit unusual, although others have also made this case, including Legewie (2015), Connelly et al. (2016), and Einav and Levin (2014). For more about the value of government administrative data for research, see Card et al. (2010), Administrative Data Taskforce (2012), and Grusky, Smeeding, and Snipp (2015).

  For a view of administrative research from inside the government statistical system, particularly the US Census Bureau, see Jarmin and O'Hara (2016). For a book-length treatment of the administrative records research at Statistics Sweden, see Wallgren and Wallgren (2007).

In the chapter, I briefly compared a traditional survey such as the General Social Survey (GSS) with a social media data source such as Twitter. For a thorough and careful comparison between traditional surveys and social media data, see Schober et al. (2016).

- **Common characteristics of big data (section 2.3)**

These 10 characteristics of big data have been described in a variety of different ways by a variety of different authors. Writing that influenced my thinking on these issues includes Lazer et al. (2009), Groves (2011), Howison, Wiggins, and Crowston (2011), boyd and Crawford (2012), Taylor (2013), Mayer-Schönberger and Cukier (2013), Golder and Macy (2014), Ruths and Pfeffer (2014), Tufekci (2014), Sampson and Small (2015), K. Lewis (2015b), Lazer (2015), Horton and Tambe (2015), Japec et al. (2015), and Goldstone and Lupyan (2016).

Throughout this chapter, I've used the term *digital traces*, which I think is relatively neutral. Another popular term for digital traces is *digital footprints* (Golder and Macy 2014), but, as Hal Abelson, Ken Ledeen, and Harry Lewis (2008) point out, a more appropriate term is probably *digital fingerprints*. When you create footprints, you are aware of what is happening and your footprints cannot generally be traced to you personally. The same is not true for your digital traces. In fact, you are leaving traces all the time, about which you have very little knowledge. And although these traces don't have your name on them, they can often be linked back to you. In other words, they are more like fingerprints: invisible and personally identifying.

- **Big (section 2.3.1)**

For more on why large datasets render statistical tests problematic, see Lin, Lucas, and Shmueli (2013) and McFarland and McFarland (2015). These issues should lead researchers to focus on practical significance rather than statistical significance.

For more about how Raj Chetty and colleagues obtained access to the tax records, see Mervis (2014).

Large datasets can also create computational problems that are generally beyond the capabilities of a single computer. Therefore, researchers making computations on large datasets often spread the work over many computers, a process sometimes called *parallel programming*. For an introduction to parallel programming, in particular a language called Hadoop, see Vo and Silvia (2016).

- **Always-on (section 2.3.2)**

When considering always-on data, it is important to consider whether you are comparing the exact same people over time or whether you are comparing some changing group of people; see, for example, Diaz et al. (2016).

- **Nonreactive (section 2.3.3)**

  A classic book on nonreactive measures is Webb et al. (1966). The examples in that book predate the digital age, but they are still illuminating. For examples of people changing their behavior because of the presence of mass surveillance, see Penney (2016) and Brayne (2014).

  Reactivity is closely related to what researchers call demand effects (Orne 1962, Zizzo 2010) and the Hawthorne effect (Adair 1984; Levitt and List 2011).

- **Incomplete (section 2.3.4)**

  For more on record linkage, see Dunn (1946) and Fellegi and Sunter (1969) (historical) and Larsen and Winkler (2014) (modern). Similar approaches have also been developed in computer science under names such as data deduplication, instance identification, name matching, duplicate detection, and duplicate record detection (Elmagarmid, Ipeirotis, and Verykios 2007). There are also privacy-preserving approaches to record linkage that do not require the transmission of personally identifying information (Schnell 2013). Facebook also has developed a process to link their records to voting behavior; this was done to evaluate an experiment that I'll tell you about in chapter 4 (Bond et al. 2012; Jones et al. 2013).

  For more on construct validity, see chapter 3 of Shadish, Cook, and Campbell (2001).

- **Inaccessible (section 2.3.5)**

  For more on the AOL search log debacle, see Ohm (2010). I offer advice about partnering with companies and governments in chapter 4 when I describe experiments. A number of authors have expressed concerns about research that relies on inaccessible data, see Huberman (2012) and boyd and Crawford (2012).

  One good way for university researchers to acquire data access is to work at a company as an intern or visiting researcher. In addition to enabling data access, this process will also help the researcher learn more about how the data was created, which is important for analysis.

  In terms of gaining access to government data, Mervis (2014) discusses how Raj Chetty and colleagues obtained access to the tax records used in their research on social mobility.

- **Nonrepresentative (section 2.3.6)**

  For more on the history of "representativeness" as a concept, see Kruskal and Mosteller (1979a,b,c, 1980).

  My summaries of the work of Snow and the work of Doll and Hill were brief. For more on Snow's work on cholera, see Freedman (1991). For more on the British Doctors Study see Doll et al. (2004) and Keating (2014).

Many researchers will be surprised to learn that although Doll and Hill had collected data from female doctors and from doctors under 35, they intentionally did not use this data in their first analysis. As they argued: "Since lung cancer is relatively rare in women and men under 35, useful figures are unlikely to be obtained in these groups for some years to come. In this preliminary report we have therefore confined our attention to men aged 35 and above." Rothman, Gallacher, and Hatch (2013), which has the provocative title "Why representativeness should be avoided," make a more general argument for the value of intentionally creating nonrepresentative data.

Nonrepresentativeness is a major problem for researchers and governments who wish to make statements about an entire population. This is less of a concern for companies, which are typically focused on their users. For more on how Statistics Netherlands considers the issue of nonrepresentativeness of business big data, see Buelens et al. (2014).

For examples of researchers expressing concern about nonrepresentative nature of big data sources, see boyd and Crawford (2012), Lewis (2015b), and Hargittai (2015).

For a more detailed comparison of the goals of social surveys and epidemiological research, see Keiding and Louis (2016).

For more on attempts to use Twitter to make out-of-sample generalizations about voters, especially the case from the 2009 German election, see Jungherr (2013, 2015). Subsequent to the work of Tumasjan et al. (2010), researchers around the world have used fancier methods—such as using sentiment analysis to distinguish between positive and negative mentions of the parties—in order to improve the ability of Twitter data to predict a variety of different types of elections (Gayo-Avello 2013; Jungherr 2015, chapter 7). Here's how Huberty (2015) summarized the results of these attempts to predict elections:

> "All known forecasting methods based on social media have failed when subjected to the demands of true forward-looking electoral forecasting. These failures appear to be due to fundamental properties of social media, rather than to methodological or algorithmic difficulties. In short, social media do not, and probably never will, offer a stable, unbiased, representative picture of the electorate; and convenience samples of social media lack sufficient data to fix these problems post hoc."

In chapter 3, I'll describe sampling and estimation in much greater detail. Even if data is nonrepresentative, under certain conditions, it can be weighted to produce good estimates.

- **Drifting (section 2.3.7)**

System drift is very hard to see from the outside. However, the MovieLens project (discussed more in chapter 4) has been run for more than 15 years by an academic research group. Thus, they have been able to document and share information about the way that the system has evolved over time and how this might impact analysis (Harper and Konstan 2015).

A number of scholars have focused on drift in Twitter: Liu, Kliman-Silver, and Mislove (2014) and Tufekci (2014).

One approach to dealing with population drift is to create a panel of users, which allows researchers to study the same people over time; see Diaz et al. (2016).

- **Algorithmically confounded (section 2.3.8)**

I first heard the term "algorithmically confounded" used by Jon Kleinberg in a talk, but unfortunately I don't remember when or where the talk was given. The first time that I saw the term in print was in Anderson et al. (2015), which is an interesting discussion of how the algorithms used by dating sites might complicate researchers' ability to use data from these websites to study social preferences. This concern was raised by Lewis (2015a) in response to Anderson et al. (2014).

In addition to Facebook, Twitter also recommends people for users to follow based on the idea of triadic closure; see Su, Sharma, and Goel (2016). So the level of triadic closure in Twitter is a combination of some human tendency toward triadic closure and some algorithmic tendency to promote triadic closure.

For more on performativity—in particular the idea that some social science theories are "engines not cameras" (i.e., they shape the world rather than just describing it)—see Mackenzie (2008).

- **Dirty (section 2.3.9)**

Governmental statistical agencies call data cleaning *statistical data editing*. De Waal, Puts, and Daas (2014) describe statistical data editing techniques developed for survey data and examine the extent to which they are applicable to big data sources, and Puts, Daas, and Waal (2015) present some of the same ideas for a more general audience.

For an overview of social bots, see Ferrara et al. (2016). For some examples of studies focused on finding spam in Twitter, see Clark et al. (2016) and Chu et al. (2012). Finally, Subrahmanian et al. (2016) describe the results of the DARPA Twitter Bot Challenge, a mass collaboration designed to compare approaches for detecting bots on Twitter.

- **Sensitive (section 2.3.10)**

Ohm (2015) reviews earlier research on the idea of sensitive information and offers a multi-factor test. The four factors he proposes are the magnitude of harm, the probability of harm, the presence of a confidential relationship, and whether the risk reflects majoritarian concerns.

- **Counting things (section 2.4.1)**

Farber's study of taxis in New York was based on an earlier study by Camerer et al. (1997) that used three different convenience samples of paper trip sheets. This earlier study found that drivers seemed to be target earners: they worked less on days where their wages were higher.

In subsequent work, King and colleagues have further explored online censorship in China (King, Pan, and Roberts 2014, 2016). For a related approach to measuring online censorship in China, see Bamman, O'Connor, and Smith (2012). For more on statistical methods like the one used in King, Pan, and Roberts (2013) to estimate the sentiment of the 11 million posts, see Hopkins and King (2010). For more on supervised learning, see James et al. (2013) (less technical) and Hastie, Tibshirani, and Friedman (2009) (more technical).

- **Forecasting and nowcasting (section 2.4.2)**

Forecasting is a big part of industrial data science (Mayer-Schönberger and Cukier 2013; Provost and Fawcett 2013). One type of forecasting that is commonly done by social researchers is demographic forecasting; see, for example, Raftery et al. (2012).

Google Flu Trends was not the first project to use search data to nowcast influenza prevalence. In fact, researchers in the United States (Polgreen et al. 2008; Ginsberg et al. 2009) and Sweden (Hulth, Rydevik, and Linde 2009) have found that certain search terms (e.g., "flu") predicted national public health surveillance data before it was released. Subsequently many, many other projects have tried to use digital trace data for disease surveillance detection; see Althouse et al. (2015) for a review.

In addition to using digital trace data to predict health outcomes, there has also been a huge amount of work using Twitter data to predict election outcomes; for reviews, see Gayo-Avello (2011), Gayo-Avello (2013), Jungherr (2015, chapter 7), and Huberty (2015). Nowcasting of economic indicators, such as gross domestic product (GDP), is also common in central banks, see Bańbura et al. (2013). Table 2.8 includes a few examples of studies that use some kind of digital trace to predict some kind of event in the world.

Finally, Jon Kleinberg and colleagues (2015) have pointed out that forecasting problems fall into two, subtly different categories and that social scientists have tended to focus on one and ignore the other. Imagine one policy maker, I'll call her Anna, who is facing a drought and must decide whether to hire a shaman to do a rain dance to increase the chance of rain. Another policy maker, I'll call her Betty, must decide whether to take an umbrella to work to avoid getting wet on the way home. Both Anna and Betty can make a better decision if they understand weather, but they need to know different things. Anna needs to understand whether the rain dance causes rain. Betty, on the other hand, does

Table 2.8: Studies That Use a Big Data Source to Predict Some Event

Digital trace	Outcome	Reference
Twitter	Box office revenue of movies in the United States	Asur and Huberman (2010)
Search logs	Sales of movies, music, books, and video games in the United States	Goel et al. (2010)
Twitter	Dow Jones Industrial Average (US stock market)	Bollen, Mao, and Zeng (2011)
Social media and search logs	Surveys of investor sentiment and stock markets in the United States, United Kingdom, Canada, and China	Mao et al. (2015)
Search logs	Prevalence of Dengue fever in Singapore and Bangkok	Althouse, Ng, and Cummings (2011)

not need to understand anything about causality; she just needs an accurate forecast. Social researchers often focus on the problems like the one faced by Anna—which Kleinberg and colleagues call "rain dance–like" policy problems—because they involve questions of causality. Questions like the one faced by Betty—which Kleinberg and colleagues call "umbrella-like" policy problems—can be quite important too, but have received much less attention from social researchers.

- **Approximating experiments (section 2.4.3)**

The journal *P.S. Political Science* had a symposium on big data, causal inference, and formal theory, and Clark and Golder (2015) summarize each contribution. The journal *Proceedings of the National Academy of Sciences of the United States of America* had a symposium on causal inference and big data, and Shiffrin (2016) summarizes each contribution. For machine learning approaches that attempt to automatically discover natural experiments inside of big data sources, see Jensen et al. (2008) and Sharma, Hofman, and Watts (2015, 2016).

In terms of natural experiments, Dunning (2012) provides an introductory, book-length treatment with many examples. For a skeptical view of natural experiments, see Rosenzweig and Wolpin (2000) (economics) or Sekhon and Titiunik (2012) (political science). Deaton (2010) and Heckman and Urzúa (2010) argue that focusing on natural experiments can lead researchers to focus on estimating unimportant causal effects; Imbens (2010) counters these arguments with a more optimistic view of the value of natural experiments.

When describing how a researcher could go from estimating the effect of being drafted to the effect of serving, I was describing a technique called *instrumental variables.* Imbens and Rubin (2015), in their chapters 23 and 24, provide an introduction and use the draft lottery as an example. The effect of military service on compliers is sometimes called the complier average causal effect (CACE) and sometimes the local average treatment effect (LATE). Sovey and Green (2011), Angrist and Krueger (2001), and Bollen (2012) offer reviews of the usage of instrumental variables in political science, economics, and sociology, and Sovey and Green (2011) provides a "reader's checklist" for evaluating studies using instrumental variables.

It turns out that the 1970 draft lottery was not, in fact properly randomized; there were small deviations from pure randomness (Fienberg 1971). Berinsky and Chatfield (2015) argues that this small deviation is not substantively important and discuss the importance of properly conducted randomization.

In terms of matching, see Stuart (2010) for an optimistic review and Sekhon (2009) for a pessimistic one. For more on matching as a kind of pruning, see Ho et al. (2007). Finding a single perfect match for each person is often difficult, and this introduces a number of complexities. First, when exact matches are not available for everyone, researchers need to decide how to measure the distance between two units and if a given distance is close enough. A second complexity arises if researchers want to use multiple matches for each case in the treatment group, since this can lead to more precise estimates. Both of these issues, as well as others, are described in detail in chapter 18 of Imbens and Rubin (2015). See also Part II of Rosenbaum (2010).

See Dehajia and Wahba (1999) for an example where matching methods were able to produce estimates similar to those from a randomized controlled experiment. But see Arceneaux, Gerber, and Green (2006, 2010) for examples where matching methods failed to reproduce an experimental benchmark.

Rosenbaum (2015) and Hernán and Robins (2016) offer other advice for discovering useful comparisons within big data sources.

Activities

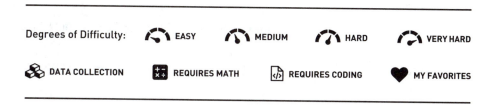

Degrees of Difficulty: EASY   MEDIUM   HARD   VERY HARD

DATA COLLECTION   REQUIRES MATH   REQUIRES CODING   MY FAVORITES

1. [, ♥] Algorithmic confounding was a problem with Google Flu Trends. Read the paper by Lazer et al. (2014), and write a short, clear email to an engineer at Google explaining the problem and offering an idea of how to fix it.

2. [⏱] Bollen, Mao, and Zeng (2011) claims that data from Twitter can be used to predict the stock market. This finding led to the creation of a hedge fund—Derwent Capital Markets—to invest in the stock market based on data collected from Twitter (Jordan 2010). What evidence would you want to see before putting your money in that fund?

3. [↘] While some public health advocates consider e-cigarettes an effective aid for smoking cessation, others warn about the potential risks, such as the high levels of nicotine. Imagine that a researcher decides to study public opinion toward e-cigarettes by collecting e-cigarettes-related Twitter posts and conducting sentiment analysis.

   a) What are the three possible biases that you are most worried about in this study?

   b) Clark et al. (2016) ran just such a study. First, they collected 850,000 tweets that used e-cigarette-related keywords from January 2012 through December 2014. Upon closer inspection, they realized that many of these tweets were automated (i.e., not produced by humans) and many of these automated tweets were essentially commercials. They developed a human detection algorithm to separate automated tweets from organic tweets. Using this algorithm, they found that 80% of tweets were automated. Does this finding change your answer to part (a)?

   c) When they compared the sentiment in organic and automated tweets, they found that the automated tweets were more positive than organic tweets (6.17 versus 5.84). Does this finding change your answer to (b)?

4. [↘] In November 2009, Twitter changed the question in the tweet box from "What are you doing?" to "What's happening?" (https://blog.twitter.com/2009/whats-happening).

   a) How do you think the change of prompts will affect who tweets and/or what they tweet?

   b) Name one research project for which you would prefer the prompt "What are you doing?" Explain why.

   c) Name one research project for which you would prefer the prompt "What's happening?" Explain why.

5. [↘] "Retweets" are often used to measure influence and spread of influence on Twitter. Initially, users had to copy and paste the tweet they liked, tag the original author with his/her handle, and manually type "RT" before the tweet to indicate that it was a retweet. Then, in 2009, Twitter added a "retweet"

button. In June 2016, Twitter made it possible for users to retweet their own tweets (https://twitter.com/twitter/status/742749353689780224). Do you think these changes should affect how you use "retweets" in your research? Why or why not?

6. [🏃, 🐎, 📖, ♥] In a widely discussed paper, Michel and colleagues (2011) analyzed the content of more than five million digitized books in an attempt to identify long-term cultural trends. The data that they used has now been released as the Google NGrams dataset, and so we can use the data to replicate and extend some of their work.

In one of the many results in the paper, Michel and colleagues argued that we are forgetting faster and faster. For a particular year, say "1883," they calculated the proportion of 1-grams published in each year between 1875 and 1975 that were "1883." They reasoned that this proportion is a measure of the interest in events that happened in that year. In their figure 3a, they plotted the usage trajectories for three years: 1883, 1910, and 1950. These three years share a common pattern: little use before that year, then a spike, then decay. Next, to quantify the rate of decay for each year, Michel and colleagues calculated the "half-life" of each year for all years between 1875 and 1975. In their figure 3a (inset), they showed that the half-life of each year is decreasing, and they argued that this means that we are forgetting the past faster and faster. They used version 1 of the English language corpus, but subsequently Google has released a second version of the corpus. Please read all the parts of the question before you begin coding.

This activity will give you practice writing reusable code, interpreting results, and data wrangling (such as working with awkward files and handling missing data). This activity will also help you get up and running with a rich and interesting dataset.

a) Get the raw data from the Google Books NGram Viewer website (http://storage.googleapis.com/books/ngrams/books/datasetsv2.html). In particular, you should use version 2 of the English language corpus, which was released on July 1, 2012. Uncompressed, this file is 1.4 GB.

b) Recreate the main part of figure 3a of Michel et al. (2011). To recreate this figure, you will need two files: the one you downloaded in part (a) and the "total counts" file, which you can use to convert the raw counts into proportions. Note that the total counts file has a structure that may make it a bit hard to read in. Does version 2 of the NGram data produce similar results to those presented in Michel et al. (2011), which are based on version 1 data?

c) Now check your graph against the graph created by the NGram Viewer (https://books.google.com/ngrams).

d) Recreate figure 3a (main figure), but change the y-axis to be the raw mention count (not the rate of mentions).

e) Does the difference between (b) and (d) lead you to reevaluate any of the results of Michel et al. (2011). Why or why not?

f) Now, using the proportion of mentions, replicate the inset of figure 3a. That is, for each year between 1875 and 1975, calculate the half-life of that year. The half-life is defined to be the number of years that pass before the proportion of mentions reaches half its peak value. Note that Michel et al. (2011) do something more complicated to estimate the half-life—see section III.6 of their Supporting Online Information—but they claim that both approaches produce similar results. Does version 2 of the NGram data produce similar results to those presented in Michel et al. (2011), which are based on version 1 data? (Hint: Don't be surprised if it doesn't.)

g) Were there any years that were outliers, such as years that were forgotten particularly quickly or particularly slowly? Briefly speculate about possible reasons for that pattern and explain how you identified the outliers.

h) Now replicate this result for version 2 of the NGrams data in Chinese, French, German, Hebrew, Italian, Russian and Spanish.

i) Comparing across all languages, were there any years that were outliers, such as years that were forgotten particularly quickly or particularly slowly? Briefly speculate about possible reasons for that pattern.

7. [📶, ♻️, 💻, ♥️] Penney (2016) explored whether the widespread publicity about NSA/PRISM surveillance (i.e., the Snowden revelations) in June 2013 was associated with a sharp and sudden decrease in traffic to Wikipedia articles on topics that raise privacy concerns. If so, this change in behavior would be consistent with a chilling effect resulting from mass surveillance. The approach of Penney (2016) is sometimes called an *interrupted time series* design, and it is related to the approaches described in section 2.4.3.

To choose the topic keywords, Penney referred to the list used by the US Department of Homeland Security for tracking and monitoring social media. The DHS list categorizes certain search terms into a range of issues, i.e., "Health Concern," "Infrastructure Security," and "Terrorism." For the study group, Penney used the 48 keywords related to "Terrorism" (see appendix table 8). He then aggregated Wikipedia article view counts on a monthly basis for the corresponding 48 Wikipedia articles over a 32-month period from the beginning of January 2012 to the end of August 2014. To strengthen his argument, he also created several comparison groups by tracking article views on other topics.

Now, you are going to replicate and extend Penney (2016). All the raw data that you will need for this activity is available from Wikipedia (https://dumps.wikimedia.org/other/pagecounts-raw/). Or you can get it from the R-package wikipediatrend (Meissner and Team 2016). When you write up your responses, please note which data source you used. (Note that this same activity also appears in chapter 6.) This activity will give you practice in data wrangling and thinking about discovering natural experiments in big data sources. It will also get you up and running with a potentially interesting data source for future projects.

a) Read Penney (2016) and replicate his figure 2, which shows the page views for "Terrorism"-related pages before and after the Snowden revelations. Interpret the findings.

b) Next, replicate figure 4A, which compares the study group ("Terrorism"-related articles) with a comparator group using keywords categorized under "DHS & Other Agencies" from the DHS list (see appendix table 10 and footnote 139). Interpret the findings.

c) In part (b) you compared the study group with one comparator group. Penney also compared with two other comparator groups: "Infrastructure Security"–related articles (appendix table 11) and popular Wikipedia pages (appendix table 12). Come up with an alternative comparator group, and test whether the findings from part (b) are sensitive to your choice of comparator group. Which choice makes most sense? Why?

d) Penney stated that keywords relating to "Terrorism" were used to select the Wikipedia articles because the US government cited terrorism as a key justification for its online surveillance practices. As a check of these 48 "Terrorism"-related keywords, Penney (2016) also conducted a survey on MTurk, asking respondents to rate each of the keywords in terms of Government Trouble, Privacy-Sensitive, and Avoidance (appendix table 7 and 8). Replicate the survey on MTurk and compare your results.

e) Based on the results in part (d) and your reading of the article, do you agree with Penney's choice of topic keywords in the study group? Why or why not? If not, what would you suggest instead?

8. [🔎] Efrati (2016) reported, based on confidential information, that "total sharing" on Facebook had declined by about 5.5% year over year while "original broadcast sharing" was down 21% year over year. This decline was particularly acute with Facebook users under 30 years of age. The report attributed the decline to two factors. One is the growth in the number of "friends" people have on Facebook. The other is that some sharing activity has shifted to messaging and to competitors such as Snapchat. The report also revealed the several tactics Facebook had tried to boost sharing, including News Feed algorithm tweaks that make original posts more prominent, as well as periodic reminders of the original posts with the "On This Day" feature. What implications, if any, do these findings have for researchers who want to use Facebook as a data source?

9. [🌓] What is the difference between a sociologist and a historian? According to Goldthorpe (1991), the main difference is control over data collection. Historians are forced to use relics, whereas sociologists can tailor their data collection to specific purposes. Read Goldthorpe (1991). How is the difference between sociology and history related to the idea of custommades and readymades?

10. [🌓] This builds on the previous question. Goldthorpe (1991) drew a number of critical responses, including one from Nicky Hart (1994) that challenged Goldthorpe's devotion to tailor-made data. To clarify the potential limitations of tailor-made data, Hart described the Affluent Worker Project, a large survey to measure the relationship between social class and voting that was conducted by Goldthorpe and colleagues in the mid-1960s. As one might expect from a scholar who favored designed data over found data, the Affluent Worker Project collected data that were tailored to address a recently proposed theory about the future of social class in an era of increasing living standards. But Goldthorpe and colleagues somehow "forgot" to collect information about the voting behavior of women. Here's how Nicky Hart (1994) summarized the whole episode:

> "... it [is] difficult to avoid the conclusion that women were omitted because this 'tailor made' dataset was confined by a paradigmatic logic which excluded female experience. Driven by a theoretical vision of class consciousness and action as male preoccupations ..., Goldthorpe and his colleagues constructed a set of empirical proofs which fed and nurtured their own theoretical assumptions instead of exposing them to a valid test of adequacy."

Hart continued:

> "The empirical findings of the Affluent Worker Project tell us more about the masculinist values of mid-century sociology than they inform the processes of stratification, politics and material life."

Can you think of other examples where tailor-made data collection has the biases of the data collector built into it? How does this compare to algorithmic confounding? What implications might this have for when researchers should use readymades and when they should use custommades?

11. [🌓] In this chapter, I have contrasted data collected by researchers for researchers with administrative records created by companies and governments.

Figure 2.12: The picture is both a duck and a rabbit; what you see depends on your perspective. Big data sources are both found and designed; again, what you see depends on your perspective. For example, the call data records collected by a mobile-phone company are found data from the perspective of a researcher. But these exact same records are designed data from the perspective of someone working in the billing department of the phone company. (Source: *Popular Science Monthly* (1899)/Wikimedia Commons).

Some people call these administrative records "found data," which they contrast with "designed data." It is true that administrative records are found by researchers, but they are also highly designed. For example, modern tech companies work very hard to collect and curate their data. Thus, these administrative records are both found and designed, it just depends on your perspective (figure 2.12).

Provide an example of data source where seeing it both as found and designed is helpful when using that data source for research.

12. [🎚️] In a thoughtful essay, Christian Sandvig and Eszter Hargittai (2015) split digital research into two broad categories depending on whether the digital system is an "instrument" or "object of study." An example of the first kind—where the system is an instrument—is the research by Bengtsson and colleagues (2011) on using mobile-phone data to track migration after the earthquake in Haiti in 2010. An example of the second kind—where the system is an object of study—is research by Jensen (2007) on how the introduction of mobile phones throughout Kerala, India impacted the functioning of the market for fish. I find this distinction helpful because it clarifies that studies using digital data sources can have quite different goals even if they are using the same kind of data source. In order to further clarify this distinction, describe four studies that you've seen: two that use a digital system as an instrument and two that use a digital system as an object of study. You can use examples from this chapter if you want.

CHAPTER 3
ASKING QUESTIONS

3.1 Introduction

Researchers who study dolphins can't ask them questions and are therefore forced to try to learn about dolphins by observing their behavior. Researchers who study humans, on the other hand, have it easier: their respondents can talk. Talking to people was an important part of social research in the past, and I expect that it will be in the future too.

In social research, talking to people typically takes two forms: surveys and in-depth interviews. Roughly speaking, research using surveys involves systematic recruitment of large numbers of participants, highly structured questionnaires, and the use of statistical methods to generalize from the participants to a larger population. Research using in-depth interviews, on the other hand, generally involves a small number of participants and semi-structured conversations, and results in a rich, qualitative description of the participants. Surveys and in-depth interviews are both powerful approaches, but surveys are much more impacted by the transition from the analog to the digital age. Therefore, in this chapter, I'll focus on survey research.

As I'll show in this chapter, the digital age creates many exciting opportunities for survey researchers to collect data more quickly and cheaply, to ask different kinds of questions, and to magnify the value of survey data with big data sources. The idea that survey research can be transformed by a technological change is not new, however. Around 1970, a similar change was taking place driven by a different communication technology: the telephone. Fortunately, understanding how the telephone changed survey research can help us imagine how the digital age will change survey research.

Survey research, as we recognize it today, began in the 1930s. During the first era of survey research, researchers would randomly sample geographic areas (such as city blocks) and then travel to those areas in order to have face-to-face conversations with people in randomly sampled households. Then, a technological development—the widespread diffusion of landline phones in wealthy countries—eventually led to the second era of survey research. This second era differed both in how people were sampled and in how conversations took place. In the second era, rather than sampling households in geographic areas, researchers randomly sampled telephone numbers in a procedure called *random-digit dialing.* And rather than traveling to talk to people face to face, researchers instead called them on the telephone. These might seem like small logistical changes, but they made survey research faster, cheaper, and more flexible. In addition to being empowering, these changes were also controversial because many researchers were concerned that changes in sampling and interviewing procedures could introduce a variety of biases. But eventually, after lots of work, researchers figured out how to collect data reliably using random-digit dialing and telephone interviews. Thus, by figuring out how to successfully harness society's technological infrastructure, researchers were able to modernize how they did survey research.

Now, another technological development—the digital age—will eventually bring us to a third era of survey research. This transition is being driven in part by the gradual decay of second-era approaches (Meyer, Mok, and Sullivan 2015). For example, for a variety of technological and social reasons, nonresponse rates—that is, the proportions of respondents who are sampled but do not participate in surveys—have been increasing for many years (National Research Council 2013). These long-term trends mean that the nonresponse rate can now exceed 90% in standard telephone surveys (Kohut et al. 2012).

On the other hand, the transition to a third era is also being driven in part by exciting new opportunities, some of which I'll describe in this chapter. Although things are not yet settled, I expect that the third era of survey research will be characterized by non-probability sampling, computer-administered interviews, and the linkage of surveys to big data sources (table 3.1).

The transition between the second and third eras of survey research has not been completely smooth, and there have been fierce debates about how researchers should proceed. Looking back on the transition between the first and second eras, I think there is one key insight for us now: *the beginning is not the end.* That is, initially many second-era telephone-based methods were ad hoc and did not work very well. But, through hard work, researchers

Table 3.1: Three Eras of Survey Research Based on Groves (2011)

	Sampling	Interviewing	Data environment
First era	Area probability sampling	Face-to-face	Stand-alone surveys
Second era	Random-digit-dialing (RDD) probability sampling	Telephone	Stand-alone surveys
Third era	Non-probability sampling	Computer-administered	Surveys linked to big data sources

solved these problems. For example, researchers had been doing random-digit dialing for many years before Warren Mitofsky and Joseph Waksberg developed a random-digit-dialing sampling method that had good practical and theoretical properties (Waksberg 1978; Brick and Tucker 2007). Thus, we should not confuse the current state of third-era approaches with their ultimate outcomes.

The history of survey research shows that the field evolves, driven by changes in technology and society. There is no way to stop that evolution. Rather, we should embrace it, while continuing to draw wisdom from earlier eras, and that is the approach that I will take in this chapter. First, I will argue that big data sources will not replace surveys and that the abundance of big data sources increases—not decreases—the value of surveys (section 3.2). Given that motivation, I'll summarize the total survey error framework (section 3.3) that was developed during the first two eras of survey research. This framework enables us to understand new approaches to representation—in particular, non-probability samples (section 3.4)— and new approaches to measurement—in particular, new ways of asking questions to respondents (section 3.5). Finally, I'll describe two research templates for linking survey data to big data sources (Section 3.6).

3.2 Asking versus observing

We are always going to need to ask people questions.

Given that more and more of our behavior is captured in big data sources, such as government and business administrative data, some people might think that asking questions is a thing of the past. But it's not that simple. There are two main reasons that I think researchers will continue to ask people questions. First, as I discussed in chapter 2, there are real problems with the accuracy, completeness, and accessibility of many big data sources. Second, in addition to these practical reasons, there is more fundamental reason: there are some things that are very hard to learn from behavioral data—even perfect behavioral data. For example, some of the most important social outcomes and predictors are *internal states*, such as emotions, knowledge, expectations, and opinions. Internal states exist inside people's heads, and sometimes the best way to learn about internal states is to ask.

The practical and fundamental limitations of big data sources, and how they can be overcome with surveys, are illustrated by Moira Burke and Robert Kraut's (2014) research on how the strength of friendships was impacted by interaction on Facebook. At the time, Burke was working at Facebook, so she had complete access to one of the most massive and detailed records of human behavior ever created. But, even so, Burke and Kraut had to use surveys in order to answer their research question. Their outcome of interest—the subjective feeling of closeness between the respondent and her friend—is an internal state that only exists inside the respondent's head. Further, in addition to using a survey to collect their outcome of interest, Burke and Kraut also had to use a survey to learn about potentially confounding factors. In particular, they wanted to separate the impact of communicating on Facebook from communication through other channels (e.g., email, phone, and face to face). Even though interactions through email and phone are automatically recorded, these traces were not available to Burke and Kraut, so they had to collect them with a survey. Combining their survey data about friendship strength and non-Facebook interaction with the Facebook log data, Burke and Kraut concluded that communication via Facebook did in fact lead to increased feelings of closeness.

As the work of Burke and Kraut illustrates, big data sources will not eliminate the need to ask people questions. In fact, I would draw the opposite lesson from this study: big data sources can actually *increase* the value of asking questions, as I will show throughout this chapter. Therefore, the best way to think about the relationship between asking and observing is that they are complements rather than substitutes; they are like peanut butter and jelly.

When there is more peanut butter, people want more jelly; when there is more big data, I think people will want more surveys.

3.3 The total survey error framework

Total survey error = representation errors + measurement errors.

Estimates that come from sample surveys are often imperfect. That is, there is usually a difference between the estimate produced by a sample survey (e.g., the estimated average height of students in a school) and the true value in the population (e.g., the actual average height of students in a school). Sometimes these errors are so small that they are unimportant, but sometimes, unfortunately, they can be big and consequential. In an attempt to understand, measure, and reduce errors, researchers gradually created a single, overarching conceptual framework for the errors that can arise in sample surveys: the *total survey error framework* (Groves and Lyberg 2010). Although the development of this framework began in the 1940s, I think it offers us two helpful ideas for survey research in the digital age.

First, the total survey error framework clarifies that there are two types of errors: *bias* and *variance*. Roughly, bias is systematic error and variance is random error. In other words, imagine running 1,000 replications of the same sample survey and then looking at the distribution of the estimates from these 1,000 replications. The bias is the difference between the mean of these replicate estimates and the true value. The variance is the variability of these estimates. All else being equal, we would like a procedure with no bias and small variance. Unfortunately, for many real problems, such no-bias, small-variance procedures do not exist, which puts researchers in the difficult position of deciding how to balance the problems introduced by bias and variance. Some researchers instinctively prefer unbiased procedures, but a single-minded focus on bias can be a mistake. If the goal is to produce an estimate that is as close as possible to the truth (i.e., with the smallest possible error), then you might be better off with a procedure that has a small bias and a small variance than with one that is unbiased but has a large variance (figure 3.1). In other words, the total survey error framework shows that when evaluating survey research procedures, you should consider *both* bias and variance.

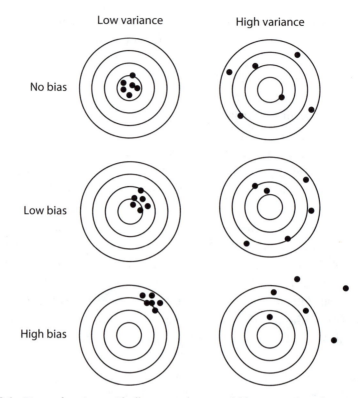

Figure 3.1: Bias and variance. Ideally, researchers would have a no-bias, low-variance estimation procedure. In reality, they often make decisions that induce a trade-off between bias and variance. Although some researchers instinctively prefer unbiased procedures, sometimes a small-bias, small-variance procedure can produce more accurate estimates than an unbiased procedure that has high variance.

The second main insight from the total survey error framework, which will organize much of this chapter, is that there are two sources of errors: problems related to who you talk to (*representation*) and problems related to what you learn from those conversations (*measurement*). For example, you might be interested in estimating attitudes about online privacy among adults living in France. Making these estimates requires two different types of inference. First, from the answers that respondents give, you have to infer their attitudes about online privacy (which is a problem of measurement). Second, from the inferred attitudes among respondents, you must infer the attitudes in the population as a whole (which is a problem of representation). Perfect sampling with bad survey questions will produce bad estimates, as will bad sampling with perfect survey questions. In other words, good estimates require sound approaches to measurement *and* representation. Given that background, I'll review how survey researchers have thought about representation and measurement in the past. Then, I'll show how ideas about representation and measurement can guide digital-age survey research.

3.3.1 Representation

Representation is about making inferences from your respondents to your target population.

In order to understand the kind of errors that can happen when inferring from respondents to the larger population, let's consider the *Literary Digest* straw poll that tried to predict the outcome of the 1936 US presidential election. Although it happened more than 75 years ago, this debacle still has an important lesson to teach researchers today.

Literary Digest was a popular general-interest magazine, and starting in 1920 they began running straw polls to predict the outcomes of presidential elections. To make these predictions, they would send ballots to lots of people and then simply tally up the ballots that were returned; *Literary Digest* proudly reported that the ballots they received were neither "weighted, adjusted, nor interpreted." This procedure correctly predicted the winners of the elections in 1920, 1924, 1928, and 1932. In 1936, in the midst of the Great Depression, *Literary Digest* sent out ballots to 10 million people, whose names came predominantly from telephone directories and automobile registration records. Here's how they described their methodology:

> "THE DIGEST's smooth-running machine moves with the swift precision of thirty years' experience to reduce guesswork to hard facts ... This week 500 pens scratched out more than a quarter of a million addresses a day. Every day, in a great room high above motor-ribboned Fourth Avenue, in New York, 400 workers deftly slide a million pieces of printed matter—enough to pave forty city blocks—into the addressed envelops [sic]. Every hour, in THE DIGEST'S own Post Office Substation, three chattering postage metering machines sealed and stamped the white oblongs; skilled postal employees flipped them into bulging mailsacks; fleet DIGEST trucks sped them to express

mail-trains ... Next week, the first answers from these ten million will begin the incoming tide of marked ballots, to be triple-checked, verified, five-times cross-classified and totaled. When the last figure has been totted and checked, if past experience is a criterion, the country will know to within a fraction of 1 percent the actual popular vote of forty million [voters]." (August 22, 1936)

Literary Digest's fetishization of size is instantly recognizable to any "big data" researcher today. Of the 10 million ballots distributed, an amazing 2.4 million were returned—that's roughly 1,000 times larger than modern political polls. From these 2.4 million respondents, the verdict was clear: Alf Landon was going to defeat the incumbent Franklin Roosevelt. But, in fact, Roosevelt defeated Landon in a landslide. How could *Literary Digest* go wrong with so much data? Our modern understanding of sampling makes *Literary Digest's* mistakes clear and helps us avoid making similar mistakes in the future.

Thinking clearly about sampling requires us to consider four different groups of people (figure 3.2). The first group is the *target population*; this is the group that the researcher defines as the population of interest. In the case of *Literary Digest*, the target population was voters in the 1936 presidential election.

After deciding on a target population, a researcher needs to develop a list of people that can be used for sampling. This list is called a *sampling frame* and the people on it are called the *frame population*. Ideally, the target population and the frame population would be exactly the same, but in practice this is often not the case. For example, in the case of *Literary Digest*, the frame population was the 10 million people whose names came predominately from telephone directories and automobile registration records. Differences between the target population and the frame population are called *coverage error*. Coverage error does not, by itself, guarantee problems. However, it can lead to *coverage bias* if people in the frame

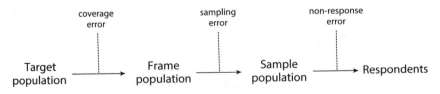

Figure 3.2: Representation errors.

population are systematically different from people in the target population who are not in the frame population. This is, in fact, exactly what happened in the *Literary Digest* poll. The people in their frame population tended to be more likely to support Alf Landon, in part because they were wealthier (recall that both telephones and automobiles were relatively new and expensive in 1936). So, in the *Literary Digest* poll, coverage error led to coverage bias.

After defining the *frame population*, the next step is for a researcher to select the *sample population*; these are the people who the researcher will attempt to interview. If the sample has different characteristics than the frame population, then sampling can introduce *sampling error.* In the case of the *Literary Digest* fiasco, however, there actually was no sampling—the magazine attempted to contact everyone in the frame population—and therefore there was no sampling error. Many researchers tend to focus on sampling error—this is typically the only kind of error captured by the margin of error reported in surveys—but the *Literary Digest* fiasco reminds us that we need to consider all sources of error, both random and systematic.

Finally, after selecting a sample population, a researcher attempts to interview all its members. Those people who are successfully interviewed are called *respondents*. Ideally, the sample population and the respondents would be exactly the same, but in practice there is nonresponse. That is, people who are selected in the sample sometimes do not participate. If the people who respond are different from those who don't respond, then there can be *nonresponse bias*. Nonresponse bias was the second main problem with the *Literary Digest* poll. Only 24% of the people who received a ballot responded, and it turned out that people who supported Landon were more likely to respond.

Beyond just being an example to introduce the ideas of representation, the *Literary Digest* poll is an oft-repeated parable, cautioning researchers about the dangers of haphazard sampling. Unfortunately, I think that the lesson that many people draw from this story is the wrong one. The most common moral of the story is that researchers can't learn anything from non-probability samples (i.e., samples without strict probability-based rules for selecting participants). But, as I'll show later in this chapter, that's not quite right. Instead, I think there are really two morals to this story; morals that are as true today as they were in 1936. First, a large amount of haphazardly collected data will not guarantee a good estimate. In general, having a large number of respondents decreases the variance of estimates, but it does not necessarily decrease the bias. With lots of data, researchers can sometimes get a precise estimate of the wrong thing; they can be *precisely inaccurate* (McFarland and McFarland 2015). The second main lesson from the *Literary Digest* fiasco is that researchers need to account for how their sample was collected when making estimates. In other words, because the sampling process in the *Literary Digest* poll was systematically skewed toward some respondents, researchers needed to use a more complex estimation process that weighted some respondents more than others. Later in this chapter, I'll show you one such weighting procedure—post-stratification—that can enable you to make better estimates from haphazard samples.

3.3.2 Measurement

> Measurement is about inferring what your respondents think and do from what they say.

In addition to problems of representation, the total survey error framework shows that the second major source of errors is *measurement*: how we make inferences from the answers that respondents give to our questions. It turns out that the answers we receive, and therefore the inferences we make, can depend critically—and in sometimes surprising ways—on exactly how we ask. Perhaps nothing illustrates this important point better than a joke in the wonderful book *Asking Questions* by Norman Bradburn, Seymour Sudman, and Brian Wansink (2004):

> Two priests, a Dominican and a Jesuit, are discussing whether it is a sin to smoke and pray at the same time. After failing to reach a conclusion, each goes off to consult his respective superior. The Dominican says, "What did your superior say?"
>
> The Jesuit responds, "He said it was alright."
> "That's funny" the Dominican replies, "My supervisor said it was a sin."
>
> The Jesuit said, "What did you ask him?" The Dominican replies, "I asked him if it was alright to smoke while praying." "Oh," said the Jesuit, "I asked if it was OK to pray while smoking."

Beyond this specific joke, survey researchers have documented many systematic ways that what you learn depends on how you ask. In fact, the very issue at the root of this joke has a name in the survey research community: *question form effects* (Kalton and Schuman 1982). To see how question form effects might impact real surveys, consider these two very similar-looking survey questions:

- "How much do you agree with the following statement: *Individuals* are more to blame than *social conditions* for crime and lawlessness in this country."
- "How much do you agree with the following statement: *Social conditions* are more to blame than *individuals* for crime and lawlessness in this country."

Although both questions appear to measure the same thing, they produced different results in a real survey experiment (Schuman and Presser 1996). When asked one way, about 60% of respondents reported that *individuals* were more to blame for crime, but when asked the other way, about 60% reported that *social conditions* were more to blame (figure 3.3). In other words, the small difference between these two questions could lead researchers to a different conclusion.

In addition to the structure of the question, respondents can also give different answers, depending on the specific words used. For example, in order to measure opinions about governmental priorities, respondents were read the following prompt:

"We are faced with many problems in this country, none of which can be solved easily or inexpensively. I'm going to name some of these problems, and for each one I'd like you to tell me whether you think we're spending too much money on it, too little money, or about the right amount."

Next, half of the respondents were asked about "welfare" and half were asked about "aid for the poor." While these might seem like two different phrases for the same thing, they elicited very different results (figure 3.4); Americans report being much more supportive of "aid to the poor" than "welfare" (Smith 1987; Rasinski 1989; Huber and Paris 2013).

As these examples about question form effects and wording effects show, the answers that researchers receive can be influenced by how they ask their

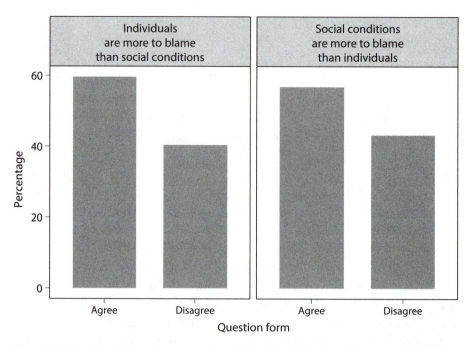

Figure 3.3: Results from a survey experiment showing that researchers can get different answers depending on exactly how they asked the question. A majority of respondents agreed that individuals are more to blame than social conditions for crime and lawlessness. And a majority of respondents agreed with the opposite: that social conditions are more responsible than individuals. Adapted from Schumann and Presser (1996), table 8.1.

questions. These examples sometimes lead researchers to wonder about the "correct" way to ask their survey questions. While I think there are some clearly wrong ways to ask a question, I don't think there is always one single correct way. That is, it is not obviously better to ask about "welfare" or "aid for the poor"; these are two different questions that measure two different things about respondents' attitudes. These examples also sometimes lead researchers to conclude that surveys should not be used. Unfortunately, sometimes there is no choice. Instead, I think the right lesson to draw from these examples is that we should construct our questions carefully and we should not accept responses uncritically.

Most concretely, this means that if you are analyzing survey data collected by someone else, make sure that you have read the actual questionnaire. And if you are creating your own questionnaire, I have four suggestions. First, I suggest that you read more about questionnaire design (e.g., Bradburn,

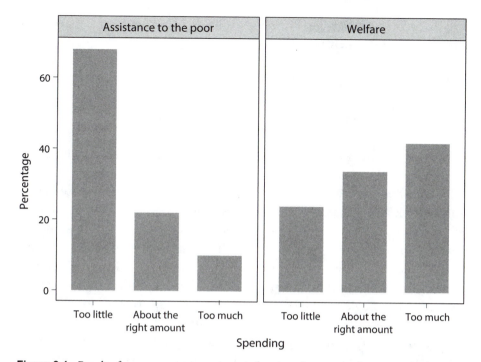

Figure 3.4: Results from a survey experiment showing that respondents are much more supportive of "aid to the poor" than "welfare." This is an example of a question wording effect whereby the answers that researchers receive depend on exactly which words they use in their questions. Adapted from Huber and Paris (2013), table A1.

Sudman, and Wansink (2004)); there is more to this than I've been able to describe here. Second, I suggest that you copy—word for word—questions from high-quality surveys. For example, if you want to ask respondents about their race/ethnicity, you could copy the questions that are used in large-scale government surveys, such as the census. Although this might sound like plagiarism, copying questions is encouraged in survey research (as long as you cite the original survey). If you copy questions from high-quality surveys, you can be sure that they have been tested, and you can compare the responses to your survey to responses from some other surveys. Third, if you think your questionnaire might contain important question wording effects or question form effects, you could run a *survey experiment* where half the respondents receive one version of the question and half receive the other version (Krosnick 2011). Finally, I suggest that you pilot-test your questions with some people from your frame population; survey researchers call this process *pre-testing* (Presser et al. 2004). My experience is that survey pre-testing is extremely helpful.

3.3.3 Cost

Surveys are not free, and this is a real constraint.

So far, I've briefly reviewed the total survey error framework, which itself is the subject of book-length treatments (Weisberg 2005; Groves et al. 2009). Although this framework is comprehensive, it generally causes researchers to overlook an important factor: cost. Although cost—which can be measured by either time or money—is rarely explicitly discussed by academic researchers, it is a real constraint that should not be ignored. In fact, cost is fundamental to the entire process of survey research (Groves 2004): it is the reason researchers interview a sample of people rather than an entire population. A single-minded devotion to minimizing error while completely ignoring cost is not always in our best interest.

The limitations of an obsession with reducing error are illustrated by the landmark project of Scott Keeter and colleagues (2000) on the effects of expensive field operations on reducing nonresponse in telephone surveys. Keeter and colleagues ran two simultaneous studies, one using "standard" recruitment procedures and one using "rigorous" recruitment procedures. The difference between the two studies was the amount of effort that went into contacting respondents and encouraging them to participate. For example, in the study with "rigorous" recruitment, researchers called the sampled households more frequently and over a longer period of time and made extra callbacks if participants initially refused to participate. These extra efforts did in fact produce a lower rate of nonresponse, but they added to the cost substantially. The study using "rigorous" procedures was twice as expensive and eight times slower. And in the end, both studies produced essentially identical estimates. This project, as well as subsequent replications with similar findings (Keeter et al. 2006), should lead you to wonder: are we better off with two reasonable surveys or one pristine survey? What about 10 reasonable surveys or one pristine survey? What about 100 reasonable surveys or one pristine survey? At some point, cost advantages must outweigh vague, nonspecific concerns about quality.

As I'll show in this rest of the chapter, many of the opportunities created by the digital age are not about making estimates that obviously have lower error. Rather, these opportunities are about estimating different quantities and about making estimates faster and cheaper, even with possibly higher errors. Researchers who insist on a single-minded obsession with minimizing error at the expense of other dimensions of quality are going to miss out on exciting opportunities. Given this background about the total survey error framework, we will now turn to three main areas of the third era of survey research: new approaches to representation (section 3.4), new approaches to measurement (section 3.5), and new strategies for combining surveys with big data sources (section 3.6).

3.4 Who to ask

The digital age is making probability sampling in practice harder and is creating new opportunities for non-probability sampling.

In the history of sampling, there have been two competing approaches: probability sampling methods and non-probability sampling methods. Although both approaches were used in the early days of sampling, probability sampling has come to dominate, and many social researchers are taught to view non-probability sampling with great skepticism. However, as I will describe below, changes created by the digital age mean that it is time for researchers to reconsider non-probability sampling. In particular, probability sampling has been getting hard to do in practice, and non-probability sampling has been getting faster, cheaper, and better. Faster and cheaper surveys are not just ends in themselves; they enable new opportunities such as more frequent surveys and larger sample sizes. For example, by using non-probability methods, the Cooperative Congressional Election Study (CCES) is able to have roughly 10 times more participants than earlier studies using probability sampling. This much larger sample enables political researchers to study variation in attitudes and behavior across subgroups and social contexts. Further, all of this added scale came without decreases in the quality of estimates (Ansolabehere and Rivers 2013).

Currently, the dominant approach to sampling for social research is *probability sampling.* In probability sampling, all members of the target population have a known, nonzero probability of being sampled, and all people who are sampled respond to the survey. When these conditions are met, elegant mathematical results offer provable guarantees about a researcher's ability to use the sample to make inferences about the target population.

In the real world, however, the conditions underlying these mathematical results are rarely met. For example, there are often coverage errors and nonresponse. Because of these problems, researchers often have to employ a variety of statistical adjustments in order to make inference from their sample to their target population. Thus, it is important to distinguish between *probability sampling in theory*, which has strong theoretical guarantees, and *probability sampling in practice*, which offers no such guarantees and depends on a variety of statistical adjustments.

Over time, the differences between probability sampling in theory and probability sampling in practice have been increasing. For example, nonresponse rates have been steadily increasing, even in high-quality, expensive surveys (figure 3.5) (National Research Council 2013; Meyer, Mok, and Sullivan 2015). Nonresponse rates are much higher in commercial telephone surveys—sometimes even as high as 90% (Kohut et al. 2012). These increases in nonresponse threaten the quality of estimates because estimates increasingly depend on the statistical models that researchers use to adjust for nonresponse. Further, these decreases in quality have happened despite increasingly expensive efforts by survey researchers to maintain high response rates. Some people fear that these twin trends of decreasing quality and increasing cost threaten the foundation of survey research (National Research Council 2013).

At the same time that there have been growing difficulties for probability sampling methods, there have also been exciting developments in *non-probability sampling methods*. There are a variety of styles of such methods, but the one thing that they have in common is that they cannot easily fit into the mathematical framework of probability sampling (Baker et al. 2013). In other words, in non-probability sampling methods, not everyone has a known and nonzero probability of inclusion. Non-probability sampling methods have a terrible reputation among social researchers, and they are associated with some of the most dramatic failures of survey researchers, such as the *Literary Digest* fiasco (discussed earlier) and "Dewey Defeats Truman," the incorrect prediction about the US presidential elections of 1948 (figure 3.6).

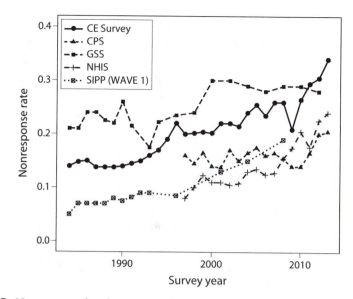

Figure 3.5: Nonresponse has been increasingly steadily, even in high-quality expensive surveys (National Research Council 2013; Meyer, Mok, and Sullivan 2015). Nonresponse rates are much higher for commercial telephones surveys, sometimes even as high as 90% (Kohut et al. 2012). These long-term trends in nonresponse mean that data collection is more expensive and estimates are less reliable. Adapted from Meyer, Mok, and Sullivan (2015), figure 1.

Figure 3.6: President Harry Truman holding up the headline of a newspaper that had incorrectly announced his defeat. This headline was based in part on estimates from non-probability samples (Mosteller 1949; Bean 1950; Freedman, Pisani, and Purves 2007). Although "Dewey Defeats Truman" happened in 1948, it is still among the reasons why many researchers are skeptical about estimates from non-probability samples. Source: Harry S. Truman Library and Museum.

One form of non-probability sampling that is particularly suited to the digital age is the use of *online panels*. Researchers using online panels depend on some panel provider—usually a company, government, or university—to construct a large, diverse group of people who agree to serve as respondents for surveys. These panel participants are often recruited using a variety of ad hoc methods such as online banner ads. Then, a researcher can pay the panel provider for access to a sample of respondents with desired characteristics (e.g., nationally representative of adults). These online panels are non-probability methods, because not everyone has a known, nonzero probability of inclusion. Although non-probability online panels are already being used by social researchers (e.g., the CCES), there is still some debate about the quality of estimates that come from them (Callegaro et al. 2014).

Despite these debates, I think there are two reasons why the time is right for social researchers to reconsider non-probability sampling. First, in the digital age, there have been many developments in the collection and analysis of non-probability samples. These newer methods are different enough from the methods that caused problems in the past that I think it makes sense to think of them as "non-probability sampling 2.0." The second reason why researchers should reconsider non-probability sampling is because probability samples in practice are becoming increasingly difficult. When there are high rates of nonresponse—as there are in real surveys now—the actual probabilities of inclusion for respondents are not known, and thus probability samples and non-probability samples are not so different as many researchers believe.

As I said earlier, non-probability samples are viewed with great skepticism by many social researchers, in part because of their role in some of the most embarrassing failures in the early days of survey research. A clear example of how far we have come with non-probability samples is the research by Wei Wang, David Rothschild, Sharad Goel, and Andrew Gelman (2015) that correctly recovered the outcome of the 2012 US election using a non-probability sample of American Xbox users—a decidedly nonrandom sample of Americans. The researchers recruited respondents from the Xbox gaming system, and, as you might expect, the sample skewed male and skewed young: 18- to 29-year-olds make up 19% of the electorate but 65% of the Xbox sample, and men make up 47% of the electorate but 93% of the Xbox sample (figure 3.7). Because of these strong demographic biases, the raw Xbox data

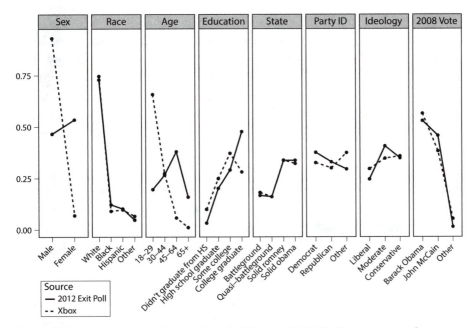

Figure 3.7: Demographics of respondents in Wang et al. (2015). Because respondents were recruited from Xbox, they were more likely to be young and more likely to be male, relative to voters in the 2012 election. Adapted from Wang et al. (2015), figure 1.

were a poor indicator of election returns. They predicted a strong victory for Mitt Romney over Barack Obama. Again, this is another example of the dangers of raw, unadjusted non-probability samples and is reminiscent of the *Literary Digest* fiasco.

However, Wang and colleagues were aware of these problems and attempted to adjust for their nonrandom sampling process when making estimates. In particular, they used *post-stratification,* a technique that is also widely used to adjust probability samples that have coverage errors and nonresponse.

The main idea of post-stratification is to use auxiliary information about the target population to help improve the estimate that comes from a sample. When using post-stratification to make estimates from their non-probability sample, Wang and colleague chopped the population into different groups, estimated the support for Obama in each group, and then took a weighted average of the group estimates to produce an overall estimate. For example, they could have split the population into two groups (men and women), estimated the support for Obama among men and women, and then estimated overall support for Obama by taking a weighted average in order to account for the fact that women make up 53% of the electorate and men 47%. Roughly, post-stratification helps correct for an imbalanced sample by bringing in auxiliary information about the sizes of the groups.

The key to post-stratification is to form the right groups. If you can chop up the population into homogeneous groups such that the response propensities are the same for everyone in each group, then post-stratification will produce unbiased estimates. In other words, post-stratifying by gender will produce unbiased estimates if all men have the same response propensity and all women have the same response propensity. This assumption is called the *homogeneous-response-propensities-within-groups* assumption, and I describe it a bit more in the mathematical notes at the end of this chapter.

Of course, it seems unlikely that the response propensities will be the same for all men and all women. However, the homogeneous-response-propensities-within-groups assumption becomes more plausible as the number of groups increases. Roughly, it becomes easier to chop the population into homogeneous groups if you create more groups. For example, it might seem implausible that all women have the same response propensity, but it might seem more plausible that there is the same response propensity for all women who are aged 18–29, who graduated from college, and who are living in California. Thus, as the number of groups used in post-stratification gets larger, the assumptions needed to support the method become more reasonable. Given this fact, researchers often want to create a huge number of groups for post-stratification. However, as the number of groups increases, researchers run into a different problem: data sparsity. If there are only a small number of people in each group, then the estimates will be more uncertain, and in the extreme case where there is a group that has no respondents, then post-stratification completely breaks down.

There are two ways out of this inherent tension between the plausibility of the homogeneous-response-propensity-within-groups assumption and the demand for reasonable sample sizes in each group. First, researchers can collect a larger, more diverse sample, which helps ensure reasonable sample sizes in each group. Second, they can use a more sophisticated statistical model for making estimates within groups. And, in fact, sometimes researchers do both, as Wang and colleagues did with their study of the election using respondents from Xbox.

Because they were using a non-probability method with computer-administered interviews (I'll talk more about computer-administered interviews in section 3.5), Wang and colleagues had very inexpensive data collection, which enabled them to collect information from 345,858 unique participants, a huge number by the standards of election polling. This massive sample size enabled them to form a huge number of post-stratification groups. Whereas post-stratification typically involves chopping the population into hundreds of groups, Wang and colleagues divided the population into 176,256 groups defined by gender (2 categories), race (4 categories), age (4 categories), education (4 categories), state (51 categories), party ID (3 categories), ideology (3 categories), and 2008 vote (3 categories). In other words, their huge sample size, which was enabled by low-cost data collection, enabled them to make a more plausible assumption in their estimation process.

Even with 345,858 unique participants, however, there were still many, many groups for which Wang and colleagues had almost no respondents. Therefore, they used a technique called *multilevel regression* to estimate the support in each group. Essentially, to estimate the support for Obama within a specific group, the multilevel regression pooled information from many closely related groups. For example, imagine trying to estimate the support for Obama among female Hispanics between 18 and 29 years old who are college graduates, who are registered Democrats, who self-identify as moderates, and who voted for Obama in 2008. This is a very, very specific group, and it is possible that there is nobody in the sample with these characteristics. Therefore, to make estimates about this group, multilevel regression uses a statistical model to pool together estimates from people in very similar groups.

Thus, Wang and colleagues used an approach that combined multilevel regression and post-stratification, so they called their strategy *multilevel regression with post-stratification* or, more affectionately, "Mr. P." When Wang and colleagues used Mr. P. to make estimates from the Xbox non-probability sample, they produced estimates very close to the overall support that Obama received in the 2012 election (figure 3.8). In fact their estimates were more accurate than an aggregate of traditional public opinion polls. Thus, in this case, statistical adjustments—specifically Mr. P.—seem to do a good job correcting the biases in non-probability data: biases that were clearly visible when you look at the estimates from the unadjusted Xbox data.

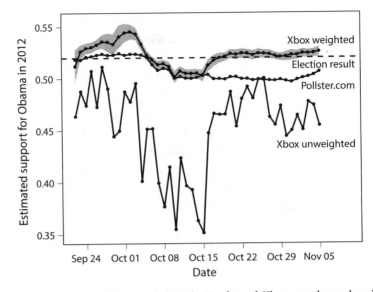

Figure 3.8: Estimates from Wang et al. (2015). Unadjusted Xbox sample produced inaccurate estimates. But the weighted Xbox sample produced estimates that were more accurate than an average of probability-based telephone surveys. Adapted from Wang et al. (2015), figures 2 and 3.

There are two main lessons from the study of Wang and colleagues. First, unadjusted non-probability samples can lead to bad estimates; this is a lesson that many researchers have heard before. The second lesson, however, is that non-probability samples, when analyzed properly, can actually produce good estimates; non-probability samples need not automatically lead to something like the *Literary Digest* fiasco.

Going forward, if you are trying to decide between using a probability sampling approach and a non-probability sampling approach, you face a difficult choice. Sometimes researchers want a quick and rigid rule (e.g., always use probability sampling methods), but it is increasingly difficult to offer such a rule. Researchers face a difficult choice between probability sampling methods in practice—which are increasingly expensive and far from the theoretical results that justify their use—and non-probability sampling methods—which are cheaper and faster, but less familiar and more varied. One thing that is clear, however, is that if you are forced to work with non-probability samples or nonrepresentative big data sources (think back to chapter 2), then there is a strong reason to believe that estimates made using post-stratification and related techniques will be better than unadjusted, raw estimates.

3.5   New ways of asking questions

Traditional surveys are closed, boring, and removed from life. Now we can ask questions that are more open, more fun, and more embedded in life.

The total survey error framework encourages researchers to think about survey research as a two-part process: recruiting respondents and asking them questions. In section 3.4, I discussed how the digital age changes how we recruit respondents, and now I'll discuss how it enables researchers to ask questions in new ways. These new approaches can be used with either probability samples or non-probability samples.

A survey *mode* is the environment in which the questions are asked, and it can have important impacts on measurement (Couper 2011). In the first era of survey research, the most common mode was face to face, while in the second era, it was telephone. Some researchers view the third era of survey research as just an expansion of survey modes to include computers and mobile phones. However, the digital age is more than just a change in the pipes through which questions and answers flow. Instead, the transition from analog to digital enables—and will likely require—researchers to change how we ask questions.

A study by Michael Schober and colleagues (2015) illustrates the benefits of adjusting traditional approaches to better match digital-age communication systems. In this study, Schober and colleagues compared different approaches to asking people questions via a mobile phone. They compared collecting data via voice conversations, which would have been a natural translation of second-era approaches, to collecting data via many microsurveys sent through text messages, an approach with no obvious precedent. They found that microsurveys sent through text messages led to higher-quality data than voice interviews. In other words, simply transferring the old approach into the new medium did not lead to the highest-quality data. Instead, by thinking clearly about the capabilities and social norms around mobile phones, Schober and colleagues were able to develop a better way of asking questions that lead to higher-quality responses.

There are many dimensions along which researchers can categorize survey modes, but I think the most critical feature of digital-age survey modes is that they are *computer-administered*, rather than *interviewer-administered* (as in telephone and face-to-face surveys). Taking human interviewers out of the data collection process offers enormous benefits and introduces some drawbacks. In terms of benefits, removing human interviewers can reduce *social desirability bias*, the tendency for respondents to try to present themselves in the best possible way by, for example, under-reporting stigmatized behavior (e.g., illegal drug use) and over-reporting encouraged behavior (e.g., voting) (Kreuter, Presser, and Tourangeau 2008). Removing human interviewers can also eliminate *interviewer effects*, the tendency for responses to be influenced in subtle ways by the characteristics of the human interviewer (West and Blom 2016). In addition to potentially improving accuracy for some types of questions, removing human interviewers also dramatically reduces costs—interview time is one of the biggest expenses in survey research—and increases flexibility because respondents can participate whenever they want, not just when an interviewer is available. However, removing the human interviewer also creates some challenges. In particular, interviewers can develop a rapport with respondents that can increase participation rates, clarify confusing questions, and maintain respondents' engagement while they slog through a long (potentially tedious) questionnaire (Garbarski, Schaeffer, and Dykema 2016). Thus, switching from an *interviewer-administered* mode to a *computer-administered* one creates both opportunities and challenges.

Next, I'll describe two approaches showing how researchers can take advantage of the tools of the digital age to ask questions differently: measuring internal states at a more appropriate time and place through *ecological momentary assessment* (section 3.5.1) and combining the strengths of open-ended and closed-ended survey questions through *wiki surveys* (section 3.5.2). However, the move toward computer-administered, ubiquitous asking will also mean that we need to design ways of asking that are more enjoyable for participants, a process sometimes called *gamification* (Section 3.5.3).

3.5.1 Ecological momentary assessments

Researchers can chop up big surveys and sprinkle them into people's lives.

Ecological momentary assessment (EMA) involves taking traditional surveys, chopping them up into pieces, and sprinkling them into the lives of participants. Thus, survey questions can be asked at an appropriate time and place, rather than in a long interview weeks after the events have occurred.

EMA is characterized by four features: (1) collection of data in real-world environments; (2) assessments that focus on individuals' current or very recent states or behaviors; (3) assessments that may be event-based, time-based, or randomly prompted (depending on the research question); and (4) completion of multiple assessments over time (Stone and Shiffman 1994). EMA is an approach to asking that is greatly facilitated by smartphones with which people interact frequently throughout the day. Further, because smartphones are packed with sensors—such as GPS and accelerometers—it is increasingly possible to trigger measurements based on activity. For example, a smartphone could be programmed to trigger a survey question if a respondent goes into a particular neighborhood.

The promise of EMA is nicely illustrated by the dissertation research of Naomi Sugie. Since the 1970s, the United States has dramatically increased the number of people that it imprisons. As of 2005, about 500 in every 100,000 Americans were in prison, a rate of incarceration higher than anywhere else in the world (Wakefield and Uggen 2010). The surge in the number of people entering prison has also produced a surge in the number leaving prison; about 700,000 people leave prison each year (Wakefield and Uggen 2010). These people face severe challenges upon leaving prison, and unfortunately many end up back there. In order to understand and reduce recidivism, social scientists and policy makers need to understand the experience of people as they re-enter society. However, these data are hard to collect with standard survey methods because ex-offenders tend to be difficult to study and their lives are extremely unstable. Measurement approaches that deploy surveys every few months miss enormous amounts of the dynamics in their lives (Sugie 2016).

In order to study the re-entry process with much greater precision, Sugie took a standard probability sample of 131 people from the complete list of individuals leaving prison in Newark, New Jersey. She provided each participant with a smartphone, which became a rich data collection platform, both for recording behavior and for asking questions. Sugie used the phones to administer two kinds of surveys. First, she sent an "experience sampling survey" at a randomly selected time between 9 a.m. and 6 p.m. asking participants about their current activities and feelings. Second, at 7 p.m., she sent a "daily survey" asking about all the activities of that day. Further, in addition to these survey questions, the phones recorded their geographic location at regular intervals and kept encrypted records of call and text metadata. Using this approach—which combines asking and observing—Sugie was able to create a detailed, high-frequency set of measurements about the lives of these people as they re-entered society.

Researchers believe that finding stable, high-quality employment helps people successfully transition back into society. However, Sugie found that, on average, her participants' work experiences were informal, temporary, and sporadic. This description of the average pattern, however, masks important heterogeneity. In particular, Sugie found four distinct patterns within her participant pool: "early exit" (those who start searching for work but then drop out of the labor market), "persistent search" (those who spend much of the period searching for work), "recurring work" (those who spend much of the period working), and "low response" (those who do not respond to the surveys regularly). The "early exit" group—those who start searching for work but then don't find it and stop searching—is particularly important, because this group is probably the least likely to have a successful re-entry.

One might imagine that searching for a job after being in prison is a difficult process, which could lead to depression and then withdrawal from the labor market. Therefore, Sugie used her surveys to collect data about the emotional state of participants—an internal state that is not easily estimated from behavioral data. Surprisingly, she found that the "early exit" group did not report higher levels of stress or unhappiness. Rather, it was the opposite: those who continued to search for work reported more feelings of emotional distress. All of this fine-grained, longitudinal detail about the behavior and emotional state of the ex-offenders is important for understanding the barriers they face and easing their transition back into society. Further, all of this fine-grained detail would have been missed in a standard survey.

Sugie's data collection with a vulnerable population, particularly the passive data collection, might raise some ethical concerns. But Sugie anticipated these concerns and addressed them in her design (Sugie 2014, 2016). Her procedures were reviewed by a third party—her university's Institutional Review Board—and complied with all existing rules. Further, consistent with the principles-based approach that I advocate in chapter 6, Sugie's approach went far beyond what was required by existing regulations. For example, she received meaningful informed consent from each participant, she enabled participants to temporarily turn off the geographic tracking, and she went to great lengths to protect the data that she was collecting. In addition to using appropriate encryption and data storage, she also obtained a Certificate of Confidentiality from the federal government, which meant that she could not be forced to turn over her data to the police (Beskow, Dame, and Costello 2008). I think that because of her thoughtful approach, Sugie's project provides a valuable model to other researchers. In particular, she did not stumble blindly into an ethical morass, nor did she avoid important research because it was ethically complex. Rather, she thought carefully, sought appropriate advice, respected her participants, and took steps to improve the risk–benefit profile of her study.

I think there are three general lessons from Sugie's work. First, new approaches to asking are completely compatible with traditional methods of sampling; recall that Sugie took a standard probability sample from a well-defined frame population. Second, high-frequency, longitudinal measurements can be particularly valuable for studying social experiences that are irregular and dynamic. Third, when survey data collection is combined with big data sources—something that I think will become increasingly common, as I'll argue later in this chapter—additional ethical issues can arise. I'll treat research ethics in more detail in chapter 6, but Sugie's work shows that these issues are addressable by conscientious and thoughtful researchers.

3.5.2 Wiki surveys

Wiki surveys enable new hybrids of closed and open questions.

In addition to asking questions at more natural times and in more natural contexts, new technology also allows us to change the form of the questions. Most survey questions are closed, with respondents choosing from a fixed set of choices written by researchers. This is a process that one prominent survey researcher calls "putting words in people's mouths." For example, here's a closed survey question:

"This next question is on the subject of work. Would you please look at this card and tell me which thing on this list you would *most* prefer in a job?

1. High income
2. No danger of being fired
3. Working hours are short, lots of free time
4. Chances for advancement
5. The work is important, and gives a feeling of accomplishment."

But are these the only possible answers? Might researchers be missing something important by limiting the responses to these five? The alternative to closed questions is an open-ended survey question. Here's the same question asked in an open form:

"This next question is on the subject of work. People look for different things in a job. What would you most prefer in a job?"

Although these two questions appear quite similar, a survey experiment by Howard Schuman and Stanley Presser (1979) revealed that they can produce very different results: nearly 60% of the responses to the open question are not included in the five researcher-created responses (figure 3.9).

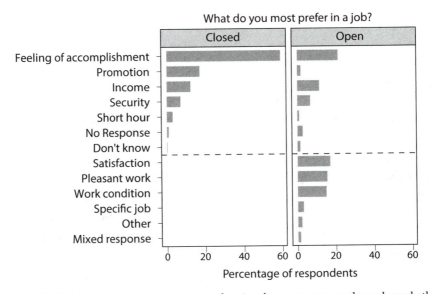

Figure 3.9: Results from a survey experiment showing that responses can depend on whether the question is asked in closed or open form. Adapted from Schuman and Presser (1979), table 1.

Although open and closed questions can yield quite different information and both were popular in the early days of survey research, closed questions have come to dominate the field. This domination is not because closed questions have been proven to provide better measurement, but rather because they are much easier to use; the process of analyzing open-ended questions is error-prone and expensive. The move away from open questions is unfortunate because it is precisely the information that researchers did not know ahead of time that can be the most valuable.

The transition from human-administered to computer-administered surveys, however, suggests a new way out of this old problem. What if we could now have survey questions that combine the best features of both open and closed questions? That is, what if we could have a survey that both is open to new information and produces easy-to-analyze responses? That's exactly what Karen Levy and I (2015) have tried to create.

In particular, Karen and I thought that websites that collect and curate user-generated content might be able to inform the design of new types of surveys. We were particularly inspired by Wikipedia—a wonderful example of an open, dynamic system driven by user-generated content—so we called our new survey a *wiki survey*. Just as Wikipedia evolves over time based on the ideas of its participants, we imagined a survey that evolves over time based on the ideas of *its* participants. Karen and I developed three properties that wiki surveys should satisfy: they should be greedy, collaborative, and adaptive. Then, with a team of web developers, we created a website that could run wiki surveys: http://www.allourideas.org.

The data collection process in a wiki survey is illustrated by a project we did with the New York City Mayor's Office in order to integrate residents' ideas into PlaNYC 2030, New York's citywide sustainability plan. To begin the process, the Mayor's Office generated a list of 25 ideas based on their previous outreach (e.g., "Require all big buildings to make certain energy efficiency upgrades" and "Teach kids about green issues as part of school curriculum"). Using these 25 ideas as seeds, the Mayor's Office asked the question "Which do you think is a better idea for creating a greener, greater New York City?" Respondents were presented with a pair of ideas (e.g., "Open schoolyards across the city as public playgrounds" and "Increase targeted tree plantings in neighborhoods with high asthma rates") and were asked to choose between them (figure 3.10). After choosing, respondents were immediately presented with another randomly selected pair of ideas.

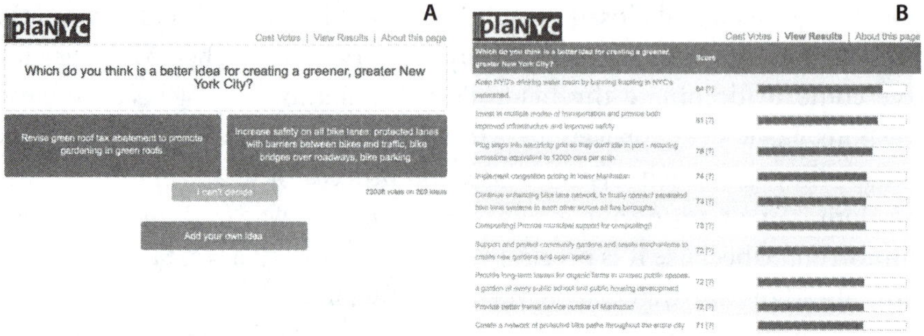

Figure 3.10: Interface for a wiki survey. Panel A shows the response screen and panel B shows the result screen. Reproduced by permission from Salganik and Levy (2015), figure 2.

They were able to continue contributing information about their preferences for as long as they wished either by voting or by choosing "I can't decide." Crucially, at any point, respondents were able to contribute their own ideas, which—pending approval by the Mayor's Office—became part of the pool of ideas to be presented to others. Thus, the questions that participants received were both open and closed simultaneously.

The Mayor's Office launched its wiki survey in October 2010 in conjunction with a series of community meetings to obtain resident feedback. Over about four months, 1,436 respondents contributed 31,893 responses and 464 new ideas. Critically, 8 of the top 10 scoring ideas were uploaded by participants rather than being part of the set of seed ideas from the Mayor's Office. And, as we describe in our paper, this same pattern, with uploaded ideas scoring better than seed ideas, happens in many wiki surveys. In other words, by being open to new information, researchers are able to learn things that would have been missed using more closed approaches.

Beyond the results of these specific surveys, our wiki survey project also illustrates how the cost structure of digital research means that researchers can now engage with the world in somewhat different ways. Academic researchers are now able to build real systems that can be used by many people: we have hosted more than 10,000 wiki surveys and have collected more than 15 million responses. This ability to create something that can be used at scale comes from the fact that once the website has been built, it costs basically nothing to make it freely available to everyone in the world (of course, this would not be true if we had human-administered interviews). Further, this scale enables different kinds of research. For example, these 15 million responses, as well as our stream of participants, provide a valuable test-bed for future methodological research. I'll describe more about other research opportunities that are created by digital-age cost structures—particularly zero variable cost data—when I discuss experiments in Chapter 4.

3.5.3 Gamification

> Standard surveys are boring for participants; that can change, and it must change.

So far, I've told you about new approaches to asking that are facilitated by computer-administered interviews. However, one downside of computer-administered interviews is that there is no human interviewer to help induce and maintain participation. This is a problem because many surveys are both time-consuming and boring. Therefore, in the future, survey designers are going to have to design around their participants and make the process of answering questions more enjoyable and game-like. This process is sometimes called *gamification*.

To illustrate what a fun survey might look like, let's consider Friendsense, a survey that was packaged as a game on Facebook. Sharad Goel, Winter Mason, and Duncan Watts (2010) wanted to estimate how much people *think* they are like their friends and how much they are *actually* like their friends. This question about real and perceived attitude similarity gets directly at people's ability to accurately perceive their social environment and has implications for political polarization and the dynamics of social change. Conceptually, real and perceived attitude similarity is an easy thing to measure. Researchers could ask lots of people about their opinions and then ask their friends about their opinions (this allows for measurement of real attitude agreement), and they could ask lots of people to guess their friends' attitudes (this allows for measurement of perceived attitude agreement). Unfortunately, it is logistically very difficult to interview both a respondent and her friend. Therefore, Goel and colleagues turned their survey into a Facebook app that was fun to play.

After a participant consented to be in a research study, the app selected a friend from the respondent's Facebook account and asked a question about the attitude of that friend (figure 3.11). Intermixed with questions about randomly selected friends, the respondent also answered questions about

Figure 3.11: Interface from the Friendsense study (Goel, Mason, and Watts 2010). The researchers turned a standard attitude survey into a fun, game-like experience. The app asked participants both serious questions and more lighthearted questions, such as the one shown in this image. The friends' faces have been intentionally blurred. Reproduced by permission from Sharad Goel.

herself. After answering a question about a friend, the respondent was told whether her answer was correct or, if her friend had not answered, the respondent was able to encourage her friend to participate. Thus, the survey spread in part through viral recruitment.

The attitude questions were adapted from the General Social Survey. For example, "Does [your friend] sympathize with the Israelis more than the Palestinians in the Middle East situation?" and "Would [your friend] pay higher taxes for the government to provide universal health care?" On top of these serious questions, the researchers mixed in more lighthearted questions: "Would [your friend] rather drink wine over beer?" and "Would [your friend] rather have the power to read minds, instead of the power to fly?" These lighthearted questions made the process more enjoyable to participants and also enabled an interesting comparison: would attitude agreement be similar for serious political questions and for lighthearted questions about drinking and superpowers?

There were three main results from the study. First, friends were more likely to give the same answer than strangers, but even close friends still disagreed on about 30% of the questions. Second, respondents overestimated their agreement with their friends. In other words, most of the diversity of opinions that exists between friends is not noticed. Finally, participants were as likely to be aware of disagreements with their friends on serious matters of politics as with lighthearted issues about drinking and superpowers.

Although the app is unfortunately no longer available to play, it was a nice example of how researchers can turn a standard attitude survey into something enjoyable. More generally, with some creativity and design work, it is possible to improve user experience for survey participants. So, next time you are designing a survey, take a moment to think about what you could do to make the experience better for your participants. Some may fear that these steps toward gamification could hurt data quality, but I think that bored participants pose a far greater risk to data quality.

The work of Goel and colleagues also illustrates the theme of the next section: linking surveys to big data sources. In this case, by linking their survey with Facebook, the researchers automatically had access to a list of the participants' friends. In the next section, we will consider the linkages between surveys and big data sources in greater detail.

3.6 Surveys linked to big data sources

Linking surveys to big data sources enables you to produce estimates that would be impossible with either data source individually.

Most surveys are stand-alone, self-contained efforts. They don't build on each other, and they don't take advantage of all of the other data that exist in the world. This will change. There is just too much to be gained by linking survey data to the big data sources discussed in chapter 2. By combining these two types of data, it is often possible to do something that was impossible with either one individually.

There are a couple of different ways in which survey data can be combined with big data sources. In this section, I'll describe two approaches that are useful and distinct, and I'll call them *enriched asking* and *amplified asking* (figure 3.12). Although I'm going to illustrate each approach with a detailed example, you should recognize that these are general recipes that could be used with different types of survey data and different types of big data. Further, you should notice that each of these examples could be viewed in two different ways. Thinking back to the ideas in chapter 1, some people will view these studies as examples of "custommade" survey data enhancing "readymade" big data, and others will view them as examples of "readymade" big data enhancing "custommade" survey data. You should be able to see both views. Finally, you should notice how these examples clarify that surveys and big data sources are complements and not substitutes.

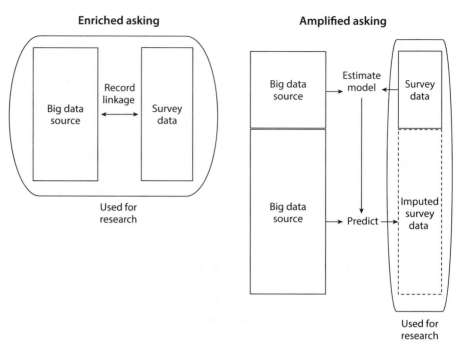

Figure 3.12: Two main ways to combine big data sources and survey data. In enriched asking (section 3.6.1), the big data source has a core measure of interest, and the survey data build the necessary context around it. In amplified asking (section 3.6.2), the big data source does not have a core measure of interest, but it is used to amplify the survey data.

3.6.1 Enriched asking

> In enriched asking, survey data build context around a big data source that contains some important measurements but lacks others.

One way to combine survey data and big data sources is a process that I'll call *enriched asking*. In enriched asking, a big data source contains some important measurements but lacks other measurements, so the researcher collects these missing measurements in a survey and then links the two data sources together. One example of enriched asking is the study by Burke and Kraut (2014) about whether interacting on Facebook increases friendship strength, which I described in section 3.2. In that case, Burke and Kraut combined survey data with Facebook log data.

The setting in which Burke and Kraut were working, however, meant that they didn't have to deal with two big problems that researchers doing enriched asking typically face. First, actually linking together the individual-level data sets, a process called *record linkage*, can be difficult if there is no unique identifier in both data sources that can be used to ensure that the correct record in one dataset is matched with the correct record in the other dataset. The second main problem with enriched asking is that the quality of the big data source will frequently be difficult for researchers to assess because the process through which the data are created may be proprietary and could be susceptible to many of the problems described in chapter 2. In other words, enriched asking will frequently involve error-prone linking of surveys to black-box data sources of unknown quality. Despite these problems, however, enriched asking can be used to conduct important research, as was demonstrated by Stephen Ansolabehere and Eitan Hersh (2012) in their research on voting patterns in the United States.

Voter turnout has been the subject of extensive research in political science, and, in the past, researchers' understanding of who votes and why has generally been based on the analysis of survey data. Voting in the United States, however, is an unusual behavior in that the government records whether each citizen has voted (of course, the government does not record who each citizen votes for). For many years, these governmental voting records were available on paper forms, scattered in various local government offices around the country. This made it very difficult, but not impossible, for political scientists to have a complete picture of the electorate and to compare what people say in surveys about voting with their actual voting behavior (Ansolabehere and Hersh 2012).

But these voting records have now been digitized, and a number of private companies have systematically collected and merged them to produce comprehensive master voting files that contain the voting behavior of all Americans. Ansolabehere and Hersh partnered with one of these companies—Catalist LCC—in order to use their master voting file to help develop a better picture of the electorate. Further, because their study relied on digital records collected and curated by a company that had invested substantial resources in data collection and harmonization, it offered a number of advantages over previous efforts that had been done without the aid of companies and by using analog records.

Like many of the big data sources in chapter 2, the Catalist master file did not include much of the demographic, attitudinal, and behavioral information that Ansolabehere and Hersh needed. In fact, they were particularly interested in comparing reported voting behavior in surveys with validated voting behavior (i.e., the information in the Catalist database). So Ansolabehere and Hersh collected the data that they wanted as part of a large social survey, the CCES, mentioned earlier in this chapter. They then gave their data to Catalist, and Catalist gave them back a merged data file that included validated voting behavior (from Catalist), the self-reported voting behavior (from CCES) and the demographics and attitudes of respondents (from CCES) (figure 3.13). In other words, Ansolabehere and Hersh combined the voting records data with survey data in order do research that was not possible with either data source individually.

With their combined data file, Ansolabehere and Hersh came to three important conclusions. First, over-reporting of voting is rampant: almost half of the nonvoters reported voting, and if someone reported voting, there is only an 80% chance that they actually voted. Second, over-reporting is not random: over-reporting is more common among high-income, well-educated, partisans who are engaged in public affairs. In other words, the people who are most likely to vote are also most likely to lie about voting. Third, and most critically, because of the systematic nature of over-reporting, the actual differences between voters and nonvoters are smaller than they appear just from surveys. For example, those with a bachelor's degree are about 22 percentage points more likely to report voting, but are only 10 percentage points more likely to actually vote. It turns out, perhaps not surprisingly, that existing resource-based theories of voting are much better at predicting who will report voting (which is the data that researchers have used in the past) than they are at predicting who actually votes. Thus, the empirical finding of Ansolabehere and Hersh (2012) call for new theories to understand and predict voting.

But how much should we trust these results? Remember, these results depend on error-prone linking to black-box data with unknown amounts of error. More specifically, the results hinge on two key steps: (1) the ability of Catalist to combine many disparate data sources to produce an accurate master datafile and (2) the ability to link the survey data to their master datafile. Each of these steps is quite difficult, and errors in either step could lead researchers to the wrong conclusions. However, both data processing

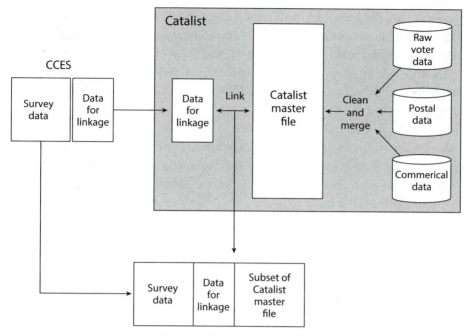

Figure 3.13: Schematic of Ansolabehere and Hersh's (2012) study. To create the master datafile, Catalist combines and harmonizes information from many different sources. This process of merging, no matter how careful, will propagate errors in the original data sources and will introduce new errors. A second source of errors is the record linkage between the survey data and the master datafile. If every person had a stable, unique identifier in both data sources, then linkage would be trivial. But, Catalist had to do the linkage using imperfect identifiers, in this case name, gender, birth year, and home address. Unfortunately, for many cases, there could be incomplete or inaccurate information; a voter named Homer Simpson might appear as Homer Jay Simpson, Homie J Simpson, or even Homer Sampsin. Despite the potential for errors in the Catalist master datafile and errors in the record linkage, Ansolabehere and Hersh were able to build confidence in their estimates through several different types of checks.

and linking are critical to the continued existence of Catalist as a company, so it can invest resources in solving these problems, often at a scale that no academic researcher can match. In their paper, Ansolabehere and Hersh go through a number of steps to check the results of these two steps— even though some of them are proprietary—and these checks might be helpful for other researchers wishing to link survey data to black-box big data sources.

What are the general lessons researchers can draw from this study? First, there is tremendous value both from enriching big data sources with survey data and from enriching survey data with big data sources (you can see this study either way). By combining these two data sources, the researchers were able to do something that was impossible with either individually. The second general lesson is that though aggregated, commercial data sources, such as the data from Catalist, should not be considered "ground truth," in some cases, they can be useful. Skeptics sometimes compare these aggregated, commercial data source with absolute Truth and point out that these data sources fall short. However, in this case, the skeptics are making the wrong comparison: all data that researchers use fall short of absolute Truth. Instead, it is better to compare aggregated, commercial data sources with other available data sources (e.g., self-reported voting behavior), which invariably have errors as well. Finally, the third general lesson of Ansolabehere and Hersh's study is that in some situations, researchers can benefit from the huge investments that many private companies are making in collecting and harmonizing complex social data sets.

3.6.2 Amplified asking

> Amplified asking using a predictive model to combine survey data from a few people with a big data source from many people.

A different way to combine survey and big data sources is a process that I'll call *amplified asking*. In amplified asking, a researcher uses a predictive model to combine a small amount of survey data with a big data source in order to produce estimates at a scale or granularity that would not be possible with either data source individually. An important example of amplified asking comes from the work of Joshua Blumenstock, who wanted to collect data that could help guide development in poor countries. In the past, researchers collecting this kind of data generally had to take one of two approaches: sample surveys or censuses. Sample surveys, where researchers interview a small number of people, can be flexible, timely, and relatively cheap. However, these surveys, because they are based on a sample, are often limited in their resolution. With a sample survey, it is often hard to make estimates about specific geographic regions or for specific demographic groups. Censuses, on the other hand, attempt to interview everyone, and so they can be used to produce estimates for small geographic regions or demographic groups. But censuses are generally expensive, narrow in focus (they only include a small number of questions), and not timely (they happen on a fixed schedule, such as every 10 years) (Kish 1979). Rather than being stuck with sample surveys or censuses, imagine if researchers could combine the best characteristics of both. Imagine if researchers could ask every question to every person every day. Obviously, this ubiquitous, always-on survey is a kind of social science fantasy. But it does appear that we can *begin* to approximate this by combining survey questions from a small number of people with digital traces from many people.

Blumenstock's research began when he partnered with the largest mobile phone provider in Rwanda, and the company provided anonymized transaction records from about 1.5 million customers between 2005 and 2009. These records contained information about each call and text message, such as the start time, duration, and approximate geographic location of the caller and receiver. Before I talk about the statistical issues, it is worth pointing out that this first step may be one of the hardest for many researchers. As I described in chapter 2, most big data sources are *inaccessible* to researchers. Telephone metadata, in particular, are especially inaccessible because they are basically impossible to anonymize and they almost certainly contain information that participants would consider sensitive (Mayer, Mutchler, and Mitchell 2016; Landau 2016). In this particular case, the researchers were careful to protect the data, and their work was overseen by a third party (i.e., their IRB). I'll return to these ethical issues in more detail in chapter 6.

Blumenstock was interested in measuring wealth and well-being. But these traits are not directly in the call records. In other words, these call records are *incomplete* for this research — a common feature of big data sources that was discussed in detail in chapter 2. However, it seems likely that the call records probably have some information that could indirectly provide information about wealth and well-being. Given this possibility, Blumenstock asked whether it was possible to train a machine learning model that could use call records to predict how someone would respond to a survey. If this was possible, then Blumenstock could use this model to predict the survey responses of all 1.5 million customers.

In order to build and train such a model, Blumenstock and research assistants from Kigali Institute of Science and Technology called a random sample of about a thousand customers. The researchers explained the goals of the project to the participants, asked for their consent to link the survey responses to the call records, and then asked them a series of questions to measure their wealth and well-being, such as "Do you own a radio?" and "Do you own a bicycle?" (see figure 3.14 for a partial list). All participants in the survey were compensated financially.

Next, Blumenstock used a two-step procedure common in machine learning: feature engineering followed by supervised learning. First, in the *feature engineering* step, for everyone that was interviewed, Blumenstock converted the call records into a set of characteristics about each person; data scientists might call these characteristics "features" and social scientists would call them "variables." For example, for each person, Blumenstock calculated the total number of days with activity, the number of distinct people a person has been in contact with, the amount of money spent on airtime, and so on. Critically, good feature engineering requires knowledge of the research setting. For example, if it is important to distinguish between domestic and international calls (we might expect people who call internationally to be wealthier), then this must be done at the feature engineering step. A researcher with little understanding of Rwanda might not include this feature, and then the predictive performance of the model would suffer.

Next, in the *supervised learning* step, Blumenstock built a model to predict the survey response for each person based on their features. In this case, Blumenstock used logistic regression, but he could have used a variety of other statistical or machine learning approaches.

So how well did it work? Was Blumenstock able to predict answers to survey questions like "Do you own a radio?" and "Do you own a bicycle?" using features derived from call records? In order to evaluate the performance of his predictive model, Blumenstock used *cross-validation*, a technique commonly used in data science but rarely in social science. The goal of cross-validation is to provide a fair assessment of a model's predictive performance by training it and testing it on different subsets of data. In particular, Blumenstock split his data into 10 chunks of 100 people each. Then, he used nine of the chunks to train his model, and the predictive performance of the trained model was evaluated on the remaining chunk. He repeated this procedure 10 times—with each chunk of data getting one turn as the validation data—and averaged the results.

The accuracy of the predictions was high for some traits (figure 3.14); for example, Blumenstock could predict with 97.6% accuracy if someone owned

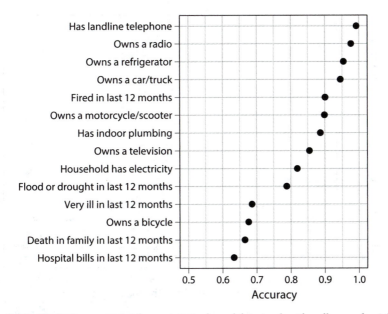

Figure 3.14: Predictive accuracy for a statistical model trained with call records. Adapted from Blumenstock (2014), table 2.

a radio. This might sound impressive, but it is always important to compare a complex prediction method against a simple alternative. In this case, a simple alternative is to predict that everyone will give the most common answer. For example, 97.3% of respondents reported owning a radio, so if Blumenstock had predicted that everyone would report owning a radio, he would have had an accuracy of 97.3%, which is surprisingly similar to the performance of his more complex procedure (97.6% accuracy). In other words, all the fancy data and modeling increased the accuracy of the prediction from 97.3% to 97.6%. However, for other questions, such as "Do you own a bicycle?", the predictions improved from 54.4% to 67.6%. More generally, figure 3.15 shows that for some traits Blumenstock did not improve much beyond just making the simple baseline prediction, but that for other traits there was some improvement. Looking just at these results, however, you might not think that this approach is particularly promising.

However, just one year later, Blumenstock and two colleagues—Gabriel Cadamuro and Robert On—published a paper in *Science* with substantially better results (Blumenstock, Cadamuro, and On 2015). There were two main technical reasons for this improvement: (1) they used more

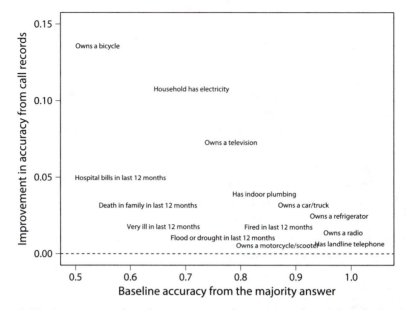

Figure 3.15: Comparison of predictive accuracy for a statistical model trained with call records to simple baseline prediction. Points are slightly jittered to avoid overlap. Adapted from Blumenstock (2014), table 2.

sophisticated methods (i.e., a new approach to feature engineering and a more sophisticated model to predict responses from features) and (2) rather than attempting to infer responses to individual survey questions (e.g., "Do you own a radio?"), they attempted to infer a composite wealth index. These technical improvements meant that they could do a reasonable job of using call records to predict wealth for the people in their sample.

Predicting the wealth of people in the sample, however, was not the ultimate goal of their research. Remember that the ultimate goal was to combine some of the best features of sample surveys and censuses to produce accurate, high-resolution estimates of poverty in developing countries. To assess their ability to achieve this goal, Blumenstock and colleagues used their model and their data to predict the wealth of all 1.5 million people in the call records. And they used the geospatial information embedded in the call data (recall that the data included the location of the nearest cell tower for each call) to estimate the approximate place of residence of each person (figure 3.16). Putting these two estimates together, Blumenstock and colleagues produced an estimate of the geographic distribution of subscriber wealth

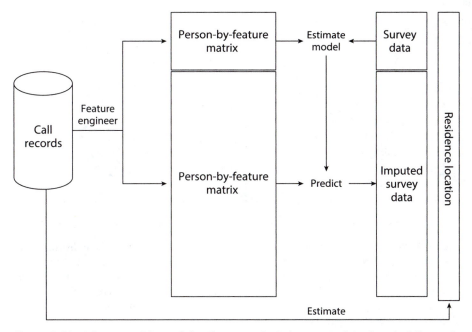

Figure 3.16: Schematic of the study by Blumenstock, Cadamuro, and On (2015). Call records from the phone company were converted to a matrix with one row for each person and one column for each feature (i.e., variable). Next, the researchers built a supervised learning model to predict the survey responses from the person-by-feature matrix. Then, the supervised learning model was used to impute the survey responses for all 1.5 million customers. Also, the researchers estimated the approximate place of residence for all 1.5 million customers based on the locations of their calls. When these two estimates—the estimated wealth and the estimated place of residence—were combined, the results were similar to estimates from the Demographic and Health Survey, a gold-standard traditional survey (figure 3.17).

at extremely fine spatial granularity. For example, they could estimate the average wealth in each of Rwanda's 2,148 cells (the smallest administrative unit in the country).

How well did these estimates match up to the actual level of poverty in these regions? Before I answer that question, I want to emphasize the fact that there are a lot of reasons to be skeptical. For example, the ability to make predictions at the individual level was pretty noisy (figure 3.17). And, perhaps more importantly, people with mobile phones might be systematically different from people without mobile phones. Thus, Blumenstock and colleagues might suffer from types of coverage errors similar to those that biased the 1936 *Literary Digest* survey that I described earlier.

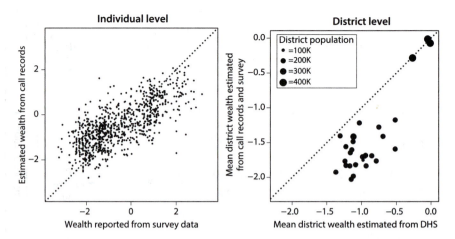

Figure 3.17: Results from Blumenstock, Cadamuro, and On (2015). At the individual level, the researchers were able to do a reasonable job at predicting someone's wealth from their call records. The estimates of district-level wealth for Rwanda's 30 districts—which were based on individual-level estimates of wealth and place of residence—were similar to results from the Demographic and Health Survey, a gold-standard traditional survey. Adapted from Blumenstock, Cadamuro, and On (2015), figures 1a and 3c.

To get a sense of the quality of their estimates, Blumenstock and colleagues needed to compare them with something else. Fortunately, around the same time as their study, another group of researchers was running a more traditional social survey in Rwanda. This other survey—which was part of the widely respected Demographic and Health Survey program—had a large budget and used high-quality, traditional methods. Therefore, the estimates from the Demographic and Health Survey could reasonably be considered gold-standard estimates. When the two estimates were compared, they were quite similar (figure 3.17). In other words, by combining a small amount of survey data with the call records, Blumenstock and colleagues were able to produce estimates comparable to those from gold-standard approaches.

A skeptic might see these results as a disappointment. After all, one way of viewing them is to say that by using big data and machine learning, Blumenstock and colleagues were able to produce estimates that could be made more reliably by already existing methods. But I don't think that this is the right way to think about this study, for two reasons. First, the estimates from Blumenstock and colleagues were about 10 times faster and 50 times cheaper (when cost is measured in terms of variable costs). As I argued earlier in this chapter, researchers ignore cost at their peril. In this case, for example, the dramatic decrease in cost means that rather than being run every few years—as is standard for Demographic and Health Surveys—this kind of survey could be run every month, which would provide numerous advantages for researchers and policy makers. The second reason not to take the skeptic's view is that this study provides a basic recipe that can be tailored to many different research situations. This recipe has only two ingredients and two steps. The ingredients are (1) a big data source that is wide but thin (i.e., it has many people but not the information that you need about each person) and (2) a survey that is narrow but thick (i.e., it has only a few people, but it does have the information that you need about those people). These ingredients are then combined in two steps. First, for the people in both data sources, build a machine learning model that uses digital trace data to predict survey answers. Next, use that model to infer the survey answers of everyone in the big data source. Thus, if there is some question that you want to ask lots of people, look for a big data source from those people that might be used to predict their answer, *even if you don't care about that big data source*. That is, Blumenstock and colleagues didn't inherently care about call records; they only cared about call records because these could be used to predict survey answers that they cared about. This characteristic—only indirect interest in the big data source—makes amplified asking different from enriched asking, which I described earlier.

In conclusion, Blumenstock's amplified asking approach combined survey data with call data to produce estimates comparable to those from a gold-standard survey. This particular example also clarifies some of the trade-offs between amplified asking and traditional survey methods. The amplified asking estimates were more timely, substantially cheaper, and more granular. But, on the other hand, there is not yet a strong theoretical basis for this kind of amplified asking. This single example does not show when this approach will work and when it won't, and researchers using this approach need to be especially concerned about possible biases caused by who is included—and who is not included—in their big data source. Further, the amplified asking approach does not yet have good ways to quantify uncertainty around its estimates. Fortunately, amplified asking has deep connections to three large areas in statistics—small area estimation (Rao and Molina 2015), imputation (Rubin 2004), and model-based post-stratification (which itself is closely related to Mr. P., the method I described earlier in the chapter) (Little 1993). Because of these deep connections, I expect that many of the methodological foundations of amplified asking will soon be improved.

Finally, comparing Blumenstock's first and second attempts also illustrates an important lesson about digital-age social research: the beginning is not the end. That is, many times, the first approach will not be the best, but if researchers continue working, things can get better. More generally, when evaluating new approaches to social research in the digital age, it is important to make two distinct evaluations: (1) How well does this work now? (2) How well will this work in the future as the data landscape changes and as researchers devote more attention to the problem? Although researchers are trained to make the first kind of evaluation (about how good a particular piece of research is), the second is often more important.

3.7 Conclusion

The transition from the analog age to the digital age is creating new opportunities for survey researchers. In this chapter, I've argued that big data sources will not replace surveys and that the abundance of big data sources increases—not decreases—the value of surveys (section 3.2). Next, I summarized the total survey error framework that was developed during the first two eras of survey research, and that can help researchers develop and evaluate third-era approaches (section 3.3). Three areas where I expect to see exciting opportunities are (1) non-probability sampling (section 3.4), (2) computer-administrated interviews (section 3.5), and (3) linking surveys and big data sources (section 3.6). Survey research has always evolved, driven by changes in technology and society. We should embrace that evolution, while continuing to draw wisdom from earlier eras.

Mathematical notes

In this appendix, I will describe some of the ideas from the chapter in a slightly more mathematical form. The goal here is to help you get comfortable with the notation and mathematical framework used by survey researchers so that you can transition to some of more technical material written on these topics. I will start by introducing probability sampling, then move to probability sampling with nonresponse, and finally, non-probability sampling.

Probability sampling

As a running example, let's consider the goal of estimating the unemployment rate in the United States. Let $U = \{1, \ldots, k, \ldots, N\}$ be the target population and let y_k be the value of the outcome variable for the person k. In this example, y_k is whether person k is unemployed. Finally, let $F = \{1, \ldots, k, \ldots, N\}$ be the frame population, which for the sake of simplicity is assumed to be the same as the target population.

A basic sampling design is simple random sampling without replacement. In this case, each person is equally likely to be included in the sample $s = \{1, \ldots, i, \ldots, n\}$. When the data are collected with this sampling design, a researchers can estimate the population unemployment rate with the sample mean:

$$\hat{\bar{y}} = \frac{\sum_{i \in s} y_i}{n} \tag{3.1}$$

where $\bar{y}$ is the unemployment rate in the population and $\hat{\bar{y}}$ is the estimate of the unemployment rate (the ^ is commonly used to indicate an estimator).

In reality, researchers rarely use simple random sampling without replacement. For a variety of reasons (one of which I'll describe in a moment), researchers often create samples with unequal probabilities of inclusion. For example, researchers might select people in Florida with higher probability of inclusion than people in California. In this case, the sample mean (eq. 3.1) might not be a good estimator. Instead, when there are unequal probabilities of inclusion, researchers use

$$\hat{\bar{y}} = \frac{1}{N} \sum_{i \in s} \frac{y_i}{\pi_i} \tag{3.2}$$

where $\hat{\bar{y}}$ is the estimate of the unemployment rate and π_i is person i's probability of inclusion. Following standard practice, I'll call the estimator in eq. 3.2 the Horvitz–Thompson estimator. The Horvitz–Thompson estimator is extremely useful because it leads to unbiased estimates for any probability sampling design (Horvitz and Thompson 1952). Because the Horvitz–Thompson estimator comes up so frequently, it is helpful to notice that it can be rewritten as

$$\hat{\bar{y}} = \frac{1}{N} \sum_{i \in s} w_i y_i \tag{3.3}$$

where $w_i = 1/\pi_i$. As eq. 3.3 reveals, the Horvitz–Thompson estimator is a weighted sample mean where the weights are inversely related to the probability of selection. In other words, the less likely a person is to be included in the sample, the more weight that person should get in the estimate.

As described earlier, researchers often sample people with unequal probabilities of inclusion. One example of a design that can lead to unequal probabilities of inclusion is *stratified sampling*, which is important to understand because it is closely related to the estimation procedure called *post-stratification*. In stratified sampling, a researcher splits the target population into H mutually exclusive and exhaustive groups. These groups are called *strata* and are indicated as $U_1, \ldots, U_h, \ldots, U_H$. In this example, the strata are states. The sizes of the groups are indicated as $N_1, \ldots, N_h, \ldots, N_H$. A researcher might want to use stratified sampling in order to make sure that she has enough people in each state to make state-level estimates of unemployment.

Once the population has been split up into *strata*, assume that the researcher selects a simple random sample without replacement of size n_h, independently from each strata. Further, assume that everyone selected in the sample becomes a respondent (I'll handle nonresponse in the next section). In this case, the probability of inclusion is

$$\pi_i = \frac{n_h}{N_h} \quad \text{for all } i \in h \tag{3.4}$$

Because these probabilities can vary from person to person, when making an estimate from this sampling design, researchers need to weight each respondent by the inverse of their probability of inclusion using the Horvitz–Thompson estimator (eq. 3.2).

Even though the Horvitz–Thompson estimator is unbiased, researchers can produce more accurate (i.e., lower-variance) estimates by combining the sample with *auxiliary information*. Some people find it surprising that this is true even when there is perfectly executed probability sampling. These techniques using auxiliary information are particularly important because, as I will show later, auxiliary information is critical for making estimates from probability samples with nonresponse and from non-probability samples.

One common technique for utilizing auxiliary information is *post-stratification*. Imagine, for example, that a researcher knows the number of men and women in each of the 50 states; we can denote these group sizes as $N_1, N_2, \ldots, N_{100}$. To combine this auxiliary information with the sample, the researcher can split the sample into H groups (in this case 100), make an estimate for each group, and then create a weighted average of these group means:

$$\hat{\bar{y}}_{post} = \sum_{h \in H} \frac{N_h}{N} \hat{\bar{y}}_h \qquad (3.5)$$

Roughly, the estimator in eq. 3.5 is likely to be more accurate, because it uses the known population information (the N_h) to correct estimates if an unbalanced sample happens to be selected. One way to think about it is that post-stratification is like approximating stratification after the data have already been collected.

In conclusion, this section has described a few sampling designs: simple random sampling without replacements, sampling with unequal probability, and stratified sampling. It has also described two main ideas about estimation: the Horvitz–Thompson estimator and post-stratification. For a more formal definition of probability sampling designs, see chapter 2 of Särndal, Swensson, and Wretman (2003). For a more formal and complete treatment of stratified sampling, see section 3.7 of Särndal, Swensson, and Wretman (2003). For a technical description of the properties of the Horvitz–Thompson estimator, see Horvitz and Thompson (1952), Overton and Stehman (1995), or section 2.8 of Särndal, Swensson, and Wretman (2003). For a more formal treatment of post-stratification, see Holt and Smith (1979), Smith (1991), Little (1993), or section 7.6 of Särndal, Swensson, and Wretman (2003).

Probability sampling with nonresponse

Almost all real surveys have nonresponse; that is, not everyone in the sample population answers every question. There are two main kinds of nonresponse: *item nonresponse* and *unit nonresponse*. In item nonresponse, some respondents don't answer some items (e.g., sometimes respondents don't want to answer questions that they consider sensitive). In unit nonresponse, some people that are selected into the sample population don't respond to the survey at all. The two most common reasons for unit nonresponse are that the sampled person cannot be contacted and that the sample person is contacted but refuses to participate. In this section, I will focus on unit nonresponse; readers interested in item nonresponse should see Little and Rubin (2002).

Researchers often think about surveys with unit nonresponse as a two-stage sampling process. In the first stage, the researcher selects a sample s such that each person has a probability of inclusion π_i (where $0 < \pi_i \leq 1$). Then, in the second stage, people who are selected into the sample respond with probability ϕ_i (where $0 < \phi_i \leq 1$). This two-stage process results in the final set of respondents r. An important difference between these two stages is that researchers control the process of selecting the sample, but they don't control which of those sampled people become respondents. Putting these two processes together, the probability that someone will be a respondent is

$$\text{pr}(i \in r) = \pi_i \phi_i \tag{3.6}$$

For the sake of simplicity, I'll consider the case where the original sample design is simple random sampling without replacement. If a researcher selects a sample of size n_s that yields n_r respondents, and if the researcher ignores nonresponse and uses the mean of the respondents, then the bias of estimate will be

$$\text{bias of sample mean} = \frac{cor(\phi, y)S(y)S(\phi)}{\bar{\phi}} \tag{3.7}$$

where $cor(\phi, y)$ is the population correlation between the response propensity and the outcome (e.g., unemployment status), $S(y)$ is the population standard deviation of the outcome (e.g., unemployment status), $S(\phi)$ is the population standard deviation of the response propensity, and $\bar{\phi}$ is the population mean response propensity (Bethlehem, Cobben, and Schouten 2011, section 2.2.4).

Equation 3.7 shows that nonresponse will not introduce bias if any of the following conditions are met:

- There is no variation in unemployment status ($S(y) = 0$).
- There is no variation in response propensities ($S(\phi) = 0$).

- There is no correlation between response propensity and unemployment status ($cor(\phi, y) = 0$).

Unfortunately, none of these conditions seems likely. It seems implausible that there will be no variation in employment status or that there will be no variation in response propensities. Thus, the key term in eq. 3.7 is the correlation, $cor(\phi, y)$. For example, if people who are unemployed are more likely to respond, then the estimated unemployment rate will be biased upward.

The trick to making estimates when there is nonresponse is to use auxiliary information. For example, one way in which you can use auxiliary information is post-stratification (recall eq. 3.5 from above). It turns out that the bias of the post-stratification estimator is

$$bias(\hat{\bar{y}}_{post}) = \frac{1}{N} \sum_{h=1}^{H} \frac{N_h \, cor(\phi, y)^{(h)} S(y)^{(h)} S(\phi)^{(h)}}{\bar{\phi}^{(h)}} \tag{3.8}$$

where $cor(\phi, y)^{(h)}$, $S(y)^{(h)}$, $S(\phi)^{(h)}$, and $\bar{\phi}^{(h)}$ are defined as above but restricted to people in group h (Bethlehem, Cobben, and Schouten 2011, section 8.2.1). Thus, the overall bias will be small if the bias in each post-stratification group is small. There are two ways that I like to think about making the bias small in each post-stratification group. First, you want to try to form homogeneous groups where there is little variation in response propensity ($S(\phi)^{(h)} \approx 0$) and the outcome ($S(y)^{(h)} \approx 0$). Second, you want to form groups where the people that you see are like the people that you don't see ($cor(\phi, y)^{(h)} \approx 0$). Comparing eqs. 3.7 and 3.8 helps clarify when post-stratification can reduce the biased caused by nonresponse.

In conclusion, this section has provided a model for probability sampling with nonresponse and has shown the bias that nonresponse can introduce both without and with post-stratification adjustments. Bethlehem (1988) offers a derivation of the bias caused by nonresponse for more general sampling designs. For more on using post-stratification to adjust for nonresponse, see Smith (1991) and Gelman and Carlin (2002). Post-stratification is part of a more general family of techniques called calibration estimators, see Zhang (2000) for an article-length treatment and Särndal and Lundström (2005) for a book-length treatment. For more on other weighting methods for adjusting for nonresponse, see Kalton and Flores-Cervantes (2003), Brick (2013), and Särndal and Lundström (2005).

Non-probability sampling

Non-probability sampling includes a huge variety of designs (Baker et al. 2013). Focusing specifically on the sample of Xbox users by Wang and colleagues (Wang et al. 2015), you can think of that kind of sample as one where the key part of the sampling design is not the π_i (the researcher-driven probability of inclusion) but the ϕ_i (the respondent-driven response propensities). Naturally, this is not ideal because the ϕ_i are unknown. But, as Wang and colleagues showed, this kind of opt-in sample—even from a sampling frame with enormous coverage error—need not be catastrophic if the researcher has good auxiliary information and a good statistical model to account for these problems.

Bethlehem (2010) extends many of the above derivations about post-stratification to include both nonresponse and coverage errors. In addition to post-stratification, other techniques for working with non-probability samples—and probability samples with coverage errors and nonresponse—include sample matching (Ansolabehere and Rivers 2013; Bethlehem 2015), propensity score weighting (Lee 2006; Schonlau et al. 2009), and calibration (Lee and Valliant 2009). One common theme among these techniques is the use of the auxiliary information.

What to read next

- **Introduction (section 3.1)**

  Many of the themes in this chapter have also been echoed in recent presidential addresses at the American Association of Public Opinion Research (AAPOR), such as those by Dillman (2002), Newport (2011), Santos (2014), and Link (2015).

  For more on the differences between survey research and in-depth interviews, see Small (2009). Related to in-depth interviews is a family of approaches called ethnography. In ethnographic research, researchers generally spend much more time with participants in their natural environment. For more on the differences between ethnography and in-depth interviews, see Jerolmack and Khan (2014). For more on digital ethnography, see Pink et al. (2015).

  My description of the history of survey research is far too brief to include many of the exciting developments that have taken place. For more historical background, see Smith (1976), Converse (1987), and Igo (2008). For more on the idea of three eras of survey research, see Groves (2011) and Dillman, Smyth, and Christian (2008) (which breaks up the three eras slightly differently).

Groves and Kahn (1979) offer a peek inside the transition from the first to the second era in survey research by doing a detailed head-to-head comparison between a face-to-face and telephone survey. Brick and Tucker (2007) look back at the historical development of random-digit-dialing sampling methods.

For more on how survey research has changed in the past in response to changes in society, see Tourangeau (2004), Mitofsky (1989), and Couper (2011).

- **Asking versus observing (section 3.2)**

The strengths and weaknesses of asking and observing have been debated by psychologists (e.g., Baumeister, Vohs, and Funder 2007) and sociologists (e.g., Jerolmack and Khan 2014; Maynard 2014; Cerulo 2014; Vaisey 2014). The difference between asking and observing also arises in economics, where researchers talk about stated and revealed preferences. For example, a researcher could ask respondents whether they prefer eating ice cream or going to the gym (stated preferences), or could observe how often people eat ice cream and go to the gym (revealed preferences). There is deep skepticism about certain types of stated preferences data in economics, as described in Hausman (2012).

A main theme from these debates is that reported behavior is not always accurate. But, as was described in chapter 2, big data sources may not be accurate, they may not be collected on a sample of interest, and they may not be accessible to researchers. Thus, I think that, in some situations, reported behavior can be useful. Further, a second main theme from these debates is that reports about emotions, knowledge, expectations, and opinions are not always accurate. But, if information about these internal states is needed by researchers—either to help explain some behavior or as the thing to be explained—then asking may be appropriate. Of course, learning about internal states by asking questions can be problematic because sometimes the respondents themselves are not aware of their internal states (Nisbett and Wilson 1977).

- **Total survey error (section 3.3)**

Chapter 1 of Groves (2004) does an excellent job reconciling the occasionally inconsistent terminology used by survey researchers to describe the total survey error framework. For a book-length treatment of the total survey error framework, see Groves et al. (2009), and for a historical overview, see Groves and Lyberg (2010).

The idea of decomposing errors into bias and variance also comes up in machine learning; see, for example, section 7.3 of Hastie, Tibshirani, and Friedman (2009). This often leads researchers to talk about a "bias–variance" trade-off.

In terms of representation, a great introduction to the issues of nonresponse and nonresponse bias is the National Research Council report Nonresponse in Social Science Surveys: A Research Agenda (2013). Another useful overview is provided by Groves (2006). Also, entire special issues of the *Journal of Official Statistics, Public Opinion Quarterly,* and the *Annals of the American Academy of Political and Social Science* have been published on the topic of nonresponse. Finally, there are actually many different ways of calculating the response rate; these approaches are described in detail in a report by the American Association of Public Opinion Researchers (AAPOR) (2016).

For more on the 1936 *Literary Digest* poll, see Bryson (1976), Squire (1988), Cahalan (1989), and Lusinchi (2012). For another discussion of this poll as a parable warning against haphazard data collection, see Gayo-Avello (2011). In 1936, George Gallup used a more sophisticated form of sampling and was able to produce more accurate estimates with a much smaller sample. Gallup's success over the *Literary Digest* was a milestone in the development of survey research, as is described in chapter 3 of Converse (1987), chapter 4 of Ohmer (2006), and chapter 3 of Igo (2008).

In terms of measurement, a great first resource for designing questionnaires is Bradburn, Sudman, and Wansink (2004). For more advanced treatments, see Schuman and Presser (1996), which is specifically focused on attitude questions, and Saris and Gallhofer (2014), which is more general. A slightly different approach to measurement is taken in psychometrics, as described in Rust and Golombok (2009). More on pretesting is available in Presser and Blair (1994), Presser et al. (2004), and chapter 8 of Groves et al. (2009). For more on survey experiments, see Mutz (2011).

In terms of cost, the classic, book-length treatment of the trade-off between survey costs and survey errors is Groves (2004).

- **Who to ask (section 3.4)**

Two classic book-length treatments of standard probability sampling and estimation are Lohr (2009) (more introductory) and Särndal, Swensson, and Wretman (2003) (more advanced). A classic book-length treatment of post-stratification and related methods is Särndal and Lundström (2005). In some digital-age settings, researchers know quite a bit about nonrespondents, which was not often true in the past. Different forms of nonresponse adjustment are possible when researchers have information about nonrespondents, as described by Kalton and Flores-Cervantes (2003) and Smith (2011).

The Xbox study by Wang et al. (2015) uses a technique called multilevel regression and post-stratification ("Mr. P.") that allows researchers to estimate group means even when there are many, many groups. Although there is some debate about the quality of the estimates from this technique, it seems like a promising area to explore. The technique was first used in Park, Gelman, and Bafumi (2004), and there has been subsequent use and debate (Gelman 2007; Lax and Phillips 2009; Pacheco 2011; Buttice and Highton 2013; Toshkov 2015). For more on the connection between individual weights and group weights, see Gelman (2007).

For other approaches to weighting web surveys, see Schonlau et al. (2009), Bethlehem (2010), and Valliant and Dever (2011). Online panels can use either probability sampling or non-probability sampling. For more on online panels, see Callegaro et al. (2014).

Sometimes, researchers have found that probability samples and non-probability samples yield estimates of similar quality (Ansolabehere and Schaffner 2014), but other comparisons have found that non-probability samples do worse (Malhotra and Krosnick 2007; Yeager et al. 2011). One possible reason for these differences is that non-probability samples have improved over time. For a more pessimistic view of non-probability sampling methods, see the AAPOR Task Force on Non-Probability Sampling (Baker et al. 2013), and I also recommend reading the commentary that follows the summary report.

- ## How to ask (section 3.5)

Conrad and Schober (2008) is an edited volume titled *Envisioning the Survey Interview of the Future*, and it offers a variety of viewpoints about the future of asking questions. Couper (2011) addresses similar themes, and Schober et al. (2015) offer a nice example of how data collection methods that are tailored to a new setting can result in higher quality data. Schober and Conrad (2015) offer a more general argument about continuing to adjust the process of survey research to match changes in society.

Tourangeau and Yan (2007) review issues of social desirability bias in sensitive questions, and Lind et al. (2013) offer some possible reasons why people might disclose more sensitive information in a computer-administered interview. For more on the role of human interviewers in increasing participation rates in surveys, see Maynard and Schaeffer (1997), Maynard, Freese, and Schaeffer (2010), Conrad et al. (2013), and Schaeffer et al. (2013). For more on mixed-mode surveys, see Dillman, Smyth, and Christian (2014).

Stone et al. (2007) offer a book-length treatment of ecological momentary assessment and related methods.

For more advice on making surveys an enjoyable and valuable experience for participants, see work on the Tailored Design Method (Dillman, Smyth, and Christian 2014). For another interesting example of using Facebook apps for social science surveys, see Bail (2015).

- ## Surveys linked to big data sources (section 3.6)

Judson (2007) describes the process of combining surveys and administrative data as "information integration" and discusses some advantages of this approach, as well as offering some examples.

Regarding enriched asking, there have been many previous attempts to validate voting. For an overview of that literature, see Belli et al. (1999),

Ansolabehere and Hersh (2012), Hanmer, Banks, and White (2014), and Berent, Krosnick, and Lupia (2016). See Berent, Krosnick, and Lupia (2016) for a more skeptical view of the results presented in Ansolabehere and Hersh (2012).

It is important to note that although Ansolabehere and Hersh were encouraged by the quality of data from Catalist, other evaluations of commercial vendors have been less enthusiastic. Pasek et al. (2014) found poor quality when data from a survey were compared with a consumer file from Marketing Systems Group (which itself merged together data from three providers: Acxiom, Experian, and InfoUSA). That is, the datafile did not match survey responses that researchers expected to be correct, the consumer file had missing data for a large number of questions, and the missing data pattern was correlated with the reported survey value (in other words, the missing data were systematic, not random).

For more on record linkage between surveys and administrative data, see Sakshaug and Kreuter (2012) and Schnell (2013). For more on record linkage in general, see Dunn (1946) and Fellegi and Sunter (1969) (historical) and Larsen and Winkler (2014) (modern). Similar approaches have also been developed in computer science under names such as data deduplication, instance identification, name matching, duplicate detection, and duplicate record detection (Elmagarmid, Ipeirotis, and Verykios 2007). There are also privacy-preserving approaches to record linkage that do not require the transmission of personally identifying information (Schnell 2013). Researchers at Facebook developed a procedure to probabilistically link their records to voting behavior (Jones et al. 2013); this linkage was done to evaluate an experiment that I'll tell you about in chapter 4 (Bond et al. 2012). For more on obtaining consent for record linkage, see Sakshaug et al. (2012).

Another example of linking a large-scale social survey to government administrative records comes from the Health and Retirement Survey and the Social Security Administration. For more on that study, including information about the consent procedure, see Olson (1996, 1999).

The process of combining many sources of administrative records into a master datafile—the process that Catalist employs—is common in the statistical offices of some national governments. Two researchers from Statistics Sweden have written a detailed book on the topic (Wallgren and Wallgren 2007). For an example of this approach in a single county in the United States (Olmsted County, Minnesota, home of the Mayo Clinic), see Sauver et al. (2011). For more on errors that can appear in administrative records, see Groen (2012).

Another way in which researchers can use big data sources in survey research is as a sampling frame for people with specific characteristics. Unfortunately, this approach can raise questions related to privacy (Beskow, Sandler, and Weinberger 2006).

Regarding amplified asking, this approach is not as new as it might appear from how I've described it. It has deep connections to three large areas in statistics: model-based post-stratification (Little 1993), imputation (Rubin 2004), and small area estimation (Rao and Molina 2015). It is also related to the use of surrogate variables in medical research (Pepe 1992).

The cost and time estimates in Blumenstock, Cadamuro, and On (2015) refer more to variable cost—the cost of one additional survey—and do not include fixed costs such as the cost of cleaning and processing the call data. In general, amplified asking will probably have high fixed costs and low variable costs similar to those of digital experiments (see chapter 4). For more on mobile phone-based surveys in developing countries, see Dabalen et al. (2016).

For ideas about how to do amplified asking better, I'd recommend learning more about multiple imputation (Rubin 2004). Also, if researchers doing amplified asking care about aggregate counts, rather than individual-level traits, then the approaches in King and Lu (2008) and Hopkins and King (2010) may be useful. Finally, for more about the machine learning approaches in Blumenstock, Cadamuro, and On (2015), see James et al. (2013) (more introductory) or Hastie, Tibshirani, and Friedman (2009) (more advanced).

One ethical issue regarding amplified asking is that it can be used to infer sensitive traits that people might not choose to reveal in a survey, as described by Kosinski, Stillwell, and Graepel (2013).

Activities

Degrees of Difficulty: 🔧 EASY   🔧 MEDIUM   🔧 HARD   🔧 VERY HARD

🧱 DATA COLLECTION   ➕ REQUIRES MATH   </> REQUIRES CODING   ♥ MY FAVORITES

1. [🔧, ➕] In the chapter, I was very positive about post-stratification. However, this does not always improve the quality of estimates. Construct a situation where post-stratification can decrease the quality of estimates. (For a hint, see Thomsen (1973).)

2. [🔧, 🧱, </>] Design and conduct a non-probability survey on Amazon Mechanical Turk to ask about gun ownership and attitudes toward gun control. So that you can compare your estimates to those derived from a probability sample, please copy the question text and response options directly from a high-

quality survey such as one of those run by the Pew Research Center.

a) How long does your survey take? How much does it cost? How do the demographics of your sample compare with the demographics of the US population?

b) What is the raw estimate of gun ownership using your sample?

c) Correct for the nonrepresentativeness of your sample using post-stratification or some other technique. Now what is the estimate of gun ownership?

d) How do your estimates compare with the latest estimate from Pew Research Center? What do you think explains the discrepancies, if there are any?

e) Repeat questions (b)–(d) for attitudes toward gun control. How do your findings differ?

3. [🔭, 🎲, 🖥] Goel and colleagues (2016) administered 49 multiple-choice attitudinal questions drawn from the General Social Survey (GSS) and select surveys by the Pew Research Center to a non-probability sample of respondents drawn from Amazon Mechanical Turk. They then adjusted for the nonrepresentativeness of data using model-based post-stratification, and compared the adjusted estimates with those from the probability-based GSS and Pew surveys. Conduct the same survey on Amazon Mechanical Turk and try to replicate figures 2a and 2b by comparing your adjusted estimates with the estimates from the most recent rounds of the GSS and Pew surveys. (See appendix table A2 for the list of 49 questions.)

a) Compare and contrast your results with those from Pew and GSS.

b) Compare and contrast your results with those from the Mechanical Turk survey in Goel, Obeng, and Rothschild (2016).

4. [🔭, 🎲, 🖥] Many studies use self-report measures of mobile phone use. This is an interesting setting in which researchers can compare self-reported behavior with logged behavior (see, e.g., Boase and Ling (2013)). Two common behaviors to ask about are calling and texting, and two common time frames are "yesterday" and "in the past week."

a) Before collecting any data, which of the self-report measures do you think is more accurate? Why?

b) Recruit five of your friends to be in your survey. Please briefly summarize how these five friends were sampled. Might this sampling procedure induce specific biases in your estimates?

c) Ask them the following microsurvey questions:

- "How many times did you use your mobile phone to call others yesterday?"
- "How many text messages did you send yesterday?"
- "How many times did you use your mobile phone to call others in the last seven days?"
- "How many times did you use your mobile phone to send or receive text messages/SMS in the last seven days?"

d) Once this microsurvey has been completed, ask to check their usage data as logged by their phone or service provider. How does self-report usage compare to log data? Which is most accurate? Which is least accurate?

e) Now combine the data that you have collected with the data from other people in your class (if you are doing this activity for a class). With this larger dataset, repeat part (d).

5. [🔾, 🎲] Schuman and Presser (1996) argue that question orders would matter for two types of questions: part–part questions where two questions are at the same level of specificity (e.g., ratings of two presidential candidates) and part–whole questions where a general question follows a more specific question (e.g., asking "How satisfied are you with your work?" followed by "How satisfied are you with your life?").

They further characterize two types of question order effect; consistency effects occur when responses to a later question are brought closer (than they would otherwise be) to those given to an earlier question; contrast effects occur when there are greater differences between responses to two questions.

a) Create a pair of part-part questions that you think will have a large question order effect; a pair of part–whole questions that you think will have a large order effect; and a pair of questions whose order you think would not matter. Run a survey experiment on MTurk to test your questions.

b) How large a part–part effect were you able to create? Was it a consistency or contrast effect?

c) How large a part–whole effect were you able to create? Was it a consistency or contrast effect?

d) Was there a question order effect in your pair where you did not think the order would matter?

6. [🎯, ♻] Building on the work of Schuman and Presser, Moore (2002) describes a separate dimension of question order effect: additive and subtractive effects. While contrast and consistency effects are produced as a consequence of respondents' evaluations of the two items in relation to each other, additive and subtractive effects are produced when respondents are made more sensitive to the larger framework within which the questions are posed. Read Moore (2002), then design and run a survey experiment on MTurk to demonstrate additive or subtractive effects.

7. [🎯, ♻] Christopher Antoun and colleagues (2015) conducted a study comparing the convenience samples obtained from four different online recruiting sources: MTurk, Craigslist, Google AdWords and Facebook. Design a simple survey and recruit participants through at least two different online recruiting sources (these sources can be different from the four sources used in Antoun et al. (2015)).

    a) Compare the cost per recruit—in terms of money and time—between different sources.

    b) Compare the composition of the samples obtained from different sources.

    c) Compare the quality of data between the samples. For ideas about how to measure data quality from respondents, see Schober et al. (2015).

    d) What is your preferred source? Why?

8. [🎯] In an effort to predict the results of the 2016 EU Referendum (i.e., Brexit), YouGov—an Internet-based market research firm—conducted online polls of a panel of about 800,000 respondents in the United Kingdom.

    A detailed description of YouGov's statistical model can be found at https://yougov.co.uk/news/2016/06/21/yougov-referendum-model/. Roughly speaking, YouGov partitioned voters into types based on 2015 general election vote choice, age, qualifications, gender, and date of interview, as well as the constituency in which they lived. First, they used data collected from the YouGov panelists to estimate, among those who voted, the proportion of people of each voter type who intended to vote Leave. They estimated the turnout of each voter type by using the 2015 British Election Study (BES), a post-election face-to-face survey, which validated turnout from the electoral rolls. Finally, they estimated how many people there were of each voter type in the electorate, based on the latest Census and Annual Population Survey (with some additional information from other data sources).

    Three days before the vote, YouGov showed a two-point lead for Leave. On the eve of voting, the poll indicated that the result was too close to call (49/51 Remain). The final on-the-day study predicted 48/52 in favor of Remain (https://yougov.co.uk/news/2016/06/23/yougov-day-poll/). In fact, this estimate missed the final result (52/48 Leave) by four percentage points.

    a) Use the total survey error framework discussed in this chapter to assess what could have gone wrong.

    b) YouGov's response after the election (https://yougov.co.uk/news/2016/06/24/brexit-follows-close-run-campaign/) explained: "This seems in a large part due to turnout—something that we have said all along would be crucial to the outcome of such a finely balanced race. Our turnout model was based, in part, on whether respondents had voted at the last general election and a turnout level above that of general elections upset the model, particularly in the North." Does this change your answer to part (a)?

9. [📟, 🖭] Write a simulation to illustrate each of the representation errors in figure 3.2.

    a) Create a situation where these errors actually cancel out.

    b) Create a situation where the errors compound each other.

10. [📟, 🖭] The research of Blumenstock and colleagues (2015) involved building a machine learning model that could use digital trace data to predict survey responses. Now, you are going to try the same thing with a different dataset. Kosinski, Stillwell, and Graepel (2013) found that Facebook likes can predict individual traits and attributes. Surprisingly, these predictions can be even more accurate than those of friends and colleagues (Youyou, Kosinski, and Stillwell 2015).

    a) Read Kosinski, Stillwell, and Graepel (2013) and replicate figure 2. Their data are available at http://mypersonality.org/.

    b) Now replicate figure 3.3.

    c) Finally, try their model on your own Facebook data: http://applymagic sauce.com/. How well does it work for you?

11. [📟] Toole et al. (2015) used call detail records (CDRs) from mobile phones to predict aggregate unemployment trends.

    a) Compare and contrast the study design of Toole et al. (2015) with that of Blumenstock, Cadamuro, and On (2015).

b) Do you think CDRs should replace traditional surveys, complement them, or not be used at all for government policymakers to track unemployment? Why?

c) What evidence would convince you that CDRs can completely replace traditional measures of the unemployment rate?

CHAPTER 4
RUNNING EXPERIMENTS

4.1 Introduction

In the approaches covered so far in this book—observing behavior (chapter 2) and asking questions (chapter 3)—researchers collect data without intentionally and systematically changing the world. The approach covered in this chapter—running experiments—is fundamentally different. When researchers run experiments, they systematically intervene in the world to create data that are ideally suited to answering questions about cause-and-effect relationships.

Cause-and-effect questions are very common in social research, and examples include questions such as: Does increasing teacher salaries increase student learning? What is the effect of minimum wage on employment rates? How does a job applicant's race affect her chance of getting a job? In addition to these explicitly causal questions, sometimes cause-and-effect questions are implicit in more general questions about maximization of some performance metric. For example, the question "What color should the donate button be on an NGO's website?" is really lots of questions about the effect of different button colors on donations.

One way to answer cause-and-effect questions is to look for patterns in existing data. For example, returning to the question about the effect of teacher salaries on student learning, you might calculate that students learn more in schools that offer high teacher salaries. But, does this correlation show that higher salaries *cause* students to learn more? Of course not. Schools where teachers earn more might be different in many ways. For example, students in schools with high teacher salaries might come from wealthier families. Thus, what looks like an effect of teachers could just come from comparing different types of students. These unmeasured differences between students are called *confounders*, and, in general, the possibility of confounders wreaks havoc on researchers' ability to answer cause-and-effect questions by looking for patterns in existing data.

One solution to the problem of confounders is to try to make fair comparisons by adjusting for observable differences between groups. For example, you might be able to download property tax data from a number of government websites. Then, you could compare student performance in schools where home prices are similar but teacher salaries are different, and you still might find that students learn more in schools with higher teacher pay. But there are still many possible confounders. Maybe the parents of these students differ in their level of education. Or maybe the schools differ in their closeness to public libraries. Or maybe the schools with higher teacher pay also have higher pay for principals, and principal pay, not teacher pay, is really what is increasing student learning. You could try to measure and adjust for these factors as well, but the list of possible confounders is essentially endless. In many situations, you just cannot measure and adjust for all the possible confounders. In response to this challenge, researchers have developed a number of techniques for making causal estimates from non-experimental data—I discussed some of them in chapter 2—but, for certain kinds of questions, these techniques are limited, and experiments offer a promising alternative.

Experiments enable researchers to move beyond the correlations in naturally occurring data in order to reliably answer certain cause-and-effect questions. In the analog age, experiments were often logistically difficult and expensive. Now, in the digital age, logistical constraints are gradually fading away. Not only is it easier to do experiments like those done in the past, it is now possible to run new kinds of experiments.

In what I've written so far I've been a bit loose in my language, but it is important to distinguish between two things: experiments and randomized controlled experiments. In an *experiment,* a researcher intervenes in the world and then measures an outcome. I've heard this approach described as "perturb and observe." In a *randomized controlled experiment* a researcher intervenes for some people and not for others, and the researcher decides which people receive the intervention by randomization (e.g., flipping a coin). Randomized controlled experiments create fair comparisons between two groups: one that has received the intervention and one that has not. In other words, randomized controlled experiments are a solution to the problems of confounders. Perturb-and-observe experiments, however, involve only a single group that has received the intervention, and therefore the results can lead researchers to the wrong conclusion (as I'll show soon). Despite the important differences between experiments and randomized controlled experiments, social researchers often use these terms interchangeably. I'll follow this convention, but, at certain points, I'll break the convention to emphasize the value of randomized controlled experiments over experiments without randomization and a control group.

Randomized controlled experiments have proven to be a powerful way to learn about the social world, and in this chapter, I'll show you more about how to use them in your research. In section 4.2, I'll illustrate the basic logic of experimentation with an example of an experiment on Wikipedia. Then, in section 4.3, I'll describe the difference between lab experiments and field experiments and the differences between analog experiments and digital experiments. Further, I'll argue that digital field experiments can offer the best features of analog lab experiments (tight control) and analog field experiments (realism), all at a scale that was not possible previously. Next, in section 4.4, I'll describe three concepts—validity, heterogeneity of treatment effects, and mechanisms—that are critical for designing rich experiments. With that background, I'll describe the trade-offs involved in the two main strategies for conducting digital experiments: doing it yourself or partnering with the powerful. Finally, I'll conclude with some design advice about how you can take advantage of the real power of digital experiments (section 4.6.1) and describe some of the responsibility that comes with that power (section 4.6.2).

4.2   What are experiments?

Randomized controlled experiments have four main ingredients: recruitment of participants, randomization of treatment, delivery of treatment, and measurement of outcomes.

Randomized controlled experiments have four main ingredients: recruitment of participants, randomization of treatment, delivery of treatment, and measurement of outcomes. The digital age does not change the fundamental nature of experimentation, but it does make it easier logistically. For example, in the past, it might have been difficult to measure the behavior of millions of people, but that is now routinely happening in many digital systems.

Researchers who can figure out how to harness these new opportunities will be able to run experiments that were impossible previously.

To make this all a bit more concrete—both what has stayed the same and what has changed—let's consider an experiment by Michael Restivo and Arnout van de Rijt (2012). They wanted to understand the effect of informal peer rewards on editorial contributions to Wikipedia. In particular, they studied the effects of *barnstars*, an award that any Wikipedian can give to any other Wikipedian to acknowledge hard work and due diligence. Restivo and van de Rijt gave barnstars to 100 deserving Wikipedians. Then, they tracked the recipients' subsequent contributions to Wikipedia over the next 90 days. Much to their surprise, the people to whom they awarded barnstars tended to make *fewer* edits after receiving one. In other words, the barnstars seemed to be discouraging rather than encouraging contribution.

Fortunately, Restivo and van de Rijt were not running a "perturb and observe" experiment; they were running a randomized controlled experiment. So, in addition to choosing 100 top contributors to receive a barnstar, they also picked 100 top contributors to whom they did not give one. These 100 served as a control group. And, critically, who was in the treatment group and who was in the control group was determined randomly.

When Restivo and van de Rijt looked at the behavior of people in the control group, they found that their contributions were decreasing too. Further, when Restivo and van de Rijt compared people in the treatment group (i.e., received barnstars) to people in the control group, they found that people in the treatment group contributed about 60% more. In other words, the contributions of both groups were decreasing, but those of the control group were doing so much faster.

As this study illustrates, the control group in experiments is critical in a way that is somewhat paradoxical. In order to precisely measure the effect of barnstars, Restivo and van de Rijt needed to observe people who did not receive barnstars. Many times, researchers who are not familiar with experiments fail to appreciate the incredible value of the control group. If Restivo and van de Rijt had not had a control group, they would have drawn exactly the wrong conclusion. Control groups are so important that the CEO of a major casino company has said that there are only three ways that employees can be fired from his company: for theft, for sexual harassment, or for running an experiment without a control group (Schrage 2011).

Restivo and van de Rijt's study illustrates the four main ingredients of an experiment: recruitment, randomization, intervention, and outcomes. Together, these four ingredients allow scientists to move beyond correlations and measure the causal effect of treatments. Specifically, randomization means that people in the treatment and control groups will be similar. This is important because it means that any difference in outcomes between the two groups can be attributed to the treatment and not a confounder.

In addition to being a nice illustration of the mechanics of experiments, Restivo and van de Rijt's study also shows that the logistics of digital experiments can be completely different from those of analog experiments. In Restivo and van de Rijt's experiment, it was easy to give the barnstar to anyone, and it was easy to track the outcome—number of edits—over an extended period of time (because edit history is automatically recorded by Wikipedia). This ability to deliver treatments and measure outcomes at no cost is *qualitatively* unlike experiments in the past. Although this experiment involved 200 people, it could have been run with 2,000 or even 20,000 people. The main thing preventing the researchers from scaling up their experiment by a factor of 100 was not cost; it was ethics. That is, Restivo and van de Rijt didn't want to give barnstars to undeserving editors, and they didn't want their experiment to disrupt the Wikipedia community (Restivo and Rijt 2012, 2014). I'll return to some of the ethical considerations raised by experiments later in this chapter and in chapter 6.

In conclusion, the experiment of Restivo and van de Rijt clearly shows that while the basic logic of experimentation has not changed, the logistics of digital-age experiments can be dramatically different. Next, in order to more clearly isolate the opportunities created by these changes, I'll compare the experiments that researchers can do now with the kinds of experiments that have been done in the past.

4.3 Two dimensions of experiments: lab–field and analog–digital

Lab experiments offer control, field experiments offer realism, and digital field experiments combine control and realism at scale.

Experiments come in many different shapes and sizes. In the past, researchers have found it helpful to organize experiments along a continuum

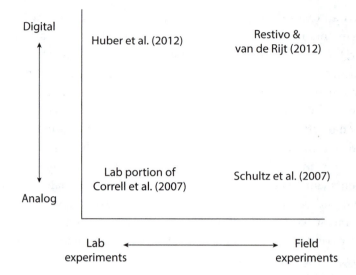

Figure 4.1: Schematic of design space for experiments. In the past, experiments varied along the lab–field dimension. Now, they also vary on the analog–digital dimension. This two-dimensional design space is illustrated by four experiments that I describe in this chapter. In my opinion, the area of greatest opportunity is digital field experiments.

between *lab experiments* and *field experiments*. Now, however, researchers should also organize experiments along a second continuum between *analog experiments* and *digital experiments*. This two-dimensional design space will help you understand the strengths and weaknesses of different approaches and highlight the areas of greatest opportunity (figure 4.1).

One dimension along which experiments can be organized is the lab–field dimension. Many experiments in the social sciences are *lab experiments* where undergraduate students perform strange tasks in a lab for course credit. This type of experiment dominates research in psychology because it enables researchers to create highly controlled settings to precisely isolate and test specific theories about social behavior. For certain problems, however, something feels a bit strange about drawing strong conclusions about human behavior from such unusual people performing such unusual tasks in such an unusual setting. These concerns have led to a movement toward *field experiments*. Field experiments combine the strong design of randomized control experiments with more representative groups of participants performing more common tasks in more natural settings.

Although some people think of lab and field experiments as competing methods, it is best to think of them as complementary, with different strengths and weaknesses. For example, Correll, Benard, and Paik (2007) used both a lab experiment and a field experiment in an attempt to find the sources of the "motherhood penalty." In the United States, mothers earn less money than childless women, even when comparing women with similar skills working in similar jobs. There are many possible explanations for this pattern, one of which is that employers are biased against mothers. (Interestingly, the opposite seems to be true for fathers: they tend to earn more than comparable childless men.) In order to assess possible bias against mothers, Correll and colleagues ran two experiments: one in the lab and one in the field.

First, in a lab experiment, they told participants, who were college undergraduates, that a company was conducting an employment search for a person to lead its new East Coast marketing department. The students were told that the company wanted their help in the hiring process, and they were asked to review resumes of several potential candidates and to rate the candidates on a number of dimensions, such as their intelligence, warmth, and commitment to work. Further, the students were asked if they would recommend hiring the applicant and what they would recommend as a starting salary. Unbeknownst to the students, however, the resumes were specifically constructed to be similar except for one thing: some of them signaled motherhood (by listing involvement in a parent–teacher association) and some did not. Correll and colleagues found that the students were less likely to recommend hiring the mothers and that they offered them a lower starting salary. Further, through a statistical analysis of both the ratings and the hiring-related decisions, Correll and colleagues found that mothers' disadvantages were largely explained by the fact that they were rated lower in terms of competence and commitment. Thus, this lab experiment allowed Correll and colleagues to measure a causal effect and provide a possible explanation for that effect.

Of course, one might be skeptical about drawing conclusions about the entire US labor market based on the decisions of a few hundred under- graduates who have probably never had a full-time job, let alone hired someone. Therefore, Correll and colleagues also conducted a complementary field experiment. They responded to hundreds of advertised job openings with fake cover letters and resumes. Similar to the materials shown to the undergraduates, some resumes signaled motherhood and some did not. Correll and colleagues found that mothers were less likely to get called back for interviews than equally qualified childless women. In other words, real employers making consequential decisions in a natural setting behaved much like the undergraduates. Did they make similar decisions for the same reason? Unfortunately, we don't know. The researchers were not able to ask the employers to rate the candidates or explain their decisions.

This pair of experiments reveals a lot about lab and field experiments in general. Lab experiments offer researchers near-total control of the environment in which participants are making decisions. So, for example, in the lab experiment, Correll and colleagues were able to ensure that all the resumes were read in a quiet setting; in the field experiment, some of the resumes might not even have been read. Further, because participants in the lab setting know that they are being studied, researchers are often able to collect additional data that can help explain why participants are making their decisions. For example, Correll and colleagues asked participants in the lab experiment to rate the candidates on different dimensions. This kind of *process data* could help researchers understand the mechanisms behind differences in how participants treat the resumes.

On the other hand, these exact same characteristics that I have just described as advantages are also sometimes considered disadvantages. Researchers who prefer field experiments argue that participants in lab experiments could act very differently because they know that they are being studied. For example, in the lab experiment, participants might have guessed the goal of the research and altered their behavior so as not to appear biased. Further, researchers who prefer field experiments might argue that small differences in resumes can only stand out in a very clean, sterile lab environment, and thus the lab experiment will overestimate the effect of motherhood on real hiring decisions. Finally, many proponents of field experiments criticize lab experiments' reliance on WEIRD participants: mainly students from Western, Educated, Industrialized, Rich, and Democratic countries (Henrich, Heine, and Norenzayan 2010a). The experiments by Correll and colleagues (2007) illustrate the two extremes on the lab–field continuum. In between these two extremes, there are also a variety of hybrid designs, including approaches such as bringing non-students into a lab or going into the field but still having participants perform an unusual task.

In addition to the lab–field dimension that has existed in the past, the digital age means that researchers now have a second major dimension along which experiments can vary: analog–digital. Just as there are pure lab experiments, pure field experiments, and a variety of hybrids in between, there are pure analog experiments, pure digital experiments, and a variety of hybrids. It is tricky to offer a formal definition of this dimension, but a useful working definition is that *fully digital experiments* are experiments that make use of digital infrastructure to recruit participants, randomize, deliver treatments, and measure outcomes. For example, Restivo and van de Rijt's (2012) study of barnstars and Wikipedia was a fully digital experiment, because it used digital systems for all four of these steps. Likewise, *fully analog experiments* do not make use of digital infrastructure for any of these four steps. Many of the classic experiments in psychology are fully analog experiments. In between these two extremes, there are *partially digital experiments* that use a combination of analog and digital systems.

When some people think of digital experiments, they immediately think of online experiments. This is unfortunate because the opportunities to run digital experiments are not just online. Researchers can run partially digital experiments by using digital devices in the physical world in order to deliver treatments or measure outcomes. For example, researchers could use smartphones to deliver treatments or sensors in the built environment to measure outcomes. In fact, as we will see later in this chapter, researchers have already used home power meters to measure outcomes in experiments about energy consumption involving 8.5 million households (Allcott 2015). As digital devices become increasingly integrated into people's lives and sensors become integrated into the built environment, these opportunities to run partially digital experiments in the physical world will increase dramatically. In other words, digital experiments are not just online experiments.

Digital systems create new possibilities for experiments everywhere along the lab–field continuum. In pure lab experiments, for example, researchers can use digital systems for finer measurement of participants' behavior; one example of this type of improved measurement is eye-tracking equipment that provides precise and continuous measures of gaze location. The digital age also creates the possibility of running lab-like experiments online. For example, researchers have rapidly adopted Amazon Mechanical Turk (MTurk) to recruit participants for online experiments (figure 4.2). MTurk matches "employers" who have tasks that need to be completed with "workers" who wish to complete those tasks for money. Unlike traditional labor markets, however, the tasks involved usually require only a few minutes to complete, and the entire interaction between employer and worker is

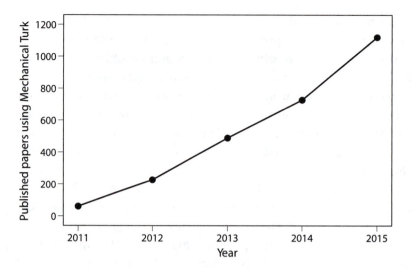

Figure 4.2: Papers published using data from Amazon Mechanical Turk (MTurk). MTurk and other online labor markets offer researchers a convenient way to recruit participants for experiments. Adapted from Bohanon (2016).

online. Because MTurk mimics aspects of traditional lab experiments—paying people to complete tasks that they would not do for free—it is naturally suited for certain types of experiments. Essentially, MTurk has created the infrastructure for managing a pool of participants—recruiting and paying people—and researchers have taken advantage of that infrastructure to tap into an always available pool of participants.

Digital systems create even more possibilities for field-like experiments. In particular, they enable researchers to combine the tight control and process data that are associated with lab experiments with the more diverse participants and more natural settings that are associated with field experiments. In addition, digital field experiments also offer three opportunities that tend to be difficult in analog experiments.

First, whereas most analog lab and field experiments have hundreds of participants, digital field experiments can have millions of participants. This change in scale is because some digital experiments can produce data at zero variable cost. That is, once researchers have created an experimental infrastructure, increasing the number of participants typically does not increase the cost. Increasing the number of participants by a factor of 100 or more is not just a *quantitative* change; it is a *qualitative* change, because it enables researchers to learn different things from experiments (e.g., heterogeneity of treatment effects) and to run entirely different experimental designs (e.g., large-group experiments). This point is so important, I'll return to it toward the end of the chapter when I offer advice about creating digital experiments.

Second, whereas most analog lab and field experiments treat participants as indistinguishable widgets, digital field experiments often use background information about participants in the design and analysis stages of the research. This background information, which is called *pre-treatment information,* is often available in digital experiments because they are run on top of always-on measurement systems (see chapter 2). For example, a researcher at Facebook has much more pre-treatment information about people in her digital field experiment than a university researcher has about the people in her analog field experiment. This pre-treatment information enables more efficient experimental designs—such as blocking (Higgins, Sävje, and Sekhon 2016) and targeted recruitment of participants (Eckles, Kizilcec, and Bakshy 2016)—and more insightful analysis—such as estimation of heterogeneity of treatment effects (Athey and Imbens 2016a) and covariate adjustment for improved precision (Bloniarz et al. 2016).

Third, whereas many analog lab and field experiments deliver treatments and measure outcomes in a relatively compressed amount of time, some digital field experiments happen over much longer timescales. For example, Restivo and van de Rijt's experiment had the outcome measured daily for 90 days, and one of the experiments I'll tell you about later in the chapter (Ferraro, Miranda, and Price 2011) tracked outcomes over three years at basically no cost. These three opportunities—size, pre-treatment information, and longitudinal treatment and outcome data—arise most commonly when experiments are run on top of always-on measurement systems (see chapter 2 for more on always-on measurement systems).

While digital field experiments offer many possibilities, they also share some weaknesses with both analog lab and analog field experiments. For example, experiments cannot be used to study the past, and they can only estimate the effects of treatments that can be manipulated. Also, although experiments are undoubtedly useful to guide policy, the exact guidance they can offer is somewhat limited because of complications such as environmental dependence, compliance problems, and equilibrium effects (Banerjee and Duflo 2009; Deaton 2010). Digital field experiments also magnify the ethical concerns created by field experiments—a topic I'll address later in this chapter and in chapter 6.

4.4 Moving beyond simple experiments

Let's move beyond simple experiments. Three concepts are useful for rich experiments: validity, heterogeneity of treatment effects, and mechanisms.

Researchers who are new to experiments often focus on a very specific, narrow question: Does this treatment "work"? For example, does a phone call from a volunteer encourage someone to vote? Does changing a website button from blue to green increase the click-through rate? Unfortunately, loose phrasing about what "works" obscures the fact that narrowly focused experiments don't really tell you whether a treatment "works" in a general sense. Rather, narrowly focused experiments answer a much more specific question: What is the average effect of this specific treatment with this specific implementation for this population of participants at this time? I'll call experiments that focus on this narrow question *simple experiments*.

Simple experiments can provide valuable information, but they fail to answer many questions that are both important and interesting, such as whether there are some people for whom the treatment had a larger or smaller effect; whether there is another treatment that would be more effective; and whether this experiment relates to broader social theories.

In order to show the value of moving beyond simple experiments, let's consider an analog field experiment by P. Wesley Schultz and colleagues on the relationship between social norms and energy consumption (Schultz et al. 2007). Schultz and colleagues hung doorhangers on 300 households in San Marcos, California, and these doorhangers delivered different messages designed to encourage energy conservation. Then, Schultz and colleagues measured the effect of these messages on electricity consumption, both after one week and after three weeks; see figure 4.3 for a more detailed description of the experimental design.

The experiment had two conditions. In the first, households received general energy-saving tips (e.g., use fans instead of air conditioners) and information about their energy usage compared with the average energy usage in their neighborhood. Schultz and colleagues called this the *descriptive normative* condition because the information about the energy use in the neighborhood provided information about typical behavior (i.e., a descriptive norm). When Schultz and colleagues looked at the resulting energy usage

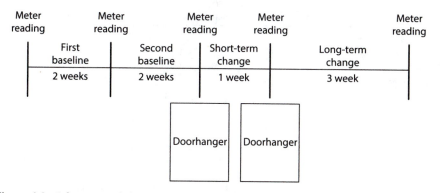

Figure 4.3: Schematic of the experimental design from Schultz et al. (2007). The field experiment involved visiting about 300 households in San Marcos, California five times over an eight-week period. On each visit, the researchers manually took a reading from the house's power meter. On two of the visits, they placed doorhangers on each house providing some information about the household's energy usage. The research question was how the content of these messages would impact energy use.

in this group, the treatment appeared to have no effect, in either the short or long term; in other words, the treatment didn't seem to "work" (figure 4.4).

Fortunately, Schultz and colleagues did not settle for this simplistic analysis. Before the experiment began, they reasoned that heavy users of electricity—people above the mean—might reduce their consumption, and that light users of electricity—people below the mean—might actually increase their consumption. When they looked at the data, that's exactly what they found (figure 4.4). Thus, what looked like a treatment that was having no effect was actually a treatment that had two offsetting effects. This counterproductive increase among the light users is an example of a *boomerang effect,* where a treatment can have the opposite effect from what was intended.

Simultaneous to the first condition, Schultz and colleagues also ran a second condition. The households in the second condition received the exact same treatment—general energy-saving tips and information about their household's energy usage compared with the average for their neighborhood—with one tiny addition: for people with below-average consumption, the researchers added a :) and for people with above-average consumption they added a :(. These emoticons were designed to trigger what the researchers called *injunctive norms.* Injunctive norms refer to perceptions of what is commonly approved (and disapproved), whereas descriptive

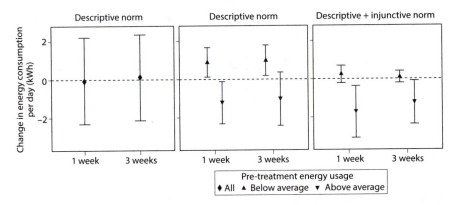

Figure 4.4: Results from Schultz et al. (2007). Panel (a) shows that the descriptive norm treatment has an estimated zero average treatment effect. However, panel (b) shows that this average treatment effect is actually composed of two offsetting effects. For heavy users, the treatment decreased usage, but for light users, the treatment increased usage. Finally, panel (c) shows that the second treatment, which used descriptive and injunctive norms, had roughly the same effect on heavy users but mitigated the boomerang effect on light users. Adapted from Schultz et al. (2007).

norms refer to perceptions of what is commonly done (Reno, Cialdini, and Kallgren 1993).

By adding this one tiny emoticon, the researchers dramatically reduced the boomerang effect (figure 4.4). Thus, by making this one simple change—a change that was motivated by an abstract social psychological theory (Cialdini, Kallgren, and Reno 1991)—the researchers were able to turn a program that didn't seem to work into one that worked, and, simultaneously, they were able to contribute to the general understanding of how social norms affect human behavior.

At this point, however, you might notice that something is a bit different about this experiment. In particular, the experiment of Schultz and colleagues doesn't really have a control group in the same way that randomized controlled experiments do. A comparison between this design and that of Restivo and van de Rijt illustrates the differences between two major experimental designs. In *between-subjects designs*, such as that of Restivo and van de Rijt, there is a treatment group and a control group. In *within-subjects designs*, on the other hand, the behavior of participants is compared before and after the treatment (Greenwald 1976; Charness, Gneezy, and Kuhn 2012). In a within-subjects experiment, it is as if each participant acts as her own control group. The strength of between-subjects designs is that they provide protection against confounders (as I described earlier), while the strength of within-subjects experiments is increased precision of estimates. Finally, to foreshadow an idea that will come later when I offer advice about designing digital experiments, a *mixed design* combines the improved precision of within-subjects designs and the protection against confounding of between-subjects designs (figure 4.5).

Overall, the design and results of the study by Schultz and colleagues (2007) show the value of moving beyond simple experiments. Fortunately, you don't need to be a creative genius to design experiments like this. Social scientists have developed three concepts that will guide you toward richer experiments: (1) validity, (2) heterogeneity of treatment effects, and (3) mechanisms. That is, if you keep these three ideas in mind while you are designing your experiment, you will naturally create a more interesting and useful experiment. In order to illustrate these three concepts in action, I'll describe a number of follow-up partially digital field experiments that built on the elegant design and exciting results of Schultz and colleagues (2007). As you will see, through more careful design, implementation, analysis, and interpretation, you too can move beyond simple experiments.

4.4.1 Validity

Validity refers to how much the results of an experiment support a more general conclusion.

No experiment is perfect, and researchers have developed an extensive vocabulary to describe possible problems. *Validity* refers to the extent to which the results of a particular experiment support some more general conclusion. Social scientists have found it helpful to split validity into four main types: statistical conclusion validity, internal validity, construct validity, and external validity (Shadish, Cook, and Campbell 2001, chapter 2). Mastering these concepts will provide you with a mental checklist for critiquing and improving the design and analysis of an experiment, and it will help you communicate with other researchers.

Statistical conclusion validity centers around whether the statistical analysis of the experiment was done correctly. In the context of Schultz et al. (2007), such a question might center on whether they computed their p-values correctly. The statistical principles needed to design and analyze

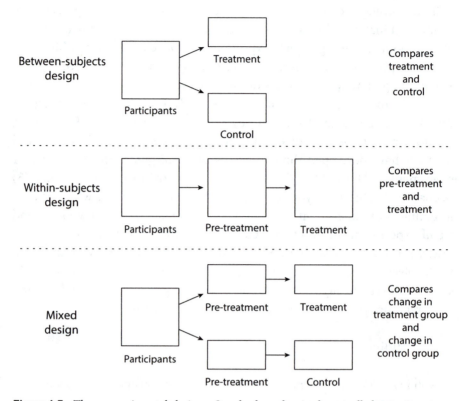

Figure 4.5: Three experimental designs. Standard randomized controlled experiments use *between-subjects* designs. An example of a between-subjects design is Restivo and van de Rijt's (2012) experiment on barnstars and contributions to Wikipedia: the researchers randomly divided participants into treatment and control groups, gave participants in the treatment group a barnstar, and compared outcomes for the two groups. The second type of design is a *within-subjects* design. The two experiments in Schultz and colleagues' (2007) study on social norms and energy use illustrate a within-subjects design: the researchers compared the electricity use of participants before and after receiving the treatment. Within-subjects designs offer improved statistical precision, but they are open to possible confounders (e.g., changes in weather between the pre-treatment and treatment periods) (Greenwald 1976; Charness, Gneezy, and Kuhn 2012). Within-subjects designs are also sometimes called repeated measures designs. Finally, *mixed designs* combine the improved precision of within-subjects designs and the protection against confounding of between-subjects designs. In a mixed design, a researcher compares the change in outcomes for people in the treatment and control groups. When researchers already have pre-treatment information, as is the case in many digital experiments, mixed designs are generally preferable to between-subjects designs because they result in improved precision of estimates.

experiments are beyond the scope of this book, but they have not fundamentally changed in the digital age. What has changed, however, is that the data environment in digital experiments has created new opportunities such as using machine learning methods to estimate heterogeneity of treatment effects (Imai and Ratkovic 2013).

Internal validity centers around whether the experimental procedures were performed correctly. Returning to the experiment of Schultz et al. (2007), questions about internal validity could center around randomization, delivery of treatment, and measurement of outcomes. For example, you might be concerned that the research assistants did not read the electric meters reliably. In fact, Schultz and colleagues were worried about this problem, and they had a sample of meters read twice; fortunately, the results were essentially identical. In general, Schultz and colleagues' experiment appears to have high internal validity, but this is not always the case: complex field and online experiments often run into problems actually delivering the right treatment to the right people and measuring the outcomes for everyone. Fortunately, the digital age can help reduce concerns about internal validity, because it is now easier to ensure that the treatment is delivered to those who are supposed to receive it and to measure outcomes for all participants.

Construct validity centers around the match between the data and the theoretical constructs. As discussed in chapter 2, constructs are abstract concepts that social scientists reason about. Unfortunately, these abstract concepts don't always have clear definitions and measurements. Returning to Schultz et al. (2007), the claim that injunctive social norms can lower electricity use requires researchers to design a treatment that would manipulate "injunctive social norms" (e.g., an emoticon) and to measure "electricity use". In analog experiments, many researchers designed their own treatments and measured their own outcomes. This approach ensures that, as much as possible, the experiments match the abstract constructs being studied. In digital experiments where researchers partner with companies or governments to deliver treatments and use always-on data systems to measure outcomes, the match between the experiment and the theoretical constructs may be less tight. Thus, I expect that construct validity will tend to be a bigger concern in digital experiments than in analog experiments.

Finally, *external validity* centers around whether the results of this experiment can be generalized to other situations. Returning to Schultz et al. (2007), one could ask whether this same idea—providing people with information about their energy usage in relationship to their peers and a signal of injunctive norms (e.g., an emoticon)—would reduce energy usage if it were done in a different way in a different setting. For most well-designed and well-run experiments, concerns about external validity are the hardest to address. In the past, these debates about external validity frequently involved nothing more than a group of people sitting in a room trying to imagine what would have happened if the procedures had been done in a different way, or in a different place, or with different participants. Fortunately, the digital age enables researchers to move beyond these data-free speculations and assess external validity empirically.

Because the results from Schultz et al. (2007) were so exciting, a company named Opower partnered with utilities in the United States to deploy the treatment more widely. Based on the design of Schultz et al. (2007), Opower created customized Home Energy Reports that had two main modules: one showing a household's electricity usage relative to its neighbors with an emoticon and one providing tips for lowering energy usage (figure 4.6). Then, in partnership with researchers, Opower ran randomized controlled experiments to assess the impact of these Home Energy Reports. Even though the treatments in these experiments were typically delivered physically— usually through old-fashioned snail mail—the outcome was measured using digital devices in the physical world (e.g., power meters). Further, rather than manually collecting this information by research assistants visiting each house, the Opower experiments were all done in partnership with power companies, enabling the researchers to access the power readings. Thus, these partially digital field experiments were run at a massive scale at low variable cost.

In a first set of experiments involving 600,000 households from 10 different sites, Allcott (2011) found that the Home Energy Report lowered electricity consumption. In other words, the results from the much larger, more geographically diverse study were qualitatively similar to the results from Schultz et al. (2007). Further, in subsequent research involving eight million additional households from 101 different sites, Allcott (2015) again found that the Home Energy Report consistently lowered electricity consumption. This much larger set of experiments also revealed an interesting new pattern that would not be visible in any single experiment: the size of the effect declined in the later experiments (figure 4.7). Allcott (2015) speculated that this decline happened because, over time, the treatment was being applied to

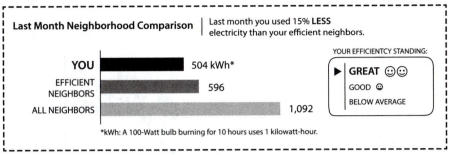

Peer Comparison Module

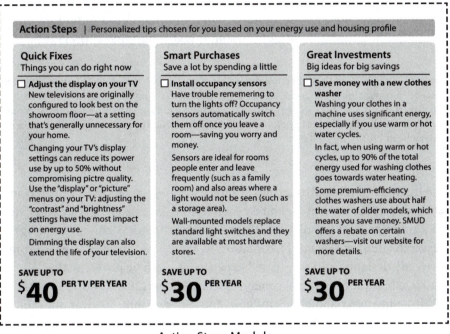

Action Steps Module

Figure 4.6: The Home Energy Reports had a Social Comparison Module and an Action Steps Module. Reproduced by permission from Elsevier from Allcott (2011), figures 1 and 2.

different types of participants. More specifically, utilities with more environmentally focused customers were more likely adopt the program earlier, and their customers were more responsive to the treatment. As utilities with less environmentally focused customers adopted the program, its effectiveness appeared to decline. Thus, just as randomization in experiments ensures that

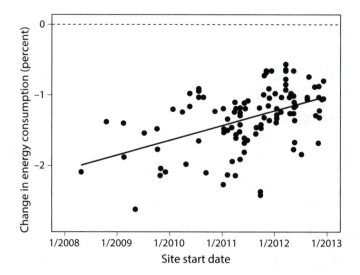

Figure 4.7: Results of 111 experiments testing the effect of the Home Energy Report on electricity consumption. At sites where the program was adopted later, it tended to have smaller effects. Allcott (2015) argues that a major source of this pattern is that sites with more environmentally focused customers were more likely to adopt the program earlier. Adapted from Allcott (2015), figure 3.

the treatment and control group are similar, randomization in research sites ensures that the estimates can be generalized from one group of participants to a more general population (think back to chapter 3 about sampling). If research sites are not sampled randomly, then generalization—even from a perfectly designed and conducted experiment—can be problematic.

Together, these 111 experiments—10 in Allcott (2011) and 101 in Allcott (2015)—involved about 8.5 million households from all over the United States. They consistently show that Home Energy Reports reduce average electricity consumption, a result that supports the original findings of Schultz and colleagues from 300 homes in California. Beyond just replicating these original results, the follow-up experiments also show that the size of the effect varies by location. This set of experiments also illustrates two more general points about partially digital field experiments. First, researchers will be able to empirically address concerns about external validity when the cost of running experiments is low, and this can occur if the outcome is already being measured by an always-on data system. Therefore, it suggests that researchers should be on the lookout for other interesting and important behaviors that are already being recorded, and then design experiments on top of this existing measuring infrastructure. Second, this set of experiments reminds us that digital field experiments are not just online; increasingly, I expect that they will be everywhere, with many outcomes measured by sensors in the built environment.

The four types of validity—statistical conclusion validity, internal validity, construct validity, and external validity—provide a mental checklist to help researchers assess whether the results from a particular experiment support a more general conclusion. Compared with analog-age experiments, in digital-age experiments, it should be easier to address external validity empirically, and it should also be easier to ensure internal validity. On the other hand, issues of construct validity will probably be more challenging in digital-age experiments, especially digital field experiments that involve partnerships with companies.

4.4.2 Heterogeneity of treatment effects

Experiments normally measure the average effect, but the effect is probably not the same for everyone.

The second key idea for moving beyond simple experiments is *heterogeneity of treatment effects*. The experiment of Schultz et al. (2007) powerfully illustrates how the same treatment can have a different effect on different kinds of people (figure 4.4). In most analog experiments, however, researchers focused on average treatment effects because there were a small number of participants and little was known about them. In digital experiments, however, there are often many more participants and more is known about them. In this different data environment, researchers who continue to estimate only average treatment effects will miss out the ways in which estimates about the heterogeneity of treatment effects can provide clues about how a treatment works, how it can be improved, and how it can be targeted to those most likely to benefit.

Two examples of heterogeneity of treatment effects come from additional research on the Home Energy Reports. First, Allcott (2011) used the large sample size (600,000 households) to further split the sample and estimate the effect of the Home Energy Report by decile of pre-treatment energy usage. While Schultz et al. (2007) found differences between heavy and light users,

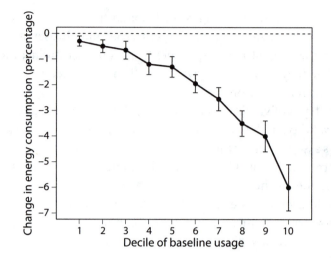

Figure 4.8: Heterogeneity of treatment effects in Allcott (2011). The decrease in energy use was different for people in different deciles of baseline usage. Adapted from Allcott (2011), figure 8.

Allcott (2011) found that there were also differences within the heavy- and light-user groups. For example, the heaviest users (those in the top decile) reduced their energy usage twice as much as someone in the middle of the heavy-user group (figure 4.8). Further, estimating the effect by pre-treatment behavior also revealed that there was no boomerang effect, even for the lightest users (figure 4.8).

In a related study, Costa and Kahn (2013) speculated that the effectiveness of the Home Energy Report could vary based on a participant's political ideology and that the treatment might actually cause people with certain ideologies to increase their electricity use. In other words, they speculated that the Home Energy Reports might be creating a boomerang effect for some types of people. To assess this possibility, Costa and Kahn merged the Opower data with data purchased from a third-party aggregator that included information such as political party registration, donations to environmental organizations, and household participation in renewable energy programs. With this merged dataset, Costa and Kahn found that the Home Energy Reports produced broadly similar effects for participants with different ideologies; there was no evidence that any group exhibited boomerang effects (figure 4.9).

As these two examples illustrate, in the digital age, we can move from esti-

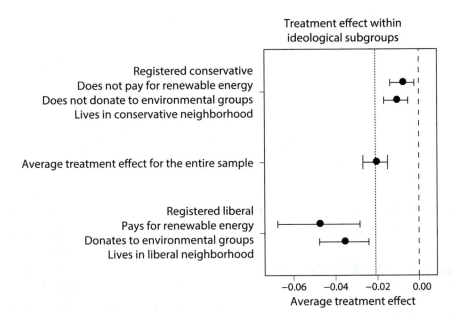

Treatment effect within
ideological subgroups

Figure 4.9: Heterogeneity of treatment effects in Costa and Kahn (2013). The estimated average treatment effect for the entire sample is −2.1% [−1.5%, −2.7%]. After combining information from the experiment with information about the households, Costa and Kahn (2013) used a series of statistical models to estimate the treatment effect for very specific groups of people. Two estimates are presented for each group because the estimates depend on the covariates they included in their statistical models (see models 4 and 6 in tables 3 and 4 in Costa and Kahn (2013)). As this example illustrates, treatment effects can be different for different people, and estimates of treatment effects that come from statistical models can depend on the details of those models (Grimmer, Messing, and Westwood 2014). Adapted from Costa and Kahn (2013), tables 3 and 4.

mating average treatment effects to estimating the heterogeneity of treatment effects, because we can have many more participants and we know more about those participants. Learning about heterogeneity of treatment effects can enable targeting of a treatment where it is most effective, provide facts that stimulate new theory development, and provide hints about possible mechanisms, the topic to which I now turn.

4.4.3 Mechanisms

Experiments measure what happened. Mechanisms explain why and how it happened.

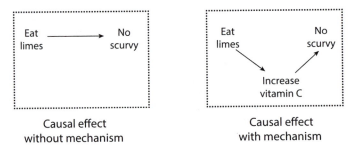

Causal effect
without mechanism

Causal effect
with mechanism

Figure 4.10: Limes prevent scurvy, and the mechanism is vitamin C.

The third key idea for moving beyond simple experiments is *mechanisms*. Mechanisms tell us *why* or *how* a treatment caused an effect. The process of searching for mechanisms is also sometimes called looking for *intervening variables* or *mediating variables*. Although experiments are good for estimating causal effects, they are often not designed to reveal mechanisms. Digital experiments can help us identify mechanisms in two ways: (1) they enable us to collect more process data and (2) they enable us to test many related treatments.

Because mechanisms are tricky to define formally (Hedström and Ylikoski 2010), I'm going to start with a simple example: limes and scurvy (Gerber and Green 2012). In the eighteenth century, doctors had a pretty good sense that when sailors ate limes, they did not get scurvy. Scurvy is a terrible disease, so this was powerful information. But these doctors did not know *why* limes prevented scurvy. It was not until 1932, almost 200 years later, that scientists could reliably show that vitamin C was the reason that lime prevented scurvy (Carpenter 1988, p. 191). In this case, vitamin C is the *mechanism* through which limes prevent scurvy (figure 4.10). Of course, identifying the mechanism is very important scientifically— lots of science is about understanding why things happen. Identifying mechanisms is also very important practically. Once we understand why a treatment works, we can potentially develop new treatments that work even better.

Unfortunately, isolating mechanisms is very difficult. Unlike limes and scurvy, in many social settings, treatments probably operate through many interrelated pathways. However, in the case of social norms and energy use, researchers have tried to isolate mechanisms by collecting process data and testing related treatments.

One way to test possible mechanisms is by collecting process data about how the treatment impacted possible mechanisms. For example, recall that Allcott (2011) showed that Home Energy Reports caused people to lower their electricity usage. But how did these reports lower electricity usage? What were the mechanisms? In a follow-up study, Allcott and Rogers (2014) partnered with a power company that, through a rebate program, had acquired information about which consumers upgraded their appliances to more energy-efficient models. Allcott and Rogers (2014) found that slightly more people receiving the Home Energy Reports upgraded their appliances. But this difference was so small that it could account for only 2% of the decrease in energy use in the treated households. In other words, appliance upgrades were not the dominant mechanism through which the Home Energy Report decreased electricity consumption.

A second way to study mechanisms is to run experiments with slightly different versions of the treatment. For example, in the experiment of Schultz et al. (2007) and all the subsequent Home Energy Report experiments, participants were provided with a treatment that had two main parts (1) tips about energy savings and (2) information about their energy use relative to their peers (figure 4.6). Thus, it is possible that the energy-saving tips were what caused the change, not the peer information. To assess the possibility that the tips alone might have been sufficient, Ferraro, Miranda, and Price (2011) partnered with a water company near Atlanta, Georgia, and ran a related experiment on water conservation involving about 100,000 households. There were four conditions:

- a group that received tips on saving water
- a group that received tips on saving water plus a moral appeal to save water
- a group that received tips on saving water plus a moral appeal to save water plus information about their water use relative to their peers
- a control group

The researchers found that the tips-only treatment had no effect on water usage in the short (one year), medium (two years), and long (three years) term. The tips plus appeal treatment caused participants to decrease water usage, but only in the short term. Finally, the tips plus appeal plus peer information treatment caused decreased usage in the short, medium,

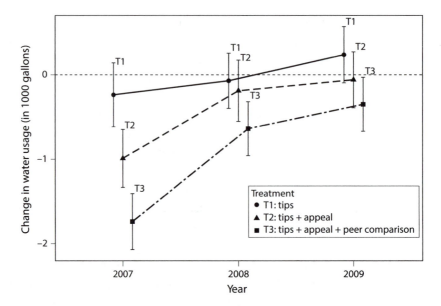

Figure 4.11: Results from Ferraro, Miranda, and Price (2011). Treatments were sent May 21, 2007, and effects were measured during the summers of 2007, 2008, and 2009. By unbundling the treatment, the researchers hoped to develop a better sense of the mechanisms. The tips-only treatment had essentially no effect in the short (one year), medium (two years), and long (three years) term. The tips plus appeal treatment caused participants to decrease water usage, but only in the short term. The advice plus appeal plus peer information treatment caused participants to decrease water usage in the short, medium, and long term. Vertical bars are estimated confidence intervals. See Bernedo, Ferraro, and Price (2014) for actual study materials. Adapted from Ferraro, Miranda, and Price (2011), table 1.

and long term (figure 4.11). These kinds of experiments with unbundled treatments are a good way to figure out which part of the treatment—or which parts together—are the ones that are causing the effect (Gerber and Green 2012, section 10.6). For example, the experiment of Ferraro and colleagues shows us that water-saving tips alone are not enough to decrease water usage.

Ideally, one would move beyond the layering of components (tips; tips plus appeal; tips plus appeal plus peer information) to a full factorial design—also sometimes called a 2^k factorial design—where each possible combination of the three elements is tested (table 4.1). By testing every possible combination of components, researchers can fully assess the effect of each component in isolation and in combination. For example, the experiment

Table 4.1: Example of Treatments in a Full Factorial Design with Three Elements: Tips, Appeal, and Peer Information

Treatment	Characteristics
1	Control
2	Tips
3	Appeal
4	Peer information
5	Tips + appeal
6	Tips + peer information
7	Appeal + peer information
8	Tips + appeal + peer information

of Ferraro and colleagues does not reveal whether peer comparison alone would have been sufficient to lead to long-term changes in behavior. In the past, these full factorial designs have been difficult to run because they require a large number of participants and they require researchers to be able to precisely control and deliver a large number of treatments. But, in some situations, the digital age removes these logistical constraints.

In summary, mechanisms—the pathways through which a treatment has an effect—are incredibly important. Digital-age experiments can help researchers learn about mechanisms by (1) collecting process data and (2) enabling full factorial designs. The mechanisms suggested by these approaches can then be tested directly by experiments specifically designed to test mechanisms (Ludwig, Kling, and Mullainathan 2011; Imai, Tingley, and Yamamoto 2013; Pirlott and MacKinnon 2016).

In total, these three concepts—validity, heterogeneity of treatment effects, and mechanisms—provide a powerful set of ideas for designing and interpreting experiments. These concepts help researchers move beyond simple experiments about what "works" to richer experiments that have tighter links to theory, that reveal where and why treatments work, and that might even help researchers design more effective treatments. Given this conceptual background about experiments, I'll now turn to how you can actually make your experiments happen.

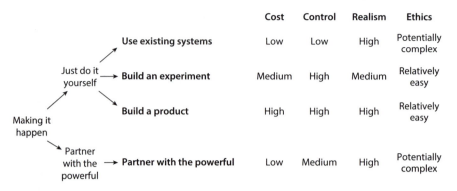

	Cost	Control	Realism	Ethics
Use existing systems	Low	Low	High	Potentially complex
Build an experiment	Medium	High	Medium	Relatively easy
Build a product	High	High	High	Relatively easy
Partner with the powerful	Low	Medium	High	Potentially complex

Figure 4.12: Summary of trade-offs for different ways that you can make your experiment happen. By *cost* I mean cost to the researcher in terms of time and money. By *control* I mean the ability to do what you want in terms of recruiting participants, randomization, delivering treatments, and measuring outcomes. By *realism* I mean the extent to which the decision environment matches those encountered in everyday life; note that high realism is not always important for testing theories (Falk and Heckman 2009). By *ethics* I mean the ability of well-intentioned researchers to manage ethical challenges that might arise.

4.5 Making it happen

> Even if you don't work at a big tech company you can run digital experiments. You can either do it yourself or partner with someone who can help you (and who you can help).

By this point, I hope that you are excited about the possibilities of doing your own digital experiments. If you work at a big tech company, you might already be doing these experiments all the time. But if you don't work at a tech company, you might think that you can't run digital experiments. Fortunately, that's wrong: with a little creativity and hard work, everyone can run a digital experiment.

As a first step, it is helpful to distinguish between two main approaches: doing it yourself or partnering with the powerful. And there are even a few different ways that you can do it yourself: you can experiment in existing environments, build your own experiment, or build your own product for repeated experimentation. As you'll see from the examples below, none of these approaches is best in all situations, and it's best to think of them as offering trade-offs along four main dimensions: cost, control, realism, and ethics (figure 4.12).

4.5.1 Use existing environments

> You can run experiments inside existing environments, often without any coding or partnership.

Logistically, the easiest way to do a digital experiment is to overlay your experiment on top of an existing environment. Such experiments can be run at a reasonably large scale and don't require partnership with a company or extensive software development.

For example, Jennifer Doleac and Luke Stein (2013) took advantage of an online marketplace similar to Craigslist in order to run an experiment that measured racial discrimination. They advertised thousands of iPods, and by systematically varying the characteristics of the seller, they were able to study the effect of race on economic transactions. Further, they used the scale of their experiment to estimate when the effect was bigger (heterogeneity of treatment effects) and to offer some ideas about why the effect might occur (mechanisms).

Doleac and Stein's iPod advertisements varied along three main dimensions. First, the researchers varied the characteristics of the seller, which was signaled by the hand photographed holding the iPod [white, black, white with tattoo] (figure 4.13). Second, they varied the asking price [$90, $110, $130]. Third, they varied the quality of the ad text [high-quality and low-quality (e.g., cApitalization errors and spelin errors)]. Thus, the authors had a $3 \times 3 \times 2$ design, which was deployed across more than 300 local markets, ranging from towns (e.g., Kokomo, Indiana and North Platte, Nebraska) to mega-cities (e.g., New York and Los Angeles).

Averaged across all conditions, the outcomes were better for the white sellers than the black sellers, with the tattooed sellers having intermediate results. For example, the white sellers received more offers and had higher final sale prices. Beyond these average effects, Doleac and Stein estimated the heterogeneity of effects. For example, one prediction from earlier theory is that discrimination would be less in markets where there is more competition between buyers. Using the number of offers in that market as a measure of the amount of buyer competition, the researchers found that black sellers did indeed receive worse offers in markets with a low degree of competition. Further, by comparing outcomes for the ads with high-quality and low-quality text, Doleac and Stein found that ad quality did not impact the

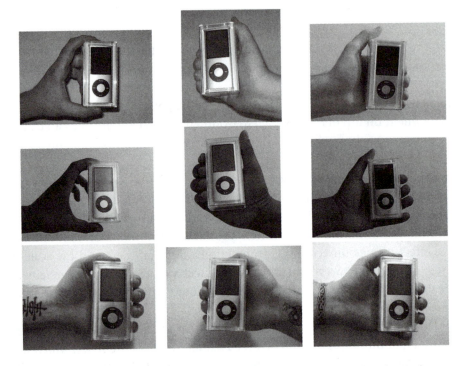

Figure 4.13: Hands used in the experiment of Doleac and Stein (2013). iPods were sold by sellers with different characteristics to measure discrimination in an online marketplace. Reproduced courtesy of John Wiley and Sons from Doleac and Stein (2013), figure 1.

disadvantage faced by black and tattooed sellers. Finally, taking advantage of the fact that advertisements were placed in more than 300 markets, the authors found that black sellers were more disadvantaged in cities with high crime rates and high residential segregation. None of these results give us a precise understanding of exactly why black sellers had worse outcomes, but, when combined with the results of other studies, they can begin to inform theories about the causes of racial discrimination in different types of economic transactions.

Another example that shows the ability of researchers to conduct digital field experiments in existing systems is the research by Arnout van de Rijt and colleagues (2014) on the keys to success. In many aspects of life, seemingly similar people end up with very different outcomes. One possible explanation for this pattern is that small—and essentially random—

advantages can lock in and grow over time, a process that researchers call *cumulative advantage*. In order to determine whether small initial successes lock in or fade away, van de Rijt and colleagues (2014) intervened in four different systems bestowing success on randomly selected participants and then measured the subsequent impacts of this arbitrary success.

More specifically, van de Rijt and colleagues (1) pledged money to randomly selected projects Kickstarter, a crowdfunding website; (2) positively rated randomly selected reviews on Epinions, a product review website; (3) gave awards to randomly chosen contributors to Wikipedia; and (4) signed randomly selected petitions on change.org. They found very similar results across all four systems: in each case, participants who were randomly given some early success went on to have more subsequent success than their otherwise completely indistinguishable peers (figure 4.14). The fact that the same pattern appeared in many systems increases the external validity of these results because it reduces the chance that this pattern is an artifact of any particular system.

Together, these two examples show that researchers can conduct digital field experiments without the need to partner with companies or to build complex digital systems. Further, table 4.2 provides even more examples that show the range of what is possible when researchers use the infrastructure of existing systems to deliver treatment and/or measure outcomes. These experiments are relatively cheap for researchers, and they offer a high degree of realism. But they offer researchers limited control over the participants, treatments, and outcomes to be measured. Further, for experiments taking place in only one system, researchers need to be concerned that the effects could be driven by system-specific dynamics (e.g., the way that Kickstarter ranks projects or the way that Change.org ranks petitions; for more information, see the discussion about algorithmic confounding in chapter 2). Finally, when researchers intervene in working systems, tricky ethical questions emerge about possible harm to participants, nonparticipants, and systems. We will consider these ethical question in more detail in chapter 6, and there is an excellent discussion of them in the appendix of van de Rijt et al. (2014). The trade-offs that come with working in an existing system are not ideal for every project, and for that reason some researchers build their own experimental system, as I'll illustrate next.

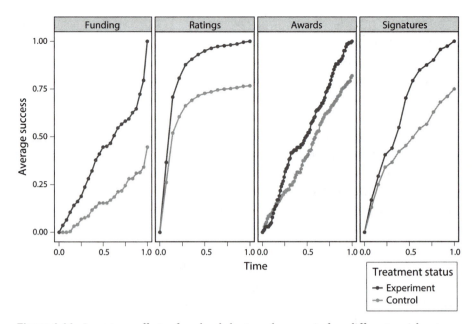

Figure 4.14: Long-term effects of randomly bestowed success in four different social systems. Arnout van de Rijt and colleagues (2014) (1) pledged money to randomly selected projects on Kickstarter, a crowdfunding website; (2) positively rated randomly selected reviews on Epinions, a produce review website; (3) gave awards to randomly chosen contributors to Wikipedia; and (4) signed randomly selected petitions on change.org. Adapted from van de Rijt et al. (2014), figure 2.

4.5.2 Build your own experiment

> Building your own experiment might be costly, but it will enable you
> to create the experiment that you want.

In addition to overlaying experiments on top of existing environments, you can also build your own experiment. The main advantage of this approach is control; if you are building the experiment, you can create the environment and treatments that you want. These bespoke experimental environments can create opportunities to test theories that are impossible to test in naturally occurring environments. The main drawbacks of building your own experiment are that it can be expensive and that the environment that you are able to create might not have the realism of a naturally occurring system. Researchers building their own experiment must also have a strategy

Table 4.2: Examples of Experiments in Existing Systems

Topic	References
Effect of barnstars on contributions to Wikipedia	Restivo and van de Rijt (2012, 2014); van de Rijt et al. (2014)
Effect of anti-harassment message on racist tweets	Munger (2016)
Effect of auction method on sale price	Lucking-Reiley (1999)
Effect of reputation on price in online auctions	Resnick et al. (2006)
Effect of race of seller on sale of baseball cards on eBay	Ayres, Banaji, and Jolls (2015)
Effect of race of seller on sale of iPods	Doleac and Stein (2013)
Effect of race of guest on Airbnb rentals	Edelman, Luca, and Svirsky (2016)
Effect of donations on the success of projects on Kickstarter	van de Rijt et al. (2014)
Effect of race and ethnicity on housing rentals	Hogan and Berry (2011)
Effect of positive rating on future ratings on Epinions	van de Rijt et al. (2014)
Effect of signatures on the success of petitions	Vaillant et al. (2015); van de Rijt et al. (2014); van de Rijt et al. (2016)

for recruiting participants. When working in existing systems, researchers are essentially bringing the experiments to their participants. But, when researchers build their own experiment, they need to bring participants to it. Fortunately, services such as Amazon Mechanical Turk (MTurk) can provide researchers with a convenient way to bring participants to their experiments.

One example that illustrates the virtues of bespoke environments for testing abstract theories is the digital lab experiment by Gregory Huber, Seth Hill, and Gabriel Lenz (2012). This experiment explores a possible practical limitation to the functioning of democratic governance. Earlier non-experimental studies of actual elections suggested that voters are not able to accurately assess the performance of incumbent politicians. In particular, voters appear to suffer from three biases: (1) they are focused on recent rather than cumulative performance; (2) they can be manipulated by rhetoric, framing, and marketing; and (3) they can be influenced by events unrelated to incumbent performance, such as the success of local sports teams and the weather. In these earlier studies, however, it was hard to isolate any of these factors from all the other stuff that happens in real, messy elections. Therefore, Huber and colleagues created a highly simplified voting environment in order to isolate, and then experimentally study, each of these three possible biases.

As I describe the experimental set-up below, it is going to sound very artificial, but remember that realism is not a goal in lab-style experiments. Rather, the goal is to clearly isolate the process that you are trying to study, and this tight isolation is sometimes not possible in studies with more realism (Falk and Heckman 2009). Further, in this particular case, the researchers argued that if voters cannot effectively evaluate performance in this highly simplified setting, then they are not going to be able to do it in a more realistic, more complex setting.

Huber and colleagues used MTurk to recruit participants. Once a participant provided informed consent and passed a short test, she was told that she was participating in a 32-round game to earn tokens that could be converted into real money. At the beginning of the game, each participant was told that she had been assigned an "allocator" that would give her free tokens each round and that some allocators were more generous than others. Further, each participant was also told that she would have a chance to either keep her allocator or be assigned a new one after 16 rounds of the game. Given what you know about Huber and colleagues' research goals, you can see that the allocator represents a government and this choice represents an election, but participants were not aware of the general goals of the research. In total, Huber and colleagues recruited about 4,000 participants, who were paid about $1.25 for a task that took about eight minutes.

Recall that one of the findings from earlier research was that voters reward and punish incumbents for outcomes that are clearly beyond their control, such as the success of local sports teams and the weather. To assess whether participants voting decisions could be influenced by purely random events in their setting, Huber and colleagues added a lottery to their experimental system. At either the 8th round or the 16th round (i.e., right before the chance to replace the allocator) participants were randomly placed in a lottery where some won 5,000 points, some won 0 points, and some lost 5,000 points.

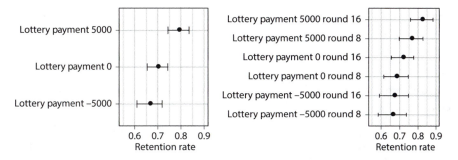

Figure 4.15: Results from Huber, Hill, and Lenz (2012). Participants who benefited from the lottery were more likely to retain their allocator, and this effect was stronger when the lottery happened in round 16—right before the replacement decision—than when it happened in round 8. Adapted from Huber, Hill, and Lenz (2012), figure 5.

This lottery was intended to mimic good or bad news that is independent of the performance of the politician. Even though participants were explicitly told that the lottery was unrelated to the performance of their allocator, the outcome of the lottery still impacted participants' decisions. Participants who benefited from the lottery were more likely to keep their allocator, and this effect was stronger when the lottery happened in round 16—right before the replacement decision—than when it happened in round 8 (figure 4.15). These results, along with those of several other experiments in the paper, led Huber and colleagues to conclude that even in a simplified setting, voters have difficulty making wise decisions, a result that impacted future research about voter decision making (Healy and Malhotra 2013). The experiment of Huber and colleagues shows that MTurk can be used to recruit participants for lab-style experiments in order to precisely test very specific theories. It also shows the value of building your own experimental environment: it is hard to imagine how these same processes could have been isolated so cleanly in any other setting.

In addition to building lab-like experiments, researchers can also build experiments that are more field-like. For example, Centola (2010) built a digital field experiment to study the effect of social network structure on the spread of behavior. His research question required him to observe the same behavior spreading in populations that had different social network structures but were otherwise indistinguishable. The only way to do this was with a bespoke, custom-built experiment. In this case, Centola built a web-based health community.

Centola recruited about 1,500 participants through advertising on health websites. When participants arrived at the online community—which was called the Healthy Lifestyle Network—they provided informed consent and were then assigned "health buddies." Because of the way Centola assigned these health buddies, he was able to knit together different social network structures in different groups. Some groups were built to have random networks (where everyone was equally likely to be connected), while others were built to have clustered networks (where connections are more locally dense). Then, Centola introduced a new behavior into each network: the chance to register for a new website with additional health information. Whenever anyone signed up for this new website, all of her health buddies received an email announcing this behavior. Centola found that this behavior—signing up for the new website—spread further and faster in the clustered network than in the random network, a finding that was contrary to some existing theories.

Overall, building your own experiment gives you much more control; it enables you to construct the best possible environment to isolate what you want to study. It is hard to imagine how the two experiments that I have just described could have been performed in an already existing environment. Further, building your own system decreases ethical concerns around experimenting in existing systems. When you build your own experiment, however, you run into many of the problems that are encountered in lab experiments: recruiting participants and concerns about realism. A final downside is that building your own experiment can be costly and time-consuming, although, as these examples show, the experiments can range from relatively simple environments (such as the study of voting by Huber, Hill, and Lenz (2012)) to relatively complex environments (such as the study of networks and contagion by Centola (2010)).

4.5.3 Build your own product

> Building your own product is a high-risk, high-reward approach. But, if it works, you can benefit from a positive feedback loop that enables distinctive research.

Taking the approach of building your own experiment one step further, some researchers actually build their own products. These products attract users and then serve as platforms for experiments and other kinds of research. For example, a group of researchers at the University of Minnesota created MovieLens, which provides free, noncommercial personalized movie recommendations. MovieLens has operated continuously since 1997, and during this time 250,000 registered users have provided more than 20 million ratings of more than 30,000 movies (Harper and Konstan 2015). MovieLens has used the active community of users to conduct wonderful research ranging from testing social science theories about contributions to public goods (Beenen et al. 2004; Cosley et al. 2005; Chen et al. 2010; Ren et al. 2012) to addressing algorithmic challenges in recommendation systems (Rashid et al. 2002; Drenner et al. 2006; Harper, Sen, and Frankowski 2007; Ekstrand et al. 2015); for a full review, see Harper and Konstan (2015). Many of these experiments would not have been possible without researchers having complete control over a real working product.

Unfortunately, building your own product is incredibly difficult, and you should think of it like creating a start-up company: high-risk, high-reward. If successful, this approach offers much of the control that comes from building your own experiment with the realism and participants that come from working in existing systems. Further, this approach is potentially able to create a positive feedback loop where more research leads to a better product, which leads to more users, which leads to more researchers, and so on (figure 4.16). In other words, once a positive feedback loop kicks in, research should get easier and easier. Even though this approach is very difficult currently, my hope is that it will become more practical as technology improves. Until then, however, if a researcher want to control a product, the more direct strategy is to partner with a company, the topic I'll address next.

4.5.4 Partner with the powerful

Partnering can reduce costs and increase scale, but it can alter the kinds of participants, treatments, and outcomes that you can use.

The alternative to doing it yourself is partnering with a powerful organization such as a company, government, or NGO. The advantage of working with a partner is that they can enable you to run experiments that you just can't do by yourself. For example, one of the experiments that I'll tell you about below

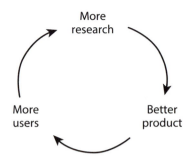

Figure 4.16: If you can successfully build your own product, you can benefit from a positive feedback loop: research leads to a better product, which leads to more users, which leads to even more research. These kinds of positive feedback loops are incredibly difficult to create, but they can enable research that would not be possible otherwise. MovieLens is an example of a research project that has succeeded in creating a positive feedback loop (Harper and Konstan 2015).

involved 61 million participants—no individual researcher could achieve that scale. At the same time that partnering increases what you can do, it also constrains you. For example, most companies will not allow you to run an experiment that could harm their business or their reputation. Working with partners also means that when it comes time to publish, you may come under pressure to "re-frame" your results, and some partners might even try to block the publication of your work if it makes them look bad. Finally, partnering also comes with costs related to developing and maintaining these collaborations.

The core challenge that has to be solved to make these partnerships successful is finding a way to balance the interests of both parties, and a helpful way to think about that balance is *Pasteur's Quadrant* (Stokes 1997). Many researchers think that if they are working on something practical— something that might be of interest to a partner—then they cannot be doing real science. This mindset will make it very difficult to create successful partnerships, and it also happens to be completely wrong. The problem with this way of thinking is wonderfully illustrated by the path-breaking research of the biologist Louis Pasteur. While working on a commercial fermentation project to convert beet juice into alcohol, Pasteur discovered a new class of microorganism that eventually led to the germ theory of disease. This discovery solved a very practical problem—it helped improve the process of fermentation—and it led to a major scientific advance. Thus, rather than thinking about research with practical applications as being in

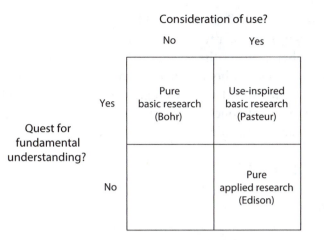

Figure 4.17: Pasteur's Quadrant (Stokes, 1997). Rather than thinking of research as either "basic" or "applied," it is better to think of it as motivated by use (or not) and seeking fundamental understanding (or not). An example of research that both is motivated by use and seeks fundamental understanding is Pasteur's work on converting beet juice into alcohol that lead to the germ theory of disease. This is the kind of work that is best suited for partnerships with the powerful. Examples of work that is motivated by use but that does not seek fundamental understanding come from Thomas Edison, and examples of work that is not motivated by use but that seeks understanding come from Niels Bohr. See Stokes (1997) for a more thorough discussion of this framework and each of these cases. Adapted from Stokes (1997), figure 3.5.

conflict with true scientific research, it is better to think of these as two separate dimensions. Research can be motivated by use (or not), and research can seek fundamental understanding (or not). Critically, some research—like Pasteur's—can be motivated by use and seeking fundamental understanding (figure 4.17). Research in Pasteur's Quadrant—research that inherently advances two goals—is ideal for collaborations between researchers and partners. Given that background, I'll describe two experimental studies with partnerships: one with a company and one with an NGO.

Large companies, particularly tech companies, have developed incredibly sophisticated infrastructure for running complex experiments. In the tech industry, these experiments are often called A/B tests because they compare the effectiveness of two treatments: A and B. Such experiments are frequently run for things like increasing click-through rates on ads, but the same experimental infrastructure can also be used for research that advances scientific understanding. An example that illustrates the potential of this kind of research is a study conducted by a partnership between researchers at Facebook and the University of California, San Diego, on the effects of different messages on voter turnout (Bond et al. 2012).

On November 2, 2010—the day of the US congressional elections—all 61 million Facebook users who lived in the United States and were 18 and older took part in an experiment about voting. Upon visiting Facebook, users were randomly assigned into one of three groups, which determined what banner (if any) was placed at the top of their News Feed (figure 4.18):

- a control group
- an informational message about voting with a clickable "I Voted" button and a counter (Info)
- an informational message about voting with a clickable "I Voted" button and a counter plus names and pictures of their friends who had already clicked the "I Voted" (Info + Social).

Bond and colleagues studied two main outcomes: reported voting behavior and actual voting behavior. First, they found that people in the Info + Social group were about two percentage points more likely than people in the Info group to click "I Voted" (about 20% versus 18%). Further, after the researchers merged their data with publicly available voting records for about six million people, they found that people in the Info + Social group were 0.39 percentage points more likely to actually vote than those in the control group and that people in the Info group were just as likely to vote as those in the control group (figure 4.18).

The results of this experiment show that some online get-out-the-vote messages are more effective than others and that a researcher's estimate of the effectiveness can depend on whether the outcome is reported voting or actual voting. This experiment unfortunately does not offer any clues about the mechanisms through which the social information—which some researchers have playfully called a "face pile"—increased voting. It could be that the social information increased the probability that someone noticed the banner or that it increased the probability that someone who noticed the banner actually voted or both. Thus, this experiment provides an interesting finding that further researchers will likely explore (see, e.g., Bakshy, Eckles, et al. (2012)).

In addition to advancing the goals of the researchers, this experiment also advanced the goal of the partner organization (Facebook). If you change the

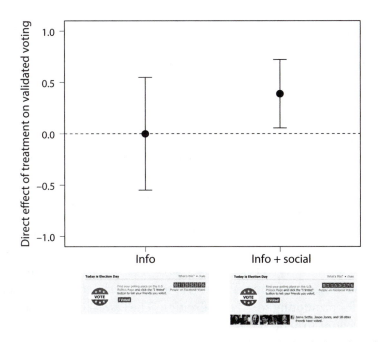

Figure 4.18: Results from a get-out-the-vote experiment on Facebook (Bond et al. 2012). Participants in the Info group voted at the same rate as those in the control group, but people in the Info + Social group voted at a slightly higher rate. Bars represent estimated 95% confidence intervals. Results in the graph are for the approximately six million participants who were matched to voting records. Adapted from Bond et al. (2012), figure 1.

behavior studied from voting to buying soap, then you can see that the study has the exact same structure as an experiment to measure the effect of online ads (see, e.g., Lewis and Rao (2015)). These ad effectiveness studies frequently measure the effect of exposure to online ads—the treatments in Bond et al. (2012) are basically ads for voting—on offline behavior. Thus, this research could advance Facebook's ability to study the effectiveness of online ads and could help Facebook convince potential advertisers that Facebook ads are effective at changing behavior.

Even though the interests of the researchers and partners were mostly aligned in this study, they were also partially in tension. In particular, the allocation of participants to the three groups—control, Info, and Info + Social—was tremendously imbalanced: 98% of the sample was assigned to Info + Social. This imbalanced allocation is inefficient statistically, and a much better allocation for the researchers would have had one-third of the participants in each group. But the imbalanced allocation happened because Facebook wanted everyone to receive the Info + Social treatment. Fortunately, the researchers convinced them to hold back 1% for a related treatment and 1% for a control group. Without the control group, it would have been basically impossible to measure the effect of the Info + Social treatment because it would have been a "perturb and observe" experiment rather than a randomized controlled experiment. This example provides a valuable practical lesson for working with partners: sometimes you create an experiment by convincing someone to deliver a treatment and sometimes you create an experiment by convincing someone not to deliver a treatment (i.e., to create a control group).

Partnership does not always need to involve tech companies and A/B tests with millions of participants. For example, Alexander Coppock, Andrew Guess, and John Ternovski (2016) partnered with an environmental NGO—the League of Conservation Voters—to run experiments testing different strategies for promoting social mobilization. The researchers used the NGO's Twitter account to send out both public tweets and private direct messages that attempted to prime different types of identities. They then measured which of these messages were most effective for encouraging people to sign a petition and retweet information about a petition.

Overall, partnering with the powerful enables to you operate at a scale that is otherwise hard to do, and table 4.3 provides other examples of partnerships between researchers and organizations. Partnering can be much easier than building your own experiment. But these advantages come with disadvantages: partnerships can limit the kinds of participants, treatments, and outcomes that you can study. Further, these partnerships can lead to ethical challenges. The best way to spot an opportunity for a partnership is to notice a real problem that you can solve while you are doing interesting science. If you are not used to this way of looking at the world, it can be hard to spot problems in Pasteur's Quadrant, but, with practice, you'll start to notice them more and more.

4.6 Advice

Whether you are doing things yourself or working with a partner, I'd like to offer four pieces of advice that I've found particularly helpful in my own

Table 4.3: Examples of Research that Comes through Partnership between Researchers and Organizations

Topic	References
Effect of Facebook News Feed on information sharing	Bakshy, Rosenn, et al. (2012)
Effect of partial anonymity on behavior on online dating website	Bapna et al. (2016)
Effect of Home Energy Reports on electricity usage	Allcott (2011, 2015); Allcott and Rogers (2014); Costa and Kahn (2013); Ayres, Raseman, and Shih (2013)
Effect of app design on viral spread	Aral and Walker (2011)
Effect of spreading mechanism on diffusion	Taylor, Bakshy, and Aral (2013)
Effect of social information in advertisements	Bakshy, Eckles, et al. (2012)
Effect of catalog frequency on sales through catalog and online for different types of customers	Simester et al. (2009)
Effect of popularity information on potential job applications	Gee (2015)
Effect of initial ratings on popularity	Muchnik, Aral, and Taylor (2013)
Effect of message content on political mobilization	Coppock, Guess, and Ternovski (2016)

Note: In some cases, the researchers work at the organizations.

work. The first two pieces of advice apply to any experiment, while the second two are much more specific to digital-age experiments.

My first piece of advice for when you are doing an experiment is that you should think as much as possible before any data have been collected. This probably seems obvious to researchers accustomed to running experiments, but it is very important for those accustomed to working with big data sources (see chapter 2). With such sources, most of the work is done *after* you have the data, but experiments are the opposite: most of the work should be done *before* you collect data. One of the best ways to force yourself to think carefully before you collect data is to create and register an pre-analysis plan for your experiment in which you basically describe the analysis that you will conduct (Schulz et al. 2010; Gerber et al. 2014; Simmons, Nelson, and Simonsohn 2011; Lin and Green 2016).

My second piece of general advice is that no single experiment is going to be perfect, and, because of that, you should consider designing a series of experiments that reinforce each other. I've heard this described as the *armada strategy*; rather than trying to build one massive battleship, you should build lots of smaller ships with complementary strengths. These kinds of multi-experiment studies are routine in psychology, but they are rare elsewhere. Fortunately, the low cost of some digital experiments makes multi-experiment studies easier.

Given that general background, I'd now like to offer two pieces of advice that are more specific to designing digital age experiments: create zero variable cost data (section 4.6.1) and build ethics into your design (section 4.6.2).

4.6.1 Create zero variable cost data

> The key to running large experiments is to drive your variable cost to zero. The best ways to do this are automation and designing enjoyable experiments.

Digital experiments can have dramatically different cost structures, and this enables researchers to run experiments that were impossible in the past. One way to think about this difference is to note that experiments generally have two types of costs: fixed costs and variable costs. *Fixed costs* are costs that remain unchanged regardless of of the number of participants. For example, in a lab experiment, fixed costs might be the costs of renting space and buying furniture. *Variable costs*, on the other hand, change depending on the number of participants. For example, in a lab experiment, variable costs might come from paying staff and participants. In general, analog experiments have low fixed costs and high variable costs, while digital experiments have high fixed costs and low variable costs (figure 4.19). Even though digital experiments have low variable costs, you can create a lot of exciting opportunities when you drive the variable cost all the way to zero.

There are two main elements of variable cost—payments to staff and payments to participants—and each of these can be driven to zero using different strategies. Payments to staff stem from the work that research

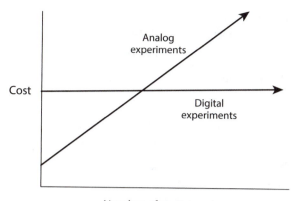

Figure 4.19: Schematic of cost structures in analog and digital experiments. In general, analog experiments have low fixed costs and high variable costs, whereas digital experiments have high fixed costs and low variable costs. The different cost structures mean that digital experiments can run at a scale that is not possible with analog experiments.

assistants do recruiting participants, delivering treatments, and measuring outcomes. For example, the analog field experiment of Schultz and colleagues (2007) on electricity usage required research assistants to travel to each home to deliver the treatment and read the electric meter (figure 4.3). All of this effort by research assistants meant that adding a new household to the study would have added to the cost. On the other hand, for the digital field experiment of Restivo and van de Rijt (2012) on the effect of awards on Wikipedia editors, researchers could add more participants at virtually no cost. A general strategy for reducing variable administrative costs is to replace human work (which is expensive) with computer work (which is cheap). Roughly, you can ask yourself: Can this experiment run while everyone on my research team is sleeping? If the answer is yes, you've done a great job of automation.

The second main type of variable cost is payments to participants. Some researchers have used Amazon Mechanical Turk and other online labor markets to decrease the payments that are needed for participants. To drive variable costs all the way to zero, however, a different approach is needed. For a long time, researchers have designed experiments that are so boring they have to pay people to participate. But what if you could create an experiment that people want to be in? This may sound far-fetched, but I'll give you an example below from my own work, and there are more

Table 4.4: Examples of Experiments with Zero Variable Cost that Compensated Participants with a Valuable Service or an Enjoyable Experience

Compensation	References
Website with health information	Centola (2010)
Exercise program	Centola (2011)
Free music	Salganik, Dodds, and Watts (2006); Salganik and Watts (2008, 2009b)
Fun game	Kohli et al. (2012)
Movie recommendations	Harper and Konstan (2015)

examples in table 4.4. Note that this idea of designing enjoyable experiments echoes some of the themes in chapter 3 regarding designing more enjoyable surveys and in chapter 5 regarding the design of mass collaboration. Thus, I think that participant enjoyment—what might also be called user experience—will be an increasingly important part of research design in the digital age.

If you want to create experiments with zero variable costs, you'll need to ensure that everything is fully automated and that participants don't require any payment. In order to show how this is possible, I'll describe my dissertation research on the success and failure of cultural products.

My dissertation was motivated by the puzzling nature of success for cultural products. Hit songs, best-selling books, and blockbuster movies are much, much more successful than average. Because of this, the markets for these products are often called "winner-take-all" markets. Yet, at the same time, which particular song, book, or movie will become successful is incredibly unpredictable. The screenwriter William Goldman (1989) elegantly summed up lots of academic research by saying that, when it comes to predicting success, "nobody knows anything." The unpredictability of winner-take-all markets made me wonder how much of success is a result of quality and how much is just luck. Or, expressed slightly differently, if we could create parallel worlds and have them all evolve independently, would the same songs become popular in each world? And, if not, what might be a mechanism that causes these differences?

In order to answer these questions, we—Peter Dodds, Duncan Watts (my dissertation advisor), and I—ran a series of online field experiments. In

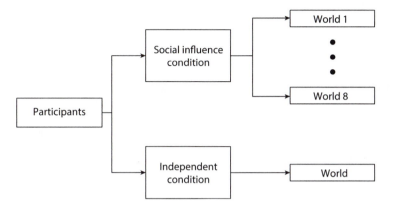

listen ★ rate ★ download ★ MUSIC LAB

Figure 4.20: An example of banner ad that my colleagues and I used to recruit participants for the MusicLab experiments (Salganik, Dodds, and Watts 2006). Reproduced by permission from Salganik (2007), figure 2.12.

Figure 4.21: Experimental design for the MusicLab experiments (Salganik, Dodds, and Watts 2006). Participants were randomly assigned to one of two conditions: independent and social influence. Participants in the independent condition made their choices without any information about what other people had done. Participants in the social influence condition were randomly assigned to one of eight parallel worlds, where they could see the popularity—as measured by downloads of previous participants—of each song in their world, but they could not see any information about, nor did they even know about the existence of, any of the other worlds. Adapted from Salganik, Dodds, and Watts (2006), figure s1.

particular, we built a website called MusicLab where people could discover new music, and we used it for a series of experiments. We recruited participants by running banner ads on a teen-interest website (figure 4.20) and through mentions in the media. Participants arriving at our website provided informed consent, completed a short background questionnaire, and were randomly assigned to one of two experimental conditions—independent and social influence. In the independent condition, participants made decisions about which songs to listen to, given only the names of the bands and the songs. While listening to a song, participants were asked to rate it after which they had the opportunity (but not the obligation) to download the song. In the social influence condition, participants had the same experience, except they could also see how many times each song had been downloaded

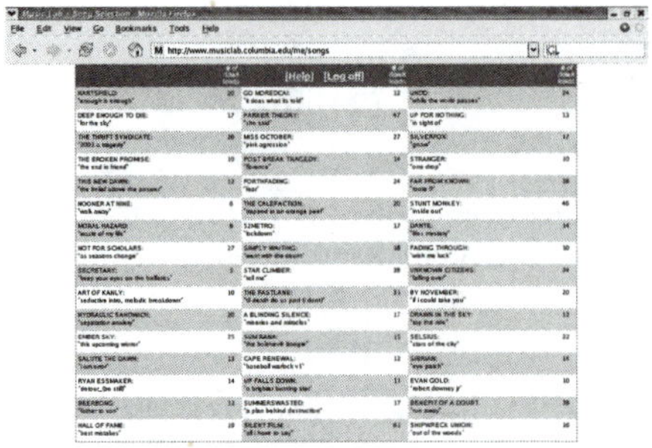

Experiment 1
Social influence condition

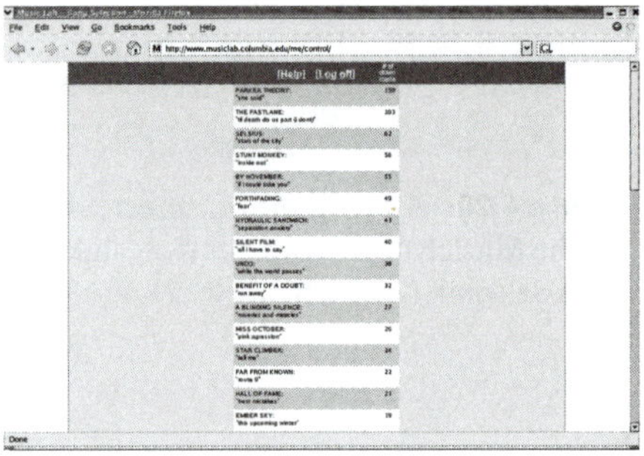

Experiment 2
Social influence condition

Figure 4.22: Screenshots from the social influence conditions in the MusicLab experiments (Salganik, Dodds, and Watts 2006). In the social influence condition in experiment 1, the songs, along with the number of previous downloads, were presented to the participants arranged in a 16×3 rectangular grid, where the positions of the songs were randomly assigned for each participant. In experiment 2, participants in the social influence condition were shown the songs, with download counts, presented in one column in descending order of current popularity. Reproduced by permission from Salganik (2007), figures 2.7 and 2.8.

by previous participants. Furthermore, participants in the social influence condition were randomly assigned to one of eight parallel worlds, each of which evolved independently (figure 4.21). Using this design, we ran two related experiments. In the first, we presented the songs in an unsorted grid, which provided a weak signal of popularity. In the second experiment, we presented the songs in a ranked list, which provided a much stronger signal of popularity (figure 4.22).

We found that the popularity of the songs differed across the worlds, suggesting that luck played an important role in success. For example, in one world the song "Lockdown" by 52Metro came in 1st out of 48 songs, while in another world it came in 40th. This was exactly the same song competing against all the same other songs, but in one world it got lucky and in the others it did not. Further, by comparing results across the two experiments, we found that social influence increases the winner-take-all nature of these markets, which perhaps suggests the importance of skill. But, looking across the worlds (which can't be done outside of this kind of parallel worlds experiment), we found that social influence actually increased the importance of luck. Further, surprisingly, it was the songs of highest appeal where luck mattered most (figure 4.23).

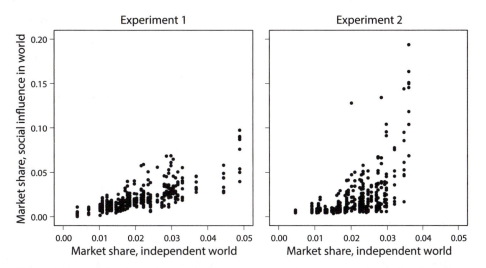

Figure 4.23: Results from the MusicLab experiments showing the relationship between appeal and success (Salganik, Dodds, and Watts 2006). The *x*-axis is the market share of the song in the independent world, which serves as a measure of the appeal of the song, and the *y*-axis is the market share of the same song in the eight social influence worlds, which serves as a measure of the success of the songs. We found that increasing the social influence that participants experienced—specifically, the change in layout from experiment 1 to experiment 2 (figure 4.22)—caused success to become more unpredictable, especially for the songs with the highest appeal. Adapted from Salganik, Dodds, and Watts (2006), figure 3.

MusicLab was able to run at essentially zero variable cost because of the way that it was designed. First, everything was fully automated so it was able to run while I was sleeping. Second, the compensation was free music, so there was no variable participant compensation cost. The use of music as compensation also illustrates how there is sometimes a trade-off between fixed and variable costs. Using music increased the fixed costs because I had to spend time securing permission from the bands and preparing reports for them about participants' reaction to their music. But in this case, increasing fixed costs in order to decrease variables costs was the right thing to do; that's what enabled us to run an experiment that was about 100 times larger than a standard lab experiment.

Further, the MusicLab experiments show that zero variable cost does not have to be an end in itself; rather, it can be a means to running a new kind of experiment. Notice that we did not use all of our participants to run a standard social influence lab experiment 100 times. Instead, we did something different, which you could think of as switching from a psychological experiment to a sociological one (Hedström 2006). Rather than focusing on individual decision-making, we focused our experiment on popularity, a collective outcome. This switch to a collective outcome meant that we required about 700 participants to produce a single data point (there were 700 people in each of the parallel worlds). That scale was only possible because of the cost structure of the experiment. In general, if researchers want to study how collective outcomes arise from individual decisions, group experiments such as MusicLab are very exciting. In the past, they have been logistically difficult, but those difficulties are fading because of the possibility of zero variable cost data.

In addition to illustrating the benefits of zero variable cost data, the MusicLab experiments also show a challenge with this approach: high fixed costs. In my case, I was extremely lucky to be able to work with a talented web developer named Peter Hausel for about six months to construct the experiment. This was only possible because my advisor, Duncan Watts, had received a number of grants to support this kind of research. Technology has improved since we built MusicLab in 2004, so it would be much easier to build an experiment like this now. But high fixed cost strategies are really only possible for researchers who can somehow cover those costs.

In conclusion, digital experiments can have dramatically different cost structures than analog experiments. If you want to run really large experiments, you should try to decrease your variable cost as much as possible and ideally all the way to zero. You can do this by automating the mechanics of your experiment (e.g., replacing human time with computer time) and designing experiments that people want to be in. Researchers who can design experiments with these features will be able to run new kinds of experiments that were not possible in the past. However, the ability to create zero variable cost experiments can raise new ethical questions, the topic that I shall now address.

4.6.2 Build ethics into your design: replace, refine, and reduce

Make your experiment more humane by replacing experiments with non-experimental studies, refining the treatments, and reducing the number of participants.

The second piece of advice that I'd like to offer about designing digital experiments concerns ethics. As the Restivo and van de Rijt experiment on barnstars in Wikipedia shows, decreased cost means that ethics will become an increasingly important part of research design. In addition to the ethical frameworks guiding human subjects research that I'll describe in chapter 6, researchers designing digital experiments can also draw on ethical ideas from a different source: the ethical principles developed to guide experiments involving animals. In particular, in their landmark book *Principles of Humane Experimental Technique*, Russell and Burch (1959) proposed three principles that should guide animal research: replace, refine, and reduce. I'd like to propose that these three R's can also be used—in a slightly modified form—to guide the design of human experiments. In particular,

- Replace: Replace experiments with less invasive methods if possible.
- Refine: Refine the treatment to make it as harmless as possible.
- Reduce: Reduce the number of participants in your experiment as much as possible.

In order to make these three R's concrete and show how they can potentially lead to better and more humane experimental design, I'll describe an online field experiment that generated ethical debate. Then, I'll describe how the three R's suggest concrete and practical changes to the design of the experiment.

One of the most ethically debated digital field experiments was conducted by Adam Kramer, Jamie Guillory, and Jeffrey Hancock (2014) and has come to be called "Emotional Contagion." The experiment took place on Facebook and was motivated by a mix of scientific and practical questions. At the time, the dominant way that users interacted with Facebook was the News Feed, an algorithmically curated set of Facebook status updates from a user's Facebook friends. Some critics of Facebook had suggested that because the News Feed has mostly positive posts—friends showing off their latest party—it could cause users to feel sad because their lives seemed less exciting in comparison. On the other hand, maybe the effect is exactly the opposite: maybe seeing your friend having a good time would make you feel happy. In order to address these competing hypotheses—and to advance our understanding of how a person's emotions are impacted by

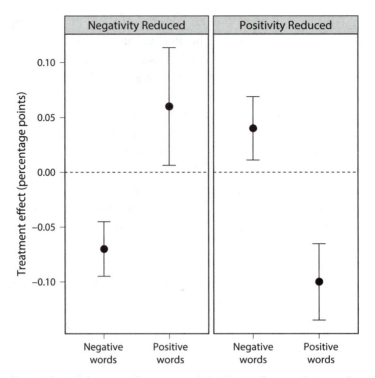

Figure 4.24: Evidence of emotional contagion (Kramer, Guillory, and Hancock 2014). Participants in the negativity-reduced condition used fewer negative words and more positive words, and participants in the positivity-reduced condition used more negative words and fewer positive words. Bars represent estimated standard errors. Adapted from Kramer, Guillory, and Hancock (2014), figure 1.

her friends' emotions—Kramer and colleagues ran an experiment. They placed about 700,000 users into four groups for one week: a "negativity-reduced" group, for whom posts with negative words (e.g., "sad") were randomly blocked from appearing in the News Feed; a "positivity-reduced" group, for whom posts with positive words (e.g., "happy") were randomly blocked; and two control groups. In the control group for the "negativity-reduced" group, posts were randomly blocked at the same rate as those in the "negativity-reduced" group, but without regard to the emotional content. The control group for the "positivity-reduced" group was constructed in a parallel fashion. The design of this experiment illustrates that the appropriate control group is not always one with no changes. Rather, sometimes, the control group receives a treatment in order to create the precise comparison that a research question requires. In all cases, the posts that were blocked from the News Feed were still available to users through other parts of the Facebook website.

Kramer and colleagues found that for participants in the positivity-reduced condition, the percentage of positive words in their status updates decreased and the percentage of negative words increased. On the other hand, for participants in the negativity-reduced condition, the percentage of positive words increased and that of negative words decreased (figure 4.24). However, these effects were quite small: the difference in positive and negative words between treatments and controls was about 1 in 1,000 words.

Before discussing the ethical issues raised by this experiment, I'd like to describe three scientific issues using some of the ideas from earlier in the chapter. First, it is not clear how the actual details of the experiment connect to the theoretical claims; in other words, there are questions about construct validity. It is not clear that the positive and negative word counts are actually a good indicator of the emotional state of participants, because (1) it is not clear that the words that people post are a good indicator of their emotions and (2) it is not clear that the particular sentiment analysis technique that the researchers used is able to reliably infer emotions (Beasley and Mason 2015; Panger 2016). In other words, there might be a bad measure of a biased signal. Second, the design and analysis of the experiment tells us nothing about who was most impacted (i.e., there is no analysis of heterogeneity of treatment effects) and what the mechanism might be. In this case, the researchers had lots of information about the participants, but they were essentially treated as widgets in the analysis. Third, the effect size in this experiment was very small; the difference between the treatment and control conditions is about 1 in 1,000 words. In their paper, Kramer and colleagues make the case that an effect of this size is important because hundreds of millions of people access their News Feed each day. In other words, they argue that even if effects are small for each person, they are big in aggregate. Even if you were to accept this argument, it is still not clear if an effect of this size is important regarding the more general scientific question about the spread of emotions (Prentice and Miller 1992).

In addition to these scientific questions, just days after this paper was published in *Proceedings of the National Academy of Sciences*, there was an enormous outcry from both researchers and the press (I'll describe the arguments in this debate in more detail in chapter 6). The issues raised in this debate caused the journal to publish a rare "editorial expression of concern" about the ethics and the ethical review process for the research (Verma 2014).

Given that background about Emotional Contagion, I would now like to show that the three R's can suggest concrete, practical improvements for real studies (whatever you might personally think about the ethics of this particular experiment). The first R is *replace*: researchers should seek to replace experiments with less invasive and risky techniques, if possible. For example, rather than running a randomized controlled experiment, the researchers could have exploited a *natural experiment*. As described in chapter 2, natural experiments are situations where something happens in the world that approximates the random assignment of treatments (e.g., a lottery to decide who will be drafted into the military). The ethical advantage of a natural experiment is that the researcher does not have to deliver treatments: the environment does that for you. For example, almost concurrently with the Emotional Contagion experiment, Coviello et al. (2014) were exploiting what could be called an Emotional Contagion natural experiment. Coviello and colleagues discovered that people post more negative words and fewer positive words on days where it is raining. Therefore, by using random variation in the weather, they were able to study the effect of changes in the News Feed without the need to intervene at all. It was as if the weather was running their experiment for them. The details of their procedure are a bit complicated, but the most important point for our purposes here is that by using a natural experiment, Coviello and colleagues were able to learn about the spread of emotions without the need to run their own experiment.

The second of the three Rs is *refine*: researchers should seek to refine their treatments to make them as harmless as possible. For example, rather than blocking content that was either positive or negative, the researchers could have boosted content that was positive or negative. This boosting design would have changed the emotional content of participants' News Feeds, but it would have addressed one of the concerns that critics expressed: that the experiments could have caused participants to miss important information in their News Feed. With the design used by Kramer and colleagues, a message that is important is as likely to be blocked as one that is not. However, with a boosting design, the messages that would be displaced would be those that are less important.

Finally, the third R is *reduce*: researchers should seek to reduce the number of participants in their experiment to the minimum needed to achieve their scientific objective. In analog experiments, this happened naturally because of the high variable costs of participants. But in digital experiments, particularly those with zero variable cost, researchers don't face a cost constraint on the size of their experiment, and this has the potential to lead to unnecessarily large experiments.

For example, Kramer and colleagues could have used pre-treatment information about their participants—such as pre-treatment posting behavior—to make their analysis more efficient. More specifically, rather than comparing the proportion of positive words in the treatment and control conditions, Kramer and colleagues could have compared the *change* in the proportion of positive words between conditions; an approach that is sometimes called a mixed design (figure 4.5) and sometimes called a difference-in-differences estimator. That is, for each participant, the researchers could have created a change score (post-treatment behavior—pre-treatment behavior) and then compared the change scores of participants in the treatment and control conditions. This difference-in-differences approach is more efficient statistically, which means that researchers can achieve the same statistical confidence using much smaller samples.

Without having the raw data, it is difficult to know exactly how much more efficient a difference-in-differences estimator would have been in this case. But we can look at other related experiments for a rough idea. Deng et al. (2013) reported that by using a form of the difference-in-differences estimator, they were able to reduce the variance of their estimates by about 50% in three different online experiments; similar results have been reported by Xie and Aurisset (2016). This 50% variance reduction means that the Emotional Contagion researchers might have been able to cut their sample in half if they had used a slightly different analysis method. In other words, with a tiny change in the analysis, 350,000 people might have been spared participation in the experiment.

At this point, you might be wondering why researchers should care if 350,000 people were in Emotional Contagion unnecessarily. There are two particular features of Emotional Contagion that make concern with excessive size appropriate, and these features are shared by many digital field experiments: (1) there is uncertainty about whether the experiment will cause harm to at least some participants and (2) participation was not voluntary.

It seems reasonable to try to keep experiments that have these features as small as possible.

To be clear, the desire to reduce the size of your experiments does not mean that you should not run large, zero variable cost experiments. It just means that your experiments should not be any larger than you need to achieve your scientific objective. One important way to make sure that an experiment is appropriately sized is to conduct a *power analysis* (Cohen 1988). In the the analog age, researchers generally did power analysis to make sure that their study was not too small (i.e., under-powered). Now, however, researchers should do power analysis to make sure that their study is not too big (i.e., over-powered).

In conclusion, the three R's—replace, refine, and reduce—provide principles that can help researchers build ethics into their experimental designs. Of course, each of these possible changes to Emotional Contagion introduces trade-offs. For example, evidence from natural experiments is not always as clean as that from randomized experiments, and boosting content might have been logistically more difficult to implement than blocking content. So, the purpose of suggesting these changes was not to second-guess the decisions of other researchers. Rather, it was to illustrate how the three R's could be applied in a realistic situation. In fact, the issue of trade-offs comes up all the time in research design, and in the digital-age, these trade-offs will increasingly involve ethical considerations. Later, in chapter 6, I'll offer some principles and ethical frameworks that can help researchers understand and discuss these trade-offs.

4.7 Conclusion

The digital age offers researchers the ability to run experiments that were not possible previously. Not only can researchers run massive experiments, they can also take advantage of the specific nature of digital experiments to improve validity, estimate heterogeneity of treatment effects, and isolate mechanisms. These experiments can be done in fully digital environments or using digital devices in the physical world.

As this chapter has shown, these experiments can be done in partnership with powerful companies, or they can be done entirely by the researcher; you don't need to work at a big tech company to run a digital experiment. If you do design your own experiment, you can drive your variable cost to zero, and you can use the three R's—replace, refine, and reduce—to build ethics into your design. Researchers' increasing power to intervene in the lives of millions of people means that we should have a corresponding increase in our attention to ethical research design. With great power comes great responsibility.

Mathematical notes

I think the best way to understand experiments is the *potential outcomes* framework (which I discussed in the mathematical notes in chapter 2). The potential outcomes framework has a close relationships to the ideas from design-based sampling that I described in chapter 3 (Aronow and Middleton 2013; Imbens and Rubin (2015), chapter 6). This appendix has been written in such a way as to emphasize that connection. This emphasis is a bit non-traditional, but I think that the connection between sampling and experiments is helpful: it means that if you know something about sampling, then you know something about experiments, and vice versa. As I'll show in these notes, the potential outcomes framework reveals the strength of randomized controlled experiments for estimating causal effects, and it shows the limitations of what can be done with even perfectly executed experiments.

In this appendix, I'll describe the potential outcomes framework, duplicating some of the material from the mathematical notes in chapter 2 in order to make these notes more self-contained. Then I'll describe some helpful results about the precision of estimates of the average treatment effects, including a discussion of optimal allocation and difference-in-differences estimators. This appendix draws heavily on Gerber and Green (2012).

Potential outcomes framework

In order to illustrate the potential outcomes framework, let's return to Restivo and van de Rijt's experiment to estimate the the effect of receiving a barnstar on future contributions to Wikipedia. The potential outcomes framework has three main elements: *units*, *treatments*, and *potential outcomes*. In the case of Restivo and van de Rijt, the *units* were deserving editors—those in the top 1% of contributors—who had not yet received a barnstar. We can index these editors by $i = 1 \ldots N$. The *treatments* in their

Table 4.5: Table of Potential Outcomes

Person	Edits in treatment condition	Edits in control condition	Treatment effect
1	$Y_1(1)$	$Y_1(0)$	τ_1
2	$Y_2(1)$	$Y_2(0)$	τ_2
⋮	⋮	⋮	⋮
N	$Y_N(1)$	$Y_N(0)$	τ_N
Mean	$\bar{Y}(1)$	$\bar{Y}(0)$	$\bar{\tau}$

experiment were "barnstar" or "no barnstar," and I'll write $W_i = 1$ if person i is in the treatment condition and $W_i = 0$ otherwise. The third element of the potential outcomes framework is the most important: the *potential outcomes*. These are bit more conceptually difficult, because they involve "potential" outcomes—things that could happen. For each Wikipedia editor, one can imagine the number of edits that she would make in the treatment condition ($Y_i(1)$) and the number that she would make in the control condition ($Y_i(0)$).

Note that this choice of units, treatments, and outcomes defines what can be learned from this experiment. For example, without any additional assumptions, Restivo and van de Rijt cannot say anything about the effects of barnstars on all Wikipedia editors or on outcomes such as edit quality. In general, the choice of units, treatments, and outcomes must be based on the goals of the study.

Given these potential outcomes—which are summarized in table 4.5—one can define the causal effect of the treatment for person i as

$$\tau_i = Y_i(1) - Y_i(0) \tag{4.1}$$

To me, this equation is the clearest way to define a causal effect, and although extremely simple, this framework turns out to generalizable in many important and interesting ways (Imbens and Rubin 2015).

If we define causality in this way, however, we run into a problem. In almost all cases, we don't get to observe both potential outcomes. That is, a specific Wikipedia editor either received a barnstar or not. Therefore, we observe one of the potential outcomes—$Y_i(1)$ or $Y_i(0)$—but not both. The inability to observe both potential outcomes is such a major problem that Holland (1986) called it the *Fundamental Problem of Causal Inference.*

Fortunately, when we are doing research, we don't just have one person, we have many people, and this offers a way around the Fundamental Problem of Causal Inference. Rather than attempting to estimate the individual-level treatment effect, we can estimate the average treatment effect:

$$\text{ATE} = \frac{1}{N} \sum_{i=1}^{N} \tau_i \tag{4.2}$$

This is still expressed in terms of the τ_i, which are unobservable, but with some algebra (eq. 2.8 of Gerber and Green (2012)), we get

$$\text{ATE} = \frac{1}{N} \sum_{i=1}^{N} Y_i(1) - \frac{1}{N} \sum_{i=1}^{N} Y_i(0) \tag{4.3}$$

This shows that if we can estimate the population average outcome under treatment $(N^{-1} \sum_{i=1}^{N} Y_i(1))$ and the population average outcome under control $(N^{-1} \sum_{i=1}^{N} Y_i(0))$, then we can estimate the average treatment effect, even without estimating the treatment effect for any particular person.

Now that I've defined our estimand—the thing we are trying to estimate— I'll turn to how we can actually estimate it with data. I like to think about this estimation challenge as a sampling problem (think back to the mathematical notes in chapter 3). Imagine that we randomly pick some people to observe in the treatment condition, and we randomly pick some people to observe in the control condition; then we can estimate the average outcome in each condition:

$$\widehat{\text{ATE}} = \underbrace{\frac{1}{N_t} \sum_{i:W_i=1} Y_i(1)}_{\text{average edits, treatment}} - \underbrace{\frac{1}{N_c} \sum_{i:W_i=0} Y_i(0)}_{\text{average edits, control}} \tag{4.4}$$

where N_t and N_c are the numbers of people in the treatment and control conditions. Equation 4.4 is a difference-of-means estimator. Because of the sampling design, we know that the first term is an unbiased estimator for the average outcome under treatment and the second term is an unbiased estimator under control.

Another way to think about what randomization enables is that it ensures that the comparison between treatment and control groups is fair because randomization ensures that the two groups will resemble each other. This resemblance holds for things we have measured (say the number of edits in the 30 days before the experiment) and the things we have not measured (say gender). This ability to ensure balance on both *observed* and *unobserved* factors is critical. To see the power of automatic balancing on unobserved factors, let's imagine that future research finds that men are more responsive to awards than women. Would that invalidate the results of Restivo and van de Rijt's experiment? No. By randomizing, they ensured that all unobservables would be balanced, in expectation. This protection against the unknown is very powerful, and it is an important way that experiments are different from the non-experimental techniques described in chapter 2.

In addition to defining the treatment effect for an entire population, it is possible to define a treatment effect for a subset of people. This is typically called a *conditional average treatment effect* (CATE). For example, in the study by Restivo and van de Rijt, let's imagine that X_i is whether the editor was above or below the median number of edits during the 90 days before the experiment. One could calculate the treatment effect separately for these light and heavy editors.

The potential outcomes framework is a powerful way to think about causal inference and experiments. However, there are two additional complexities that you should keep in mind. These two complexities are often lumped together under the term *Stable Unit Treatment Value Assumption* (SUTVA). The first part of SUTVA is the assumption that the only thing that matters for person i's outcome is whether that person was in the treatment or control condition. In other words, it is assumed that person i is not impacted by the treatment given to other people. This is sometimes called "no interference" or "no spillovers" and can be written as

$$Y_i(W_i, \mathbf{W_{-i}}) = Y_i(W_i) \quad \forall\, \mathbf{W_{-i}} \tag{4.5}$$

where $\mathbf{W_{-i}}$ is a vector of treatment statuses for everyone except person i. One way that this can be violated is if the treatment from one person spills over onto another person, either positively or negatively. Returning to Restivo and van de Rijt's experiment, imagine two friends i and j and that person i receives a barnstar and j does not. If i receiving the barnstar causes j to edit more (out of a sense of competition) or edit less (out of a sense of despair), then SUTVA has been violated. It can also be violated if the impact of the treatment depends on the total number of other people receiving the treatment. For example, if Restivo and van de Rijt had given out 1,000 or 10,000 barnstars instead of 100, this might have impacted the effect of receiving a barnstar.

The second issue lumped into SUTVA is the assumption that the only relevant treatment is the one that the researcher delivers; this assumption is sometimes called *no hidden treatments* or *excludability*. For example, in Restivo and van de Rijt, it might have been the case that by giving a barnstar the researchers caused editors to be featured on a popular editors page and that it was being on the popular editors page—rather than receiving a barnstar—that caused the change in editing behavior. If this is true, then the effect of the barnstar is not distinguishable from the effect of being on the popular editors page. Of course, it is not clear if, from a scientific perspective, this should be considered attractive or unattractive. That is, you could imagine a researcher saying that the effect of receiving a barnstar includes all the subsequent treatments that the barnstar triggers. Or you could imagine a situation where a researcher would want to isolate the effect of barnstars from all these other things. One way to think about it is to ask if there is anything that leads to what Gerber and Green (2012, p. 41) call a "breakdown in symmetry"? In other words, is there anything other than the treatment that causes people in the treatment and control conditions to be treated differently? Concerns about symmetry breaking are what lead patients in control groups in medical trials to take a placebo pill. That way, researchers can be sure that the only difference between the two conditions is the actual medicine and not the experience of taking the pill.

For more on SUTVA, see section 2.7 of Gerber and Green (2012), section 2.5 of Morgan and Winship (2014), and section 1.6 of Imbens and Rubin (2015).

Precision

In the previous section, I've described how to estimate the average treatment effect. In this section, I'll provide some ideas about the variability of those estimates.

If you think about estimating the average treatment effect as estimating the difference between two sample means, then it is possible to show that the standard error of the average treatment effect is (see Gerber and Green (2012), eq. 3.4)

$$
\text{SE}(\widehat{\text{ATE}}) = \sqrt{\frac{1}{N-1}\left[\frac{m\,\text{Var}\big(Y_i(0)\big)}{N-m} + \frac{(N-m)\,\text{Var}\big(Y_i(1)\big)}{m} + 2\,\text{Cov}\big(Y_i(0),\,Y_i(1)\big)\right]}
\tag{4.6}
$$

where m people were assigned to treatment and $N - m$ to control. Thus, when thinking about how many people to assign to treatment and how many to control, you can see that if $\text{Var}\big(Y_i(0)\big) \approx \text{Var}\big(Y_i(1)\big)$, then you want $m \approx N/2$, as long as the costs of treatment and control are the same. Equation 4.6 clarifies why the design of Bond and colleagues' (2012) experiment about the effects of social information on voting (figure 4.18) was inefficient statistically. Recall that it had 98% of participants in the treatment condition. This meant that the mean behavior in the control condition was not estimated as accurately as it could have been, which in turn meant that the estimated difference between the treatment and control conditions was not estimated as accurately as it could have been. For more on optimal allocation of participants to conditions, including when costs differ between conditions, see List, Sadoff, and Wagner (2011).

Finally, in the main text, I described how a difference-in-differences estimator, which is typically used in a mixed design, can lead to smaller variance than a difference-in-means estimator, which is typically used in a between-subjects design. The quantity that we are trying to estimate with the difference-in-differences approach is

$$
\text{ATE}' = \frac{1}{N}\sum_{i=1}^{N}\big((Y_i(1) - X_i) - (Y_i(0) - X_i)\big)
\tag{4.7}
$$

The standard error of this quantity is (see Gerber and Green (2012), eq. 4.4)

$$
\text{SE}(\widehat{\text{ATE}'}) = \sqrt{\frac{1}{N-1}\left[\text{Var}\big(Y_i(0) - X_i\big) + \text{Var}\big(Y_i(1) - X_i\big) + 2\,\text{Cov}\big(Y_i(0) - X_i,\,Y_i(1) - X_i\big)\right]}
\tag{4.8}
$$

Comparison of eqs. 4.6 and 4.8 reveals that the difference-in-differences approach will have a smaller standard error when (see Gerber and Green (2012), eq. 4.6)

$$\frac{\mathrm{Cov}\left(Y_i(0), X_i\right)}{\mathrm{Var}(X_i)} + \frac{\mathrm{Cov}\left(Y_i(1), X_i\right)}{\mathrm{Var}(X_i)} > 1$$

Roughly, when X_i is very predictive of $Y_i(1)$ and $Y_i(0)$, then you can get more precise estimates from a difference-in-differences approach than from a difference-in-means one. One way to think about this in the context of Restivo and van de Rijt's experiment is that there is a lot of natural variation in the amount that people edit, so this makes comparing the treatment and control conditions difficult: it is hard to detect a relative small effect in noisy outcome data. But if you difference-out this naturally occurring variability, then there is much less variability, and that makes it easier to detect a small effect.

See Frison and Pocock (1992) for a precise comparison of difference-in-means, difference-in-differences, and analysis of covariance (ANCOVA) in the more general setting where there are multiple measurements pre-treatment and post-treatment. In particular, they strongly recommend AN-COVA, which I have not covered here. Further, see McKenzie (2012) for a discussion of the importance of multiple post-treatment outcome measures.

What to read next

- **Introduction (section 4.1)**

  Questions about causality in social research are often complex and intricate. For a foundational approach to causality based on causal graphs, see Pearl (2009), and for a foundational approach based on potential outcomes, see Imbens and Rubin (2015). For a comparison between these two approaches, see Morgan and Winship (2014). For a formal approach to defining a confounder, see VanderWeele and Shpitser (2013).

  In this chapter, I have created what seemed like a bright line between our ability to make causal estimates from experimental and non-experimental data. However, I think that, in reality, the distinction is more blurred. For example, everyone accepts that smoking causes cancer, even though no randomized controlled experiment that forces people to smoke has ever been done. For excellent book-length treatments on making causal estimates from non-experimental data, see Rosenbaum (2002), Rosenbaum (2010), Shadish, Cook, and Campbell (2001), and Dunning (2012).

Chapters 1 and 2 of Freedman, Pisani, and Purves (2007) offer a clear introduction to the differences between experiments, controlled experiments, and randomized controlled experiments.

Manzi (2012) provides a fascinating and readable introduction to the philosophical and statistical underpinnings of randomized controlled experiments. It also provides interesting real-world examples of the power of experimentation in business. Issenberg (2012) provides a fascinating introduction to the use of experimentation in political campaigns.

- ## What are experiments? (section 4.2)

Box, Hunter, and Hunter (2005), Casella (2008), and Athey and Imbens (2016b) provide good introductions to the statistical aspects of experimental design and analysis. Further, there are excellent treatments of the use of experiments in many different fields: economics (Bardsley et al. 2009), sociology (Willer and Walker 2007; Jackson and Cox 2013), psychology (Aronson et al. 1989), political science (Morton and Williams 2010), and social policy (Glennerster and Takavarasha 2013).

The importance of participant recruitment (e.g., sampling) is often underappreciated in experimental research. However, if the effect of the treatment is heterogeneous in the population, then sampling is critical. Longford (1999) makes this point clearly when he advocates for researchers thinking of experiments as a population survey with haphazard sampling.

- ## Two dimensions of experiments: lab–field and analog–digital (section 4.3)

I have suggested that there is a continuum between lab and field experiments, and other researchers have proposed more detailed typologies, in particular ones that separate the various forms of field experiments (Harrison and List 2004; Charness, Gneezy, and Kuhn 2013).

A number of papers have compared lab and field experiments in the abstract (Falk and Heckman 2009; Cialdini 2009) and in terms of outcomes of specific experiments in political science (Coppock and Green 2015), economics (Levitt and List 2007a, b; Camerer 2011; Al-Ubaydli and List 2013), and psychology (Mitchell 2012). Jerit, Barabas, and Clifford (2013) offer a nice research design for comparing results from lab and field experiments. Parigi et al. (2017) describe how online field experiments can combine some of the characteristics of lab and field experiments.

Concerns about participants changing their behavior because they know they are being closely observed are sometimes called *demand effects*, and they have been studied in psychology (Orne 1962) and economics (Zizzo 2010). Although mostly associated with lab experiments, these same issues can cause problems for field experiments as well. In fact, *demand effects* are also sometimes called

Hawthorne effects, a term that derives from the famous illumination experiments that began in 1924 at the Hawthorne Works of the Western Electric Company (Adair 1984; Levitt and List 2011). Both *demand effects* and *Hawthorne effects* are closely related to the idea of reactive measurement discussed in chapter 2 (see also Webb et al. (1966)).

Field experiments have a long history in economics (Levitt and List 2009), political science (Green and Gerber 2003; Druckman et al. 2006; Druckman and Lupia 2012), psychology (Shadish 2002), and public policy (Shadish and Cook 2009). One area of social science where field experiments quickly became prominent is international development. For a positive review of that work within economics, see Banerjee and Duflo (2009) and for a critical assessment, see Deaton (2010). For a review of this work in political science, see Humphreys and Weinstein (2009). Finally, the ethical challenges arising in field experiments have been explored in the context of political science (Humphreys 2015; Desposato 2016b) and development economics (Baele 2013).

In this section, I suggested that pre-treatment information can be used to improve the precision of estimated treatment effects, but there is some debate about this approach; see Freedman (2008), Lin (2013), Berk et al. (2013), and Bloniarz et al. (2016) for more information.

Finally, there are two other types of experiments performed by social scientists that don't fit neatly along the lab–field dimension: survey experiments and social experiments. *Survey experiments* are experiments using the infrastructure of existing surveys and compare responses to alternative versions of the same questions (some survey experiments are presented in chapter 3); for more on survey experiments, see Mutz (2011). *Social experiments* are experiments where the treatment is some social policy that can only be implemented by a government. Social experiments are closely related to program evaluation. For more on policy experiments, see Heckman and Smith (1995), Orr (1998), and Glennerster and Takavarasha (2013).

- **Moving beyond simple experiments (section 4.4)**

I've chosen to focus on three concepts: validity, heterogeneity of treatment effects, and mechanisms. These concepts have different names in different fields. For example, psychologists tend to move beyond simple experiments by focusing on *mediators* and *moderators* (Baron and Kenny 1986). The idea of mediators is captured by what I call mechanisms, and the idea of moderators is captured by what I call external validity (e.g., would the results of the experiment be different if it were run in different situations) and heterogeneity of treatment effects (e.g., are the effects larger for some people than for others).

The experiment by Schultz et al. (2007) shows how social theories can be used to design effective interventions. For a more general argument about the role of theory in designing effective interventions, see Walton (2014).

- **Validity (section 4.4.1)**

The concepts of internal and external validity were first introduced by Campbell (1957). See Shadish, Cook, and Campbell (2001) for a more detailed history and a careful elaboration of statistical conclusion validity, internal validity, construct validity, and external validity.

For an overview of issues related to statistical conclusion validity in experiments, see Gerber and Green (2012) (from a social science perspective) and Imbens and Rubin (2015) (from a statistical perspective). Some issues of statistical conclusion validity that arise specifically in online field experiments include issues such as computationally efficient methods for creating confidence intervals with dependent data (Bakshy and Eckles 2013).

Internal validity can be difficult to ensure in complex field experiments. See, for example, Gerber and Green (2000), Imai (2005), and Gerber and Green (2005) for debate about the implementation of a complex field experiment about voting. Kohavi et al. (2012, 2013) provide an introduction to the challenges of interval validity in online field experiments.

One major threat to internal validity is the possibility of failed randomization. One potential way to detect such problems is to compare the treatment and control groups on observable traits. This kind of comparison is called a *balance check*. See Hansen and Bowers (2008) for a statistical approach to balance checks and Mutz and Pemantle (2015) for concerns about balance checks. For example, using a balance check, Allcott (2011) found some evidence that randomization was not implemented correctly in three of the Opower experiments (see table 2; sites 2, 6, and 8). For other approaches, see chapter 21 of Imbens and Rubin (2015).

Other major concerns related to internal validity are (1) one-sided non-compliance, where not everyone in the treatment group actually received the treatment, (2) two sided noncompliance, where not everyone in the treatment group receives the treatment and some people in the control group receive the treatment, (3) attrition, where outcomes are not measured for some participants, and (4) interference, where the treatment spills over from people in the treatment condition to people in the control condition. See chapters 5, 6, 7, and 8 of Gerber and Green (2012) for more on each of these issues.

For more on construct validity, see Westen and Rosenthal (2003), and for more on construct validity in big data sources, Lazer (2015) and chapter 2 of this book.

One aspect of external validity is the setting in which an intervention is tested. Allcott (2015) provides a careful theoretical and empirical treatment of site selection bias. This issue is also discussed by Deaton (2010). Another aspect of external validity is whether alternative operationalizations of the same intervention will have similar effects. In this case, a comparison between Schultz et al. (2007) and Allcott (2011) shows that the Opower experiments had a smaller estimated treated effect than the original experiments by Schultz and colleagues (1.7% versus 5%). Allcott (2011) speculated that the follow-up experiments had a smaller effect because of the ways in which the treatment differed: a handwritten emoticon as part of a study sponsored by a university, compared with a printed emoticon as part of a mass-produced report from a power company.

- **Heterogeneity of treatment effects (section 4.4.2)**

For an excellent overview of heterogeneity of treatment effects in field experiments, see chapter 12 of Gerber and Green (2012). For introductions to heterogeneity of treatment effects in medical trials, see Kent and Hayward (2007), Longford (1999), and Kravitz, Duan, and Braslow (2004). Considerations of heterogeneity of treatment effects generally focus on differences based on pre-treatment characteristics. If you are interested in heterogeneity based on post-treatment outcomes, then more complex approaches are needed, such as principal stratification (Frangakis and Rubin 2002); see Page et al. (2015) for a review.

Many researchers estimate the heterogeneity of treatment effects using linear regression, but newer methods rely on machine learning; see, for example, Green and Kern (2012), Imai and Ratkovic (2013), Taddy et al. (2016), and Athey and Imbens (2016a).

There is some skepticism about findings of heterogeneity of effects because of multiple comparison problems and "fishing." There are a variety of statistical approaches that can help address concerns about multiple comparison (Fink, McConnell, and Vollmer 2014; List, Shaikh, and Xu 2016). One approach to concerns about "fishing" is pre-registration, which is becoming increasingly common in psychology (Nosek and Lakens 2014), political science (Humphreys, Sierra, and Windt 2013; Monogan 2013; Anderson 2013; Gelman 2013; Laitin 2013), and economics (Olken 2015).

In the study by Costa and Kahn (2013) only about half of the households in the experiment could be linked to the demographic information. Readers interested in these details should refer to the original paper.

- **Mechanisms (section 4.4.3)**

Mechanisms are incredibly important, but they turn out to be very difficult to study. Research about mechanisms is closely related to the study of mediators in psychology (but see also VanderWeele (2009) for a precise comparison between the two ideas). Statistical approaches to finding mechanisms, such as the approach developed in Baron and Kenny (1986), are quite common. Unfortunately, it turns out that those procedures depend on some strong assumptions (Bullock, Green, and Ha 2010) and suffer when there are multiple mechanisms, as one might expect in many situations (Imai and Yamamoto 2013; VanderWeele and Vansteelandt 2014). Imai et al. (2011) and Imai and Yamamoto (2013) offer some improved statistical methods. Further, VanderWeele (2015) offers a book-length treatment with a number of important results, including a comprehensive approach to sensitivity analysis.

A separate approach focuses on experiments that attempt to manipulate the mechanism directly (e.g., giving sailors vitamin C). Unfortunately, in many social science settings, there are often multiple mechanisms, and it is hard to design treatments that change one without changing the others. Some approaches to experimentally altering mechanisms are described by Imai, Tingley, and Yamamoto (2013), Ludwig, Kling, and Mullainathan (2011), and Pirlott and MacKinnon (2016).

Researchers running fully factorial experiments will need to be concerned about multiple hypothesis testing; see Fink, McConnell, and Vollmer (2014) and List, Shaikh, and Xu (2016) for more information.

Finally, mechanisms also have a long history in the philosophy of science, as described by Hedström and Ylikoski (2010).

- ## Using existing environments (section 4.5.1)

For more on the use of correspondence studies and audit studies to measure discrimination, see Pager (2007).

- ## Build your own experiment (section 4.5.2)

The most common way to recruit participants to experiments that you build is Amazon Mechanical Turk (MTurk). Because MTurk mimics aspects of traditional lab experiments—paying people to complete tasks that they would not do for free—many researchers have already begun using Turkers (the workers on MTurk) as experimental participants, resulting in faster and cheaper data collection than can be achieved in traditional on-campus laboratory experiments (Paolacci, Chandler, and Ipeirotis 2010; Horton, Rand, and Zeckhauser 2011; Mason and Suri 2012; Rand 2012; Berinsky, Huber, and Lenz 2012).

Generally, the biggest advantages of using participants recruited from MTurk are logistical. Whereas lab experiments can take weeks to run and field experiments can take months to set up, experiments with participants recruited from MTurk can be run in days. For example, Berinsky, Huber, and Lenz (2012) were able to recruit 400 subjects in a single day to participate in an eight-minute experiment. Further, these participants can be recruited for virtually any purpose (including surveys and mass collaboration, as discussed in chapters 3 and 5). This ease of recruitment means that researchers can run sequences of related experiments in rapid succession.

Before recruiting participants from MTurk for your own experiments, there are four important things that you need to know. First, many researchers have a nonspecific skepticism of experiments involving Turkers. Because this skepticism is not specific, it is hard to counter with evidence. However, after several years of studies using Turkers, we can now conclude that this skepticism is not particularly justified. There have been many studies comparing the demographics of Turkers with those of other populations and many studies comparing the results of experiments with Turkers with those from other populations. Given all this work, I think that the best way for you to think about it is that Turkers are a reasonable convenience sample, much like students but slightly more diverse (Berinsky, Huber, and Lenz 2012). Thus, just as students are a reasonable population for some, but not all, research, Turkers are a reasonable population for some, but not all, research. If you are going to work with Turkers, then it makes sense to read many of these comparative studies and understand their nuances.

Second, researchers have developed best practices for increasing the internal validity of MTurk experiments, and you should learn about and follow these best-practices (Horton, Rand, and Zeckhauser 2011; Mason and Suri 2012). For example, researchers using Turkers are encouraged to use screeners to remove inattentive participants (Berinsky, Margolis, and Sances 2014, 2016) (but see also D. J. Hauser and Schwarz (2015a, b)). If you don't remove inattentive participants, then any effect of the treatment can be washed out by the noise that they introduce, and in practice the number of inattentive participants can be substantial. In the experiment by Huber and colleagues (2012), about 30% of participants failed basic attention screeners. Other problems that commonly arise when Turkers are used are non-naive participants (Chandler et al. 2015) and attrition (Zhou and Fishbach 2016).

Third, relative to some other forms of digital experiments, MTurk experiments cannot scale; Stewart et al. (2015) estimate that at any given time there are only about 7,000 people on MTurk.

Finally, you should know that MTurk is a community with its own rules and norms (Mason and Suri 2012). In the same way that you would try to find out about the culture of a country where you were going to run your experiments, you should try to find out more about the culture and norms of Turkers (Salehi et al. 2015). And you should know that the Turkers will be talking about your experiment if you do something inappropriate or unethical (Gray et al. 2016).

MTurk is an incredibly convenient way to recruit participants to your experiments, whether they are lab-like, such as that of Huber, Hill, and Lenz (2012), or more field-like, such as those of Mason and Watts (2009), Goldstein, McAfee, and Suri (2013), Goldstein et al. (2014), Horton and Zeckhauser (2016), and Mao et al. (2016).

- **Build your own product (section 4.5.3)**

If you are thinking of trying to create your own product, I recommend that you read the advice offered by the MovieLens group in Harper and Konstan (2015). A key insight from their experience is that for each successful project there are many, many failures. For example, the MovieLens group launched other products, such as GopherAnswers, that were complete failures (Harper and Konstan 2015). Another example of a researcher failing while attempting to build a product is Edward Castronova's attempt to build an online game called Arden. Despite $250,000 in funding, the project was a flop (Baker 2008). Projects like GopherAnswers and Arden are unfortunately much more common than projects like MovieLens.

- **Partner with the powerful (section 4.5.4)**

  I've heard the idea of Pasteur's Quadrant discussed frequently at tech companies, and it helps organize research efforts at Google (Spector, Norvig, and Petrov 2012).

  Bond and colleagues' study (2012) also attempts to detect the effect of these treatments on the friends of those who received them. Because of the design of the experiment, these spillovers are difficult to detect cleanly; interested readers should see Bond et al. (2012) for a more thorough discussion. Jones and colleagues (2017) also conducted a very similar experiment during the 2012 election. These experiments are part of a long tradition of experiments in political science on efforts to encourage voting (Green and Gerber 2015). These get-out-the-vote experiments are common, in part because they are in Pasteur's Quadrant. That is, there are many people who are motivated to increase voting, and voting can be an interesting behavior to test more general theories about behavior change and social influence.

  For advice about running field experiments with partner organizations such as political parties, NGOs, and businesses, see Loewen, Rubenson, and Wantchekon (2010), List (2011), and Gueron (2002). For thoughts about how partnerships with organizations can impact research designs, see King et al. (2007) and Green, Calfano, and Aronow (2014). Partnership can also lead to ethical questions, as discussed by Humphreys (2015) and Nickerson and Hyde (2016).

- **Advice (section 4.6)**

  If you are going create an analysis plan before running your experiment, I suggest that you start by reading reporting guidelines. The CONSORT (Consolidated Standard Reporting of Trials) guidelines were developed in medicine (Schulz et al. 2010) and modified for social research (Mayo-Wilson et al. 2013). A related set of guidelines has been developed by the editors of the *Journal of Experimental Political Science* (Gerber et al. 2014) (see also Mutz and Pemantle (2015) and Gerber et al. (2015)). Finally, reporting guidelines have been developed in psychology (APA Working Group 2008), and see also Simmons, Nelson, and Simonsohn (2011).

  If you create an analysis plan, you should consider pre-registering it because pre-registration will increase the confidence that others have in your results. Further, if you are working with a partner, it will limit your partner's ability to change the analysis after seeing the results. Pre-registration is becoming increasingly common in psychology (Nosek and Lakens 2014), political science (Humphreys, Sierra, and Windt 2013; Monogan 2013; Anderson 2013; Gelman 2013; Laitin 2013), and economics (Olken 2015).

Design advice specifically for online field experiments is also presented in Konstan and Chen (2007) and Chen and Konstan (2015).

What I've called the armada strategy is sometimes called *programmatic research*; see Wilson, Aronson, and Carlsmith (2010).

- **Create zero variable cost data (section 4.6.1)**

For more on the MusicLab experiments, see Salganik, Dodds, and Watts (2006), Salganik and Watts (2008, 2009a, b), and Salganik (2007). For more on winner-take-all markets, see Frank and Cook (1996). For more on untangling luck and skill more generally, see Mauboussin (2012), Watts (2012), and Frank (2016).

There is another approach to eliminating participant payments that researchers should use with caution: conscription. In many online field experiments, participants are basically drafted into experiments and never compensated. Examples of this approach include Restivo and van de Rijt's (2012) experiment on rewards in Wikipedia and Bond and colleague's (2012) experiment on encouraging people to vote. These experiments don't really have zero variable cost—rather, they have zero variable cost *to researchers*. In such experiments, even if the cost to each participant is extremely small, the aggregate cost can be quite large. Researchers running massive online experiments often justify the importance of small estimated treatment effects by saying that these small effects can become important when applied to many people. The exact same thinking applies to costs that researchers impose on participants. If your experiment causes one million people to waste one minute, the experiment is not very harmful to any particular person, but in aggregate it has wasted almost two years of time.

Another approach to creating zero variable cost payment to participants is to use a lottery, an approach that has also been used in survey research (Halpern et al. 2011). For more about designing enjoyable user experiences, see Toomim et al. (2011). For more about using bots to create zero variable cost experiments, see Krafft, Macy, and Pentland (2016).

- **Replace, refine, and reduce (section 4.6.2)**

The three R's as originally proposed by Russell and Burch (1959) are as follows:

> "Replacement means the substitution for conscious living higher animals of insentient material. Reduction means reduction in the numbers of animals used to obtain information of a given amount and precision. Refinement means any decrease in the incidence or severity of inhumane procedures applied to those animals which still have to be used."

The three R's that I propose don't override the ethical principles described in chapter 6. Rather, they are a more elaborated version of one of those principles—beneficence—specifically in the setting of human experiments.

In terms of the first R ("replacement"), comparing the emotional contagion experiment (Kramer, Guillory, and Hancock 2014) and the emotional contagion natural experiment (Coviello et al. 2014) offers some general lessons about the trade-offs involved in moving from experiments to natural experiments (and other approaches like matching that attempt to approximate experiments in non-experimental data; see chapter 2). In addition to the ethical benefits, switching from experimental to non-experimental studies also enables researchers to study treatments that they are logistically unable to deploy. These ethical and logistical benefits come at a cost, however. With natural experiments, researchers have less control over things like recruitment of participants, randomization, and the nature of the treatment. For example, one limitation of rainfall as a treatment is that it both increases positivity and decreases negativity. In the experimental study, however, Kramer and colleagues were able to adjust positivity and negativity independently. The particular approach used by Coviello et al. (2014) was further elaborated by Coviello, Fowler, and Franceschetti (2014). For an introduction to instrumental variables, which is the approach used by Coviello et al. (2014), see Angrist and Pischke (2009) (less formal) or Angrist, Imbens, and Rubin (1996) (more formal). For a skeptical appraisal of instrumental variables, see Deaton (2010), and for an introduction to instrumental variables with weak instruments (rain is a weak instrument), see Murray (2006). More generally, a good introduction to natural experiments is given by Dunning (2012), while Rosenbaum (2002), Rosenbaum (2010), and Shadish, Cook, and Campbell (2001) offer good ideas about estimating causal effects without experiments.

In terms of the second R ("refinement"), there are scientific and logistical trade-offs when considering changing the design of Emotional Contagion from blocking posts to boosting posts. For example, it may be the case that the technical implementation of the News Feed makes it substantially easier to do an experiment in which posts are blocked rather than one in which they are boosted (note that an experiment involving blocking of posts could be implemented as a layer on top of the News Feed system without any need for alterations of the underlying system). Scientifically, however, the theory addressed by the experiment did not clearly suggest one design over the other.

Unfortunately, I am not aware of substantial prior research about the relative merits of blocking and boosting content in the News Feed. Also, I have not seen much research about refining treatments to make them less harmful; one exception is Jones and Feamster (2015), which considers the case of measurement of Internet censorship (a topic I discuss in chapter 6 in relationship to the Encore study (Burnett and Feamster 2015; Narayanan and Zevenbergen 2015)).

In terms of the third R ("reduction"), good introductions to traditional power analysis are given by Cohen (1988) (book) and Cohen (1992) (article), while Gelman and Carlin (2014) offer a slightly different perspective. Pre-treatment covariates can be included in the design and analysis stages of experiments; chapter 4 of Gerber and Green (2012) provides a good introduction to both approaches, and Casella (2008) provides a more in-depth treatment. Techniques that use this pre-treatment information in the randomization are typically called either blocked experimental designs or stratified experimental designs (the terminology is not used consistently across communities); these techniques are closely related to the stratified sampling techniques discussed in chapter 3. See Higgins, Sävje, and Sekhon (2016) for more on using these designs in massive experiments. Pre-treatment covariates can also be included in the analysis stage. McKenzie (2012) explores the difference-in-differences approach to analyzing field experiments in greater detail. See Carneiro, Lee, and Wilhelm (2016) for more on the trade-offs between different approaches to increase precision in estimates of treatment effects. Finally, when deciding whether to try to include pre-treatment covariates at the design or analysis stage (or both), there are a few factors to consider. In a setting where researchers want to show that they are not "fishing" (Humphreys, Sierra, and Windt 2013), using pre-treatment covariates in the design stage can be helpful (Higgins, Sävje, and Sekhon 2016). In situations where participants arrive sequentially, especially online field experiments, using pre-treatment information in the design stage may be difficult logistically; see, for example, Xie and Aurisset (2016).

It is worth adding a bit of intuition about why a difference-in-differences approach can be so much more effective than a difference-in-means one. Many online outcomes have very high variance (see e.g., Lewis and Rao (2015) and Lamb et al. (2015)) and are relatively stable over time. In this case, the change score will have substantially smaller variance, increasing the power of the statistical test. One reason this approach is not used more often is that prior to the digital age, it was not common to have pre-treatment outcomes. A more concrete way to think about this is to imagine an experiment to measure whether a specific exercise routine causes weight loss. If you adopt a difference-in-means approach, your estimate will have variability arising from the variability in weights in the population. If you do a difference-in-differences approach, however, that naturally occurring variation in weights is removed, and you can more easily detect a difference caused by the treatment.

Finally, I considered adding a fourth R: "repurpose". That is, if researchers find themselves with more experimental data than they need to address their original research question, they should repurpose the data to ask new questions. For example, imagine that Kramer and colleagues had used a difference-in-differences estimator and found themselves with more data than they needed to address their research question. Rather than not using the data to the fullest extent, they could have studied the size of the effect as a function of pre-treatment emotional expression. Just as Schultz et al. (2007) found that the effect of the treatment was different for light and heavy users, perhaps the effects of the News Feed were different for people who already tended to post happy (or sad) messages. Repurposing could lead to "fishing" (Humphreys, Sierra, and Windt 2013) and "p-hacking" (Simmons, Nelson, and Simonsohn 2011), but these are largely addressable with a combination of honest reporting (Simmons, Nelson, and Simonsohn 2011), pre-registration (Humphreys, Sierra, and Windt 2013), and machine learning methods that attempt to avoid over-fitting.

Activities

Degrees of Difficulty: ⌒ EASY   ⌒ MEDIUM   ⌒ HARD   ⌒ VERY HARD

⬡ DATA COLLECTION   ⊞ REQUIRES MATH   </> REQUIRES CODING   ♥ MY FAVORITES

1. [⌒, ⬡] Berinsky and colleagues (2012) evaluated MTurk in part by replicating three classic experiments. Replicate the classic Asian Disease framing experiment by Tversky and Kahneman (1981). Do your results match Tversky and Kahneman's? Do your results match those of Berinsky and colleagues? What—if anything—does this teach us about using MTurk for survey experiments?

2. [⌒, ♥] In a somewhat tongue-in-cheek paper titled "We Have to Break Up," the social psychologist Robert Cialdini, one of the authors of Schultz et al. (2007), wrote that he was retiring early from his job as a professor, in part because of the challenges he faced doing field experiments in a discipline (psychology) that mainly conducts lab experiments (Cialdini 2009). Read Cialdini's paper, and write him an email urging him to reconsider his break-up in light of the possibilities of digital experiments. Use specific examples of research that address his concerns.

3. [⌒] In order to determine whether small initial successes lock in or fade away, van de Rijt and and colleagues (2014) intervened into four different systems bestowing success on randomly selected participants, and then measured the long-term impacts of this arbitrary success. Can you think of other systems in which you could run similar experiments? Evaluate these systems in terms of issues of scientific value, algorithmic confounding (see chapter 2), and ethics.

4. [📡, 🎲] The results of an experiment can depend on the participants. Create an experiment and then run it on MTurk using two different recruitment strategies. Try to pick the experiment and recruitment strategies so that the results will be as *different* as possible. For example, your recruitment strategies could be to recruit participants in the morning and the evening or to compensate participants with high and low pay. These kinds of differences in recruitment strategy could lead to different pools of participants and different experimental outcomes. How different did your results turn out? What does that reveal about running experiments on MTurk?

5. [🎚️, ⬛, 💻] Imagine that you were planning the Emotional Contagion experiment (Kramer, Guillory, and Hancock 2014). Use the results from an earlier observational study by Kramer (2012) to decide the number of participants in each condition. These two studies don't match perfectly, so be sure to explicitly list all the assumptions that you make

> **a**) Run a simulation that will decide how many participants would have been needed to detect an effect as large as the effect in Kramer (2012) with $\alpha = 0.05$ and $1 - \beta = 0.8$.
>
> **b**) Do the same calculation analytically.
>
> **c**) Given the results from Kramer (2012), was Emotional Contagion (Kramer, Guillory, and Hancock 2014) over-powered (i.e., did it have more participants than needed)?
>
> **d**) Of the assumptions that you made, which have the biggest effect on your calculation?

6. [🎚️, ⬛, 💻] Answer the previous question again, but this time, rather than using the earlier observational study by Kramer (2012), use the results from an earlier natural experiment by Coviello et al. (2014).

7. [📡] Both Margetts et al. (2011) and van de Rijt et al. (2014) performed experiments studying the process of people signing a petition. Compare and contrast the designs and findings of these studies.

8. [📡] Dwyer, Maki, and Rothman (2015) conducted two field experiments on the relationship between social norms and pro-environmental behavior. Here's the abstract of their paper:

> "How might psychological science be utilized to encourage proenvironmental behavior? In two studies, interventions aimed at promoting energy conservation behavior in public bathrooms examined the influences of

descriptive norms and personal responsibility. In Study 1, the light status (i.e., on or off) was manipulated before someone entered an unoccupied public bathroom, signaling the descriptive norm for that setting. Participants were significantly more likely to turn the lights off if they were off when they entered. In Study 2, an additional condition was included in which the norm of turning off the light was demonstrated by a confederate, but participants were not themselves responsible for turning it on. Personal responsibility moderated the influence of social norms on behavior; when participants were not responsible for turning on the light, the influence of the norm was diminished. These results indicate how descriptive norms and personal responsibility may regulate the effectiveness of proenvironmental interventions."

Read their paper and design a replication of study 1.

9. [⏱, ✎] Building on the previous question, now carry out your design.

   a) How do the results compare?

   b) What might explain these differences?

10. [⏱] There has been substantial debate about experiments using participants recruited from MTurk. In parallel, there has also been substantial debate about experiments using participants recruited from undergraduate student populations. Write a two-page memo comparing and contrasting Turkers and undergraduates as research participants. Your comparison should include a discussion of both scientific and logistical issues.

11. [⏱] Jim Manzi's book *Uncontrolled* (2012) is a wonderful introduction to the power of experimentation in business. In the book, he related the following story:

"I was once in a meeting with a true business genius, a self-made billionaire who had a deep, intuitive understating of the power of experiments. His company spent significant resources trying to create great store window displays that would attract consumers and increases sales, as conventional wisdom said they should. Experts carefully tested design after design, and in individual test review sessions over a period of years kept showing no significant causal effect of each new display design on sales. Senior marketing and merchandising executives met with the CEO to review these historical test results in toto. After presenting all of the experimental data, they concluded that the conventional wisdom was wrong—that window displays don't drive sales. Their recommended action was to reduce costs and effort in this area. This dramatically demonstrated the ability of experimentation to overturn conventional wisdom. The CEO's response was simple: 'My conclusion is that your designers aren't very good.' His solution was to increase effort in store display design, and to get new people to do it." (Manzi 2012, pp. 158–9)

Which type of validity is the concern of the CEO?

12. [⚙] Building on the previous question, imagine that you were at the meeting where the results of the experiments were discussed. What are four questions that you could ask—one for each type of validity (statistical, construct, internal, and external)?

13. [⚙] Bernedo, Ferraro, and Price (2014) studied the seven-year effect of the water-saving intervention described by Ferraro, Miranda, and Price (2011) (see figure 4.11). In this paper, Bernedo and colleagues also sought to understand the mechanism behind the effect by comparing the behavior of households that have and have not moved after the treatment was delivered. That is, roughly, they tried to see whether the treatment impacted the home or the homeowner.

   a) Read the paper, describe their design, and summarize their findings.

   b) Do their findings impact how you should assess the cost-effectiveness of similar interventions? If so, why? If not, why not?

14. [⚙] In a follow-up to Schultz et al. (2007), Schultz and colleagues performed a series of three experiments on the effect of descriptive and injunctive norms on a different environmental behavior (towel reuse) in two contexts (a hotel and a timeshare condominium) (Schultz, Khazian, and Zaleski 2008).

   a) Summarize the design and findings of these three experiments.

   b) How, if at all, do they change your interpretation of Schultz et al. (2007)?

15. [⚙] In response to Schultz et al. (2007), Canfield, Bruine de Bruin, and Wong-Parodi (2016) ran a series of lab-like experiments to study the design of electric bills. Here's how they describe it in the abstract:

"In a survey-based experiment, each participant saw a hypothetical electricity bill for a family with relatively high electricity use, covering information about (a) historical use, (b) comparisons to neighbors, and (c) historical use with appliance breakdown. Participants saw all information types in one of three formats including (a) tables, (b) bar graphs, and (c) icon graphs. We report on three main findings. First, consumers understood each type of electricity-use information the most when it was presented in a table, perhaps because tables facilitate simple point reading. Second, preferences and intentions to save electricity were the strongest for the historical use information, independent of format. Third, individuals with lower energy literacy understood all information less."

Unlike other follow-up studies, the main outcome of interest in Canfield, Bruine de Bruin, and Wong-Parodi (2016) is reported behavior, not actual behavior. What are the strengths and weaknesses of this type of study in a broader research program promoting energy savings?

16. [🎯, ❤️] Smith and Pell (2003) presented a satirical meta-analysis of studies demonstrating the effectiveness of parachutes. They concluded:

"As with many interventions intended to prevent ill health, the effectiveness of parachutes has not been subjected to rigorous evaluation by using randomised controlled trials. Advocates of evidence based medicine have criticised the adoption of interventions evaluated by using only observational data. We think that everyone might benefit if the most radical protagonists of evidence based medicine organised and participated in a double blind, randomised, placebo controlled, crossover trial of the parachute."

Write an op-ed suitable for a general-readership newspaper, such as the *New York Times*, arguing against the fetishization of experimental evidence. Provide specific, concrete examples. Hint: See also Deaton (2010) and Bothwell et al. (2016).

17. [🎯, 🖥️, ❤️] Difference-in-differences estimators of a treatment effect can be more precise than difference-in-mean estimators. Write a memo to an engineer in charge of A/B testing at a start-up social media company explaining the value of the difference-in-differences approach for running an online experiment. The memo should include a statement of the problem, some intuition about the conditions under which the difference-in-difference estimator will outperform the difference-in-mean estimator, and a simple simulation study.

18. [🎯, ❤️] Gary Loveman was a professor at Harvard Business School before becoming the CEO of Harrah's, one of the largest casino companies in the world. When he moved to Harrah's, Loveman transformed the company with a frequent-flier-like loyalty program that collected tremendous amounts of

data about customer behavior. On top of this always-on measurement system, the company began running experiments. For example, they might run an experiment to evaluate the effect of a coupon for a free hotel night for customers with a specific gambling pattern. Here's how Loveman described the importance of experimentation to Harrah's everyday business practices:

> "It's like you don't harass women, you don't steal, and you've got to have a control group. This is one of the things that you can lose your job for at Harrah's—not running a control group." (Manzi 2012, p. 146)

Write an email to a new employee explaining why Loveman thinks it is so important to have a control group. You should try to include an example—either real or made up—to illustrate your point.

19. [🌀, ➕] A new experiment aims to estimate the effect of receiving text message reminders on vaccination uptake. One hundred and fifty clinics, each with 600 eligible patients, are willing to participate. There is a fixed cost of $100 for each clinic you want to work with, and it costs $1 for each text message that you want to send. Further, any clinics that you are working with will measure the outcome (whether someone received a vaccination) for free. Assume that you have a budget of $1,000.

   a) Under what conditions might it be better to focus your resources on a small number of clinics and under what conditions might it be better to spread them more widely?

   b) What factors would determine the smallest effect size that you will be able to reliably detect with your budget?

   c) Write a memo explaining these trade-offs to a potential funder.

20. [🌀, ➕] A major problem with online courses is attrition: many students who start courses end up dropping out. Imagine that you are working at an online learning platform, and a designer at the platform has created a visual progress bar that she thinks will help prevent students from dropping out of the course. You want to test the effect of the progress bar on students in a large computational social science course. After addressing any ethical issues that might arise in the experiment, you and your colleagues get worried that the course might not have enough students to reliably detect the effects of the progress bar. In the following calculations, you can assume that half of the students will receive the progress bar and half not. Further, you can assume that there is no interference. In other words, you can assume that participants are only affected by whether they received the treatment or control; they are not effected by whether other people received the treatment or control (for a more

formal definition, see chapter 8 of Gerber and Green (2012)). Keep track of any additional assumptions that you make.

a) Suppose the progress bar is expected to increase the proportion of students who finish the class by 1 percentage point; what is the sample size needed to reliably detect the effect?

b) Suppose the progress bar is expected to increase the proportion of students who finish the class by 10 percentage points; what is the sample size needed to reliably detect the effect?

c) Now imagine that you have run the experiment, and students who have completed all the course materials have taken a final exam. When you compare the final exam scores of students who received the progress bar with the scores of those who didn't, you find, much to your surprise, that students who did not receive the progress bar actually scored higher. Does this mean that the progress bar caused students to learn less? What can you learn from these outcome data? (Hint: See chapter 7 of Gerber and Green (2012).)

21. [⌖, ⟨/⟩, ♥] Imagine that you are working as a data scientist at a tech company. Someone from the marketing department asks for your help in evaluating an experiment that they are planning in order to measure the return on investment (ROI) for a new online ad campaign. ROI is defined as the net profit from the campaign divided by the cost of the campaign. For example, a campaign that had no effect on sales would have an ROI of -100%; a campaign where profits generated were equal to costs would have an ROI of 0; and a campaign where profits generated were double the cost would have an ROI of 200%.

Before launching the experiment, the marketing department provides you with the following information based on their earlier research (in fact, these values are typical of the real online ad campaigns reported in Lewis and Rao (2015)):

- The mean sales per customer follows a log-normal distribution with a mean of $7 and a standard deviation of $75.
- The campaign is expected to increase sales by $0.35 per customer, which corresponds to an increase in profit of $0.175 per customer.
- The planned size of the experiment is 200,000 people: half in the treatment group and half in the control group.
- The cost of the campaign is $0.14 per participant.
- The expected ROI for the campaign is 25% $[(0.175 - 0.14)/0.14]$. In other words, the marketing department believes that for each 100 dollars spent on marketing, the company will earn an additional $25 in profit.

Write a memo evaluating this proposed experiment. Your memo should use evidence from a simulation that you create, and it should address two major issues: (1) Would you recommend launching this experiment as planned? If so, why? If not, why not? Be sure to be clear about the criteria that you are using to make this decision. (2) What sample size would you recommend for this experiment? Again please be sure to be clear about the criteria that you are using to make this decision.

A good memo will address this specific case; a better memo will generalize from this case in one way (e.g., show how the decision changes as a function of the size of the effect of the campaign); and a great memo will present a fully generalized result. Your memo should use graphs to help illustrate your results.

Here are two hints. First, the marketing department might have provided you with some unnecessary information, and they might have failed to provide you with some necessary information. Second, if you are using R, be aware that the rlnorm() function does not work the way that many people expect.

This activity will give you practice with power analysis, creating simulations, and communicating your results with words and graphs. It should help you conduct power analysis for any kind of experiment, not just experiments designed to estimate ROI. This activity assumes that you have some experience with statistical testing and power analysis. If you are not familiar with power analysis, I recommend that you read "A Power Primer" by Cohen (1992).

This activity was inspired by a lovely paper by Lewis and Rao (2015), which vividly illustrates a fundamental statistical limitation of even massive experiments. Their paper—which originally had the provocative title "On the Near-Impossibility of Measuring the Returns to Advertising"—shows how difficult it is to measure the return on investment of online ads, even with digital experiments involving millions of customers. More generally, Lewis and Rao (2015) illustrate a fundamental statistical fact that is particularly important for digital-age experiments: it is hard to estimate small treatment effects amidst noisy outcome data.

22. [🏃, ➕] Do the same as the previous question, but, rather than simulation, you should use analytical results.

23. [🏃, ➕, </>] Do the same as the previous question, but use both simulation and analytical results.

24. [🏃, ➕, </>] Imagine that you have written the memo described above, and someone from the marketing department provides one piece of new information: they expect a 0.4 correlation between sales before and after the experiment. How does this change the recommendations in your memo? (Hint: see section 4.6.2 for more on the difference-of-means estimator and the difference-in-differences estimator.)

Table 4.6: Simple View of Data from the Career Services Experiment

Group	Size	Employment rate
Granted access to website	5,000	70%
Not granted access to website	5,000	70%

25. [⟨icon⟩, ⟨icon⟩] In order to evaluate the effectiveness of a new web-based employment-assistance program, a university career services office conducted a randomized control trial among 10,000 students entering their final year of school. A free subscription with unique log-in information was sent through an exclusive email invitation to 5,000 of the randomly selected students, while the other 5,000 students were in the control group and did not have a subscription. Twelve months later, a follow-up survey (with no nonresponse) showed that in both the treatment and control groups, 70% of the students had secured full-time employment in their chosen field (table 4.6). Thus, it seemed that the web-based service had no effect.

However, a clever data scientist at the university looked at the data a bit more closely and found that only 20% of the students in the treatment group ever logged into the account after receiving the email. Further, and somewhat surprisingly, among those who did log into the website, only 60% had secured full-time employment in their chosen field, which was lower than the rate for people who didn't log in and lower than the rate for people in the control condition (table 4.7).

    a) Provide an explanation for what might have happened.

    b) What are two different ways to calculate the effect of the treatment in this experiment?

    c) Given this result, should the university career service provide this service to all students? Just to be clear, this is not a question with a simple answer.

    d) What should they do next?

Hint: This question goes beyond the material covered in this chapter, but addresses issues common in experiments. This type of experimental design is sometimes called an *encouragement design* because participants are encouraged to engage in the treatment. This problem is an example of what is called *one-sided noncompliance* (see chapter 5 of Gerber and Green (2012)).

26. [⟨icon⟩] After further examination, it turned out that the experiment described in the previous question was even more complicated. It turned out that 10% of the people in the control group paid for access to the service, and they ended up

Table 4.7: More Complete View of Data from the Career Services Experiment

Group	Size	Employment rate
Granted access to website and logged in	1,000	60%
Granted access to website and never logged in	4,000	72.5%
Not granted access to website	5,000	70%

Table 4.8: Full View of Data from the Career Services Experiment

Group	Size	Employment rate
Granted access to website and logged in	1,000	60%
Granted access to website and never logged in	4,000	72.5%
Not granted access to website and paid for it	500	65%
Not granted access to website and did not pay for it	4,500	70.56%

with an employment rate of 65% (table 4.8).

Write an email summarizing what you think is happening and recommend a course of action.

Hint: This question goes beyond the material covered in this chapter, but addresses issues common in experiments. This problem is an example of what is called *two-sided noncompliance* (see chapter 6 of Gerber and Green (2012)).

CHAPTER 5
CREATING MASS COLLABORATION

5.1 Introduction

Wikipedia is amazing. A mass collaboration of volunteers created a fantastic encyclopedia that is available to everyone. The key to Wikipedia's success was not new knowledge; rather, it was a new form of collaboration. The digital age, fortunately, enables many new forms of collaboration. Thus, we should now ask: What massive scientific problems—problems that we could not solve individually—can we now tackle together?

Collaboration in research is nothing new, of course. What is new, however, is that the digital age enables collaboration with a much larger and more diverse set of people: the billions of people around the world with Internet access. I expect that these new mass collaborations will yield amazing results not just because of the number of people involved but also because of their diverse skills and perspectives. How can we incorporate everyone with an Internet connection into our research process? What could you do with 100 research assistants? What about 100,000 skilled collaborators?

There are many forms of mass collaboration, and computer scientists typically organize them into a large number of categories based on their technical characteristics (Quinn and Bederson 2011). In this chapter, how-ever, I'm going to categorize mass collaboration projects based on how they can be used for social research. In particular, I think it is helpful to roughly distinguish between three types of projects: *human computation, open call,* and *distributed data collection* (figure 5.1).

I'll describe each of these types in greater detail later in the chapter, but for now let me describe each one briefly. *Human computation* projects are ideally suited for easy-task–big-scale problems such as labeling a million

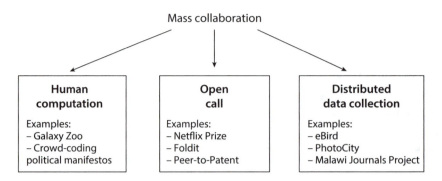

Figure 5.1: Mass collaboration schematic. This chapter is organized around three main forms of mass collaboration: human computation, open call, and distributed data collection. More generally, mass collaboration combines ideas from fields such as citizen science, crowdsourcing, and collective intelligence.

images. These are projects that in the past might have been performed by undergraduate research assistants. Contributions don't require task-related skills, and the final output is typically an average of all of the contributions. A classic example of a human computation project is Galaxy Zoo, where a hundred thousand volunteers helped astronomers classify a million galaxies. *Open call* projects, on the other hand, are ideally suited for problems where you are looking for novel and unexpected answers to clearly formulated questions. These are projects that in the past might have involved asking colleagues. Contributions come from people who have special task-related skills, and the final output is usually the best of all of the contributions. A classic example of an open call is the Netflix Prize, where thousands of scientists and hackers worked to develop new algorithms to predict customers' ratings of movies. Finally, *distributed data collection* projects are ideally suited for large-scale data collection. These are projects that in the past might have been performed by undergraduate research assistants or survey research companies. Contributions typically come from people who have access to locations that researchers do not, and the final product is a simple collection of the contributions. A classic example of a distributed data collection is eBird, in which hundreds of thousands of volunteers contribute reports about birds they see.

Mass collaboration has a long, rich history in fields such as astronomy (Marshall, Lintott, and Fletcher 2015) and ecology (Dickinson, Zuckerberg, and Bonter 2010), but it is not yet common in social research. However, by describing successful projects from other fields and providing a few key organizing principles, I hope to convince you of two things. First, mass collaboration *can* be harnessed for social research. And second, researchers who use mass collaboration will be able to solve problems that had previously seemed impossible. Although mass collaboration is often promoted as a way to save money, it is much more than that. As I will show, mass collaboration doesn't just allow us to do research *cheaper*, it allows us to do research *better*.

In the previous chapters, you have seen what can be learned by engaging with people in three different ways: observing their behavior (chapter 2), asking them questions (chapter 3), and enrolling them in experiments (chapter 4). In this chapter, I'll show you what can be learned by engaging people as research collaborators. For each of the three main forms of mass collaboration, I will describe a prototypical example, illustrate important additional points with further examples, and finally describe how this form of mass collaboration might be used for social research. The chapter will conclude with five principles that can help you design your own mass collaboration project.

5.2   Human computation

> Human computation projects take a big problem, break it into simple pieces, send them to many workers, and then aggregate the results.

Human computation projects combine the efforts of many people working on simple microtasks in order to solve problems that are impossibly big for one person. You might have a research problem suitable for human computation if you've ever thought: "I could solve this problem if I had a thousand research assistants."

The prototypical example of a human computation project is Galaxy Zoo. In this project, more than one hundred thousand volunteers classified images of about a million galaxies with similar accuracy to earlier—and substantially smaller—efforts by professional astronomers. This increased scale provided by mass collaboration led to new discoveries about how galaxies form, and it turned up an entirely new class of galaxies called "Green Peas."

Although Galaxy Zoo might seem far from social research, there are actually many situations where social researchers want to code, classify, or label images or texts. In some cases, this analysis can be done by computers, but there are still certain forms of analysis that are hard for computers but easy for people. It is these easy-for-people yet hard-for-computers microtasks that we can turn over to human computation projects.

Not only is the microtask in Galaxy Zoo quite general, but the structure of the project is general as well. Galaxy Zoo, and other human computation projects, typically use a *split–apply–combine* strategy (Wickham 2011), and once you understand this strategy you'll be able to use it to solve lots of problems. First, a big problem is *split* into lots of little problem chunks. Then, human work is *applied* to each little problem chunk, independently of the other chunks. Finally, the results of this work are *combined* to produce a consensus solution. Given that background, let's see how the split–apply–combine strategy was used in Galaxy Zoo.

5.2.1 Galaxy Zoo

> Galaxy Zoo combined the efforts of many non-expert volunteers to classify a million galaxies.

Galaxy Zoo grew out of a problem faced by Kevin Schawinski, a graduate student in Astronomy at the University of Oxford in 2007. Simplifying quite a bit, Schawinski was interested in galaxies, and galaxies can be classified by their morphology—elliptical or spiral—and by their color—blue or red. At the time, the conventional wisdom among astronomers was that spiral galaxies, like our Milky Way, were blue in color (indicating youth) and elliptical galaxies were red (indicating old age). Schawinski doubted this conventional wisdom. He suspected that while this pattern might be true in general, there were probably a sizable number of exceptions, and that by studying lots of these unusual galaxies—the ones that did not fit the expected pattern—he could learn something about the process through which galaxies formed.

Thus, what Schawinski needed in order to overturn conventional wisdom was a large set of morphologically classified galaxies; that is, galaxies that had been classified as either spiral or elliptical. The problem, however, was that existing algorithmic methods for classification were not yet good enough to be used for scientific research; in other words, classifying galaxies was, at that time, a problem that was hard for computers. Therefore, what was needed was a large number of *human*-classified galaxies. Schawinski undertook

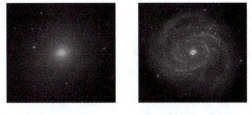

Elliptical galaxy   Spiral galaxy

Figure 5.2: Examples of the two main types of galaxies: spiral and elliptical. The Galaxy Zoo project used more than 100,000 volunteers to categorize more than 900,000 images. Reproduced by permission from http://www.GalaxyZoo.org and Sloan Digital Sky Survey.

this classification problem with the enthusiasm of a graduate student. In a marathon session of seven 12-hour days, he was able to classify 50,000 galaxies. While 50,000 galaxies may sound like a lot, it is actually only about 5% of the almost one million galaxies that had been photographed in the Sloan Digital Sky Survey. Schawinski realized that he needed a more scalable approach.

Fortunately, it turns out that the task of classifying galaxies does not require advanced training in astronomy; you can teach someone to do it pretty quickly. In other words, even though classifying galaxies is a task that was hard for computers, it was pretty easy for humans. So, while sitting in a pub in Oxford, Schawinski and fellow astronomer Chris Lintott dreamed up a website where volunteers would classify images of galaxies. A few months later, Galaxy Zoo was born.

At the Galaxy Zoo website, volunteers would undergo a few minutes of training; for example, learning the difference between a spiral and elliptical galaxy (figure 5.2). After this training, each volunteer had to pass a relatively easy quiz—correctly classifying 11 of 15 galaxies with known classifications—and then would begin real classification of unknown galaxies through a simple web-based interface (figure 5.3). The transition from volunteer to astronomer would take place in less than 10 minutes and only required passing the lowest of hurdles, a simple quiz.

Galaxy Zoo attracted its initial volunteers after the project was featured in a news article, and in about six months the project grew to involve more than 100,000 citizen scientists, people who participated because they enjoyed the task and they wanted to help advance astronomy. Together, these 100,000 volunteers contributed a total of more than 40 million classifications, with

Figure 5.3: Input screen where volunteers were asked to classify a single image. Reproduced by permission from Chris Lintott based on an image from the Sloan Digital Sky Survey Collection.

the majority of the classifications coming from a relatively small core group of participants (Lintott et al. 2008).

Researchers who have experience hiring undergraduate research assistants might immediately be skeptical about data quality. While this skepticism is reasonable, Galaxy Zoo shows that when volunteer contributions are correctly cleaned, debiased, and aggregated, they can produce high-quality results (Lintott et al. 2008). An important trick for getting the crowd to create professional-quality data is *redundancy*, that is, having the same task performed by many different people. In Galaxy Zoo, there were about 40 classifications per galaxy; researchers using undergraduate research assistants could never afford this level of redundancy and therefore would need to be much more concerned with the quality of each individual classification. What the volunteers lacked in training, they made up for with redundancy.

Even with multiple classifications per galaxy, however, combining the set of volunteer classifications to produce a consensus classification was tricky. Because very similar challenges arise in most human computation projects, it is helpful to briefly review the three steps that the Galaxy Zoo researchers used to produce their consensus classifications. First, the researchers "cleaned" the data by removing bogus classifications. For example, people who repeatedly classified the same galaxy—something that would happen if they were trying to manipulate the results—had all their classifications discarded. This and other similar cleaning removed about 4% of all classifications.

Second, after cleaning, the researchers needed to remove systematic biases in classifications. Through a series of bias detection studies embedded within the original project—for example, showing some volunteers the galaxy in monochrome instead of color—the researchers discovered several systematic biases, such as a systematic bias to classify faraway spiral galaxies as elliptical galaxies (Bamford et al. 2009). Adjusting for these systematic biases is extremely important because redundancy does not automatically remove systematic bias; it only help removes random error.

Finally, after debiasing, the researchers needed a method to combine the individual classifications to produce a consensus classification. The simplest way to combine classifications for each galaxy would have been to choose the most common classification. However, this approach would have given each volunteer equal weight, and the researchers suspected that some volunteers were better at classification than others. Therefore, the researchers developed a more complex iterative weighting procedure that attempted to detect the best classifiers and give them more weight.

Thus, after a three-step process—cleaning, debiasing, and weighting—the Galaxy Zoo research team had converted 40 million volunteer classifications into a set of consensus morphological classifications. When these Galaxy Zoo classifications were compared with three previous smaller-scale attempts by professional astronomers, including the classification by Schawinski that helped to inspire Galaxy Zoo, there was strong agreement. Thus, the volunteers, in aggregate, were able to provide high-quality classifications and at a scale that the researchers could not match (Lintott et al. 2008). In fact, by having human classifications for such a large number of galaxies, Schawinski, Lintott, and others were able to show that only about 80% of galaxies follow the expected pattern—blue spirals and red ellipticals—and numerous papers have been written about this discovery (Fortson et al. 2011).

Given this background, you can now see how Galaxy Zoo follows the split–apply–combine recipe, the same recipe that is used for most human computation projects. First, a big problem was *split* into chunks. In this case, the problem of classifying a million galaxies is split into a million problems of classifying one galaxy. Next, an operation is *applied* to each chunk independently. In this case, volunteers classified each galaxy as either spiral or elliptical. Finally, the results are *combined* to produce a consensus result. In this case, the combine step included the cleaning, debiasing, and weighting to produce a consensus classification for each galaxy. Even though most projects use this general recipe, each step needs to be customized to the specific problem being addressed. For example, in the human computation project described below, the same recipe will be followed, but the apply and combine steps will be quite different.

For the Galaxy Zoo team, this first project was just the beginning. Very quickly, they realized that even though they were able to classify close to a million galaxies, this scale is not enough to work with newer digital sky surveys, which can produce images of about 10 billion galaxies (Kuminski et al. 2014). To handle an increase from 1 million to 10 billion—a factor of 10,000—Galaxy Zoo would need to recruit roughly 10,000 times more participants. Even though the number of volunteers on the Internet is large, it is not infinite. Therefore, the researchers realized that if they were going to handle ever-growing amounts of data, a new, even more scalable, approach was needed.

Therefore, Manda Banerji—working with Schawinski, Lintott, and other members of the Galaxy Zoo team (2010)—started teaching computers to classify galaxies. More specifically, using the human classifications created by Galaxy Zoo, Banerji built a machine learning model that could predict the human classification of a galaxy based on the characteristics of the image. If this model could reproduce the human classifications with high accuracy, then it could be used by Galaxy Zoo researchers to classify an essentially infinite number of galaxies.

The core of Banerji and colleagues' approach is actually pretty similar to techniques commonly used in social research, although that similarity might not be clear at first glance. First, Banerji and colleagues converted each image into a set of numerical *features* that summarized its properties. For example, for images of galaxies, there could be three features: the amount of blue in the image, the variance in the brightness of the pixels, and the proportion of nonwhite pixels. The selection of the correct features is an important part of the problem, and it generally requires subject-area expertise. This first step, commonly called *feature engineering*, results in a data matrix with one row per image and three columns describing that image. Given the data matrix and the desired output (e.g., whether the image was classified by a human as an elliptical galaxy), the researcher creates a statistical or machine learning model—for example, logistic regression—that predicts the human classification based on the features of the image. Finally, the researcher uses the parameters in this statistical model to produce estimated classifications of new galaxies (figure 5.4). In machine learning, this approach—using labeled examples to create a model that can then label new data—is called *supervised learning*.

The features in Banerji and colleagues' machine learning model were more complex than those in my toy example—for example, she used features like "de Vaucouleurs fit axial ratio"—and her model was not logistic regression, it was an artificial neural network. Using her features, her model, and the consensus Galaxy Zoo classifications, she was able to create weights on each feature and then use these weights to make predictions about the classification of galaxies. For example, her analysis found that images with low de Vaucouleurs fit axial ratio were more likely to be spiral galaxies. Given these weights, she was able to predict the human classification of a galaxy with reasonable accuracy.

The work of Banerji and colleagues turned Galaxy Zoo into what I would call a *computer-assisted human computation system*. The best way to think about these hybrid systems is that rather than having humans solve a problem, they have humans build a dataset that can be used to train a computer to solve the problem. Sometimes, training a computer to solve the problem can require lots of examples, and the only way to produce a sufficient number of examples is a mass collaboration. The advantage of this computer-assisted approach is that it enables you to handle essentially infinite amounts of data using only a finite amount of human effort. For example, a researcher with a million human classified galaxies can build a predictive model that can then be used to classify a billion or even a trillion galaxies. If there are enormous numbers of galaxies, then this kind of human–computer hybrid is really the only possible solution. This infinite scalability is not free, however. Building a machine learning model that can correctly reproduce the human classifications is itself a hard problem, but fortunately there are already excellent books dedicated to this topic (Hastie, Tibshirani, and Friedman 2009; Murphy 2012; James et al. 2013).

Galaxy Zoo is a good illustration of how many human computation projects evolve. First, a researcher attempts the project by herself or with a small team of research assistants (e.g., Schawinski's initial classification effort). If this approach does not scale well, the researcher can move to

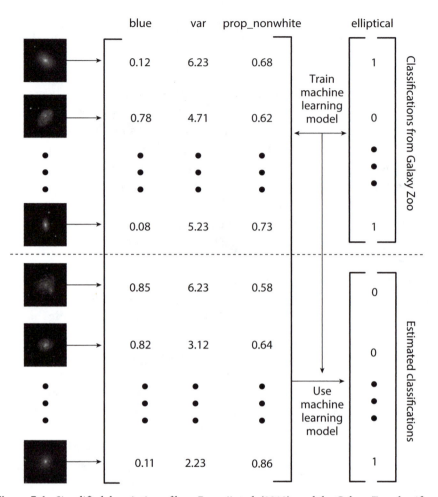

Figure 5.4: Simplified description of how Banerji et al. (2010) used the Galaxy Zoo classifications to train a machine learning model to do galaxy classification. Images of galaxies were converted in a matrix of features. In this simplified example, there are three features (the amount of blue in the image, the variance in the brightness of the pixels, and the proportion of nonwhite pixels). Then, for a subset of the images, the Galaxy Zoo labels are used to train a machine learning model. Finally, the machine learning model is used to estimate classifications for the remaining galaxies. I call this a computer-assisted human computation project because, rather than having humans solve a problem, it has humans build a dataset that can be used to train a computer to solve the problem. The advantage of this computer-assisted human computation system is that it enables you to handle essentially infinite amounts of data using only a finite amount of human effort. Images of galaxies reproduced by permission from Sloan Digital Sky Survey.

a human computation project with many participants. But, for a certain volume of data, pure human effort will not be enough. At that point, researchers need to build a computer-assisted human computation system in which human classifications are used to train a machine learning model that can then be applied to virtually unlimited amounts of data.

5.2.2 Crowd-coding of political manifestos

Coding political manifestos, something typically done by experts, can be performed by a human computation project resulting in greater reproducibility and flexibility.

Similar to Galaxy Zoo, there are many situations where social researchers want to code, classify, or label an image or piece of text. An example of this kind of research is the coding of political manifestos. During elections, political parties produce manifestos describing their policy positions and guiding philosophies. For example, here's a piece of the manifesto of the Labour Party in the United Kingdom from 2010:

"Millions of people working in our public services embody the best values of Britain, helping empower people to make the most of their own lives while protecting them from the risks they should not have to bear on their own. Just as we need to be bolder about the role of government in making markets work fairly, we also need to be bold reformers of government."

These manifestos contain valuable data for political scientists, particularly those studying elections and the dynamics of policy debates. In order to systematically extract information from these manifestos, researchers created the Manifesto Project, which collected 4,000 manifestos from nearly 1,000 parties in 50 countries and then organized political scientists to systematically code them. Each sentence in each manifesto was coded by an expert using a 56-category scheme. The result of this collaborative effort was a massive dataset summarizing the information embedded in these manifestos, and this dataset has been used in more than 200 scientific papers.

Kenneth Benoit and colleagues (2016) decided to take the manifesto coding task that had previously been performed by experts and turn it into a

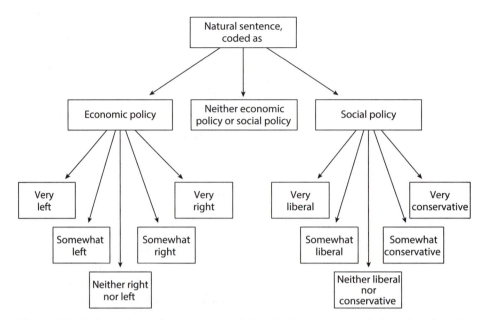

Figure 5.5: Coding scheme from Benoit et al. (2016). Readers were asked to classify each sentence as referring to economic policy (left or right), to social policy (liberal or conservative), or to neither. Adapted from Benoit et al. (2016), figure 1.

human computation project. As a result, they created a coding process that is more reproducible and more flexible, not to mention cheaper and faster.

Working with 18 manifestos generated during six recent elections in the United Kingdom, Benoit and colleagues used the split–apply–combine strategy with workers from a microtask labor market (Amazon Mechanical Turk and CrowdFlower are examples of microtask labor markets; for more on such markets, see chapter 4). The researchers took each manifesto and *split* it into sentences. Next, a person *applied* the coding scheme to each sentence. In particular, readers were asked to classify each sentence as referring to economic policy (left or right), to social policy (liberal or conservative), or to neither (figure 5.5). Each sentence was coded by about five different people. Finally, these ratings were *combined* using a statistical model that accounted for both individual-rater effects and difficulty-of-sentence effects. In all, Benoit and colleagues collected 200,000 ratings from about 1,500 people.

In order to assess the quality of the crowd coding, Benoit and colleagues also had about 10 experts—professors and graduate students in political

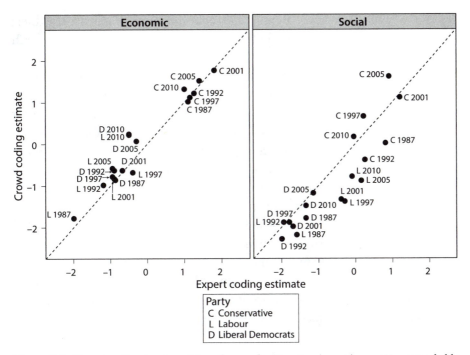

Figure 5.6: Expert estimates (*x*-axis) and crowd estimates (*y*-axis) were in remarkable agreement when coding 18 party manifestos from the United Kingdom (Benoit et al. 2016). The manifestos coded were from three political parties (Conservative, Labour, and Liberal Democrats) and six general elections (1987, 1992, 1997, 2001, 2005, and 2010). Adapted from Benoit et al. (2016), figure 3.

science—rate the same manifestos using a similar procedure. Although the ratings from members of the crowd were more variable than the ratings from the experts, the consensus crowd rating had remarkable agreement with the consensus expert rating (figure 5.6). This comparison shows that, as with Galaxy Zoo, human computation projects can produce high-quality results.

Building on this result, Benoit and colleagues used their crowd-coding system to do research that was impossible with the expert-run coding system used by the Manifesto Project. For example, the Manifesto Project did not code the manifestos on the topic of immigration, because that was not a salient topic when the coding scheme was developed in the mid-1980s. And, at this point, it is logistically infeasible for the Manifesto Project to go back and recode their manifestos to capture this information. Therefore, it would appear that researchers interested in studying the politics of immigration are out of luck. However, Benoit and colleagues were able to use their human computation system to do this coding—customized to their research question—quickly and easily.

In order to study immigration policy, they coded the manifestos for eight parties in the 2010 general election in the United Kingdom. Each sentence in each manifesto was coded as to whether it related to immigration, and if so, whether it was pro-immigration, neutral, or anti-immigration. Within 5 hours of launching their project, the results were in. They had collected more than 22,000 responses at a total cost of $360. Further, the estimates from the crowd showed remarkable agreement with an earlier survey of experts. Then, as a final test, two months later, the researchers reproduced their crowd-coding. Within a few hours, they had created a new crowd-coded dataset that closely matched their original crowd-coded data set. In other words, human computation enabled them to generate coding of political texts that agreed with expert evaluations and was reproducible. Further, because the human computation was quick and cheap, it was easy for them to customize their data collection to their specific research question about immigration.

5.2.3 Conclusion

> Human computation enables you to have a thousand research
> assistants.

Human computation projects combine the work of many non-experts to solve easy-task–big-scale problems that are not easily solved by computers. They use the split–apply–combine strategy to break a big problem into lots of simple microtasks that can be solved by people without specialized skills. Computer-assisted human computation systems also use machine learning in order to amplify the human effort.

In social research, human computation projects are most likely to be used in situations where researchers want to classify, code, or label images, video, or texts. These classifications are usually not the final product of the research; instead, they are the raw material for analysis. For example, the crowd-coding of political manifestos could be used as part of analysis about the dynamics of political debate. These kinds of classification microtasks are likely to work best when they do not require specialized training and when there is broad agreement about the correct answer. If the classification task

Table 5.1: Examples of Human Computation Projects in Social Research

Summary	Data	Participants	Reference
Code political party manifestos	Text	Microtask labor market	Benoit et al. (2016)
Extract event information from news articles on the Occupy protests in 200 US cities	Text	Microtask labor market	Adams (2016)
Classify newspaper articles	Text	Microtask labor market	Budak, Goel, and Rao (2016)
Extract event information from diaries of soldiers in World War 1	Text	Volunteers	Grayson (2016)
Detect changes in maps	Images	Microtask labor market	Soeller et al. (2016)
Check algorithmic coding	Text	Microtask labor market	Porter, Verdery, and Gaddis (2016)

is more subjective—such as "Is this news story biased?"—then it becomes increasingly important to understand who is participating and what biases they might bring. In the end, the quality of the output of human computation projects rests on the quality of the inputs that the human participants provide: garbage in, garbage out.

In order to further build your intuition, table 5.1 provides additional examples of how human computation has been used in social research. This table shows that, unlike Galaxy Zoo, many other human computation projects use microtask labor markets (e.g., Amazon Mechanical Turk) and rely on paid workers rather than volunteers. I'll return to this issue of participant motivation when I provide advice about creating your own mass collaboration project.

Finally, the examples in this section show that human computation can have a democratizing impact on science. Recall that Schawinski and Lintott were graduate students when they started Galaxy Zoo. Prior to the digital age, a project to classify a million galaxies would have required so much time and money that it would have only been practical for well-funded and patient professors. That's no longer true. Human computation projects combine the work of many non-experts to solve easy-task–big-scale problems. Next, I'll show you that mass collaboration can also be applied to problems that require expertise, expertise that even the researcher herself might not have.

5.3 Open calls

Open calls solicit new ideas for a clearly specified goal. They work on problems where a solution is easier to check than to create.

In the human computation problems described in the previous section, the researchers knew how to solve the problems given sufficient time. That is, Kevin Schawinski could have classified all million galaxies himself, if he had unlimited time. Sometimes, however, researchers encounter problems where the challenge comes not from the scale but from the inherent difficulty of the task itself. In the past, a researcher facing one of these intellectually challenging tasks might have asked colleagues for advice. Now, these problems can also be tackled by creating an open call project. You might have a research problem suitable for an open call if you've ever thought: "I don't know how to solve this problem, but I'm sure that someone else does."

In open call projects, the researcher poses a problem, solicits solutions from lots of people, and then picks the best. It may seem strange to take a problem that is challenging to you and turn it over to the crowd, but I hope to convince you with three examples—one from computer science, one from biology, and one from law—that this approach can work well. These three examples show that a key to creating a successful open call project is to formulate your question so that solutions are easy to check, even if they are difficult to create. Then, at the end of the section, I'll describe more about how these ideas can be applied to social research.

5.3.1 Netflix Prize

The Netflix Prize uses an open call to predict which movies people will like.

The most well known open call project is the Netflix Prize. Netflix is an online movie rental company, and in 2000 it launched Cinematch, a service to recommend movies to customers. For example, Cinematch might notice that you liked *Star Wars* and *The Empire Strikes Back* and then recommend that you watch *Return of the Jedi*. Initially, Cinematch worked poorly. But, over the course of many years, it continued to improve its ability to predict what movies customers would enjoy. By 2006, however, progress on Cinematch had plateaued. The researchers at Netflix had tried pretty much everything they could think of, but, at the same time, they suspected that there were other ideas that might help them improve their system. Thus, they came up with what was, at the time, a radical solution: an open call.

Critical to the eventual success of the Netflix Prize was how the open call was designed, and this design has important lessons for how open calls can be used for social research. Netflix did not just put out an unstructured request for ideas, which is what many people imagine when they first consider an open call. Rather, Netflix posed a clear problem with a simple evaluation procedure: they challenged people to use a set of 100 million movie ratings to predict 3 million held-out ratings (ratings that users had made but that Netflix did not release). The first person to create an algorithm that predicted the 3 million held-out ratings 10% better than Cinematch would win a million dollars. This clear and easy to apply evaluation procedure—comparing predicted ratings with held-out ratings—meant that the Netflix Prize was framed in such a way that solutions were easier to check than generate; it turned the challenge of improving Cinematch into a problem suitable for an open call.

In October of 2006, Netflix released a dataset containing 100 million movie ratings from about 500,000 customers (we will consider the privacy implications of this data release in chapter 6). The Netflix data can be conceptualized as a huge matrix that is approximately 500,000 customers by 20,000 movies. Within this matrix, there were about 100 million ratings on a scale from one to five stars (table 5.2). The challenge was to use the observed data in the matrix to predict the 3 million held-out ratings.

Researchers and hackers around the world were drawn to the challenge, and by 2008 more than 30,000 people were working on it (Thompson 2008). Over the course of the contest, Netflix received more than 40,000 proposed solutions from more than 5,000 teams (Netflix 2009). Obviously, Netflix could not read and understand all these proposed solutions. The whole thing ran smoothly, however, because the solutions were easy to check. Netflix could just have a computer compare the predicted ratings with the held-out

Table 5.2: Schematic of Data from the Netflix Prize

	Movie 1	Movie 2	Movie 3	...	Movie 20,000
Customer 1	2	5		...	?
Customer 2		2	?	...	3
Customer 3		?	2	...	
⋮	⋮	⋮	⋮		⋮
Customer 500,000	?		2	...	1

ratings using a prespecified metric (the particular metric they used was the square root of the mean squared error). It was this ability to quickly evaluate solutions that enabled Netflix to accept solutions from everyone, which turned out to be important because good ideas came from some surprising places. In fact, the winning solution was submitted by a team started by three researchers who had no prior experience building movie recommendation systems (Bell, Koren, and Volinsky 2010).

One beautiful aspect of the Netflix Prize is that it enabled all the proposed solutions to be evaluated fairly. That is, when people uploaded their predicted ratings, they did not need to upload their academic credentials, their age, race, gender, sexual orientation, or anything about themselves. The predicted ratings of a famous professor from Stanford were treated exactly the same as those from a teenager in her bedroom. Unfortunately, this is not true in most social research. That is, for most social research, evaluation is very time-consuming and partially subjective. So, most research ideas are never seriously evaluated, and when ideas are evaluated, it is hard to detach those evaluations from the creator of the ideas. Open call projects, on the other hand, have easy and fair evaluation, so they can discover ideas that would be missed otherwise.

For example, at one point during the Netflix Prize, someone with the screen name Simon Funk posted on his blog a proposed solution based on a singular value decomposition, an approach from linear algebra that had not been used previously by other participants. Funk's blog post was simultaneously technical and weirdly informal. Was this blog post describing a good solution or was it a waste of time? Outside of an open call project, the solution might never have received serious evaluation. After all, Simon Funk was not a professor at MIT; he was a software developer who, at the time, was backpacking around New Zealand (Piatetsky 2007). If he had emailed this idea to an engineer at Netflix, it almost certainly would not have been read.

Fortunately, because the evaluation criteria were clear and easy to apply, Funk's predicted ratings were evaluated, and it was instantly clear that his approach was very powerful: he rocketed to fourth place in the competition, a tremendous result given that other teams had already been working for months on the problem. In the end, parts of his approach were used by virtually all serious competitors (Bell, Koren, and Volinsky 2010).

The fact that Simon Funk chose to write a blog post explaining his approach, rather than trying to keep it secret, also illustrates that many participants in the Netflix Prize were not exclusively motivated by the million-dollar prize. Rather, many participants also seemed to enjoy the intellectual challenge and the community that developed around the problem (Thompson 2008), feelings that I expect many researchers can understand.

The Netflix Prize is a classic example of an open call. Netflix posed a question with a specific goal (predicting movie ratings) and solicited solutions from many people. Netflix was able to evaluate all these solutions because they were easier to check than to create, and ultimately Netflix picked the best solution. Next, I'll show you how this same approach can be used in biology and law, and without a million-dollar prize.

5.3.2 Foldit

Foldit is a protein-folding game that enables non-experts to participate in a way that is fun.

The Netflix Prize, while evocative and clear, does not illustrate the full range of open call projects. For example, in the Netflix Prize, most of the serious participants had years of training in statistics and machine learning. But open call projects can also involve participants who have no formal training, as was illustrated by Foldit, a protein-folding game.

Protein folding is the process through which a chain of amino acids takes on its shape. With a better understanding of this process, biologists could design proteins with specific shapes that could be used as medicines. Simplifying quite a bit, proteins tend to move to their

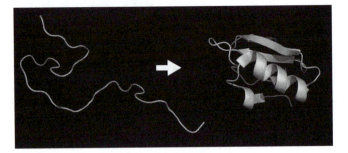

Figure 5.7: Protein folding. Image courtesy of "DrKjaergaard"/Wikimedia Commons.

lowest-energy configuration, a configuration that balances the various pushes and pulls within the protein (figure 5.7). So, if a researcher wants to predict the shape into which a protein will fold, the solution sounds simple: just try all possible configurations, calculate their energies, and predict that the protein will fold into the lowest-energy configuration. Unfortunately, trying all possible configurations is computationally impossible because there are billions and billions of potential configurations. Even with the most powerful computers available today—and in the foreseeable future—brute force is just not going to work. Therefore, biologists have developed many clever algorithms to efficiently search for the lowest-energy configuration. But, despite massive amounts of scientific and computational effort, these algorithms are still far from perfect.

David Baker and his research group at the University of Washington were part of the community of scientists working to create computational approaches to protein folding. In one project, Baker and colleagues developed a system that allowed volunteers to donate unused time on their computers to help simulate protein folding. In return, the volunteers could watch a screensaver showing the protein folding that was happening on their computer. Several of these volunteers wrote to Baker and colleagues saying that they thought that they could improve on the computer's performance if they could get involved in the calculation. And thus began Foldit (Hand 2010).

Foldit turns the process of protein folding into a game that can be played by anyone. From the perspective of the player, Foldit appears to be a puzzle (figure 5.8). Players are presented with a three-dimensional tangle of protein structure and can perform operations—"tweak," "wiggle," "rebuild"—that

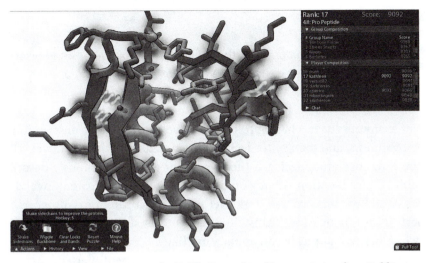

Figure 5.8: Game screen for Foldit. Reproduced by permission from Foldit.

change its shape. By performing these operations, players change the shape of the protein, which in turn increases or decreases their score. Critically, the score is calculated based on the energy level of the current configuration; lower-energy configurations result in higher scores. In other words, the score helps guide the players as they search for low-energy configurations. This game is only possible because—just like predicting movie ratings in the Netflix Prize—protein folding is also a situation where it is easier to check solutions than generate them.

Foldit's elegant design enables players with little formal knowledge of biochemistry to compete with the best algorithms designed by experts. While most players are not particularly good at the task, there are a few individual players and small teams of players who are exceptional. In fact, in a head-to-head competition between Foldit players and state-of-the-art algorithms, the players created better solutions for 5 out of 10 proteins (Cooper et al. 2010).

Foldit and the Netflix prize are different in many ways, but they both involve open calls for solutions that are easier to check than generate. Now, we will see the same structure in yet another very different setting: patent law. This final example of an open call problem shows that this approach can also be used in settings that are not obviously amenable to quantification.

5.3.3 Peer-to-Patent

> Peer-to-Patent is an open call that helps patent examiners find prior
> art; it shows that open calls can be used for problems that are not
> amenable to quantification.

Patent examiners have a hard job. They receive terse, lawyerly descriptions of
new inventions, and then must decide if the stated invention is "novel." That
is, the examiner must decide if there is "prior art"—a previously described
version of this invention—that would render the proposed patent invalid. To
understand how this process works, let's consider a patent examiner named
Albert, in honor of Albert Einstein, who got his start in the Swiss Patent
Office. Albert could receive an application like US Patent 20070118658 filed
by Hewlett Packard for a "User-selectable management alert format" and
described extensively in Beth Noveck's book *Wiki Government* (2009). Here's
the first claim from the application:

> "A computer system, comprising: a processor; a basic input/output
> system (BIOS) including logic instructions which, when executed by the
> processor, configure the processor to: initiate power on self test (POST)
> processing in the basic input/output system of a computing device;
> present one or more management alert formats in a user interface;
> receive a selection signal from the user interface identifying one of
> the management alert formats presented in the user interface; and
> configure a device coupled to the computing system with the identified
> management alert format."

Should Albert award 20-year monopoly rights to this patent or has there been
prior art? The stakes in many patent decisions are high, but unfortunately,
Albert will have to make this decision without much of the information that
he might need. Because of the huge backlog of patents, Albert is working
under intense time pressure and must make his decision based on only 20
hours of work. Further, because of the need to keep the proposed invention
secret, Albert is not allowed to consult with outside experts (Noveck 2006).

This situation struck law professor Beth Noveck as completely broken.
In July 2005, inspired in part by Wikipedia, she created a blog post titled
"Peer-to-Patent: A Modest Proposal" that called for an open peer-review

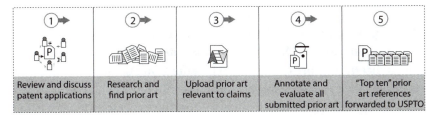

①	②	③	④	⑤
Review and discuss patent applications	Research and find prior art	Upload prior art relevant to claims	Annotate and evaluate all submitted prior art	"Top ten" prior art references forwarded to USPTO

Figure 5.9: Peer-to-Patent workflow. Reproduced from Bestor and Hamp (2010).

system for patents. After collaboration with the US Patent and Trademark Office and leading technology companies such as IBM, Peer-to-Patent was launched in June 2007. A nearly 200-year-old governmental bureaucracy and a group of lawyers seems like an unlikely place to look for innovation, but Peer-to-Patent does a lovely job of balancing everyone's interest.

Here's how it works (figure 5.9). After an inventor agrees to have her application go through community review (more on why she might do that in a moment), the application is posted to a website. Next, the application is discussed by community reviewers (again, more on why they might participate in a moment), and examples of possible prior art are located, annotated, and uploaded to a website. This process of discussion, research, and uploading continues, until, ultimately, the community of reviewers votes to select the top 10 pieces of suspected prior art that are then sent to the patent examiner for review. The patent examiner then conducts her own research and in combination with the input from Peer-to-Patent renders a judgment.

Let's return to US Patent 20070118658 for a "User-selectable management alert format." This patent was uploaded to Peer-to-Patent in June 2007, where it was read by Steve Pearson, a senior software engineer for IBM. Pearson was familiar with this area of research and identified a piece of prior art: a manual from Intel entitled "Active Management Technology: Quick Reference Guide" that had been published two years earlier. Armed with this document, as well as other prior art and the discussion from the Peer-to-Patent community, a patent examiner began a thorough review of the case, and ultimately threw out the patent application, in part because of the Intel manual that was located by Pearson (Noveck 2009). Of the 66 cases that have completed Peer-to-Patent, nearly 30% have been rejected primarily based on prior art found through Peer-to-Patent (Bestor and Hamp 2010).

What makes the design of Peer-to-Patent especially elegant is the way that it gets people with many conflicting interests to all dance together. Inventors have an incentive to participate because the patent office reviews the Peer-to-Patent applications more quickly than patents going through the traditional, secret review process. Reviewers have an incentive to participate in order to prevent bad patents, and many seem to find the process enjoyable. Finally, the patent office and patent examiners have an incentive to participate because this approach can only improve their results. That is, if the community review process finds 10 unhelpful pieces of prior art, these unhelpful pieces can be ignored by the patent examiner. In other words, Peer-to-Patent and a patent examiner working together should be as good as or better than a patent examiner working in isolation. Thus, open calls do not always replace experts; sometimes they help experts do their work better.

Although Peer-to-Patent may seem different than the Netflix Prize and Foldit, it has a similar structure in that solutions are easier to check than generate. Once someone has produced the manual "Active Management Technology: Quick Reference Guide," it is relatively easy—for a patent examiner, at least—to verify that this document is prior art. However, finding that manual is quite difficult. Peer-to-Patent also shows that open call projects are possible even for problems that are not obviously amenable to quantification.

5.3.4 Conclusion

Open calls enable you to find solutions to problems that you can state clearly but that you cannot solve yourself.

In all three open call projects described here—Netflix Prize, Foldit, Peer-to-Patent—researchers posed questions of a specific form, solicited solutions, and then picked the best solutions. The researchers didn't even need to know the best expert to ask, and sometimes the good ideas came from unexpected places.

Now I can also highlight two important differences between open call projects and human computation projects. First, in open call projects, the researcher specifies a goal (e.g., predicting movie ratings), whereas in human computation, the researcher specifies a microtask (e.g., classifying a galaxy). Second, in open calls, the researchers want the best contribution—such as the best algorithm for predicting movie ratings, the lowest-energy configuration of a protein, or the most relevant piece of prior art—not some sort of simple combination of all of the contributions.

Given the general template for open calls and these three examples, what kinds of problems in social research might be suitable for this approach? At this point, I should acknowledge that there have not been many successful examples yet (for reasons that I'll explain in a moment). In terms of direct analogs, one could imagine a Peer-to-Patent style open call being used by a historical researcher searching for the earliest document to mention a specific person or idea. An open call approach to this kind of problem could be especially valuable when the potentially relevant documents are not in a single archive but are widely distributed.

More generally, many governments and companies have problems that might be amenable to open calls because open calls can generate algorithms that can be used for predictions, and these predictions can be an important guide for action (Provost and Fawcett 2013; Kleinberg et al. 2015). For example, just as Netflix wanted to predict ratings on movies, governments might want to predict outcomes such as which restaurants are most likely to have health-code violations in order to allocate inspection resources more efficiently. Motivated by this kind of problem, Edward Glaeser and colleagues (2016) used an open call to help the City of Boston predict restaurant hygiene and sanitation violations based on data from Yelp reviews and historical inspection data. They estimated that the predictive model that won the open call would improve the productivity of restaurant inspectors by about 50%.

Open calls can also potentially be used to compare and test theories. For example, the Fragile Families and Child Wellbeing Study has tracked about 5,000 children since birth in 20 different US cities (Reichman et al. 2001). Researchers have collected data about these children, their families, and their broader environment at birth and at ages 1, 3, 5, 9, and 15. Given all the information about these children, how well could researchers predict outcomes such as who will graduate from college? Or, expressed in a way that would be more interesting to some researchers, which data and theories would be most effective in predicting these outcomes? Since none of these children are currently old enough to go to college, this would be a true forward-looking prediction, and there are many different strategies that researchers might employ. A researcher who believes that neighborhoods are critical in shaping life outcomes might take one approach, while a researcher who focuses on families might do something completely different. Which of these approaches would work better? We don't know, and in the process of finding out, we might learn something important about families, neighborhoods, education, and social inequality. Further, these predictions might be used to guide future data collection. Imagine that there were a small number of college graduates who were not predicted to graduate by any of the models; these people would be ideal candidates for follow-up qualitative interviews and ethnographic observation. Thus, in this kind of open call, the predictions are not the end; rather, they provide a new way to compare, enrich, and combine different theoretical traditions. This kind of open call is not specific to using data from the Fragile Families and Child Wellbeing Study to predict who will go to college; it could be used to predict any outcome that will eventually be collected in any longitudinal social data set.

As I wrote earlier in this section, there have not been many examples of social researchers using open calls. I think that this is because open calls are not well suited to the way that social scientists typically ask their questions. Returning to the Netflix Prize, social scientists wouldn't usually ask about predicting tastes; rather, they would ask about how and why cultural tastes differ for people from different social classes (see, e.g., Bourdieu (1987)). Such "how" and "why" questions do not lead to easily verifiable solutions, and therefore seem poorly fit to open calls. Thus, it appears that open calls are more appropriate for questions of *prediction* than questions of *explanation*. Recent theorists, however, have called on social scientists to reconsider the dichotomy between explanation and prediction (Watts 2014). As the line between prediction and explanation blurs, I expect open calls to become increasingly common in social research.

5.4   Distributed data collection

> Mass collaboration can also help with data collection, but it is tricky
> to ensure data quality and systematic approaches to sampling.

In addition to creating human computation projects and open calls, researchers can also create distributed data collection projects. In fact, much of quantitative social science already relies on distributed data collection using paid staff. For example, to collect the data for the General Social Survey, a company hires interviewers to collect information from respondents. But what if we could somehow enlist volunteers as data collectors?

As the examples below—from ornithology and computer science—show, distributed data collection enables researchers to collect data more frequently and in more places than were possible previously. Further, given appropriate protocols, these data can be reliable enough to be used for scientific research. In fact, for certain research questions, distributed data collection is better than anything that would realistically be possible with paid data collectors.

5.4.1 eBird

eBird collects data on birds from birders; volunteers provide scale that no research team can match.

Birds are everywhere, and ornithologists would like to know where every bird is at every moment. Given such a perfect dataset, ornithologists could address many fundamental questions in their field. Of course, collecting these data is beyond the scope of any particular researcher. At the same time that ornithologists desire richer and more complete data, "birders"—people who go bird watching for fun—are constantly observing birds and documenting what they see. These two communities have a long history of collaborating, but now these collaborations have been transformed by the digital age. eBird is a distributed data collection project that solicits information from birders around the world, and it has already received over 260 million bird sightings from 250,000 participants (Kelling, Fink, et al. 2015).

Prior to the launch of eBird, most of the data created by birders were unavailable to researchers:

"In thousands of closets around the world today lie countless notebooks, index cards, annotated checklists, and diaries. Those of us involved with birding institutions know well the frustration of hearing over and over again about 'my late-uncle's bird records' [sic] We know how valuable they could be. Sadly, we also know we can't use them." (Fitzpatrick et al. 2002)

Rather than having these valuable data sit unused, eBird enables birders to upload them to a centralized, digital database. Data uploaded to eBird contain six key fields: who, where, when, what species, how many, and effort. For non-birding readers, "effort" refers to the methods used while making observations. Data quality checks begin even before the data are uploaded. Birders trying to submit unusual reports—such as reports of very rare species, very high counts, or out-of-season reports—are flagged, and the website automatically requests additional information, such as photographs. After collecting this additional information, the flagged reports are sent to one of hundreds of volunteer regional experts for further review. After investigation by the regional expert—including possible additional correspondence with the birder—the flagged reports are either discarded as unreliable or entered into the eBird database (Kelling et al. 2012). This database of screened observations is then made available to anyone in the world with an Internet connection, and, so far, almost 100 peer-reviewed publications have used it (Bonney et al. 2014). eBird clearly shows that volunteer birders are able to collect data that are useful for real ornithology research.

One of the beauties of eBird is that it captures "work" that is already happening—in this case, birding. This feature enables the project to collect data at a tremendous scale. However, the "work" done by birders does not exactly match the data needed by ornithologists. For example, in eBird, data collection is determined by the location of birders, not the location of the birds. This means that, for example, most observations tend to occur close to roads (Kelling et al. 2012; Kelling, Fink, et al. 2015). In addition to this unequal distribution of effort over space, the actual observations made by birders are not always ideal. For example, some birders only upload information about species that they consider interesting, rather than information on all species that they observed.

eBird researchers have two main solutions to these data quality issues—solutions that might be helpful in other distributed data collection projects as well. First, eBird researchers are constantly trying to upgrade the quality of the data submitted by birders. For example, eBird offers education to participants, and it has created visualizations of each participant's data that, by their design, encourage birders to upload information about all species that they observed, not just the most interesting (Wood et al. 2011; Wiggins 2011). Second, eBird researchers use statistical models that attempt to correct for the noisy and heterogeneous nature of the raw data (Fink et al. 2010; Hurlbert and Liang 2012). It is not yet clear if these statistical models fully remove biases from the data, but ornithologists are confident enough in the quality of adjusted eBird data that, as had been mentioned earlier, these data have been used in almost 100 peer-reviewed scientific publications.

Many non-ornithologists are initially extremely skeptical when they hear about eBird for the first time. In my opinion, part of this skepticism comes from thinking about eBird in the wrong way. Many people first think "Are the eBird data perfect?", and the answer is "absolutely not." However, that's not the right question. The right question is "For certain research questions, are the eBird data better than existing ornithology data?" For that question, the answer is "definitely yes," in part because, for many questions of interest—such as questions about large-scale seasonal migration—there are no realistic alternatives to distributed data collection.

The eBird project demonstrates that it is possible to involve volunteers in the collection of important scientific data. However, eBird, and related projects, indicate that challenges related to sampling and data quality are concerns for distributed data collection projects. As we will see in the next section, however, with clever design and technology, these concerns can be minimized in some settings.

5.4.2 PhotoCity

PhotoCity solves the data quality and sampling problems in distributed data collection.

Websites such as Flickr and Facebook enable people to share pictures with their friends and family, and they also create huge repositories of photos that can be used for other purposes. For example, Sameer Agarwal and colleagues (2011) attempted to use these photos to "Build Rome in a Day" by repurposing 150,000 pictures of Rome to create a 3D reconstruction of the city. For some heavily photographed buildings—such as the Coliseum (figure 5.10)—the researchers were partially successful, but the reconstructions suffered because most photos were taken from the same iconic perspectives, leaving portions of the buildings unphotographed. Thus, the images from photo repositories were not enough. But what if volunteers could be enlisted to collect the necessary photos to enrich those already available? Thinking back to the art analogy in chapter 1, what if the readymade images could be enriched by custommade images?

Figure 5.10: A 3D reconstruction of the Coliseum from a large set of 2D images from the project "Building Rome in a Day." The triangles represent the locations from which the photographs were taken. Reproduced by permission from the Association for Computing Machinery, Inc. from Agarwal et al. (2011).

Figure 5.11: PhotoCity turned the potentially laborious task of collecting data (i.e., uploading photos) and turned it into a game. Reproduced by permission from the Association for Computing Machinery, Inc. from Tuite et al. (2011), figure 2.

In order to enable the targeted collection of large numbers of photos, Kathleen Tuite and colleagues developed PhotoCity, a photo-uploading game. PhotoCity turned the potentially laborious task of data collection—uploading photos—into a game-like activity involving teams, castles, and flags (figure 5.11), and it was first deployed to create a 3D reconstruction of two universities: Cornell University and the University of Washington. Researchers started the process by uploading seed photos from some

a. Lewis Hall (UW)   **b.** Sage Chapel (Cornell)   **c.** Uris Library (Cornell)

Figure 5.12: The PhotoCity game enabled researchers and participants to create high-quality 3D models of buildings using photos uploaded by participants. Reproduced by permission from the Association for Computing Machinery, Inc. from Tuite et al. (2011), figure 8.

buildings. Then, players on each campus inspected the current state of the reconstruction and earned points by uploading images that improved the reconstruction. For example, if the current reconstruction of Uris Library (at Cornell) was very patchy, a player could earn points by uploading new pictures of it. Two features of this uploading process are very important. First, the number of points a player received was based on the amount that their photo added to reconstruction. Second, the photos that were uploaded had to overlap with existing reconstruction so that they could be validated. In the end, the researchers were able to create high-resolution 3D models of buildings on both campuses (figure 5.12).

The design of PhotoCity solved two problems that often arise in distributed data collection: data validation and sampling. First, photos were validated by comparing them against previous photos, which were in turn compared with previous photos all the way back to the seed photos that were uploaded by researchers. In other words, because of this built-in redundancy, it was very difficult for someone to upload a photo of the wrong building, either accidentally or intentionally. This design feature meant that the system protected itself against bad data. Second, the scoring system naturally trained participants to collect the most valuable—not the most convenient—data. In fact, here are some of the strategies that players described using in order to earn more points, which is equivalent to collecting more valuable data (Tuite et al. 2011):

- "[I tried to] approximate the time of day and the lighting that some pictures were taken; this would help prevent rejection by the game. With that said, cloudy days were the best by far when dealing with corners because less contrast helped the game figure out the geometry from my pictures."

- "When it was sunny, I utilized my camera's anti-shake features to allow myself to take photos while walking around a particular zone. This allowed me to take crisp photos while not having to stop my stride. Also bonus: less people stared at me!"

- "Taking many pictures of one building with 5 megapixel camera, then coming home to submit, sometimes up to 5 gigs on a weekend shoot, was primary photo capture strategy. Organizing photos on external hard drive folders by campus region, building, then face of building provided good hierarchy to structure uploads."

These statements show that when participants are provided with appropriate feedback, they can become quite expert at collecting data of interest to researchers.

Overall, the PhotoCity project shows that sampling and data quality are not insurmountable problems in distributed data collection. Further, it shows that distributed data collection projects are not limited to tasks that people are already doing anyway, such as watching birds. With the right design, volunteers can be encouraged to do other things too.

5.4.3 Conclusion

Distributed data collection is possible, and in the future it will likely involve technology and passive participation.

As eBird demonstrates, distributed data collection can be used for scientific research. Further, PhotoCity shows that problems related to sampling and data quality are potentially solvable. How might distributed data collection work for social research? One example comes from the work of Susan Watkins and her colleagues on the Malawi Journals Project (Watkins and Swidler 2009; Kaler, Watkins, and Angotti 2015). In this project, 22 local residents—called "journalists"—kept "conversational journals" that recorded, in detail, the conversations they overheard about AIDS in the daily lives of ordinary people (at the time the project began, about 15% of adults in Malawi were infected with HIV (Bello, Chipeta, and Aberle-Grasse 2006)). Because of their insider status, these journalists were able to overhear conversations that might have been inaccessible to Watkins and

Table 5.3: Examples of Distributed Data Collection Projects in Social Research

Data collected	Reference
Discussions about HIV/AIDS in Malawi	Watkins and Swidler (2009); Kaler, Watkins, and Angotti (2015)
Street begging in London	Purdam (2014)
Conflict events in Eastern Congo	Windt and Humphreys (2016)
Economic activity in Nigeria and Liberia	Blumenstock, Keleher, and Reisinger (2016)
Influenza surveillance	van Noort et al. (2015)

her Western research collaborators (I'll discuss the ethics of this later in the chapter when I offer advice about designing your own mass collaboration project). The data from the Malawi Journals Project have led to a number of important findings. For example, before the project started, many outsiders believed that there was silence about AIDS in sub-Saharan Africa, but the conversational journals demonstrated that this was clearly not the case: journalists overheard hundreds of discussions of the topic, in locations as diverse as funerals, bars, and churches. Further, the nature of these conversations helped researchers better understand some of the resistance to condom use; the way that condom use was framed in public health messages was inconsistent with the way that it was discussed in everyday life (Tavory and Swidler 2009).

Of course, like the data from eBird, the data from the Malawi Journals Project are not perfect, an issue discussed in detail by Watkins and colleagues. For example, the recorded conversations are not a random sample of all possible conversations. Rather, they are an incomplete census of conversations about AIDS. In terms of data quality, the researchers believed that their journalists were high-quality reporters, as evidenced by the consistency within journals and across journals. That is, because enough journalists were deployed in a small enough setting and focused on a specific topic, it was possible to use redundancy to assess and ensure data quality. For example, a sex worker named "Stella" showed up several times in the journals of four different journalists (Watkins and Swidler 2009). In order to further build your intuition, table 5.3 shows other examples of distributed data collection for social research.

All of the examples described in this section have involved active participation: journalists transcribed conversations that they heard; birders uploaded their birding checklists; or players uploaded their photos. But what if the participation was automatic and did not require any specific skill or time to submit? This is the promise offered by "participatory sensing" or "people-centric sensing." For example, the Pothole Patrol, a project by scientists at MIT, mounted GPS-equipped accelerometers inside seven taxi cabs in the Boston area (Eriksson et al. 2008). Because driving over a pothole leaves a distinct accelerometer signal, these devices, when placed inside of moving taxis, can create pothole maps of Boston. Of course, taxis don't randomly sample roads, but, given enough taxis, there may be sufficient coverage to provide information about large portions of the city. A second benefit of passive systems that rely on technology is that they de-skill the process of contributing data: while it requires skill to contribute to eBird (because you need to be able to reliably identify bird species), it requires no special skills to contribute to Pothole Patrol.

Going forward, I suspect that many distributed data collection projects will begin to make use of capabilities of the mobile phones that are already carried by billions of people around the world. These phones already have a large number of sensors important for measurement, such as microphones, cameras, GPS devices, and clocks. Further, they support third-party apps enabling researchers some control over the underlying data collection protocols. Finally, they have Internet-connectivity, making it possible for them to off-load the data they collect. There are numerous technical challenges, ranging from inaccurate sensors to limited battery life, but these problems will likely diminish over time as technology develops. Issues related to privacy and ethics, on the other hand, might get more complicated; I'll return to questions of ethics when I offer advice about designing your own mass collaboration.

In distributed data collection projects, volunteers contribute data about the world. This approach has already been used successfully, and future uses will likely have to address sampling and data quality concerns. Fortunately, existing projects such as PhotoCity and Pothole Patrol suggest solutions to these problems. As more projects take advantage of technology that enables de-skilled and passive participation, distributed data collection projects should dramatically increase in scale, enabling researchers to collect data that were simply off limits in the past.

5.5   Designing your own

> Five principles for designing a mass collaboration project: motivate
> participants, leverage heterogeneity, focus attention, enable surprise,
> and be ethical.

Now that you might be excited about the potential for mass collaboration to solve your scientific problem, I'd like to offer you some advice on how to actually do it. Although mass collaborations may be less familiar than the techniques described in earlier chapters, such as surveys and experiments, they are not inherently any more difficult. Because the technologies that you will be able to harness are developing rapidly, the most helpful advice that I can offer is expressed in terms of general principles, rather than step-by-step instructions. More specifically, there are five general principles that I think will help you design a mass collaboration project: motivate participants, leverage heterogeneity, focus attention, enable surprise, and be ethical.

5.5.1 Motivate participants

The biggest challenge in designing a scientific mass collaboration is matching a meaningful scientific problem to a group of people who are willing and able to solve that problem. Sometimes, the problem comes first, as in Galaxy Zoo: given the task of categorizing galaxies, the researchers found people who could help. However, other times, the people come first and the problem second. For example, eBird attempts to harness the "work" that people are already doing to help scientific research.

The simplest way to motivate participants is money. For example, any researcher creating a human computation project on a microtask labor market (e.g., Amazon Mechanical Turk) is going to motivate participants with money. Financial motivation may be sufficient for some human computation problems, but many of the examples of mass collaboration in this chapter did not use money to motivate participation (Galaxy Zoo, Foldit, Peer-to-Patent, eBird, and PhotoCity). Instead, many of the more complex projects rely on a combination of personal value and collective value. Roughly, personal value comes from things like fun and competition (Foldit and PhotoCity), and collective value can come from knowing that your contribution is helping a greater good (Foldit, Galaxy Zoo, eBird, and Peer-to-Patent) (table 5.4).

Table 5.4: Likely Motivations of Participants in the Main Projects Described in this Chapter

Project	Motivation
Galaxy Zoo	Helping science, fun, community
Crowd-coding political manifestos	Money
Netflix Prize	Money, intellectual challenge, competition, community
Foldit	Helping science, fun, competition, community
Peer-to-Patent	Helping society, fun, community
eBird	Helping science, fun
PhotoCity	Fun, competition, community
Malawi Journals Project	Money, helping science

If you are building your own project, you should think what will motivate people to participate and the ethical issues raised by those motivations (more on ethics later in this section).

5.5.2 Leverage heterogeneity

Once you have motivated a lot of people to work on a real scientific problem, you will discover that your participants will be heterogeneous in two main ways: they will vary both in their skill and in their level of effort. The first reaction of many social researchers is to fight against this heterogeneity by trying to exclude low-quality participants and then attempting to collect a fixed amount of information from everyone left. This is the wrong way to design a mass collaboration project. Instead of fighting heterogeneity, you should leverage it.

First, there is no reason to exclude low-skilled participants. In open calls, low-skilled participants cause no problems; their contributions don't hurt anyone and they don't require any time to evaluate. In human computation and distributed data collection projects, moreover, the best form of quality control comes through redundancy, not through a high bar for participation. In fact, rather than excluding low-skilled participants, a better approach is to help them make better contributions, much as the researchers at eBird have done.

Second, there is no reason to collect a fixed amount of information from each participant. Participation in many mass collaboration projects is incredibly unequal (Sauermann and Franzoni 2015), with a small number of people contributing a lot—sometimes called the *fat head*—and a lot of people contributing a little—sometimes called the *long tail*. If you don't collect information from the fat head and the long tail, you are leaving masses of information uncollected. For example, if Wikipedia accepted 10 and only 10 edits per editor, it would lose about 95% of edits (Salganik and Levy 2015). Thus, with mass collaboration projects, it is best to leverage heterogeneity rather than try to eliminate it.

5.5.3 Focus attention

Given that you have found a way to motivate participation and you are able to leverage participants with wide-ranging interests and skills, the next major challenge you have as a designer is to focus participants' attention where it will be the most valuable, a point developed extensively in Michael Nielsen's book *Reinventing Discovery* (2012). In human computation projects, such as Galaxy Zoo, where researchers have explicit control of the tasks, the focus of attention is easiest to maintain. For example, in Galaxy Zoo, the researchers could have shown each galaxy until there was agreement about its shape. Further, in distributed data collection, a scoring system can also be used to focus individuals on providing the most useful input, as was done in PhotoCity.

5.5.4 Enable surprise

Now that you have heterogeneous people working together on a meaningful scientific problem, and you have their attention focused on where it can be most valuable, be sure to leave room for them to surprise you. It is pretty cool that citizen scientists have labeled galaxies at Galaxy Zoo and folded proteins at Foldit. But, of course, that is what these projects were designed to enable. What is even more amazing, in my opinion, is that these communities have produced scientific results that were unanticipated even by their creators. For example, the Galaxy Zoo community has discovered a new class of astronomical object that they called "Green Peas."

Very early in the Galaxy Zoo project, a few people had noticed unusual green objects, but interest in them crystallized when Hanny van Arkel, a Dutch school teacher, started a thread in the Galaxy Zoo discussion forum with the catchy title: "Give Peas a Chance." The thread, which began August 12, 2007, started with jokes: "Are you collecting them for dinner?," "Peas stop," and so on. But pretty soon, other Zooites started posting their own peas. Over time, the posts became more technical and detailed, until posts like this started showing up: "The OIII line (the 'pea' line, at 5007 angstrom) that you are following shifts towards the red as z increases and disappears into the infra-red at about $z = 0.5$, ie is invisible" (Nielsen 2012).

Over time, the Zooites were gradually understanding and systematizing their observations of the peas. Finally, on July 8, 2008—almost a full year later—Carolin Cardamone, an astronomy graduate student at Yale and member of the Galaxy Zoo team, joined the thread to help organize the "Pea Hunt." More enthusiastic work ensued, and by July 9, 2009, a paper had been published in the *Monthly Notices of the Royal Astronomical Society* with the title "Galaxy Zoo Green Peas: Discovery of a Class of Compact Extremely Star-Forming Galaxies" (Cardamone et al. 2009). But interest in the peas didn't end there. Subsequently, they have been the subject of further research by astronomers around the world (Izotov, Guseva, and Thuan 2011; Chakraborti et al. 2012; Hawley 2012; Amorín et al. 2012). Then, in 2016, less than 10 years after the first post by a Zooite, a paper published in *Nature* proposed Green Peas as a possible explanation for an important and puzzling pattern in the ionization of the universe. None of this was ever imagined when Kevin Schawinski and Chris Lintott first discussed Galaxy Zoo in a pub in Oxford. Fortunately, Galaxy Zoo enabled these kinds of unexpected surprises by allowing participants to communicate with each other.

5.5.5 Be ethical

The exhortation to be ethical applies to all the research described in this book. In addition to the more general issues of ethics—discussed in chapter 6— some specific ethical issues arise in the case of mass collaboration projects, and since mass collaboration is so new to social research, these problems might not be fully apparent at first.

In all mass collaboration projects, issues of compensation and credit are complex. For example, some people consider it unethical that thousands of people worked for years on the Netflix Prize and ultimately received no compensation. Similarly, some people consider it unethical to pay workers on microtask labor markets extremely small amounts of money. In addition to these issues of compensation, there are related issues of credit. Should all participants in a mass collaboration be authors of the eventual scientific papers? Different projects take different approaches. Some projects give authorship credit to all members of the mass collaboration; for example, the final author of the first Foldit paper was "Foldit players" (Cooper et al. 2010). In the Galaxy Zoo family of projects, extremely active and important contributors are sometimes invited to be coauthors on papers. For example, Ivan Terentev and Tim Matorny, two Radio Galaxy Zoo participants were coauthors on one of the papers that arose from that project (Banfield et al. 2016; Galaxy Zoo 2016). Sometimes projects merely acknowledge contributions without coauthorship. Decisions about coauthorship will obviously vary from case to case.

Open calls and distributed data collection can also raise complex questions about consent and privacy. For example, Netflix released customers' movie ratings to everyone. Although movie ratings might not appear sensitive, they can reveal information about customers' political preferences or sexual orientation, information that customers did not agree to make public. Netflix attempted to anonymize the data so that the ratings could not be linked to any specific individual, but just weeks after the release of the Netflix data, it was partially re-identified by Arvind Narayanan and Vitaly Shmatikov (2008) (see chapter 6). Further, in distributed data collection, researchers could collect data about people without their consent. For example, in the Malawi Journals Projects, conversations about a sensitive topic (AIDS) were transcribed without the consent of the participants. None of these ethical problems are insurmountable, but they should be considered in the design phase of a project. Remember, your "crowd" is made up of people.

5.5.6 Final design advice

In addition to these five general design principles, I'd like to offer two other pieces of advice. First, the immediate reaction that you might encounter when you propose a mass collaboration project is "Nobody would participate." Of course that might be true. In fact, lack of participation is the biggest risk that mass collaboration projects face. However, this objection usually arises from thinking about the situation in the wrong way. Many people start with themselves and work out: "I'm busy; I wouldn't do that. And I don't know anyone that would do that. So, nobody would do that." Instead of starting with yourself and working out, however, you should start with the entire population of people connected to the Internet and work in. If only one in a million of these people participate, then your project could be a success. But, if only one in a billion participate, then your project will probably be a failure. Since our intuition is not good at distinguishing between one in a million and one in a billion, we have to acknowledge that it is very hard to know if projects will generate sufficient participation.

To make this a bit more concrete, let's return to Galaxy Zoo. Imagine Kevin Schawinski and Chris Linton, two astronomers sitting in a pub in Oxford thinking about Galaxy Zoo. They would never have guessed—and never could have guessed—that Aida Berges, a stay-at-home mother of two living in Puerto Rico, would end up classifying hundreds of galaxies a week (Masters 2009). Or consider the case of David Baker, the biochemist working in Seattle developing Foldit. He could never have anticipated that someone from McKinney, Texas named Scott "Boots" Zaccanelli, who worked by day as a buyer for a valve factory, would spend his evenings folding proteins, eventually rising to a number-six ranking on Foldit, and that Zaccaenlli would, through the game, submit a design for a more stable variant of fibronectin that Baker and his group found so promising that they decided to synthesize it in their lab (Hand 2010). Of course, Aida Berges and Scott Zaccanelli are atypical, but that is the power of the Internet: with billions of people, it is typical to find the atypical.

Second, given this difficulty with predicting participation, I'd like to remind you that creating a mass collaboration project can be risky. You could invest a lot of effort in building a system that nobody will want to use. For example, Edward Castronova—a leading researcher in the field of economics of virtual worlds, armed with a grant of $250,000 from the MacArthur Foundation, and supported by a team of developers—spent nearly two years trying to build a virtual world within which he could conduct economic experiments. In the end, the whole effort was a failure because nobody wanted to play in Castonova's virtual world; it just wasn't very much fun (Baker 2008).

Given the uncertainty about participation, which is hard to eliminate, I suggest that you try to use lean start-up techniques (Blank 2013): build simple prototypes using off-the-shelf software and see if you can demonstrate viability before investing in lots of custom software development. In other words, when you start pilot testing, your project will not—and should not—look as polished as Galaxy Zoo or eBird. These projects, as they are now, are the results of years of effort by large teams. If your project is going to fail—and that is a real possibility—then you want to fail fast.

5.6 Conclusion

> Mass collaboration will enable researchers to solve scientific problems that were impossible to solve before.

The digital age enables mass collaboration in scientific research. Rather than just collaborating with a small number of colleagues or research assistants, as in the past, we can now collaborate with everyone in the world who has an Internet connection. As the examples in this chapter show, these new forms of mass collaboration have already enabled real progress on important problems. Some skeptics may doubt the applicability of mass collaboration for social research, but I am optimistic. Quite simply, there are a lot of people in the world, and if our talents and energies can be harnessed, we can do amazing things together. In other words, in addition to learning from people by observing their behavior (chapter 2), asking them questions (chapter 3), or enrolling them in experiments (chapter 4), we can also learn from people by making them research collaborators.

For the purposes of social research, I think it is helpful to divide mass collaboration projects into three rough groups:

- In **human computation** projects, researchers combine the efforts of many people working on simple microtasks in order to solve problems that are impossibly big for one person.
- In **open call** projects, researchers pose a problem with an easy-to-check solution, solicit solutions from many people, and then pick the best.
- In **distributed data collection** projects, researchers enable participants to contribute new measurements of the world.

In addition to advancing social research, mass collaboration projects also have democratizing potential. These projects broaden both the range of people who can organize large-scale projects and the range of people who can contribute to them. Just as Wikipedia changed what we thought was possible, future mass collaboration projects will change what we think is possible in scientific research.

What to read next

- **Introduction (section 5.1)**

    Mass collaboration blends ideas from *citizen science, crowdsourcing,* and *collective intelligence.* Citizen science usually means involving "citizens" (i.e., nonscientists) in the scientific process; for more, see Crain, Cooper, and Dickinson (2014) and Bonney et al. (2014). Crowdsourcing usually means taking a problem ordinarily solved within an organization and instead outsourcing it to a crowd; for more, see Howe (2009). Collective intelligence usually means groups of individuals acting collectively in ways that seem intelligent; for more, see Malone and Bernstein (2015). Nielsen (2012) is a book-length introduction to the power of mass collaboration for scientific research.

    There are many types of mass collaboration that don't fit neatly into the three categories that I have proposed, and I think three of these deserve special attention because they might be useful in social research. One example is prediction markets, where participants buy and trade contracts that are redeemable based on outcomes that occur in the world. Predicting markets are often used by firms and governments for forecasting, and they have also been used by social researchers to predict the replicability of published studies in psychology (Dreber et al. 2015). For an overview of prediction markets, see Wolfers and Zitzewitz (2004) and Arrow et al. (2008).

    A second example that does not fit well into my categorization scheme is the PolyMath project, where researchers collaborated using blogs and wikis to prove new math theorems. The PolyMath project is in some ways similar to the Netflix Prize, but in this project participants more actively built on the partial solutions of others. For more on the PolyMath project, see Gowers and Nielsen (2009), Cranshaw and Kittur (2011), Nielsen (2012), and Kloumann et al. (2016).

    A third example that does not fit well into my categorization scheme is that of time-dependent mobilizations such as the Defense Advanced Research Projects Agency (DARPA) Network Challenge (i.e., the Red Balloon Challenge). For more on these time-sensitive mobilizations see Pickard et al. (2011), Tang et al. (2011), and Rutherford et al. (2013).

- **Human computation (section 5.2)**

The term "human computation" comes out of work done by computer scientists, and understanding the context behind this research will improve your ability to pick out problems that might be suitable for it. For certain tasks, computers are incredibly powerful, with capabilities far exceeding those of even expert humans. For example, in chess, computers can beat even the best grandmasters. But—and this is less well appreciated by social scientists—for other tasks, computers are actually much worse than people. In other words, right now you are better than even the most sophisticated computer at certain tasks involving processing of images, video, audio, and text. Computer scientists working on these hard-for-computers–easy-for-human tasks therefore realized that they could include humans in their computational process. Here's how Luis von Ahn (2005) described human computation when he first coined the term in his dissertation: "a paradigm for utilizing human processing power to solve problems that computers cannot yet solve." For a book-length treatment of human computation, in the most general sense of the term, see Law and von Ahn (2011).

According to the definition proposed in von Ahn (2005), Foldit—which I described in the section on open calls—could be considered a human computation project. However, I choose to categorize Foldit as an open call, because it requires specialized skills (although not necessarily formal training) and it takes the best solution contributed, rather than using a split–apply–combine strategy.

The term "split–apply–combine" was used by Wickham (2011) to describe a strategy for statistical computing, but it perfectly captures the process of many human computation projects. The split–apply–combine strategy is similar to the MapReduce framework developed at Google; for more on MapReduce, see Dean and Ghemawat (2004) and Dean and Ghemawat (2008). For more on other distributed computing architectures, see Vo and Silvia (2016). Chapter 3 of Law and von Ahn (2011) has a discussion of projects with more complex combine steps than those in this chapter.

In the human computation projects that I have discussed in this chapter, participants were aware of what was happening. Some other projects, however, seek to capture "work" that is already happening (similar to eBird) and without participant awareness. See, for example, the ESP Game (von Ahn and Dabbish 2004) and reCAPTCHA (von Ahn et al. 2008). However, both of these projects also raise ethical questions because participants did not know how their data were being used (Zittrain 2008; Lung 2012).

Inspired by the ESP Game, many researchers have attempted to develop other "games with a purpose" (von Ahn and Dabbish 2008) (i.e., "human-based computation games" (Pe-Than, Goh, and Lee 2015)) that can be used to solve a variety of other problems. What these "games with a purpose" have in common is that they try to make the tasks involved in human computation enjoyable.

Thus, while the ESP Game shares the same split–apply–combine structure as Galaxy Zoo, it differs in how participants are motivated—fun versus desire to help science. For more on games with a purpose, see von Ahn and Dabbish (2008).

My description of Galaxy Zoo draws on Nielsen (2012), Adams (2012), Clery (2011), and Hand (2010), and my presentation of the research goals of Galaxy Zoo was simplified. For more on the history of galaxy classification in astronomy and how Galaxy Zoo continues this tradition, see Masters (2012) and Marshall, Lintott, and Fletcher (2015). Building on Galaxy Zoo, the researchers completed Galaxy Zoo 2, which collected more than 60 million more complex morphological classifications from volunteers (Masters et al. 2011). Further, they branched out into problems outside of galaxy morphology, including exploring the surface of the Moon, searching for planets, and transcribing old documents. Currently, all their projects are collected at the Zooniverse website (Cox et al. 2015). One of the projects—Snapshot Serengeti—provides evidence that Galaxy Zoo-type image classification projects can also be done for environmental research (Swanson et al. 2016).

For researchers planning to use a microtask labor market (e.g., Amazon Mechanical Turk) for a human computation project, Chandler, Paolacci, and Mueller (2013) and Wang, Ipeirotis, and Provost (2015) offer good advice on task design and other related issues. Porter, Verdery, and Gaddis (2016) offer examples and advice focused specifically on uses of microtask labor markets for what they call "data augmentation." The line between data augmentation and data collection is somewhat blurry. Finally, for more on collecting and using labels for supervised learning for text, see Grimmer and Stewart (2013).

Researchers interested in creating what I've called computer-assisted human computation systems (e.g., systems that use human labels to train a machine learning model) might be interested in Shamir et al. (2014) (for an example using audio) and Cheng and Bernstein (2015). Also, the machine learning models in these projects can be solicited with open calls, whereby researchers compete to create machine learning models with the greatest predictive performance. For example, the Galaxy Zoo team ran an open call and found a new approach that outperformed the one developed in Banerji et al. (2010); see Dieleman, Willett, and Dambre (2015) for details.

- **Open calls (section 5.3)**

Open calls are not new. In fact, one of the most well-known open calls dates back to 1714 when Britain's Parliament created The Longitude Prize for anyone that could develop a way to determine the longitude of a ship at sea. The problem stumped many of the greatest scientists of the days, including Isaac Newton, and the winning solution was eventually submitted by John Harrison, a clockmaker from the countryside who approached the problem differently from scientists who were focused on a solution that would somehow involve astronomy; for more information, see Sobel (1996). As this example illustrates, one reason that open calls are thought to work so well is that they provide access to people with different perspectives and skills (Boudreau and Lakhani 2013). See Hong and Page (2004) and Page (2008) for more on the value of diversity in problem solving.

Each of the open call cases in the chapter requires a bit of further explanation for why it belongs in this category. First, one way that I distinguish between human computation and open call projects is whether the output is an average of all the solutions (human computation) or the best solution (open call). The Netflix Prize is somewhat tricky in this regard because the best solution turned out to be a sophisticated average of individual solutions, an approach called an ensemble solution (Bell, Koren, and Volinsky 2010; Feuerverger, He, and Khatri 2012). From the perspective of Netflix, however, all they had to do was pick the best solution. For more on the Netflix Prize, see Bennett and Lanning (2007), Thompson (2008), Bell, Koren, and Volinsky (2010), and Feuerverger, He, and Khatri (2012).

Second, by some definitions of human computation (e.g., von Ahn (2005)), Foldit should be considered a human computation project. However, I choose to categorize it as an open call because it requires specialized skills (although not necessarily specialized training) and it takes the best solution, rather than using a split–apply–combine strategy. For more on Foldit, see Cooper et al. (2010), Khatib et al. (2011), and Andersen et al. (2012); my description of Foldit draws on descriptions in Bohannon (2009), Hand (2010), and Nielsen (2012).

Finally, one could argue that Peer-to-Patent is an example of distributed data collection. I choose to include it as an open call because it has a contest-like structure and only the best contributions are used, whereas with distributed data collection, the idea of good and bad contributions is less clear. For more on Peer-to-Patent, see Noveck (2006), Ledford (2007), Noveck (2009), and Bestor and Hamp (2010).

In terms of using open calls in social research, results similar to those of Glaeser et al. (2016) are reported in chapter 10 of Mayer-Schönberger and Cukier (2013), whereby New York City was able to use predictive modeling to produce large gains in the productivity of housing inspectors. In New York City, these predictive models were built by city employees, but in other cases, one could imagine that they could be created or improved with open calls (e.g., Glaeser et al. (2016)). However, one major concern with predictive models being used to allocate resources is that these models have the potential to reinforce existing biases. Many researchers already know "garbage in, garbage out," and with predictive models it can be "bias in, bias out." See Barocas and Selbst (2016) and O'Neil (2016) for more on the dangers of predictive models built with biased training data.

One problem that might prevent governments from using open calls is that this requires data release, which could lead to privacy violations. For more about privacy and data release in open calls, see Narayanan, Huey, and Felten (2016) and the discussion in chapter 6.

For more on the differences and similarities between prediction and explanation, see Breiman (2001), Shmueli (2010), Watts (2014), and Kleinberg et al. (2015). For more on the role of prediction in social research, see Athey (2017), Cederman and Weidmann (2017), Hofman et al. (2017), Subrahmaniian and Kumar (2017), and Yarkoni and Westfall (2017).

For a review of open call projects in biology, including design advice, see Saez-Rodriguez et al. (2016).

- **Distributed data collection (section 5.4)**

My description of eBird draws on descriptions in Bhattacharjee (2005), Robbins (2013), and Sullivan et al. (2014). For more on how researchers use statistical models to analyze eBird data, see Fink et al. (2010) and Hurlbert and Liang (2012). For more on estimating the skill of eBird participants, see Kelling, Johnston, et al. (2015). For more on the history of citizen science in ornithology, see Greenwood (2007).

For more on the Malawi Journals Project, see Watkins and Swidler (2009) and Kaler, Watkins, and Angotti (2015). For more on a related project in South Africa, see Angotti and Sennott (2015). For more examples of research using data from the Malawi Journals Project, see Kaler (2004) and Angotti et al. (2014).

- **Designing your own (section 5.5)**

My approach to offering design advice was inductive, based on the examples of successful and failed mass collaboration projects that I've heard about. There has also been a stream of research attempts to apply more general social psychological theories to designing online communities that is relevant to the design of mass collaboration projects, see, for example, Kraut et al. (2012).

Regarding motivating participants, it is actually quite tricky to figure out exactly why people participate in mass collaboration projects (Cooper et al. 2010; Nov, Arazy, and Anderson 2011; Tuite et al. 2011; Raddick et al. 2013; and Preist, Massung, and Coyle 2014). If you plan to motivate participants with payment on a microtask labor market (e.g., Amazon Mechanical Turk), Kittur et al. (2013) offers some advice.

Regarding enabling surprise, for more examples of unexpected discoveries coming out of Zooniverse projects, see Marshall, Lintott, and Fletcher (2015).

Regarding being ethical, some good general introductions to the issues involved are Gilbert (2015), Salehi et al. (2015), Schmidt (2013), Williamson (2016), Resnik, Elliott, and Miller (2015), and Zittrain (2008). For issues specifically related to legal issues with crowd employees, see Felstiner (2011). O'Connor (2013) addresses questions about ethical oversight of research when the roles of researchers and participants blur. For issues related to sharing data while protecting participants in citizen science projects, see Bowser et al. (2014). Both Purdam (2014) and Windt and Humphreys (2016) have some discussion about the ethical issues in distributed data collection. Finally, most projects acknowledge contributions, but do not give authorship credit to participants. In Foldit, the players are often listed as an author (Cooper et al. 2010; Khatib et al. 2011). In other open call projects, the winning contributor can often write a paper describing their solutions (e.g., Bell, Koren, and Volinsky (2010) and Dieleman, Willett, and Dambre (2015)).

Activities

Degrees of Difficulty: EASY   MEDIUM   HARD   VERY HARD

DATA COLLECTION   REQUIRES MATH   REQUIRES CODING   MY FAVORITES

1. [, , ,] One of the most exciting claims from Benoit and colleagues' (2016) research on crowd-coding of political manifestos is that the results are reproducible. Merz, Regel, and Lewandowski (2016) provides access to the Manifesto Corpus. Try to reproduce figure 2 from Benoit et al. (2016) using workers from Amazon Mechanical Turk. How similar were your results?

2. [ ] In the InfluenzaNet project, a volunteer panel of people report the incidence, prevalence, and health-seeking behavior related to influenza-like-illness (Tilston et al. 2010; van Noort et al. 2015).

   a) Compare and contrast the design, costs, and likely errors in InfluenzaNet, Google Flu Trends, and traditional influenza tracking systems.

   b) Consider an unsettled time, such as an outbreak of a novel form of influenza. Describe the possible errors in each system.

3. [, ,] The *Economist* is a weekly news magazine. Create a human computation project to see if the ratio of women to men on the cover has changed over time. The magazine can have different covers in eight different

regions (Africa, Asia Pacific, Europe, European Union, Latin America, Middle East, North America, and United Kingdom) and they can all be downloaded from the magazine's website. Pick one of these regions and perform the analysis. Be sure to describe your procedures with enough detail that they could be replicated by someone else.

This question was inspired by a similar project by Justin Tenuto, a data scientist at the crowdsourcing company CrowdFlower; see "Time Magazine Really Likes Dudes" (http://www.crowdflower.com/blog/time-magazine-cover-data).

4. [📟, 🔖, 🎲] Building on the previous question, now perform the analysis for all eight regions.

   a) What differences did you find across regions?

   b) How much extra time and money did it take to scale up your analysis to all eight of the regions?

   c) Imagine that the *Economist* has 100 different covers each week. Estimate how much extra time and money would it take to scale up your analysis to 100 covers per week.

5. [📟, 🔖] There are several websites that host open call projects, such as Kaggle. Participate in one of those projects, and describe what you learn about that particular project and about open calls in general.

6. [📟] Look through a recent issue of a journal in your field. Are there any papers that could have been reformulated as open call projects? Why or why not?

7. [📟] Purdam (2014) describes a distributed data collection about begging in London. Summarize the strengths and weaknesses of this research design.

8. [📟] Redundancy is an important way to assess the quality of distributed data collection. Van der Windt and Humphreys (2016) developed and tested a system to collect reports of conflict events from people in Eastern Congo. Read the paper.

   a) How does their design ensure redundancy?

   b) They offered several approaches to validate the data collected from their project. Summarize them. Which was most convincing to you?

   c) Propose a new way that the data could be validated. Suggestions should try to increase the confidence that you would have in the data in a way that is cost-effective and ethical.

9. [🎯] Karim Lakhani and colleagues (2013) created an open call to solicit new algorithms to solve a problem in computational biology. They received more than 600 submissions containing 89 novel computational approaches. Of these submissions, 30 exceeded the performance of the US National Institutes of Health's MegaBLAST, and the best submission achieved both greater accuracy and speed (1,000 times faster).

   a) Read their paper, and then propose a social research problem that could use the same kind of open contest. In particular, this kind of open contest is focused on speeding up and improving the performance of an existing algorithm. If you can't think of a problem like this in your field, try to explain why not.

10. [🎯, ❤️] Many human computation projects rely on participants from Amazon Mechanical Turk. Sign up to become a worker on Amazon Mechanical Turk. Spend one hour working there. How does this impact your thoughts about the design, quality, and ethics of human computation projects?

CHAPTER 6
ETHICS

6.1 Introduction

The previous chapters have shown that the digital age creates new opportunities for collecting and analyzing social data. The digital age has also created new ethical challenges. The goal of this chapter is to give you the tools that you need to handle these ethical challenges responsibly.

There is currently uncertainty about the appropriate conduct of some digital-age social research. This uncertainty has led to two related problems, one of which has received much more attention than the other. On the one hand, some researchers have been accused of violating people's privacy or enrolling participants in unethical experiments. These cases—which I'll describe in this chapter—have been the subject of extensive debate and discussion. On the other hand, the ethical uncertainty has also had a chilling effect, preventing ethical and important research from happening, a fact that I think is much less appreciated. For example, during the 2014 Ebola outbreak, public health officials wanted information about the mobility of people in the most heavily infected countries in order to help control the outbreak. Mobile phone companies had detailed call records that could have provided some of this information. Yet ethical and legal concerns bogged down researchers' attempts to analyze the data (Wesolowski et al. 2014; McDonald 2016). If we, as a community, can develop ethical norms and standards that are shared by both researchers and the public—and I think we can do this—then we can harness the capabilities of the digital age in ways that are responsible and beneficial to society.

One barrier to creating these shared standards is that social scientists and data scientists tend to have different approaches to research ethics. For social scientists, thinking about ethics is dominated by Institutional Review Boards (IRBs) and the regulations that they are tasked with enforcing. After all, the only way that most empirical social scientists experience ethical debate is through the bureaucratic process of IRB review. Data scientists, on the other hand, have little systematic experience with research ethics because it is not commonly discussed in computer science and engineering. Neither of these approaches—the *rules-based approach* of social scientists or the *ad hoc approach* of data scientists—is well suited for social research in the digital age. Instead, I believe that we, as a community, will make progress if we adopt a *principles-based approach*. That is, researchers should evaluate their research through existing rules—which I will take as given and assume should be followed—*and* through more general ethical principles. This principles-based approach helps researchers make reasonable decisions for cases where rules have not yet been written, and it helps researchers communicate their reasoning to each other and the public.

The principles-based approach that I am advocating is not new. It draws on decades of previous thinking, much of which was crystallized in two landmark reports: the Belmont Report and the Menlo Report. As you will see, in some cases, the principles-based approach leads to clear, actionable solutions. And when it does not lead to such solutions, it clarifies the trade-offs involved, which is critical for striking an appropriate balance. Further, the principles-based approach is sufficiently general that it will be helpful no matter where you work (e.g., university, government, NGO, or company).

This chapter has been designed to help a well-meaning individual researcher. How should you think about the ethics of your own work? What can you do to make your own work more ethical? In section 6.2, I'll describe three digital-age research projects that have generated ethical debate. Then, in section 6.3, I'll abstract from those specific examples to describe what I think is the fundamental reason for ethical uncertainty: rapidly increasing power for researchers to observe and experiment on people without their consent or even awareness. These capabilities are changing faster than our norms, rules, and laws. Next, in section 6.4, I'll describe four existing principles that can guide your thinking: Respect for Persons, Beneficence, Justice, and Respect for Law and Public Interest. Then, in section 6.5, I'll summarize two broad ethical frameworks—consequentialism and deontology—that can help you with one of the deepest challenges that you might face: when is it appropriate for you to use ethically questionable means in order to achieve an ethically appropriate end. These principles and ethical frameworks—

Ethical frameworks		Principles		Rules
Consequentialism Deontology	→	Respect for Persons Beneficence Justice Respect for Law and Public Interest	→	Common Rule

Figure 6.1: The rules governing research are derived from principles that in turn are derived from ethical frameworks. A main argument of this chapter is that researchers should evaluate their research through existing rules—which I will take as given and assume should be followed—*and* through more general ethical principles. The Common Rule is the set of regulations currently governing most federally funded research in the United States (for more information, see the historical appendix to this chapter). The four principles come from two blue-ribbon panels that were created to provide ethical guidance to researchers: the Belmont Report and the Menlo Report (for more information, see the historical appendix). Finally, consequentialism and deontology are ethical frameworks that have been developed by philosophers for hundreds of years. A quick and crude way to distinguish the two frameworks is that deontologists focus on means and consequentialists focus on ends.

summarized in figure 6.1—will enable you to move beyond focusing on what is permitted by existing regulations and increase your ability to communicate your reasoning with other researchers and the public.

With that background, in section 6.6, I will discuss four areas that are particularly challenging for digital age social researchers: informed consent (section 6.6.1), understanding and managing informational risk (section 6.6.2), privacy (section 6.6.3), and making ethical decisions in the face of uncertainty (section 6.6.4). Finally, in section 6.7, I'll offer three practical tips for working in an area with unsettled ethics. The chapter concludes with a historical appendix, where I briefly summarize the evolution of research ethics oversight in the United States, including discussions of the Tuskegee Syphilis Study, the Belmont Report, the Common Rule, and the Menlo Report.

6.2 Three examples

> Digital-age social research will involve situations where reasonable, well-meaning people will disagree about ethics.

To keep things concrete, I'll start with three examples of digital-age studies that have generated ethical controversy. I've selected these particular studies for two reasons. First, there are no easy answers about any of them. That is, reasonable, well-meaning people disagree about whether these studies should have happened and what changes might improve them. Second, these studies embody many of the principles, frameworks, and areas of tension that will follow later in the chapter.

6.2.1 Emotional Contagion

> 700,000 Facebook users were put into an experiment that may have altered their emotions. The participants did not give consent, and the study was not subject to meaningful third-party ethical oversight.

For one week in January 2012, approximately 700,000 Facebook users were placed in an experiment to study "emotional contagion," the extent to which a person's emotions are impacted by the emotions of the people with whom they interact. I've discussed this experiment in chapter 4, but I'll review it again now. Participants in the Emotional Contagion experiment were put into four groups: a "negativity-reduced" group, for whom posts with negative words (e.g., sad) were randomly blocked from appearing in the News Feed; a "positivity-reduced" group, for whom posts with positive words (e.g., happy) were randomly blocked; and two control groups, one for the positivity-reduced group and one for the negativity-reduced group. The researchers found that people in the positivity-reduced group used slightly fewer positive words and slightly more negative words relative to the control group. Likewise, they found that people in the negativity-reduced group used slightly more positive words and slightly fewer negative words. Thus, the researchers found evidence of emotional contagion (Kramer, Guillory, and Hancock 2014); for a more complete discussion of the design and results of the experiment, see chapter 4.

After this paper was published in *Proceedings of the National Academy of Sciences*, there was an enormous outcry from both researchers and the press. Outrage around the paper focused on two main points: (1) participants did not provide any consent beyond the standard Facebook terms of service and (2) the study had not undergone meaningful third-party ethical review (Grimmelmann 2015). The ethical questions raised in this debate caused the journal to quickly publish a rare "editorial expression of concern" about the ethics and ethical review process for the research (Verma 2014). In subsequent years, this experiment has continued to be a source of intense debate and disagreement, and the criticism of this experiment may have had the unintended effect of driving this kind of research into the shadows (Meyer 2014). That is, some have argued that companies have not stopped running these kinds of experiments—they have merely stopped talking about them in public. This debate may have helped spur the creation of an ethical review process for research at Facebook (Hernandez and Seetharaman 2016; Jackman and Kanerva 2016).

6.2.2 Tastes, Ties, and Time

> Researchers scraped students' data from Facebook, merged it with university records, used these merged data for research, and then shared them with other researchers.

Beginning in 2006, each year, a team of professors and research assistants scraped the Facebook profiles of members of the Class of 2009 at a "diverse private college in the Northeastern U.S." The researchers then merged these data from Facebook, which included information about friendships and cultural tastes, with data from the college, which included information about academic majors and where the students lived on campus. These merged data were a valuable resource, and they were used to create new knowledge about topics such as how social networks form (Wimmer and Lewis 2010) and how social networks and behavior co-evolve (Lewis, Gonzalez, and Kaufman 2012). In addition to using these data for their own work, the Tastes, Ties, and Time researchers made them available to other researchers, after taking some steps to protect the students' privacy (Lewis et al. 2008).

Unfortunately, just days after the data were made available, other researchers deduced that the school in question was Harvard College (Zimmer 2010). The Tastes, Ties, and Time researchers were accused of a "failure to adhere to ethical research standards" (Zimmer 2010), in part because the students had not provided informed consent (all procedures were reviewed and approved by Harvard's IRB and Facebook). In addition to criticism from academics, newspaper articles appeared with headlines such as "Harvard Researchers Accused of Breaching Students' Privacy" (Parry 2011). Ultimately, the dataset was removed from the Internet, and it can no longer be used by other researchers.

6.2.3 Encore

Researchers caused people's computers to secretly visit websites that were potentially blocked by repressive governments.

In March 2014, Sam Burnett and Nick Feamster launched Encore, a system to provide real-time and global measurements of Internet censorship. To do this, the researchers, who were at Georgia Tech, encouraged website owners to install this small code snippet into the source files of their web pages:

```
<iframe src="//encore.noise.gatech.edu/task.html"
        width="0" height="0"
        style="display: none"></iframe>
```

If you happen to visit a web page with this code snippet in it, your web browser will try to contact a website that the researchers were monitoring for possible censorship (e.g., the website of a banned political party). Then, your web browser will report back to the researchers about whether it was able to contact the potentially blocked website (figure 6.2). Further, all of this will be invisible unless you check the HTML source file of the web page. Such invisible third-party page requests are actually quite common on the web (Narayanan and Zevenbergen 2015), but they rarely involve explicit attempts to measure censorship.

This approach to measuring censorship has some very attractive technical properties. If a sufficient number of websites include this simple code snippet, then Encore can provide a real-time, global-scale measure of which websites are censored. Before launching the project, the researchers conferred with their IRB, which declined to review the project because it was not "human subjects research" under the Common Rule (the set of regulations governing most federally funded research in the United States; for more information, see the historical appendix to this chapter).

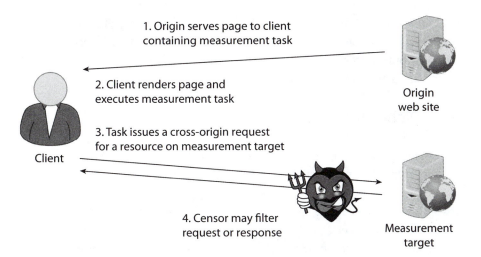

1. Origin serves page to client containing measurement task

2. Client renders page and executes measurement task

3. Task issues a cross-origin request for a resource on measurement target

Client

Origin web site

4. Censor may filter request or response

Measurement target

Figure 6.2: Schematic of the research design of Encore (Burnett and Feamster 2015). The origin website has a small code snippet embedded in it (step 1). Your computer renders the web page, which triggers the measurement task (step 2). Your computer attempts to access a measurement target, which could be the website of a banned political group (step 3). A censor, such as a government, may then block your access to the measurement target (step 4). Finally, your computer reports the results of this request to the researchers (not shown in the figure). Reproduced by permission from the Association for Computing Machinery, Inc. from Burnett and Feamster (2015), figure 1.

Soon after Encore was launched, however, Ben Zevenbergen, then a graduate student, contacted to the researchers to raise questions about the ethics of the project. In particular, Zevenbergen was concerned that people in certain countries could be exposed to risk if their computer attempted to visit certain sensitive websites, and these people did not consent to participate in the study. Based on these conversations, the Encore team modified the project to attempt to measure the censorship of only Facebook, Twitter, and YouTube, because third-party attempts to access these sites are common during normal web browsing (Narayanan and Zevenbergen 2015).

After collecting data using this modified design, a paper describing the methodology and some results was submitted to SIGCOMM, a prestigious computer science conference. The program committee appreciated the technical contribution of the paper, but expressed concern about the lack of informed consent from participants. Ultimately, the program committee decided to publish the paper, but with a signing statement expressing ethical concerns (Burnett and Feamster 2015). Such a signing statement had never been used before at SIGCOMM, and this case has led to additional debate among computer scientists about the nature of ethics in their research (Narayanan and Zevenbergen 2015; Jones and Feamster 2015).

6.3 Digital is different

Social research in the digital age has different characteristics and therefore raises different ethical questions.

In the analog age, most social research had a relatively limited scale and operated within a set of reasonably clear rules. Social research in the digital age is different. Researchers—often in collaboration with companies and governments—have more power over participants than in the past, and the rules about how that power should be used are not yet clear. By power, I mean simply the ability to do things to people without their consent or even awareness. The kinds of things that researchers can do to people include observing their behavior and enrolling them in experiments. As the power of researchers to observe and perturb is increasing, there has not been an equivalent increase in clarity about how that power should be used. In fact, researchers must decide how to exercise their power based on inconsistent and overlapping rules, laws, and norms. This combination of powerful capabilities and vague guidelines creates difficult situations.

One set of powers that researchers now have is the ability to observe people's behavior without their consent or awareness. Researchers could, of course, do this in past, but in the digital age, the scale is completely different, a fact that has been proclaimed repeatedly by many fans of big data sources. In particular, if we move from the scale of an individual student or professor and instead consider the scale of a company or government—institutions with which researchers increasingly collaborate—the potential ethical issues become complex. One metaphor that I think helps people visualize the idea of mass surveillance is the *panopticon.* Originally proposed by Jeremy Bentham as an architecture for prisons, the panopticon is a circular building with cells built around a central watchtower (figure 6.3). Whoever occupies this watchtower can observe the behavior of all the people in the rooms without being seen herself. The person in the watchtower is thus an *unseen seer*

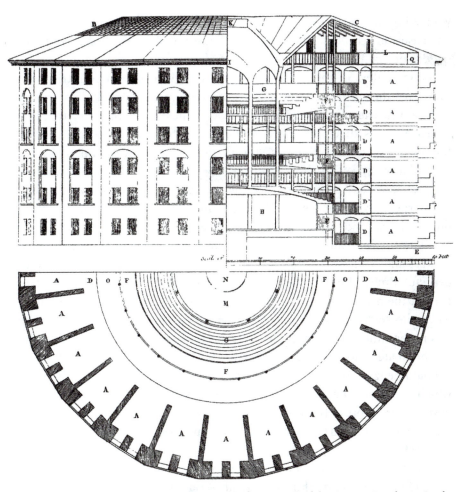

Figure 6.3: Design for the panopticon prison, first proposed by Jeremy Bentham. In the center, there is an unseen seer who can observe the behavior of everyone but cannot be observed. Drawing by Willey Reveley, 1791. (Source: *The Works of Jeremy Bentham*, vol. 4/Wikimedia Commons).

(Foucault 1995). To some privacy advocates, the digital age has moved us into a panoptic prison where tech companies and governments are constantly watching and recording our behavior.

To carry this metaphor a bit further, when many social researchers think about the digital age, they imagine themselves inside of the watchtower, observing behavior and creating a master database that could be used to do all kinds of exciting and important research. But now, rather than imagining yourself in the watchtower, imagine yourself in one of the cells. That master database starts to look like what Paul Ohm (2010) has called a *database of ruin,* which could be used in unethical ways.

Some readers of this book are lucky enough to live in countries where they trust their unseen seers to use their data responsibly and to protect it from adversaries. Other readers are not so lucky, and I'm sure that issues raised by mass surveillance are very clear to them. But I believe that even for the lucky readers there is still an important concern raised by mass surveillance: *unanticipated secondary use.* That is, a database created for one purpose—say targeting ads—might one day be used for a very different purpose. A horrific example of unanticipated secondary use happened during the Second World War, when government census data were used to facilitate the genocide that was taking place against Jews, Roma, and others (Seltzer and Anderson 2008). The statisticians who collected the data during peaceful times almost certainly had good intentions, and many citizens trusted them to use the data responsibly. But, when the world changed—when the Nazis came to power—these data enabled a secondary use that was never anticipated. Quite simply, once a master database exists, it is hard to anticipate who may gain access to it and how it will be used. In fact, William Seltzer and Margo Anderson (2008) have documented 18 cases in which population data systems have been involved or potentially involved in human rights abuses (table 6.1). Further, as Seltzer and Anderson point out, this list is almost certainly an underestimate, because most abuses happen in secret.

Ordinary social researchers are very, very far from anything like participating in human rights abuses through secondary use. I've chosen to discuss it, however, because I think it will help you understand how some people might react to your work. Let's return to the Tastes, Ties, and Time project as an example. By merging together complete and granular data from Facebook with complete and granular data from Harvard, the researchers created an amazingly rich view of the social and cultural life of the students (Lewis et al. 2008). To many social researchers, this seems like the master database, which could be used for good. But to some others, it looks like the beginning of the database of ruin, which could be used unethically. In fact, it is probably a bit of both.

In addition to mass surveillance, researchers—again in collaboration with companies and governments—can increasingly intervene in people's lives in

Table 6.1: Cases where Population Data Systems Have Been Involved or Potentially Involved in Human Rights Abuses

Place	Time	Targeted individuals or groups	Data system	Human rights violation or presumed state intention
Australia	19th and early 20th century	Aborigines	Population registration	Forced migration, elements of genocide
China	1966–76	Bad-class origin during cultural revolution	Population registration	Forced migration, instigated mob violence
France	1940–44	Jews	Population registration, special censuses	Forced migration, genocide
Germany	1933–45	Jews, Roma, and others	Numerous	Forced migration, genocide
Hungary	1945–46	German nationals and those reporting German mother tongue	1941 population census	Forced migration
Netherlands	1940–44	Jews and Roma	Population registration systems	Forced migration, genocide
Norway	1845–1930	Samis and Kvens	Population censuses	Ethnic cleansing
Norway	1942–44	Jews	Special census and proposed population register	Genocide
Poland	1939–43	Jews	Primarily special censuses	Genocide
Romania	1941–43	Jews and Roma	1941 population census	Forced migration, genocide

continued.

Table 6.1: *Continued*

Place	Time	Targeted individuals or groups	Data system	Human rights violation or presumed state intention
Rwanda	1994	Tutsi	Population registration	Genocide
South Africa	1950–93	African and "Colored" populations	1951 population census and population registration	Apartheid, voter disenfranchisement
United States	19th century	Native Americans	Special censuses, population registers	Forced migration
United States	1917	Suspected draft law violators	1910 census	Investigation and prosecution of those avoiding registration
United States	1941–45	Japanese Americans	1940 census	Forced migration and internment
United States	2001–08	Suspected terrorists	NCES surveys and administrative data	Investigation and prosecution of domestic and international terrorists
United States	2003	Arab Americans	2000 census	Unknown
USSR	1919–39	Minority populations	Various population censuses	Forced migration, punishment of other serious crimes

Note: This table is based on one compiled by Seltzer and Anderson (2008), from which I have included a subset of the columns. See Seltzer and Anderson (2008) for more information about each case and inclusion criteria. Some, but not all, of these cases involved unanticipated secondary use.

order to create randomized controlled experiments. For example, in Emotional Contagion, researchers enrolled 700,000 people in an experiment without their consent or awareness. As I described in chapter 4, this kind of secret conscription of participants into experiments is not uncommon, and it does not require the cooperation of large companies. In fact, in chapter 4, I taught you how to do it.

In the face of this increased power, researchers are subject to *inconsistent and overlapping rules, laws, and norms.* One source of this inconsistency is that the capabilities of the digital age are changing more quickly than rules, laws, and norms. For example, the Common Rule (the set of regulations governing most government-funded research in the United States) has not changed much since 1981, and a recent effort to modernize it took almost five and a half years to complete (Jaschik 2017). A second source of inconsistency is that norms around abstract concepts such as privacy are still being actively debated by researchers, policy makers, and activists. If specialists in these areas cannot reach a uniform consensus, we should not expect empirical researchers or participants to do so. A third and final source of inconsistency is that digital-age research is increasingly mixed into other contexts, which leads to potentially overlapping norms and rules. For example, Emotional Contagion was a collaboration between a data scientist at Facebook and a professor and graduate student at Cornell. At that time, it was common at Facebook to run large experiments without third-party oversight, as long as the experiments complied with Facebook's terms of service. At Cornell, the norms and rules are quite different; virtually all experiments must be reviewed by the Cornell IRB. So, which set of rules should govern Emotional Contagion—Facebook's or Cornell's? When there are inconsistent and overlapping rules, laws, and norms, even well-meaning researchers might have trouble doing the right thing. In fact, because of the inconsistency, there might not even be a single right thing.

Overall, these two features—increasing power and lack of agreement about how that power should be used—mean that researchers working in the digital age are going to be facing ethical challenges for the foreseeable future. Fortunately, when dealing with these challenges, it is not necessary to start from scratch. Instead, researchers can draw wisdom from previously developed ethical principles and frameworks, the topics of the next two sections.

6.4 Four principles

Four principles that can guide researchers facing ethical uncertainty are: Respect for Persons, Beneficence, Justice, and Respect for Law and Public Interest.

The ethical challenges that researchers face in the digital age are somewhat different than those in the past. However, researchers can address these challenges by building on earlier ethical thinking. In particular, I believe that the principles expressed in two reports—the Belmont Report (Belmont Report 1979) and the Menlo Report (Dittrich, Kenneally, and others 2011)—can help researchers reason about the ethical challenges that they face. As I describe in more detail in the historical appendix to this chapter, both of these reports were the results of many years of deliberation by panels of experts with many opportunities for input from a variety of stakeholders.

First, in 1974, in response to ethical failures by researchers—such as the notorious Tuskegee Syphilis Study in which almost 400 African American men were actively deceived by researchers and denied access to safe and effective treatment for almost 40 years (see the historical appendix)—the US Congress created a national commission to produce ethical guidelines for research involving human subjects. After four years of meeting at the Belmont Conference Center, the group produced the *Belmont Report,* a slender but powerful document. The Belmont Report is the intellectual basis for the *Common Rule,* the set of regulations governing human subjects research that IRBs are tasked with enforcing (Porter and Koski 2008).

Then, in 2010, in response to the ethical failures of computer security researchers and the difficulty of applying the ideas in the Belmont Report to digital-age research, the US Government—specifically the Department of Homeland Security—created a blue-ribbon commission to produce a guiding ethical framework for research involving information and communication technologies (ICT). The result of this effort was the *Menlo Report* (Dittrich, Kenneally, and others 2011).

Together, the Belmont Report and the Menlo Report offer four principles that can guide ethical deliberations by researchers: *Respect for Persons,* *Beneficence, Justice,* and *Respect for Law and Public Interest.* Applying these four principles in practice is not always straightforward, and it can require difficult balancing. The principles, however, help clarify trade-offs, suggest improvements to research designs, and enable researchers to explain their reasoning to each other and the public.

6.4.1 Respect for Persons

Respect for Persons is about treating people as autonomous and honoring their wishes.

The Belmont Report argues that the principle of Respect for Persons consists of two distinct parts: (1) individuals should be treated as autonomous and (2) individuals with diminished autonomy should be entitled to additional protections. Autonomy roughly corresponds to letting people control their own lives. In other words, Respect for Persons suggests that researchers should not do things to people without their consent. Critically, this holds even if the researcher thinks that the thing that is happening is harmless, or even beneficial. Respect for Persons leads to the idea that participants—not researchers—get to decide.

In practice, the principle of Respect for Persons has been interpreted to mean that researchers should, if possible, receive informed consent from participants. The basic idea with informed consent is that participants should be presented with relevant information in a comprehensible format and then should voluntarily agree to participate. Each of these terms has itself been the subject of substantial additional debate and scholarship (Manson and O'Neill 2007), and I'll devote section 6.6.1 to informed consent.

Applying the principle of Respect for Persons to the three examples from the beginning of the chapter highlights areas of concern with each of them. In each case, researchers did things to participants—used their data (Tastes, Ties, or Time), used their computer to perform a measurement task (Encore), or enrolled them in an experiment (Emotional Contagion)—without their consent or awareness. The violation of the principle of Respect for Persons does not automatically make these studies ethically impermissible; Respect for Persons is one of four principles. But thinking about Respect for Persons does suggest some ways in which the studies could be improved ethically. For example, researchers could have obtained some form of consent from participants before the study began or after it ended; I'll return to these options when I discuss informed consent in section 6.6.1.

6.4.2 Beneficence

> Beneficence is about understanding and improving the risk/benefit profile of your study, and then deciding if it strikes the right balance.

The Belmont Report argues that the principle of Beneficence is an obligation that researchers have to participants, and that it involves two parts: (1) do not harm and (2) maximize possible benefits and minimize possible harms. The Belmont Report traces the idea of "do not harm" to the Hippocratic tradition in medical ethics, and it can be expressed in a strong form where researchers "should not injure one person regardless of the benefits that might come to others" (Belmont Report 1979). However, the Belmont Report also acknowledges that learning what is beneficial may involve exposing some people to risk. Therefore, the imperative of not doing harm can be in conflict with the imperative to learn, leading researchers to occasionally make difficult decisions about "when it is justifiable to seek certain benefits despite the risks involved, and when the benefits should be foregone because of the risks" (Belmont Report 1979).

In practice, the principle of Beneficence has been interpreted to mean that researchers should undertake two separate processes: a risk/benefit analysis and then a decision about whether the risks and benefits strike an appropriate ethical balance. This first process is largely a technical matter requiring substantive expertise, while the second is largely an ethical matter where substantive expertise may be less valuable, or even detrimental.

A risk/benefit analysis involves both understanding *and* improving the risks and benefits of a study. Analysis of risk should include two elements: the probability of adverse events and the severity of those events. As the result of a risk/benefit analysis, a researcher could adjust the study design to reduce the probability of an adverse event (e.g., screen out participants who are vulnerable) or reduce the severity of an adverse event if it occurs (e.g., make counseling available to participants who request it). Further, during the risk/benefit analysis, researchers need to keep in mind the impact of their work not just on participants, but also on nonparticipants and social systems. For example, consider the experiment by Restivo and van de Rijt (2012) on the effect of awards on Wikipedia editors (discussed in chapter 4). In this experiment, the researchers gave awards to a small number of editors whom they considered deserving and then tracked their contributions to Wikipedia compared with a control group of equally deserving editors to whom the researchers did not give an award. Imagine, if, instead of giving a small number of awards, Restivo and van de Rijt flooded Wikipedia with many, many awards. Although this design might not harm any individual participant, it could disrupt the entire award ecosystem in Wikipedia. In other words, when doing a risk/benefit analysis, you should think about the impacts of your work not just on participants but on the world more broadly.

Next, once the risks have been minimized and the benefits maximized, researchers should assess whether the study strikes a favorable balance. Ethicists do not recommend a simple summation of costs and benefits. In particular, some risks render the research impermissible, no matter the benefits (e.g., the Tuskegee Syphilis Study described in the historical appendix). Unlike the risk/benefit analysis, which is largely technical, this second step is deeply ethical and may in fact be enriched by people who do not have specific subject-area expertise. In fact, because outsiders often notice different things from insiders, IRBs in the United States are required to include at least one nonresearcher. In my experience serving on an IRB, these outsiders can be helpful for preventing group-think. So if you are having trouble deciding whether your research project strikes an appropriate risk/benefit analysis don't just ask your colleagues, try asking some nonresearchers—their answers might surprise you.

Applying the principle of Beneficence to the three examples that we are considering suggests some changes that might improve their risk/benefit balance. For example, in Emotional Contagion, the researchers could have attempted to screen out people under 18 years old and people who might be especially likely to react badly to the treatment. They could also have tried to minimize the number of participants by using efficient statistical methods (as described in detail in chapter 4). Further, they could have attempted to monitor participants and offered assistance to anyone that appeared to have been harmed. In Tastes, Ties, and Time, the researchers could have put extra safeguards in place when they released the data (although their procedures were approved by Harvard's IRB, which suggests that they were consistent with common practice at that time); I'll offer some more specific suggestions about data release later when I describe informational risk (section 6.6.2). Finally, in Encore, the researchers could have attempted to minimize the number of risky requests that were created in order to achieve the measurement goals of the project, and they could have excluded participants who are most in danger from repressive governments. Each of these possible changes would introduce trade-offs into the design of these projects, and my goal is not to suggest that these researchers should have made these changes. Rather, it is to show the kinds of changes that the principle of Beneficence can suggest.

Finally, although the digital age has generally made the weighing of risks and benefits more complex, it has actually made it easier for researchers to increase the benefits of their work. In particular, the tools of the digital age greatly facilitate open and reproducible research, where researchers make their research data and code available to other researchers and make their papers available to the public through open access publishing. This change to open and reproducible research, while by no means simple, offers a way for researchers to increase the benefits of their research without exposing participants to any additional risk (data sharing is an exception that will be discussed in detail in section 6.6.2 on informational risk).

6.4.3 Justice

> Justice is about ensuring that the risks and benefits of research are distributed fairly.

The Belmont Report argues that the principle of Justice addresses the distribution of the burdens and benefits of research. That is, it should not be the case that one group in society bears the costs of research while another group reaps its benefits. For example, in the nineteenth and early twentieth century, the burdens of serving as research subjects in medical trials fell largely on the poor, while the benefits of improved medical care flowed primarily to the rich.

In practice, the principle of Justice was initially interpreted to mean that vulnerable people should be protected from researchers. In other words, researchers should not be allowed to intentionally prey on the powerless. It is a troubling pattern that, in the past, a large number of ethically problematic studies involved extremely vulnerable participants, including poorly educated and disenfranchised citizens (Jones 1993); prisoners (Spitz 2005); institutionalized, mentally disabled children (Robinson and Unruh 2008); and old and debilitated hospital patients (Arras 2008).

Around 1990, however, views of Justice began to swing from *protection to access* (Mastroianni and Kahn 2001). For example, activists argued that children, women, and ethnic minorities needed to be explicitly included in clinical trials so that these groups could benefit from the knowledge gained from these trials (Epstein 2009).

In addition to questions about protection and access, the principle of Justice is often interpreted to raise questions about appropriate compensation for participants—questions that are subject to intense debate in medical ethics (Dickert and Grady 2008).

Applying the principle of Justice to our three examples offers yet another way to view them. In none of the studies were participants compensated financially. Encore raises the most complex questions about the principle of Justice. While the principle of Beneficence might suggest excluding participants from countries with repressive governments, the principle of Justice could argue for allowing these people to participate in—and benefit from— accurate measurements of Internet censorship. The case of Tastes, Ties, and Time also raises questions because one group of students bore the burdens of the research and only society as a whole benefited. Finally, in Emotional Contagion, the participants who bore the burden of the research were a random sample from the population most likely to benefit from the results (namely, Facebook users). In this sense, the design of Emotional Contagion was well aligned with the principle of Justice.

6.4.4 Respect for Law and Public Interest

> Respect for Law and Public Interest extends the principle of Beneficence beyond specific research participants to include all relevant stakeholders.

The fourth and final principle that can guide your thinking is Respect for Law and Public Interest. This principle comes from the Menlo Report, and therefore may be less well known to social researchers. The Menlo Report argues that the principle of Respect for Law and Public Interest is implicit in the principle of Beneficence, but it also argues that the former deserves explicit consideration. In particular, while Beneficence tends to focus on participants, Respect for Law and Public Interest explicitly encourages researchers to take a wider view and to include law in their considerations.

In the Menlo Report, Respect for Law and Public Interest has two distinct components: (1) compliance and (2) transparency-based accountability. *Compliance* means that researchers should attempt to identify and obey relevant laws, contracts, and terms of service. For example, compliance would mean that a researcher considering scraping the content of a website should read and consider the terms-of-service agreement of that website. There may, however, be situations where it is permissible to violate the terms of service; remember, Respect for Law and Public Interest is just one of four principles. For example, at one time, both Verizon and AT&T had terms of service that prevented customers from criticizing them (Vaccaro et al. 2015). I don't think researchers should not be automatically bound by such terms-of-service agreements. Ideally, if researchers violate terms-of-service agreements, they should explain their decision openly (see, e.g., Soeller et al. (2016)), as suggested by transparency-based accountability. But this openness may expose researchers to added legal risk; in the United States, for example, the Computer Fraud and Abuse Act may make it illegal to violate terms-of-service agreements (Sandvig and Karahalios 2016; Krafft, Macy, and Pentland 2016). At this brief discussion illustrates, including compliance in ethical deliberations can raise complex questions.

In addition to compliance, Respect for Law and Public Interest also encourages *transparency-based accountability*, which means that researchers should be clear about their goals, methods, and results at all stages of their research and take responsibility for their actions. Another way to think about transparency-based accountability is that it is trying to prevent the research community from doing things in secret. This transparency-based accountability enables a broader role for the public in ethical debates, which is important for both ethical and practical reasons.

Applying the principle of Respect for Law and Public Interest to the three studies considered here illustrates some of the complexity researchers face when it comes to law. For example, Grimmelmann (2015) has argued that Emotional Contagion may have been illegal in the State of Maryland. In particular, Maryland House Bill 917, passed in 2002, extends Common Rule protections to all research conducted in Maryland, independent of funding source (many experts believe that Emotional Contagion was not subject to the Common Rule under Federal Law because it was conducted at Facebook, an institution that does not receive research funds from the US Government). However, some scholars believe that Maryland House Bill 917 is itself unconstitutional (Grimmelmann 2015, pp. 237–38). Practicing social researchers are not judges, and therefore are not equipped to understand and assess the constitutionality of the laws of all 50 US states. These complexities are compounded in international projects. Encore, for example, involved participants from 170 countries, which makes legal compliance incredibly difficult. In response to the ambiguous legal environment, researchers might benefit from third-party review of their work, both as a source of advice about legal requirements and as a personal protection in case their research is unintentionally illegal.

On the other hand, all three studies published their results in academic journals, enabling transparency-based accountability. In fact, Emotional Contagion was published in open access form, so the research community and the broader public were informed—after the fact—about the design and results of the research. One quick and crude way to assess transparency-based accountability is to ask yourself: would I be comfortable if my research procedures were written about on the front page of my home town newspaper? If the answer is no, then that is a sign that your research design may need changes.

In conclusion, the Belmont Report and Menlo Report propose four principles that can be used to assess research: Respect for Persons, Beneficence, Justice, and Respect for Law and Public Interest. Applying these four principles in practice is not always straightforward, and it can require difficult balancing. For example, with regard to the decision whether to debrief participants from Emotional Contagion, it might be considered that Respect for Persons encourages debriefing, whereas Beneficence discourages it (if the debriefing could itself do harm). There is no automatic way to balance these competing principles, but the four principles help clarify trade-offs, suggest changes to research designs, and enable researchers to explain their reasoning to each other and the public.

6.5 Two ethical frameworks

Most debates about research ethics reduce to disagreements between consequentialism and deontology.

These four ethical principles of Respect for Persons, Beneficence, Justice, and Respect for Law and Public Interest are themselves largely derived from two more abstract ethical frameworks: *consequentialism* and *deontology*. Understanding these frameworks is helpful because it will enable you identify and then reason about one of the most fundamental tensions in research ethics: using potentially unethical means to achieve ethical ends.

Consequentialism, which has roots in the work of Jeremy Bentham and John Stuart Mill, focuses on taking actions that lead to better states in the world (Sinnott-Armstrong 2014). The principle of Beneficence, which focuses on balancing risk and benefits, is deeply rooted in consequentialist thinking. On the other hand, deontology, which has roots in the work of Immanuel Kant, focuses on ethical duties, independent of their consequences (Alexander and Moore 2015). The principle of Respect for Persons, which focuses on the autonomy of participants, is deeply rooted in deontological thinking. A quick and crude way to distinguish the two frameworks is that deontologists focus on *means* and consequentialists focus on *ends*.

To see how these two frameworks operate, consider informed consent. Both frameworks could be used to support informed consent, but for different reasons. A consequentialist argument for informed consent is that it helps to prevent harm to participants by prohibiting research that does not properly balance risk and anticipated benefit. In other words, consequentialist thinking would support informed consent because it helps prevent bad outcomes for participants. However, a deontological argument for informed consent focuses on a researcher's duty to respect the autonomy of her participants. Given these approaches, a pure consequentialist might be willing to waive the requirement for informed consent in a setting where there was no risk, whereas a pure deontologist might not.

Both consequentialism and deontology offer important ethical insight, but each can be taken to absurd extremes. For consequentialism, one of these extreme cases could be called *Transplant*. Imagine a doctor who has five patients dying of organ failure and one healthy patient whose organs can save all five. Under certain conditions, a consequentialist doctor will be permitted—and even required—to kill the healthy patient to obtain his organs. This complete focus on ends, without regard to means, is flawed.

Likewise, deontology can also be taken to awkward extremes, such as in the case that could be called *Time Bomb*. Imagine a police officer who has captured a terrorist who knows the location of a ticking time bomb that will kill millions of people. A deontological police officer would not lie in order to trick a terrorist into revealing the location of the bomb. This complete focus on means, without regards to ends, also is flawed.

In practice, most social researchers implicitly embrace a blend of these two ethical frameworks. Noticing this blending of ethical schools helps clarify why many ethical debates—which tend to be between those who are more consequentialist and those who are more deontological—don't make much progress. Consequentialists generally offer arguments about ends—arguments that are not convincing to deontologists, who are worried about means. Likewise, deontologists tend to offer arguments about means, which are not convincing to consequentialists, who are focused on ends. Arguments between consequentialists and deontologists are like two ships passing in the night.

One solution to these debates would be for social researchers to develop a consistent, morally solid, and easy-to-apply blend of consequentialism and deontology. Unfortunately, that's unlikely to happen; philosophers have been struggling with these problems for a long time. However, researchers can use these two ethical frameworks—and the four principles they imply—to reason about ethical challenges, clarify trade-offs, and suggest improvements to research designs.

6.6 Areas of difficulty

The four ethical principles—Respect for Persons, Beneficence, Justice, and Respect for Law and Public Interest—and the two ethical frameworks—consequentialism and deontology—should help you reason about any research ethics problems that you are facing. However, based on the characteristics of digital-age research described earlier in this chapter and based on the ethical debates we have considered so far, I see four areas of particular difficulty: *informed consent, understanding and managing informational risk, privacy*, and *making decisions in the face of uncertainty.* In the next sections, I will describe these four issues in more detail and offer advice about how to handle them.

6.6.1 Informed consent

Researchers should, can, and do follow the rule: some form of consent for most research.

Informed consent is a foundational idea—some might say a near obsession (Emanuel, Wendler, and Grady 2000; Manson and O'Neill 2007)—in research ethics. The simplest version of research ethics says: "informed consent for everything." This simple rule, however, is not consistent with existing ethical principles, ethical regulation, or research practice. Instead, researchers should, can, and do follow a more complex rule: "some form of consent for most research."

First, in order to move beyond overly simplistic ideas about informed consent, I want to tell you more about field experiments to study discrimination. In these studies, fake applicants who have different characteristics—say, some men and some women—apply for different jobs. If one type of applicant gets hired more often, then researchers can conclude that there may be discrimination in the hiring process. For the purposes of this chapter, the most important thing about these experiments is that the participants in these experiments—the employers—never provide consent. In fact, these participants are actively deceived. Yet field experiments to study discrimination have 117 studies in 17 countries (Riach and Rich 2002; Rich 2014).

Researchers who use field experiments to study discrimination have identified four features of these studies that, collectively, make them ethically permissible: (1) the limited harm to the employers; (2) the great social benefit of having a reliable measure of discrimination; (3) the weakness of other methods of measuring discrimination; and (4) the fact that deception does not strongly violate the norms of that setting (Riach and Rich 2004). Each of these conditions is critical, and if any of them are not satisfied, the ethical case will be more challenging. Three of these features can be derived from the ethical principles in the Belmont Report: limited harm (Respect for Persons and Beneficence) and great benefit and weakness of other methods (Beneficence and Justice). The final feature, nonviolation of contextual norms, can be derived from the Menlo Report's Respect for Law and Public Interest. In other words, employment applications are a setting where there is already some expectation of possible deception. Thus, these experiments do not pollute an already pristine ethical landscape.

In addition to this principles-based argument, dozens of IRBs have also concluded that the lack of consent in these studies is consistent with existing rules, in particular Common Rule §46.116, part (d). Finally, US courts have also supported the lack of consent and use of deception in field experiments to measure discrimination (No. 81-3029. United States Court of Appeals, Seventh Circuit). Thus, the use of field experiments without consent is consistent with existing ethical principles and existing rules (at least the rules in the United States). This reasoning has been supported by the broad social research community, dozens of IRBs, and by the US Court of Appeals. Thus, we must reject the simple rule "informed consent for everything." This is not a rule that researchers follow, nor is it one that they should follow.

Moving beyond "informed consent for everything" leaves researchers with a difficult question: What forms of consent are needed for what kinds of research? Naturally, there has been substantial debate around this question, although most of it is in the context of medical research in the analog age. Summarizing that debate, Nir Eyal (2012) writes:

> "The more risky the intervention, the more it is a high-impact or a definitive 'critical life choice,' the more it is value-laden and controversial, the more private the area of the body that the intervention directly affects, the more conflicted and unsupervised the practitioner, the higher the need for robust informed consent. On other occasions, the need for very robust informed consent, and indeed, for consent of any form, is lesser. On those occasions, high costs may easily override that need." [internal citations excluded]

An important insight from this debate is that informed consent is not all or nothing: there are stronger and weaker forms of consent. In some situations, robust informed consent seems necessary, but in others, weaker forms of consent may be appropriate. Next, I'll describe three reasons why researchers might struggle to obtain informed consent, and I'll describe a few options in those cases.

First, sometimes asking participants to provide informed consent may increase the risks that they face. For example, in Encore, asking people living under repressive governments to provide consent to have their computer used for measurement of Internet censorship might place those who agree at increased risk. When consent leads to increased risk, researchers can ensure that information about what they are doing is public and that it is possible for participants to opt out. Also, they could seek consent from groups that represent the participants (e.g., NGOs).

Second, sometimes having fully informed consent before the study begins could compromise the scientific value of the study. For example, in Emotional Contagion, if participants had known that researchers were doing an experiment about emotions, this might have changed their behavior. Withholding information from participants, and even deceiving them, is not uncommon in social research, especially in lab experiments in psychology. If informed consent is not possible before a study begins, researchers could (and usually do) *debrief* participants after the study is over. Debriefing generally includes explaining what actually happened, remediating any harms, and obtaining consent after the fact. There is some debate, however, about whether debriefing in field experiments is appropriate, if the debriefing itself might harm participants (Finn and Jakobsson 2007).

Third, sometimes it is logistically impractical to obtain informed consent from everyone impacted by your study. For example, imagine a researcher who wishes to study the Bitcoin blockchain (Bitcoin is a crypto-currency and the blockchain is a public record of all Bitcoin transactions (Narayanan et al. 2016)). Unfortunately, it is impossible to obtain consent from everyone who uses Bitcoin because many of these people are anonymous. In this case, the researcher could try to contact a sample of Bitcoin users and ask for their informed consent.

These three reasons why researchers might not be able to obtain informed consent—increasing risk, compromising research goals, and logistical limitations—are not the only reasons why researchers struggle to obtain informed consent. And the solutions that I've suggested—informing the public about the research, enabling an opt-out, seeking consent from third parties, debriefing, and seeking consent from a sample of participants—may not be possible in all cases. Further, even if these alternatives are possible, they may not be sufficient for the given study. What these examples do show, however, is that informed consent is not all or nothing, and that creative solutions can improve the ethical balance of studies that cannot receive full informed consent from all impacted parties.

To conclude, rather than "informed consent for everything," researchers should, can, and do follow a more complex rule: "some form of consent for most things." Expressed in terms of principles, informed consent is neither necessary nor sufficient for the principles of Respect for Persons (Humphreys 2015, p. 102). Further, Respect for Persons is just one of the principles that need to be balanced when considering research ethics; it should not automatically overwhelm Beneficence, Justice, and Respect for Law and Public Interest, a point made repeatedly by ethicists over the past 40 years (Gillon 2015, pp. 112–13). Expressed in terms of ethical frameworks, informed consent for everything is an overly deontological position that falls victim to situations such as *Time Bomb* (see section 6.5).

Finally, as a practical matter, if you are considering doing research without any kind of consent, then you should know that you are in a gray area. Be careful. Look back at the ethical argument that researchers have made in order to conduct experimental studies of discrimination without consent. Is your justification as strong? Because informed consent is central to many lay ethical theories, you should know that you will likely be called on to defend your decisions.

6.6.2 Understanding and managing informational risk

Informational risk is the most common risk in social research; it has increased dramatically; and it is the hardest risk to understand.

The second ethical challenge for digital-age social research is *informational risk,* the potential for harm from the disclosure of information (National Research Council 2014). Informational harms from the disclosure of personal information could be economic (e.g., losing a job), social (e.g., embarrassment), psychological (e.g., depression), or even criminal (e.g., arrest for illegal behavior). Unfortunately, the digital age increases informational risk dramatically—there is just so much more information about our behavior. And informational risk has proven very difficult to understand and manage compared with risks that were concerns in analog-age social research, such as physical risk.

One way that social researchers decrease informational risk is "*anonymization*" of data. "Anonymization" is the process of removing obvious personal identifiers such as name, address, and telephone number from the data. However, this approach is much less effective than many people realize, and it is, in fact, deeply and fundamentally limited. For that reason, whenever I describe "anonymization," I'll use quotation marks to remind you that this process creates the appearance of anonymity but not true anonymity.

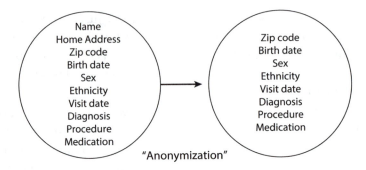

Figure 6.4: "Anonymization" is the process of removing obviously identifying information. For example, when releasing the medical insurance records of state employees, the Massachusetts Group Insurance Commission (GIC) removed names and addresses from the files. I use the quotation marks around the word "anonymization" because the process provides the appearance of anonymity but not actual anonymity.

A vivid example of the failure of "anonymization" comes from the late 1990s in Massachusetts (Sweeney 2002). The Group Insurance Commission (GIC) was a government agency responsible for purchasing health insurance for all state employees. Through this work, the GIC collected detailed health records about thousands of state employees. In an effort to spur research, the GIC decided to release these records to researchers. However, they did not share all of their data; rather, they "anonymized" these data by removing information such as names and addresses. However, they left other information that they thought could be useful for researchers, such as demographic information (zip code, birth date, ethnicity, and sex) and medical information (visit data, diagnosis, and procedure) (figure 6.4) (Ohm 2010). Unfortunately, this "anonymization" was not sufficient to protect the data.

To illustrate the shortcomings of the GIC "anonymization", Latanya Sweeney—then a graduate student at MIT—paid $20 to acquire the voting records from the city of Cambridge, the hometown of Massachusetts governor William Weld. These voting records included information such as name, address, zip code, birth date, and gender. The fact that the medical data file and the voter file shared fields—zip code, birth date, and sex—meant that Sweeney could link them. Sweeney knew that Weld's birthday was July 31, 1945, and the voting records included only six people in Cambridge with that birthday. Further, of those six people, only three were male. And, of

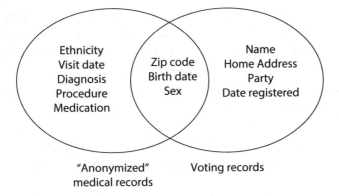

"Anonymized"   Voting records
medical records

Figure 6.5: Re-idenification of "anonymized" data. Latanya Sweeney combined the "anonymized" health records with voting records in order to find the medical records of Governor William Weld. Adapted from Sweeney (2002), figure 1.

those three men, only one shared Weld's zip code. Thus, the voting data showed that anyone in the medical data with Weld's combination of birth date, gender, and zip code was William Weld. In essence, these three pieces of information provided a *unique fingerprint* to him in the data. Using this fact, Sweeney was able to locate Weld's medical records, and, to inform him of her feat, she mailed him a copy of his records (Ohm 2010).

Sweeney's work illustrates the basic structure of *re-identification attacks*—to adopt a term from the computer security community. In these attacks, two datasets, neither of which by itself reveals sensitive information, are linked, and, through this linkage, sensitive information is exposed.

In response to Sweeney's work, and other related work, researchers now generally remove much more information—all so-called "personally identifying information" (PII) (Narayanan and Shmatikov 2010)—during the process of "anonymization." Further, many researchers now realize that certain data—such as medical records, financial records, answers to survey questions about illegal behavior—are probably too sensitive to release even after "anonymization." However, the examples that I'm about to give suggest that social researchers need to change their thinking. As a first step, it is wise to assume that all data are *potentially* identifiable and all data are *potentially* sensitive. In other words, rather than thinking that informational risk applies to a small subset of projects, we should assume that it applies—to some degree—to all projects.

Both aspects of this reorientation are illustrated by the Netflix Prize. As described in chapter 5, Netflix released 100 million movie ratings provided by almost 500,000 members, and had an open call where people from all over the world submitted algorithms that could improve Netflix's ability to recommend movies. Before releasing the data, Netflix removed any obvious personally identifying information, such as names. They also went an extra step and introduced slight perturbations in some of the records (e.g., changing some ratings from 4 stars to 3 stars). They soon discovered, however, that, despite their efforts, the data were still by no means anonymous.

Just two weeks after the data were released, Arvind Narayanan and Vitaly Shmatikov (2008) showed that it was possible to learn about specific people's movie preferences. The trick to their re-identification attack was similar to Sweeney's: merge together two information sources, one with potentially sensitive information and no obviously identifying information and one that contains people's identities. Each of these data sources may be individually safe, but when they are combined, the merged dataset can create informational risk. In the case of the Netflix data, here's how it could happen. Imagine that I choose to share my thoughts about action and comedy movies with my co-workers, but that I prefer not to share my opinion about religious and political movies. My co-workers could use the information that I've shared with them to find my records in the Netflix data; the information that I share could be a unique fingerprint just like William Weld's birth date, zip code, and sex. Then, if they found my unique fingerprint in the data, they could learn my ratings about all movies, including movies that I choose not to share. In addition to this kind of *targeted attack* focused on a single person, Narayanan and Shmatikov also showed that it was possible to do a *broad attack*—one involving many people—by merging the Netflix data with personal and movie rating data that some people have chosen to post on the Internet Movie Database (IMDb). Quite simply, any information that is a unique fingerprint to a specific person—even their set of movie ratings—can be used to identify them.

Even though the Netflix data can be re-identified in either a targeted or broad attack, it still might appear to be low risk. After all, movie ratings don't seem very sensitive. While that might be true in general, for some of the 500,000 people in the dataset, movie ratings might be quite sensitive. In fact, in response to the re-identification, a closeted lesbian woman joined a class-action suit against Netflix. Here's how the problem was expressed in their lawsuit (Singel 2009):

> "[M]ovie and rating data contains information of a ... highly personal and sensitive nature. The member's movie data exposes a Netflix member's personal interest and/or struggles with various highly personal issues, including sexuality, mental illness, recovery from alcoholism, and victimization from incest, physical abuse, domestic violence, adultery, and rape."

The re-identification of the Netflix Prize data illustrates both that all data are potentially identifiable and that all data are potentially sensitive. At this point, you might think that this only applies to data that purport to be about people. Surprisingly, that is not the case. In response to a Freedom of Information Law request, the New York City Government released records of every taxi ride in New York in 2013, including the pickup and drop off times, locations, and fare amounts (recall from chapter 2 that Farber 2015 used similar data to test important theories in labor economics). These data about taxi trips might seem benign because they do not seem to provide information about people, but Anthony Tockar realized that this taxi dataset actually contained lots of potentially sensitive information about people. To illustrate, he looked at all trips starting at the Hustler Club—a large strip club in New York—between midnight and 6 a.m. and then found their drop-off locations. This search revealed—in essence—a list of addresses of some people who frequented the Hustler Club (Tockar 2014). It is hard to imagine that the city government had this in mind when it released the data. In fact, this same technique could be used to find the home addresses of people who visit any place in the city—a medical clinic, a government building, or a religious institution.

These two cases of the Netflix Prize and the New York City taxi data show that relatively skilled people can fail to correctly estimate the informational risk in the data that they release—and these cases are by no means unique (Barbaro and Zeller 2006; Zimmer 2010; Narayanan, Huey, and Felten 2016). Further, in many such cases, the problematic data are still freely available online, indicating the difficulty of ever undoing a data release. Collectively, these examples—as well as research in computer science about privacy—lead to an important conclusion. Researchers should assume that all data are *potentially* identifiable and all data are *potentially* sensitive.

Table 6.2: The "Five Safes" are Principles for Designing and Executing a Data Protection Plan (Desai, Ritchie, and Welpton 2016)

Safe	Action
Safe projects	Limits projects with data to those that are ethical
Safe people	Access is restricted to people who can be trusted with data (e.g., people who have undergone ethical training)
Safe data	Data are de-identified and aggregated to the extent possible
Safe settings	Data are stored in computers with appropriate physical (e.g., locked room) and software (e.g., password protection, encrypted) protection
Safe output	Research output is reviewed to prevent accidental privacy breaches

Unfortunately, there is no simple solution to the facts that all data are potentially identifiable and that all data are potentially sensitive. However, one way to reduce informational risk while you are working with data is to create and follow a *data protection plan.* This plan will decrease the chance that your data will leak and will decrease the harm if a leak does somehow occur. The specifics of data protection plans, such as which form of encryption to use, will change over time, but the UK Data Services helpfully organizes the elements of a data protection plan into five categories that they call the *five safes*: safe projects, safe people, safe settings, safe data, and safe outputs (table 6.2) (Desai, Ritchie, and Welpton 2016). None of the five safes individually provide perfect protection. But together they form a powerful set of factors that can decrease informational risk.

In addition to protecting your data while you are using them, one step in the research process where informational risk is particularly salient is data sharing with other researchers. Data sharing among scientists is a core value of the scientific endeavor, and it greatly facilitates the advancement of knowledge. Here's how the UK House of Commons described the importance of data sharing (Molloy 2011):

"Access to data is fundamental if researchers are to reproduce, verify and build on results that are reported in the literature. The presumption must be that, unless there is a strong reason otherwise, data should be fully disclosed and made publicly available."

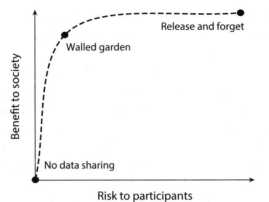

Figure 6.6: Data release strategies can fall along a continuum. Where you should be on this continuum depends on the specific details of your data, and third-party review may help you decide the appropriate balance of risk and benefit in your case. The exact shape of this curve depends on the specifics of the data and research goals (Goroff 2015).

Yet, by sharing your data with another researcher, you may be increasing informational risk to your participants. Thus, it may seem that data sharing creates a fundamental tension between the obligation to share data with other scientists and the obligation to minimize informational risk to participants. Fortunately, this dilemma is not as severe as it appears. Rather, it is better to think about data sharing as falling along a continuum, with each point on that continuum providing a different mix of benefits to society and risk to participants (figure 6.6).

At one extreme, you can share your data with no one, which minimizes risk to participants but also minimizes gains to society. At the other extreme, you can *release and forget,* where data are "anonymized" and posted for everyone. Relative to not releasing data, release and forget offers both higher benefits to society and higher risk to participants. In between these two extreme cases are a range of hybrids, including what I'll call a *walled garden* approach. Under this approach, data are shared with people who meet certain criteria and who agree to be bound by certain rules (e.g., oversight from an IRB and a data protection plan). The walled garden approach provides many of the benefits of release and forget with less risk. Of course, such an approach creates many questions—who should have access, under what conditions and for how long, who should pay to maintain and police the walled garden, etc.—but these are not insurmountable. In fact, there are already working walled gardens in place that researchers can use right now, such as the data archive of the Inter-university Consortium for Political and Social Research at the University of Michigan.

So, where should the data from your study be on the continuum of no sharing, walled garden, and release and forget? This depend on the details of your data: researchers must balance Respect for Persons, Beneficence, Justice, and Respect for Law and Public Interest. Viewed from this perspective, data sharing is not a distinctive ethical conundrum; it is just one of the many aspects of research in which researchers have to find an appropriate ethical balance.

Some critics are generally opposed to data sharing because, in my opinion, they are focused on its risks—which are undoubtedly real—and are ignoring its benefits. So, in order to encourage focus on both risks and benefits, I'd like to offer an analogy. Every year, cars are responsible for thousands of deaths, but we do not attempt to ban driving. In fact, a call to ban driving would be absurd because driving enables many wonderful things. Rather, society places restrictions on who can drive (e.g., the need to be a certain age and to have passed certain tests) and how they can drive (e.g., under the speed limit). Society also has people tasked with enforcing these rules (e.g., police), and we punish people who are caught violating them. This same kind of balanced thinking that society applies to regulating driving can also be applied to data sharing. That is, rather than making absolutist arguments for or against data sharing, I think we will make the most progress by focusing on how we can decrease the risks and increase the benefits from data sharing.

To conclude, informational risk has increased dramatically, and it is very hard to predict and quantify. Therefore, it is best to assume that all data are potentially identifiable and potentially sensitive. To decrease informational risk while doing research, researchers can create and follow a data protection plan. Further, informational risk does not prevent researchers from sharing data with other scientists.

6.6.3 Privacy

Privacy is a right to the appropriate flow of information.

A third area where researchers may struggle is *privacy*. As Lowrance (2012) put it quite succinctly: "privacy should be respected because people should be respected." Privacy, however, is a notoriously messy concept (Nissenbaum 2010, chapter 4), and, as such, it is a difficult one to use when trying to make specific decisions about research.

A common way to think about privacy is with a public/private dichotomy. By this way of thinking, if information is publicly accessible, then it can be used by researchers without concerns about violating people's privacy. But this approach can run into problems. For example, in November 2007, Costas Panagopoulos sent letters about an upcoming election to everyone in three towns. In two towns—Monticello, Iowa and Holland, Michigan—Panagopoulos promised/threatened to publish a list of people who had voted in the newspaper. In the other town—Ely, Iowa—Panagopoulos promised/threatened to publish a list of people who had not voted in the newspaper. These treatments were designed to induce pride and shame (Panagopoulos 2010) because these emotions had been found to impact turnout in earlier studies (Gerber, Green, and Larimer 2008). Information about who votes and who doesn't is public in the United States; anyone can access it. So, one could argue that because this voting information is already public, there is no problem with a researcher publishing it in the newspaper. On the other hand, something about that argument feels wrong to some people.

As this example illustrates, the public/private dichotomy is too blunt (boyd and Crawford 2012; Markham and Buchanan 2012). A better way to think about privacy—one especially designed to handle issues raised by the digital age—is the idea of *contextual integrity* (Nissenbaum 2010). Rather than considering information as public or private, contextual integrity focuses on the flow of information. According to Nissenbaum (2010), "a right to privacy is neither a right to secrecy or a right to control but a right to *appropriate flow* of personal information."

The key concept underlying contextual integrity is *context-relative informational norms* (Nissenbaum 2010). These are norms that govern the flow of information in specific settings, and they are determined by three parameters:

- actors (subject, sender, recipient)
- attributes (types of information)
- transmission principles (constraints under which information flows)

Thus, when you as a researcher are deciding whether to use data without permission, it is helpful to ask, "Does this use violate context-relative informational norms?" Returning to the case of Panagopoulos (2010), in this case, having an outside researcher publish lists of voters or nonvoters in the newspaper seems likely to violate informational norms. This is probably not how people expect information to flow. In fact, Panagopoulos did not follow through on his promise/threat, because local election officials traced the letters to him and persuaded him that it was not a good idea (Issenberg 2012, p. 307).

The idea of context-relative informational norms can also help evaluate the case I discussed at the beginning of the chapter regarding the use of mobile phone call logs to track mobility during the Ebola outbreak in West Africa in 2014 (Wesolowski et al. 2014). In this setting, one could imagine two different situations:

- Situation 1: sending complete call log data [attributes]; to governments of incomplete legitimacy [actors]; for any possible future use [transmission principles]
- Situation 2: sending partially anonymized records [attributes]; to respected university researchers [actors]; for use in response to the Ebola outbreak and subject to the oversight of university ethical boards [transmission principles]

Even though in both of these situations, call data are flowing out of the company, the informational norms concerning these two situations are not the same because of differences between the actors, attributes, and transmission principles. Focusing on only one of these parameters can lead to overly simplistic decision-making. In fact, Nissenbaum (2015) emphasizes that none of these three parameters can be reduced to the others, nor can any one of them individually define informational norms. This three-dimensional nature of informational norms explains why past efforts—which have focused on either attributes or transmission principles—have been ineffective at capturing common-sense notions of privacy.

One challenge with using the idea of context-relative informational norms to guide decisions is that researchers might not know them ahead of time and they are very hard to measure (Acquisti, Brandimarte, and Loewenstein 2015). Further, even if some research would violate contextual-relative informational norms, that does not automatically mean that the research should not happen. In fact, chapter 8 of Nissenbaum (2010) is entirely about "Breaking Rules for Good." Despite these complications, context-relative informational norms are still a useful way to reason about questions related to privacy.

Finally, privacy is an area where I've seen misunderstandings between researchers who prioritize Respect for Persons and those who prioritize Beneficence. Imagine the case of a public health researcher who, in an effort to prevent the spread of a novel infectious disease, secretly watched people taking showers. Researchers focusing on Beneficence would focus on the benefits to society from this research and might argue that there was no harm to participants if the researcher did her spying without detection. On the other hand, researchers who prioritize Respect for Persons would focus on the fact that the researcher was not treating people with respect and might argue that harm was created by violating the privacy of participants, even if the participants were not aware of the spying. In other words, to some, violating people's privacy is a harm in and of itself.

In conclusion, when reasoning about privacy, it is helpful to move beyond the overly simplistic public/private dichotomy and to reason instead about context-relative informational norms, which are made up of three elements: actors (subject, sender, recipient), attributes (types of information), and transmission principles (constraints under which information flows) (Nissenbaum 2010). Some researchers evaluate privacy in terms of the harm that could result from its violation, whereas other researchers view the violation of privacy as a harm in and of itself. Because notions of privacy in many digital systems are changing over time, vary from person to person, and vary from situation to situation (Acquisti, Brandimarte, and Loewenstein 2015), privacy is likely to be a source of difficult ethical decisions for researchers for some time to come.

6.6.4 Making decisions in the face of uncertainty

Uncertainty need not lead to inaction.

The fourth and final area where I expect researchers to struggle is making decisions in the face of uncertainty. That is, after all the philosophizing and balancing, research ethics involves making decisions about what to do and what not to do. Unfortunately, these decisions often must be made based on incomplete information. For example, when designing Encore, researchers might have wished to know the probability that it would cause someone to be visited by the police. Or, when designing Emotional Contagion, researchers might have wished to know the probability that it could trigger depression in some participants. These probabilities were probably extremely low, but they were unknown before the research takes place. And, because neither project publicly tracked information about adverse events, these probabilities are still not generally known.

Uncertainties are not unique to social research in the digital age. When the Belmont Report described the systematic assessment of risks and benefits, it explicitly acknowledged these would be difficult to quantify exactly. These uncertainties, however, are more severe in the digital age, in part because we have less experience with this type of research and in part because of the characteristics of the research itself.

Given these uncertainties, some people seem to advocate for something like "better safe than sorry," which is a colloquial version of the *Precautionary Principle*. While this approach appears reasonable—perhaps even wise—it can actually cause harm; it is chilling to research; and it causes people to take an excessively narrow view of the situation (Sunstein 2005). In order to understand the problems with the Precautionary Principle, let's consider Emotional Contagion. The experiment was planned to involve about 700,000 people, and there was certainly some chance that people in the experiment would suffer harm. But there was also some chance that the experiment could yield knowledge that would be beneficial to Facebook users and to society. Thus, while allowing the experiment was a risk (as has been amply discussed), preventing the experiment would also have been a risk, because it could have produced valuable knowledge. Of course, the choice was not between doing the experiment as it occurred and not doing the experiment; there were many possible modifications to the design that might have brought it into a different ethical balance. However, at some point, researchers will have the choice between doing a study and not doing it, and there are risks in both action and inaction. It is inappropriate to focus only on the risks of action. Quite simply, there is no risk-free approach.

Moving beyond the Precautionary Principle, one important way to think about making decisions given uncertainty is the *minimal risk standard*. This standard attempts to benchmark the risk of a particular study against the risks that participants undertake in their daily lives, such as playing sports and driving cars (Wendler et al. 2005). This approach is valuable because assessing whether something meets the minimal risk standard is easier than assessing the actual level of risk. For example, in Emotional Contagion, before the study began, the researchers could have compared the emotional content of News Feeds in the experiment with that of other News Feeds on Facebook. If they had been similar, then the researchers could have concluded that the experiment met the minimal risk standard (Meyer 2015). And they could have made this decision *even if they didn't know the absolute level of risk*. The same approach could have been applied to Encore. Initially, Encore triggered requests to websites that were known to be sensitive, such as those of banned political groups in countries with repressive governments. As such, it was not minimal risk for participants in certain countries. However, the revised version of Encore—which only triggered requests to Twitter, Facebook, and YouTube—was minimal risk because requests to those sites are triggered during normal web browsing (Narayanan and Zevenbergen 2015).

A second important idea when making decisions about studies with unknown risk is *power analysis*, which allows researchers to calculate the sample size they will need to reliably detect an effect of a given size (Cohen 1988). If your study might expose participants to risk—even minimal risk— then the principle of Beneficence suggests that you should impose the smallest amount of risk needed to achieve your research goals. (Think back to the Reduce principle in chapter 4.) Even though some researchers have an obsession with making their studies as *big* as possible, research ethics suggests that researchers should make their studies as *small* as possible. Power analysis is not new, of course, but there is an important difference between the way that it was used in the analog age and how it should be used today. In the analog age, researchers generally did power analysis to make sure that their study was not too small (i.e., under-powered). Now, however, researchers should do power analysis to make sure that their study is not too big (i.e., over-powered).

The minimal risk standard and power analysis help you reason about and design studies, but they don't provide you with any new information about how participants might feel about your study and what risks they might experience from participating in it. Another way to deal with uncertainty is to collect additional information, which leads to ethical-response surveys and staged trials.

In *ethical-response surveys*, researchers present a brief description of a proposed research project and then ask two questions:

- (Q1) "If someone you cared about were a candidate participant for this experiment, would you want that person to be included as a participant?": [Yes], [I have no preferences], [No]
- (Q2) "Do you believe that the researchers should be allowed to proceed with this experiment?": [Yes], [Yes, but with caution], [I'm not sure], [No]

Following each question, respondents are provided a space in which they can explain their answer. Finally, respondents—who could be potential participants or people recruited from a microtask labor markets (e.g., Amazon Mechanical Turk)—answer some basic demographic questions (Schechter and Bravo-Lillo 2014).

Ethical-response surveys have three features that I find particularly attractive. First, they happen before a study has been conducted, and therefore they can prevent problems before the research starts (as opposed to approaches that monitor for adverse reactions). Second, the respondents in ethical-response surveys are typically not researchers, and so this helps researchers see their study from the perspective of the public. Finally, ethical-response surveys enable researchers to pose multiple versions of a research project in order to assess the perceived ethical balance of different versions of the same project. One limitation, however, of ethical-response surveys is that it is not clear how to decide between different research designs given the survey results. But, despite these limitations, ethical-response surveys appear to be helpful; in fact, Schechter and Bravo-Lillo (2014) report abandoning a planned study in response to concerns raised by participants in an ethical-response survey.

While ethical-response surveys can be helpful for assessing reactions to proposed research, they cannot measure the probability or severity of adverse events. One way that medical researchers deal with uncertainty in high-risk settings is to perform *staged trials*—an approach that might be helpful in some social research. When testing the effectiveness of a new drug, researchers do not immediately jump to a large randomized clinical trial. Rather, they run two types of studies first. Initially, in a phase I trial, researchers are particularly focused on finding a safe dose, and these studies involve a small number of people. Once a safe dose has been determined, phase II trials assess the efficacy of the drug, that is, its ability to work in a best-case situation (Singal, Higgins, and Waljee 2014). Only after phase I and II studies have been completed is a new drug allowed to be assessed in a large randomized controlled trial. While the exact structure of staged trials used in the development of new drugs may not be a good fit for social research, when faced with uncertainty, researchers could run smaller studies explicitly focused on safety and efficacy. For example, with Encore, you could imagine the researchers starting with participants in countries with a strong rule of law.

Together, these four approaches—the minimal risk standard, power analysis, ethical-response surveys, and staged trials—can help you proceed in a sensible way, even in the face of uncertainty. Uncertainty need not lead to inaction.

6.7 Practical tips

In addition to high-minded ethical principles, there are practical issues in research ethics.

In addition to the ethical principles and frameworks described in this chapter, I'd also like to offer three practical tips based on my personal experience conducting, reviewing, and discussing social research in the digital age: *the IRB is a floor, not a ceiling*; *put yourself in everyone else's shoes*; and *think of research ethics as continuous, not discrete*.

6.7.1 The IRB is a floor, not a ceiling

Many researchers seem to hold contradictory views of the IRB. On the one hand, they consider it to be a bumbling bureaucracy. Yet, at the same time, they also consider it to be the final arbitrator of ethical decisions. That is, many researchers seem to believe that if the IRB approves it, then it must be OK. If we acknowledge the very real limitations of IRBs as they currently exist—and there are many of them (Schrag 2010, 2011; Hoonaard 2011; Klitzman 2015; King and Sands 2015; Schneider 2015)—then we as researchers must take on additional responsibility for the ethics of our research. The IRB is a floor not a ceiling, and this idea has two main implications.

First, *the IRB is a floor* means that if you are working at an institution that requires IRB review, then you should follow those rules. This may seem obvious, but I've noticed that some people seem to want to avoid the IRB. In fact, if you are working in ethically unsettled areas, the IRB can be a powerful ally. If you follow their rules, they should stand behind you should something go wrong with your research (King and Sands 2015). And if you don't follow their rules, you could end up out on your own in a very difficult situation.

Second, *the IRB is not a ceiling* means that just filling out your forms and following the rules is not enough. In many situations, you as the researcher are the one who knows the most about how to act ethically. Ultimately, you are the researcher, and the ethical responsibility lies with you; it is your name on the paper.

One way to ensure that you treat the IRB as a floor and not a ceiling is to include an ethical appendix in your papers. In fact, you could draft your ethical appendix before your study even begins, in order to force yourself to think about how you will explain your work to your peers and the public. If you find yourself uncomfortable while writing your ethical appendix, then your study might not strike the appropriate ethical balance. In addition to helping you diagnose your own work, publishing your ethical appendices will help the research community discuss ethical issues and establish appropriate norms based on examples from real empirical research. Table 6.3 presents empirical research papers that I think have good discussions of research ethics. I don't agree with every claim by the authors in these discussions, but they are all examples of researchers acting with *integrity* in the sense defined by Carter (1996): in each case, (1) the researchers decide what they think is right and what is wrong; (2) they act based on what they have decided, even at personal cost; and (3) they publicly show that they are acting based on their ethical analysis of the situation.

6.7.2 Put yourself in everyone else's shoes

Often researchers are so focused on the scientific aims of their work that they see the world only through that lens. This myopia can lead to bad ethical judgment. Therefore, when you are thinking about your study, try to imagine

Table 6.3: Papers with Interesting Discussions of the Ethics of their Research

Study	Issue addressed
van de Rijt et al. (2014)	Field experiments without consent
	Avoiding contextual harm
Paluck and Green (2009)	Field experiments in developing country
	Research on sensitive topic
	Complex consent issues
	Remediation of possible harms
Burnett and Feamster (2015)	Research without consent
	Balancing risks and benefits when risks are hard to quantify
Chaabane et al. (2014)	Social implications of research
	Using leaked data files
Jakobsson and Ratkiewicz (2006)	Field experiments without consent
Soeller et al. (2016)	Violated terms of service

how your participants, other relevant stakeholders, and even a journalist might react to your study. This perspective taking is different than imaging how *you* would feel in each of these positions. Rather, it is trying to imagine how these *other people* will feel, a process that is likely to induce empathy (Batson, Early, and Salvarani 1997). Thinking through your work from these different perspectives can help you foresee problems and move your work into better ethical balance.

Further, when imagining your work from the perspective of others, you should expect that they are likely to fixate on vivid worst-case scenarios. For example, in response to Emotional Contagion, some critics focused on the possibility that it might have triggered suicide, a low-probability but extremely vivid worst-case scenario. Once people's emotions have been activated and they focus on worst-case scenarios, they may completely lose track of the probability of this worst-case event occurring (Sunstein 2002). The fact that people might respond emotionally, however, does not mean that you should dismiss them as uninformed, irrational, or stupid. We should all be humble enough to realize that none of us have a perfect view of ethics.

6.7.3 Think of research ethics as continuous, not discrete

Debate about the ethics of social research in the digital age frequently happens in binary terms; for example, Emotional Contagion was either ethical or it was not ethical. This binary thinking polarizes discussion, hinders efforts to develop shared norms, promotes intellectual laziness, and absolves researchers whose research is labeled "ethical" from their responsibility to act more ethically. The most productive conversations that I've seen involving research ethics move beyond this binary thinking to a continuous notion about research ethics.

A major practical problem with a binary conception of research ethics is that it polarizes discussion. Calling Emotional Contagion "unethical" lumps it together with true atrocities in a way that is not helpful. Rather, it is more helpful and appropriate to talk specifically about the aspects of the study that you find problematic. Moving away from binary thinking and polarizing language is not a call for us to use muddled language to hide unethical behavior. Rather, a continuous notion of ethics will, I think, lead to more careful and precise language. Further, a continuous notion of research ethics clarifies that everyone—even researchers who are doing work that is already considered "ethical"—should strive to create an even better ethical balance in their work.

A final benefit of a move toward continuous thinking is that it encourages intellectual humility, which is appropriate in the face of difficult ethical challenges. The questions of research ethics in the digital age are difficult, and no single person should be overly confident in her own ability to diagnose the correct course of action.

6.8 Conclusion

Social research in the digital age raises new ethical issues. But these issues are not insurmountable. If we, as a community, can develop shared ethical norms and standards that are supported both by researchers and the public, then we can harness the capabilities of the digital age in ways that are responsible and beneficial to society. This chapter represents my attempt to move us in that direction, and I think the key will be for researchers to adopt principles-based thinking, while continuing to follow appropriate rules.

In section 6.2, I described three digital-age research projects that have generated ethical debate. Then, in section 6.3, I described what I think is the fundamental reason for ethical uncertainty in digital-age social research: rapidly increasing power for researchers to observe and experiment on people without their consent or even awareness. These capabilities are changing faster than our norms, rules, and laws. Next, in section 6.4, I described four existing principles that can guide your thinking: Respect for Persons, Beneficence, Justice, and Respect for Law and Public Interest. Then, in section 6.5, I summarized two broad ethical frameworks—consequentialism and deontology—that can help you with one of the deepest challenges that you might face: when is it appropriate for you to take ethically questionable means in order to achieve an ethically appropriate end. These principles and ethical frameworks will enable you to move beyond focusing on what is permitted by existing regulations and increase your ability to communicate your reasoning with other researchers and the public.

With that background, in section 6.6, I discussed four areas that are particularly challenging for digital-age social researchers: informed consent (section 6.6.1), understanding and managing informational risk (section 6.6.2), privacy (section 6.6.3), and making ethical decisions in the face of uncertainty (section 6.6.4). Finally, in section 6.7, I concluded with three practical tips for working in an area with unsettled ethics.

In terms of scope, this chapter has focused on the perspective of an individual researcher seeking generalizable knowledge. As such, it leaves out important questions about improvements to the system of ethical oversight of research; questions about regulation of the collection and use of data by companies; and questions about mass surveillance by governments. These other questions are obviously complex and difficult, but it is my hope that some of the ideas from research ethics will be helpful in these other contexts.

Historical appendix

This historical appendix provides a very brief review of research ethics in the United States.

Any discussion of research ethics needs to acknowledge that, in the past, researchers have done awful things in the name of science. One of the worst

Table 6.4: Partial Time Line of the Tuskegee Syphilis Study, adapted from Jones (2011)

Date	Event
1932	Approximately 400 men with syphilis are enrolled in the study; they are not informed of the nature of the research
1937–38	The PHS sends mobile treatment units to the area, but treatment is withheld for the men in the study
1942–43	In order to prevent the men in the study from receiving treatment, the PHS intervenes to prevent them from being drafted for World War II
1950s	Penicillin becomes a widely available and effective treatment for syphilis; the men in the study are still not treated (Brandt 1978)
1969	The PHS convenes an ethical review of the study; the panel recommends that the study continue
1972	Peter Buxtun, a former PHS employee, tells a reporter about the study, and the press breaks the story
1972	The US Senate holds hearings on human experimentation, including the Tuskegee Study
1973	The government officially ends the study and authorizes treatment for survivors
1997	US President Bill Clinton publicly and officially apologizes for the Tuskegee Study

of these was the Tuskegee Syphilis Study (table 6.4). In 1932, researchers from the US Public Health Service (PHS) enrolled about 400 black men infected with syphilis in a study to monitor the effects of the disease. These men were recruited from the area around Tuskegee, Alabama. From the outset, the study was nontherapeutic; it was designed to merely document the history of the disease in black males. The participants were deceived about the nature of the study—they were told that it was a study of "bad blood"—and they were offered false and ineffective treatment, even though syphilis is a deadly disease. As the study progressed, safe and effective treatments for syphilis were developed, but the researchers actively intervened to prevent the participants from getting treatment elsewhere. For example, during World War II, the research team secured draft deferments for all men in the study in order to prevent the treatment the men would have received had they entered the Armed

Forces. Researchers continued to deceive participants and deny them care for 40 years.

The Tuskegee Syphilis Study took place against a backdrop of racism and extreme inequality that was common in the southern part of the United States at the time. But, over its 40-year history, the study involved dozens of researchers, both black and white. And, in addition to researchers directly involved, many more must have read one of the 15 reports of the study published in the medical literature (Heller 1972). In the mid-1960s—about 30 years after the study began—a PHS employee named Robert Buxtun began pushing within the PHS to end the study, which he considered morally outrageous. In response to Buxtun, in 1969, the PHS convened a panel to do a complete ethical review of the study. Shockingly, the ethical review panel decided that researchers should continue to withhold treatment from the infected men. During the deliberations, one member of the panel even remarked: "You will never have another study like this; take advantage of it" (Brandt 1978). The all-white panel, which was mostly made up of doctors, did decide that some form of informed consent should be obtained. But the panel judged the men themselves incapable of providing informed consent because of their age and low level of education. The panel recommended, therefore, that the researchers receive "surrogate informed consent" from local medical officials. So, even after a full ethical review, the withholding of care continued. Eventually, Buxtun took the story to a journalist, and, in 1972, Jean Heller wrote a series of newspaper articles that exposed the study to the world. It was only after widespread public outrage that the study was finally ended and care was offered to the men who had survived.

The victims of this study included not just the 399 men, but also their families: at least 22 wives, 17 children, and 2 grandchildren with syphilis may have contracted the disease as a result of the withholding of treatment (Yoon 1997). Further, the harm caused by the study continued long after it ended. The study—justifiably—decreased the trust that African Americans had in the medical community, an erosion in trust that may have led African Americans to avoid medical care to the detriment of their health (Alsan and Wanamaker 2016). Further, the lack of trust hindered efforts to treat HIV/AIDS in the 1980s and 90s (Jones 1993, chapter 14).

Although it is hard to imagine research so horrific happening today, I think there are three important lessons from the Tuskegee Syphilis Study for people conducting social research in the digital age. First, it reminds us that there are some studies that simply should not happen. Second, it shows us that research can harm not just participants, but also their families and entire communities long after the research has been completed. Finally, it shows that researchers can make terrible ethical decisions. In fact, I think it should induce some fear in researchers today that so many people involved in this study made such awful decisions over such a long period of time. And, unfortunately, Tuskegee is by no means unique; there were several other examples of problematic social and medical research during this era (Katz, Capron, and Glass 1972; Emanuel et al. 2008).

In 1974, in response to the Tuskegee Syphilis Study and these other ethical failures by researchers, the US Congress created the National Commission for the Protection of Human Subjects of Biomedical and Behavioral Research and tasked it to develop ethical guidelines for research involving human subjects. After four years of meeting at the Belmont Conference Center, the group produced the *Belmont Report*, a report that has had a tremendous impact on both abstract debates in bioethics and the everyday practice of research.

The Belmont Report has three sections. In the first—Boundaries Between Practice and Research—the report sets out its purview. In particular, it argues for a distinction between *research*, which seeks generalizable knowledge, and *practice*, which includes everyday treatment and activities. Further, it argues that the ethical principles of the Belmont Report apply only to research. It has been argued that this distinction between research and practice is one way that the Belmont Report is not well suited to social research in the digital age (Metcalf and Crawford 2016; boyd 2016).

The second and third parts of the Belmont Report lay out three ethical principles—Respect for Persons; Beneficence; and Justice—and describe how these principles can be applied in research practice. These are the principles that I described in more detail in the main text of this chapter.

The Belmont Report sets broad goals, but it is not a document that can be easily used to oversee day-to-day activities. Therefore, the US Government created a set of regulations that are colloquially called the *Common Rule* (their official name is Title 45 Code of Federal Regulations, Part 46, Subparts A–D) (Porter and Koski 2008). These regulations describe the process for reviewing, approving, and overseeing research, and they are the regulations that Institutional Review Boards (IRBs) are tasked with enforcing. To understand the difference between the Belmont Report and the Common Rule, consider how each discusses informed consent: the Belmont Report describes the philosophical reasons for informed consent and broad characteristics that would represent true informed consent, while the Common Rule lists the eight required and six optional elements of an informed consent document. By law, the Common Rule governs almost all research that receives funding from the US Government. Further, many institutions that receive funding from the US Government typically apply the Common Rule to all research happening at that institution, regardless of the funding source. But the Common Rule does not automatically apply to companies that do not receive research funding from the US Government.

I think that almost all researchers respect the broad goals of ethical research as expressed in the Belmont Report, but there is widespread annoyance with the Common Rule and the process of working with IRBs (Schrag 2010, 2011; Hoonaard 2011; Klitzman 2015; King and Sands 2015; Schneider 2015). To be clear, those critical of IRBs are not against ethics. Rather, they believe that the current system does not strike an appropriate balance or that it could better achieve its goals through other methods. I, however, will take these IRBs as given. If you are required to follow the rules of an IRB, then you should do so. However, I would encourage you to *also* take a principles-based approach when considering the ethics of your research.

This background very briefly summarizes how we arrived at the rules-based system of IRB review in the United States. When considering the Belmont Report and the Common Rule today, we should remember that they were created in a different era and were—quite sensibly—responding to the problems of that era, in particular breaches in medical ethics during and after World War II (Beauchamp 2011).

In addition to efforts by medical and behavioral scientists to create ethical codes, there were also smaller and less well-known efforts by computer scientists. In fact, the first researchers to run into the ethical challenges created by digital-age research were not social scientists: they were computer scientists, specifically researchers in computer security. During the 1990s and 2000s, computer security researchers conducted a number of ethically questionable studies that involved things like taking over botnets and hacking into thousands of computers with weak passwords (Bailey, Dittrich, and Kenneally 2013; Dittrich, Carpenter, and Karir 2015). In response to these studies, the US Government—specifically the Department of Homeland Security—created a blue-ribbon commission to write a guiding ethical framework for research involving information and communication technologies (ICT). The result of this effort was the *Menlo Report* (Dittrich, Kenneally, and others 2011). Although the concerns of computer security researchers are not exactly the same as those of social researchers, the Menlo Report provides three important lessons for social researchers.

First, the Menlo Report reaffirms the three Belmont principles—Respect for Persons, Beneficence, and Justice—and adds a fourth: *Respect for Law and Public Interest*. I described this fourth principle and how it should be applied to social research in the main text of this chapter (section 6.4.4).

Second, the Menlo Report calls on researchers to move beyond the narrow definition of "research involving human subjects" from the Belmont Report to a more general notion of "research with human-harming potential." The limitations of the scope of the Belmont Report are well illustrated by Encore. The IRBs at Princeton and Georgia Tech ruled that Encore was not "research involving human subjects," and therefore was not subject to review under the Common Rule. However, Encore clearly has human-harming potential; at its most extreme, Encore could potentially result in innocent people being jailed by repressive governments. A principles-based approach means that researchers should not hide behind a narrow, legal definition of "research involving human subjects," even if IRBs allow it. Rather, they should adopt a more general notion of "research with human-harming potential," and they should subject all of their own research with human-harming potential to ethical consideration.

Third, the Menlo Report calls on researchers to expand the stakeholders that are considered when applying the Belmont principles. As research has moved from a separate sphere of life to something that is more embedded in day-to-day activities, ethical considerations must be expanded beyond just specific research participants to include nonparticipants and the environment in which the research takes place. In other words, the Menlo Report calls for researchers to broaden their ethical field of view beyond just their participants.

This historical appendix has provided a very brief review of research ethics in the social and medical sciences and in computer science. For a book-length treatment of research ethics in medical science, see Emanuel et al. (2008) or Beauchamp and Childress (2012).

What to read next

- **Introduction (section 6.1)**

Research ethics has traditionally also included topics such as scientific fraud and allocation of credit. These are discussed in greater detail in *On Being a Scientist*, by the Institute of Medicine and the National Academy of Science and National Academy of Engineering (2009).

This chapter is heavily influenced by the situation in the United States. For more on the ethical review procedures in other countries, see chapters 6–9 of Desposato (2016b). For an argument that the biomedical ethical principles that have influenced this chapter are excessively American, see Holm (1995). For a further historical review of Institutional Review Boards in the United States, see Stark (2012). The journal *PS: Political Science and Politics* held a professional symposium on the relationship between political scientists and IRBs; see Martinez-Ebers (2016) for a summary.

The Belmont Report and subsequent regulations in the United States tend to make a distinction between research and practice. I have not made such a distinction in this chapter, because I think the ethical principles and frameworks apply to both settings. For more on this distinction and the problems it introduces, see Beauchamp and Saghai (2012), Meyer (2015), boyd (2016), and Metcalf and Crawford (2016).

For more on research oversight at Facebook, see Jackman and Kanerva (2016). For ideas about research oversight at companies and NGOs, see Calo (2013), Polonetsky, Tene, and Jerome (2015), and Tene and Polonetsky (2016).

In relation to the use of mobile phone data to help address the 2014 Ebola outbreak in West Africa (Wesolowski et al. 2014; McDonald 2016), for more about the privacy risks of mobile phone data, see Mayer, Mutchler, and Mitchell (2016). For examples of earlier crisis-related research using mobile phone data, see Bengtsson et al. (2011) and Lu, Bengtsson, and Holme (2012), and for more on the ethics of crisis-related research, see Crawford and Finn (2015).

- **Three examples (section 6.2)**

Many people have written about Emotional Contagion. The journal *Research Ethics* devoted their entire issue in January 2016 to discussing the experiment; see Hunter and Evans (2016) for an overview. The *Proceedings of the National Academy of Sciences* published two pieces about the experiment: Kahn, Vayena, and Mastroianni (2014) and Fiske and Hauser (2014). Other pieces about the experiment include Puschmann and Bozdag (2014), Meyer (2014, 2015),

Grimmelmann (2015), Selinger and Hartzog (2015), Kleinsman and Buckley (2015), Shaw (2015), and Flick (2015).

- **Digital is different (section 6.3)**

In terms of mass surveillance, broad overviews are provided in Mayer-Schönberger (2009) and Marx (2016). For a concrete example of the changing costs of surveillance, Bankston and Soltani (2013) estimate that tracking a criminal suspect using mobile phones is about 50 times cheaper than using physical surveillance. See also Ajunwa, Crawford, and Schultz (2016) for a discussion of surveillance at work. Bell and Gemmell (2009) provide a more optimistic perspective on self-surveillance.

In addition to being able to track observable behavior that is public or partially public (e.g., Tastes, Ties, and Time), researchers can increasingly infer things that many participants consider to be private. For example, Michal Kosinski and colleagues (2013) showed that they could infer sensitive information about people, such as sexual orientation and use of addictive substances, from seemingly ordinary digital trace data (Facebook Likes). This might sound magical, but the approach Kosinski and colleagues used—which combined digital traces, surveys, and supervised learning—is actually something that I've already told you about. Recall that in chapter 3, I told you how Joshua Blumenstock and colleagues (2015) combined survey data with mobile phone data to estimate poverty in Rwanda. This exact same approach, which can be used to efficiently measure poverty in a developing country, can also be used for potentially privacy-violating inferences.

For more on the possible unintended secondary uses of health data, see O'Doherty et al. (2016). In addition to the potential for unintended secondary uses, the creation of even an incomplete master database could have a chilling effect on social and political life if people became unwilling to read certain materials or discuss certain topics; see Schauer (1978) and Penney (2016).

In situations with overlapping rules, researcher sometimes engage in "regulatory shopping" (Grimmelmann 2015; Nickerson and Hyde 2016). In particular, some researchers who wish to avoid IRB oversight can form partnerships with researchers who are not covered by IRBs (e.g., people at companies or NGOs), and have those colleagues collect and de-identify data. Then, the IRB-covered researcher can analyze this de-identified data without IRB oversight because the research is no longer considered "human subjects research," at least according to some interpretations of current rules. This kind of IRB evasion is probably not consistent with a principles-based approach to research ethics.

In 2011, an effort began to update the Common Rule, and this process was finally completed in 2017 (Jashchik 2017). For more on these efforts to update the Common Rule, see Evans (2013), National Research Council (2014), Hudson and Collins (2015), and Metcalf (2016).

- **Four principles (section 6.4)**

The classic principles-based approach to biomedical ethics is that of Beauchamp and Childress (2012). They propose that four main principles should guide biomedical ethics: Respect for Autonomy, Nonmaleficence, Beneficence, and Justice. The principle of nonmaleficence urges one to abstain from causing harm to other people. This concept is deeply connected to the Hippocratic idea of "Do not harm." In research ethics, this principle is often combined with the principle of Beneficence, but see chapter 5 of Beauchamp and Childress (2012) for more on the distinction between the two. For a criticism that these principles are overly American, see Holm (1995). For more on balancing when the principles conflict, see Gillon (2015).

The four principles in this chapter have also been proposed to guide ethical oversight for research being done at companies and NGOs (Polonetsky, Tene, and Jerome 2015) through bodies called "Consumer Subject Review Boards" (CSRBs) (Calo 2013).

- **Respect for Persons (section 6.4.1)**

In addition to respecting autonomy, the Belmont Report also acknowledges that not every human is capable of true self-determination. For example, children, people suffering from illness, or people living in situations of severely restricted liberty may not be able to act as fully autonomous individuals, and these people are therefore subject to extra protection.

Applying the principle of Respect for Persons in the digital age can be challenging. For example, in digital-age research, it can be difficult to provide extra protections for people with diminished capability of self-determination because researchers often know very little about their participants. Further, informed consent in digital-age social research is a huge challenge. In some cases, truly informed consent can suffer from the *transparency paradox* (Nissenbaum 2011), where *information* and *comprehension* are in conflict. Roughly, if researchers provide full information about the nature of the data collection, data analysis, and data security practices, it will be difficult for many participants to comprehend. But if researchers provide comprehensible information, it may lack important technical details. In medical research in the analog age—the dominant setting considered by the Belmont Report—one could imagine a doctor talking individually with each participant to help resolve the transparency paradox. In online studies involving thousands or millions of people, such a face-to-face approach is impossible. A second problem with consent in the digital age is that in some studies, such as analyses of massive data repositories, it would be impractical to obtain informed consent from all participants. I discuss these and other questions about informed consent in more detail in section 6.6.1. Despite these difficulties, however, we should remember that informed consent is neither necessary nor sufficient for Respect for Persons.

For more on medical research before informed consent, see Miller (2014). For a book-length treatment of informed consent, see Manson and O'Neill (2007). See also the suggested readings about informed consent below.

- ## Beneficence (section 6.4.2)

Harms to context are the harms that research can cause not to specific people but to social settings. This concept is a bit abstract, but I'll illustrate it with a classic example: the Wichita Jury Study (Vaughan 1967; Katz, Capron, and Glass 1972, chapter 2)—also sometimes called the Chicago Jury Project (Cornwell 2010). In this study, researchers from the University of Chicago, as part of a larger study of social aspects of the legal system, secretly recorded six jury deliberations in Wichita, Kansas. The judges and lawyers in the cases had approved the recordings, and there was strict oversight of the process. However, the jurors were unaware that recordings were occurring. Once the study was discovered, there was public outrage. The Justice Department began an investigation of the study, and the researchers were called to testify in front of Congress. Ultimately, Congress passed a new law that makes it illegal to secretly record jury deliberation.

The concern of critics of the Wichita Jury Study was not the risk of harm to the participants; rather, it was the risk of harms to the context of jury deliberation. That is, people thought that if jury members did not believe that they were having discussions in a safe and protected space, it would be harder for jury deliberations to proceed in the future. In addition to jury deliberation, there are other specific social contexts that society provides with extra protection, such as attorney–client relationships and psychological care (MacCarthy 2015).

The risk of harms to context and the disruption of social systems also arise in some field experiments in political science (Desposato 2016b). For an example of a more context-sensitive cost–benefit calculation for a field experiment in political science, see Zimmerman (2016).

- ## Justice (section 6.4.3)

Compensation for participants has been discussed in a number of settings related to digital-age research. Lanier (2014) proposes paying participants for digital traces that they generate. Bederson and Quinn (2011) discuss payments in online labor markets. Finally, Desposato (2016a) proposes paying participants in field experiments. He points out that even if participants cannot be paid directly, a donation could be made to a group working on their behalf. For example, in Encore, the researchers could have made a donation to a group working to support access to the Internet.

- **Respect for Law and Public Interest (section 6.4.4)**

Terms-of-service agreements should have less weight than contracts negotiated between equal parties and than laws created by legitimate governments. Situations where researchers have violated terms-of-service agreements in the past have generally involved using automated queries to audit the behavior of companies (much like field experiments to measure discrimination). For additional discussions, see Vaccaro et al. (2015) and Bruckman (2016a, b). For an example of empirical research that discusses terms of service, see Soeller et al. (2016). For more on the possible legal problems researchers face if they violate terms of service, see Sandvig and Karahalios (2016). Finally, for a slightly different approach to the idea of transparency, see Neuhaus and Webmoor (2012).

- **Two ethical frameworks (section 6.5)**

Obviously, an enormous amount has been written about consequentialism and deontology. For an example of how these ethical frameworks, and others, can be used to reason about digital-age research, see Zevenbergen et al. (2015). For an example of how they can be applied to field experiments in development economics, see Baele (2013).

- **Informed consent (section 6.6.1)**

For more on audit studies of discrimination, see Pager (2007) and Riach and Rich (2004). Not only do these studies not have informed consent, they also involve deception without debriefing.

Both Desposato (2016a) and Humphreys (2015) offer advice about field experiments without consent.

Sommers and Miller (2013) review many arguments in favor of not debriefing participants after deception, and argue that researchers should forgo debriefing

> "under a very narrow set of circumstances, namely, in field research in which debriefing poses considerable practical barriers but researchers would have no qualms about debriefing if they could. Researchers should not be permitted to forgo debriefing in order to preserve a naive participant pool, shield themselves from participant anger, or protect participants from harm."

Others argue that, in some situations, if debriefing causes more harm than good, it should be avoided (Finn and Jakobsson 2007). Debriefing is a case where some researchers prioritize Respect for Persons over Beneficence, whereas some researchers do the opposite. One possible solution would be to find ways to make debriefing a learning experience for the participants. That is, rather than thinking of debriefing as something that can cause harm, perhaps debriefing can also be something that benefits participants. For an example of this kind of educational debriefing, see Jagatic et al. (2007). Psychologists have developed techniques for debriefing (Holmes 1976a, b; Mills 1976; Baumrind 1985; Oczak and Nied¹wie«ska 2007), and some of these may be usefully applied to digital-age research. Humphreys (2015) offers interesting thoughts about *deferred consent*, which is closely related to the debriefing strategy that I described.

The idea of asking a sample of participants for their consent is related to what Humphreys (2015) calls *inferred consent*.

A further idea related to informed consent that has been proposed is to build a panel of people who agree to be in online experiments (Crawford 2014). Some have argued that this panel would be a nonrandom sample of people. But chapter 3 shows that these problems are potentially addressable using post-stratification. Also, consent to be on the panel could cover a variety of experiments. In other words, participants might not need to consent to each experiment individually, a concept called *broad consent* (Sheehan 2011). For more on the differences between one-time consent and consent for each study, as well as a possible hybrid, see Hutton and Henderson (2015).

- **Understanding and managing informational risk (section 6.6.2)**

Far from unique, the Netflix Prize illustrates an important technical property of datasets that contain detailed information about people, and thus offers important lessons about the possibility of "anonymization" of modern social datasets. Files with many pieces of information about each person are likely to be *sparse*, in the sense defined formally in Narayanan and Shmatikov (2008). That is, for each record, there are no records that are the same, and in fact there are no records that are very similar: each person is far away from their nearest neighbor in the dataset. One can imagine that the Netflix data might be sparse because, with about 20,000 movies on a five-star scale, there are about $6^{20,000}$ possible values that each person could have (6 because, in addition to 1 to 5 stars, someone might have not rated the movie at all). This number is so large, it is hard to even comprehend.

Sparsity has two main implications. First, it means that attempting to "anonymize" the dataset based on random perturbation will likely fail. That is, even if Netflix were to randomly adjust some of the ratings (which they did), this would not be sufficient, because the perturbed record is still the closest possible record to the information that the attacker has. Second, the sparsity means that re-identification is possible even if the attacker has imperfect or partial knowledge. For example, in the Netflix data, let's imagine the attacker knows your ratings for two movies and the dates you made those ratings $\pm$ 3 days; just that information alone is sufficient to uniquely identify 68% of people in the Netflix data. If the attacker knows eight movies that you have rated $\pm$ 14 days, then even if two of these known ratings are completely wrong, 99% of records can be uniquely identified in the dataset. In other words, sparsity is a fundamental problem for efforts to "anonymize" data, which is unfortunate because most modern social datasets are sparse. For more on "anonymization" of sparse data, see Narayanan and Shmatikov (2008).

Telephone metadata also might appear to be "anonymous" and not sensitive, but that is not the case. Telephone metadata are identifiable and sensitive (Mayer, Mutchler, and Mitchell 2016; Landau 2016).

In figure 6.6, I sketched out a trade-off between risk to participants and benefits to society from data release. For a comparison between restricted access approaches (e.g., a walled garden) and restricted data approaches (e.g., some form of "anonymization"), see Reiter and Kinney (2011). For a proposed categorization system of risk levels of data, see Sweeney, Crosas, and Bar-Sinai (2015). For a more a general discussion of data sharing, see Yakowitz (2011).

For more detailed analysis of this trade-off between the risk and utility of data, see Brickell and Shmatikov (2008), Ohm (2010), Reiter (2012), Wu (2013), and Goroff (2015). To see this trade-off applied to real data from massively open online courses (MOOCs), see Daries et al. (2014) and Angiuli, Blitzstein, and Waldo (2015).

Differential privacy also offers an alternative approach that can combine both low risk to participants and high benefit to society; see Dwork and Roth (2014) and Narayanan, Huey, and Felten (2016).

For more on the concept of personally identifying information (PII), which is central to many of the rules about research ethics, see Narayanan and Shmatikov (2010) and Schwartz and Solove (2011). For more on all data being potentially sensitive, see Ohm (2015).

In this section, I've portrayed the linkage of different datasets as something that can lead to informational risk. However, it can also create new opportunities for research, as argued in Currie (2013).

For more on the five safes, see Desai, Ritchie, and Welpton (2016). For an example of how outputs can be identifying, see Brownstein, Cassa, and Mandl (2006), which shows how maps of disease prevalence can be identifying. Dwork et al. (2017) also consider attacks against aggregate data, such as statistics about how many individuals have a certain disease.

Questions about data use and data release also raise questions about data ownership. For more on data ownership, see Evans (2011) and Pentland (2012).

- **Privacy (section 6.6.3)**

Warren and Brandeis (1890) is a landmark legal article about privacy and is most associated with the idea that privacy is a right to be left alone. Book-length treatments of privacy that I would recommend include Solove (2010) and Nissenbaum (2010).

For a review of empirical research on how people think about privacy, see Acquisti, Brandimarte, and Loewenstein (2015). Phelan, Lampe, and Resnick (2016) propose a dual-system theory—that people sometimes focus on intuitive concerns and sometimes focus on considered concerns—to explain how people can make apparently contradictory statements about privacy. For more on the idea of privacy in online settings such as Twitter, see Neuhaus and Webmoor (2012).

The journal *Science* published a special section titled "The End of Privacy," which addresses the issues of privacy and informational risk from a variety of different perspectives; for a summary, see Enserink and Chin (2015). Calo (2011) offers a framework for thinking about the harms that come from privacy violations. An early example of concerns about privacy at the very beginnings of the digital age is Packard (1964).

- **Making decisions under uncertainty (section 6.6.4)**

  One challenge when trying to apply the minimal risk standard is that it is not clear whose daily life is to be used for benchmarking (National Research Council 2014). For example, homeless people have higher levels of discomfort in their daily lives. But that does not imply that it is ethically permissible to expose homeless people to higher-risk research. For this reason, there seems to be a growing consensus that minimal risk should be benchmarked against a *general-population* standard, not a *specific-population* standard. While I generally agree with the idea of a general-population standard, I think that for large online platforms such as Facebook, a specific-population standard is reasonable. Thus, when considering Emotional Contagion, I think that it is reasonable to benchmark against everyday risk on Facebook. A specific-population standard in this case is much easier to evaluate and is unlikely to conflict with the principle of Justice, which seeks to prevent the burdens of research failing unfairly on disadvantaged groups (e.g., prisoners and orphans).

- **Practical tips (section 6.7)**

  Other scholars have also called for more papers to include ethical appendices (Schultze and Mason 2012; Kosinski et al. 2015; Partridge and Allman 2016). King and Sands (2015) also offers practical tips. Zook and colleagues (2017) offer "ten simple rules for responsible big data research."

Activities

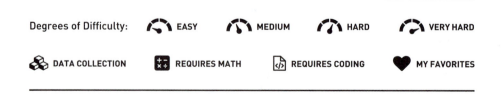

Degrees of Difficulty: EASY   MEDIUM   HARD   VERY HARD

DATA COLLECTION   REQUIRES MATH   REQUIRES CODING   MY FAVORITES

1. [⟨⟩] In arguing against the Emotional Contagion experiment, Kleinsman and Buckley (2015) wrote:

   "Even if it is true that the risks for the Facebook experiment were low and even if, in hindsight, the results are judged to be useful, there is an important principle at stake here that must be upheld. In the same way that stealing is stealing no matter what amounts are involved, so we all have a right not to be experimented on without our knowledge and consent, whatever the nature of the research."

   a) Which of the two ethical frameworks discussed in this chapter—consequentialism or deontology—is this argument most clearly associated with?

   b) Now, imagine that you wanted to argue against this position. How would you argue the case to a reporter for the *New York Times*?

   c) How, if at all, would your argument be different if you were discussing this with a colleague?

2. [⟨⟩] Maddock, Mason, and Starbird (2015) consider the question of whether researchers should use tweets that have been deleted. Read their paper to learn about the background.

   a) Analyze this decision from deontological perspective.

   b) Analyze the exact same decision from a consequentialist perspective.

   c) Which do you find more convincing in this case?

3. [⟨⟩] In an article on the ethics of field experiments, Humphreys (2015) proposed the following hypothetical experiment to highlight the ethical challenges of interventions that are done without consent of all impacted parties and that harms some and helps others:

   "Say a researcher is contacted by a set of community organizations that want to figure out whether placing street lights in slums will reduce violent crime. In this research the subjects are the criminals: seeking informed consent of the criminals would likely compromise the research and it would likely not be forthcoming anyhow (violation of respect for persons); the criminals will likely bear the costs of the research without benefiting (violation of justice); and there will be disagreement regarding the benefits of the research—if it is effective, the criminals in particular will not value it (producing a difficulty for assessing benevolence).

... The special issues here are not just around the subjects however. Here there are also risks that obtain to non-subjects, if for example criminals retaliate against the organizations putting the lamps in place. The organization may be very aware of these risks but be willing to bear them because they erroneously put faith in the ill-founded expectations of researchers from wealthy universities who are themselves motivated in part to publish."

a) Write an email to the community organization offering your ethical assessment of the experiment as designed? Would you help them do the experiment as proposed? What factors might impact your decision?

b) Are there some changes that might improve your assessment of the ethics of this experimental design.

4. [⏱] In the 1970s, 60 men participated in a field experiment that took place in the men's bathroom at a university in the midwestern part of the United States (the researchers don't name the university) (Middlemist, Knowles, and Matter 1976). The researchers were interested in how people respond to violations of their personal space, which Sommer (1969) defined as the "area with invisible boundaries surrounding a person's body into which intruders may not come." More specifically, the researchers chose to study how a man's urination was impacted by the presence of others nearby. After conducting a purely observational study, the researchers conducted a field experiment. Participants were forced to use the left-most urinal in a three-urinal bathroom (the researchers do not explain exactly how this was done). Next, participants were assigned to one of three levels of interpersonal distance. For some men, a confederate used a urinal right next to them; for some men, a confederate used a urinal one space away from them; and for some men, no confederate entered the bathroom. The researchers measured their outcome variables—delay time and persistence—by stationing a research assistant inside the toilet stall adjacent to the participant's urinal. Here's how the researchers described the measurement procedure:

"An observer was stationed in the toilet stall immediately adjacent to the subjects' urinal. During pilot tests of these procedures it became clear that auditory cues could not be used to signal the initiation and cessation of [urination]. ... Instead, visual cues were used. The observer used a periscopic prism imbedded in a stack of books lying on the floor of the toilet stall. An 11-inch (28-cm) space between the floor and the wall of the toilet stall provided a view, through the periscope, of the user's lower torso and made possible direct visual sightings of the stream of urine. The observer, however, was unable to see a subject's face. The observer

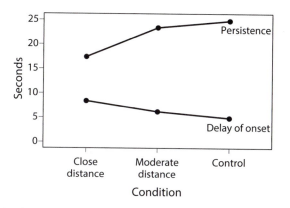

Figure 6.7: Results from Middlemist, Knowles, and Matter (1976). Men who entered the bathroom were assigned to one of three conditions: close distance (a confederate was placed in the immediately adjacent urinal), moderate distance (a confederate was placed one urinal removed), or control (no confederate). An observer stationed in a toilet stall used a custom-built periscope to observe and time the delay and persistence of urination. Standard errors around estimates are not available. Adapted from Middlemist, Knowles, and Matter (1976), figure 1.

started two stop watches when a subject stepped up to the urinal, stopped one when urination began, and stopped the other when urination was terminated."

The researchers found that decreased physical distance leads to increased delay of onset and decreased persistence (figure 6.7).

a) Do you think the participants were harmed by this experiment?

b) Do you think that the researchers should have conducted this experiment?

c) What changes, if any, would you recommend to improve the ethical balance?

5. [🎭, ♥] In August 2006, about 10 days prior to the primary election, 20,000 people living in Michigan received a mailing that showed their voting behavior and the voting behavior of their neighbors (figure 6.8). (As discussed in this chapter, in the United States, state governments keep records of who votes in each election, and this information is available to the public.) One-piece mailings typically increase voter turnout by about one percentage point, but this one increased turnout by 8.1 percentage points, the largest effect seen up to that point (Gerber, Green, and Larimer 2008). The effect was so large that a political operative named Hal Malchow offered Donald Green $100,000 not to publish the result of the experiment (presumably so that Malchow could make use of this

30423-3 ||| || || | |||

For more information: (517) 351-1975
email: etov@grebner.com
Practical Political Consulting
P.O. Box 6249
East Lansing, MI 48826

PRSRT STD
U.S. Postage
PAID
Lansing, MI
Permit #444

ECRLOT **C050
THE JACKSON FAMILY
9999 MAPLE DR
FLINT MI 48507

Dear Registered Voter:

WHAT IF YOUR NEIGHBORS KNEW WHETHER YOU VOTED?

Why do so many people fail to vote? We've been talking about the problem for years, but it only seems to get worse. This year, we're taking a new approach. We're sending this mail to you and your neighbors to publicize who does and does not vote.

The chart shows the names of some of your neighbors, showing which have voted in the past. After the August 8 election, we intend to mail an updated chart. You and your neighbors will all know who voted and who did not.

DO YOUR CIVIC DUTY — VOTE!

MAPLE DR		Aug 04	Nov 04	Aug 06
9995	JOSEPH JAMES SMITH	Voted	Voted	_____
9995	JENNIFER KAY SMITH		Voted	_____
9997	RICHARD B JACKSON		Voted	_____
9999	KATHY MARIE JACKSON		Voted	_____
9999	BRIAN JOSEPH JACKSON		Voted	_____
9991	JENNIFER KAY THOMPSON		Voted	_____
9991	BOB R THOMPSON		Voted	_____
9993	BILL S SMITH			_____
9989	WILLIAM LUKE CASPER		Voted	_____
9989	JENNIFER SUE CASPER		Voted	_____
9987	MARIA S JOHNSON	Voted	Voted	_____
9987	TOM JACK JOHNSON	Voted	Voted	_____
9987	RICHARD TOM JOHNSON		Voted	_____
9985	ROSEMARY S SUE		Voted	_____
9985	KATHRYN L SUE		Voted	_____
9985	HOWARD BEN SUE		Voted	_____
9983	NATHAN CHAD BERG		Voted	_____
9983	CARRIE ANN BERG		Voted	_____
9981	EARL JOEL SMITH			_____
9979	DEBORAH KAY WAYNE		Voted	_____
9979	JOEL R WAYNE		Voted	_____

Figure 6.8: Neighbor mailer from Gerber, Green, and Larimer (2008). This mailer increased turnout rates by 8.1 percentage points, the largest effect that had ever been observed for a single-piece mailer. Reproduced by permission from Cambridge University Press from Gerber, Green, and Larimer (2008), appendix A.

information himself) (Issenberg 2012, p. 304). But Alan Gerber, Donald Green, and Christopher Larimer did publish the paper in 2008 in the *American Political Science Review*.

When you carefully inspect the mailer in figure 6.8 you may notice that the researchers' names do not appear on it. Rather, the return address is to Practical Political Consulting. In the acknowledgment to the paper, the authors explain: "Special thanks go to Mark Grebner of Practical Political Consulting, who designed and administered the mail program studied here."

a) Assess the use of this treatment in terms of the four ethical principles described in this chapter.

b) Assess the treatment in terms of the idea of contextual integrity.

c) What changes, if any, would you recommend to this experiment?

d) Would it impact your answers to the questions above if Mark Grebner was already sending similar mailings at this time? More generally, how should researchers think about evaluating existing interventions created by practitioners?

e) Imagine that you decide to try to receive informed consent from people in the treatment group but not those in the control group. What impact might this decision have on your ability to understand the cause of a difference in voting rates between the treatment and control groups?

f) Write an ethical appendix that could appear with this paper when it was published.

6. [✎] This builds on the previous question. Once the 20,000 mailers had been sent (figure 6.8), as well as 60,000 other potentially less sensitive mailers, there was a backlash from participants. In fact, Issenberg (2012) (p. 198) reports that "Grebner [the director of Practical Political Consulting] was never able to calculate how many people took the trouble to complain by phone, because his office answering machine filled so quickly that new callers were unable to leave a message." In fact, Grebner noted that the backlash could have been even larger if they had scaled up the treatment. He said to Alan Gerber, one of the researchers, "Alan if we had spent five hundred thousand dollars and covered the whole state you and I would be living with Salman Rushdie." (Issenberg 2012, p. 200)

a) Does this information change your answers to the previous question?

b) What strategies for dealing with decision making in the face of uncertainty would you recommend for similar studies in the future?

7. [✎, ♥] In practice, most ethical debate occurs about studies where researchers do not have true informed consent from participants (e.g., the three case studies described in this chapter). However, ethical debate can also arise for studies that have true informed consent. Design a hypothetical study where you would have true informed consent from participants, but which you still think would be unethical. (Hint: If you are struggling, you can try reading Emanuel, Wendler, and Grady (2000).)

8. [✎, ♥] Researchers often struggle to describe their ethical thinking to each other and to the general public. After it was discovered that Tastes, Ties, and Time was re-identified, Jason Kauffman, the leader of the research team, made a few public comments about the ethics of the project. Read Zimmer (2010) and then rewrite Kauffman's comments using the principles and ethical frameworks that are described in this chapter.

9. [✎] Banksy is one of the most famous contemporary artists in the United Kingdom and is known particularly for politically oriented street graffiti (figure 6.9). His precise identity, however, is a mystery. Banksy has a personal website, so he could make his identity public if he wanted, but he has chosen not to. In 2008, the *Daily Mail* newspaper published an article claiming to identify

Figure 6.9: Photograph of *Spy Booth* by Banksy in Cheltenham, England by Kathryn Yengel, 2014. (Source: Kathryn Yengel/Flickr).

Banksy's real name. Then, in 2016, Michelle Hauge, Mark Stevenson, D. Kim Rossmo and Steven C. Le Comber (2016) attempted to verify this claim using a Dirichlet process mixture model of geographic profiling. More specifically, they collected the geographic locations of Banksy's public graffiti in Bristol and London. Next, by searching through old newspaper articles and public voting records, they found past addresses of the named individual, his wife, and his football (i.e., soccer) team. The author's summarize the finding of their paper as follows:

> "With no other serious 'suspects' [sic] to investigate, it is difficult to make conclusive statements about Banksy's identity based on the analysis presented here, other than saying the peaks of the geoprofiles in both Bristol and London include addresses known to be associated with [name redacted]."

Following Metcalf and Crawford (2016), I have decided not to include the name of the individual when discussing this study.

a) Assess this study using the principles and ethical frameworks in this chapter.

b) Would you have done this study?

c) The authors justify this study in the abstract of their paper with the following sentence: "More broadly, these results support previous suggestions that the analysis of minor terrorism-related acts (e.g., graffiti) could be used to help locate terrorist bases before more serious incidents occur, and provides a fascinating example of the application of the model to a complex, real-world problem." Does this change your opinion of the paper? If so, how?

d) The authors included the following ethical note at the end of their paper: "The authors are aware of, and respectful of, the privacy of [name redacted] and his relatives and have thus only used data in the public domain. We have deliberately omitted precise addresses." Does this change your opinion of the paper? If so, how? Do you think the public/private dichotomy makes sense in this case?

10. [🔾🔾] Metcalf (2016) makes the argument that "publicly available datasets containing private data are among the most interesting to researchers and most risky to subjects."

    a) What are two concrete examples that support this claim?

    b) In this same article, Metcalf also claims that it is anachronistic to assume that "any information harm has already been done by a public dataset." Give one example of where this could be the case.

11. [🔾🔾, ♥] In this chapter, I have proposed a rule of thumb that *all* data are potentially identifiable and *all* data are potentially sensitive. Table 6.5 provides a list of examples of data that have no obviously personally identifying information but that can still be linked to specific people.

    a) Pick two of these examples and describe how the re-identification attack in both cases has a similar structure.

    b) For each of the two examples in part (a), describe how the data could reveal sensitive information about the people in the dataset.

    c) Now pick a third dataset from the table. Write an email to someone considering releasing it. Explain to them how this data could be potentially identifiable and potentially sensitive.

12. [🔾🔾] Putting yourself in everyone's shoes includes your participants and the general public, not just your peers. This distinction is illustrated in the case of the Jewish Chronic Disease Hospital (Katz, Capron, and Glass 1972, chapter 1; Lerner 2004; Arras 2008).

Table 6.5: Examples of Social Data that Do Not Have Any Obvious Personally Identifying Information but Can Still Be Linked to Specific People

Data	Reference
Health insurance records	Sweeney (2002)
Credit card transaction data	Montjoye et al. (2015)
Netflix movie rating data	Narayanan and Shmatikov (2008)
Phone call metadata	Mayer, Mutchler, and Mitchell (2016)
Search log data	Barbaro and Zeller (2006)
Demographic, administrative, and social data about students	Zimmer (2010)

Dr. Chester M. Southam was a distinguished physician and researcher at the Sloan-Kettering Institute for Cancer Research and an Associate Professor of Medicine at the Cornell University Medical College. On July 16, 1963, Southam and two colleagues injected live cancer cells into the bodies of 22 debilitated patients at the Jewish Chronic Disease Hospital in New York. These injections were part of Southam's research to understand the immune system of cancer patients. In earlier research, Southam had found that healthy volunteers were able to reject injected cancer cells in roughly four to six weeks, whereas it took patients who already had cancer much longer. Southam wondered whether the delayed response in the cancer patients was because they had cancer or because they were elderly and already debilitated. To address these possibilities, Southam decided to inject live cancer cells into a group of people who were elderly and debilitated but who did not have cancer. When word of the study spread, triggered in part by the resignation of three physicians who were asked to participate, some made comparisons to Nazi concentration camp experiments, but others—based in part on assurances by Southam—found the research unproblematic. Eventually, the New York State Board of Regents reviewed the case in order to decide if Southam should be able to continue to practice medicine. Southam argued in his defense that he was acting in "the best tradition of responsible clinical practice." His defense was based on a number of claims, all of which were supported by several distinguished experts who testified on his behalf: (1) his research was of high scientific and social merit; (2) there were no appreciable risks to participants; a claim based in part of Southam's 10 years of prior experience with more than 600 subjects; (3) the level of disclosure should be adjusted according to the level of risk posed by the researcher; (4) the research was in conformity with the standard of medical practice at that time. Ultimately, the Regent's board found Southam guilty of fraud, deceit, and unprofessional conduct, and suspended his medical license for one year. Yet, just a few years later, Southam was elected president of the American Association of Cancer Research.

a) Assess Southam's study using the four principles in this chapter.

b) It appears that Southam took the perspective of his colleagues and correctly anticipated how they might respond to his work; in fact, many of them testified on his behalf. But he was unable or unwilling to understand how his research might be troubling to the public. What role do you think public opinion—which could be distinct from the opinions of participants or peers—should have in research ethics? What should happen if popular opinion and peer opinion differ?

13. [🔾] In a paper titled "Crowdseeding in Eastern Congo: Using Cell Phones to Collect Conflict Events Data in Real Time," van der Windt and Humphreys (2016) describe a distributed data collection system (see chapter 5) that they created in Eastern Congo. Describe how the researchers dealt with the uncertainty about possible harms to participants.

14. [🔾] In October 2014, three political scientists sent mailers to 102,780 registered voters in Montana—roughly 15% of registered voters in the state (Willis 2014)—as part of an experiment to measure whether voters who are given more information are more likely to vote. The mailers—which were labeled "2014 Montana General Election Voter Information Guide"—placed Montana Supreme Court Justice candidates, in what is a nonpartisan election, on a scale from liberal to conservative, which included Barack Obama and Mitt Romney as comparisons. The mailer also included a reproduction of the Great Seal of the State of Montana (figure 6.10).

The mailers generated complaints from Montana voters, and they caused Linda McCulloch, Montana's Secretary of State, to file a formal complaint with the Montana state government. The universities that employed the researchers—Dartmouth and Stanford—sent a letter to everyone who had received the mailer, apologizing for any potential confusion and making clear that the mailer "was not affiliated with any political party, candidate or organization, and was not intended to influence any race." The letter also clarified that the ranking "relied upon public information about who had donated to each of the campaigns" (figure 6.11).

In May 2015, the Commissioner of Political Practices of the State of Montana, Jonathan Motl, determined that the researchers had violated Montana law: "The Commissioner determines that there are sufficient facts to show that Stanford, Dartmouth and/or its researchers violated Montana campaign practice laws requiring registration, reporting and disclosure of independent expenditures" (Sufficient Finding Number 3 in Motl (2015)). The Commissioner also recommended that the County Attorney investigate whether the unauthorized use of the Great Seal of Montana violated Montana state law (Motl 2015).

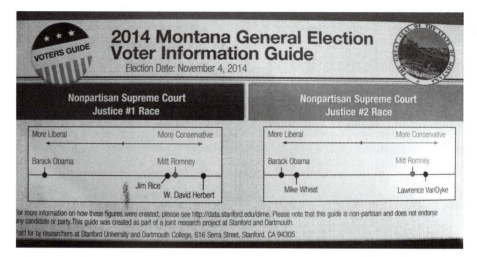

Figure 6.10: Mailer sent by three political scientists to 102,780 registered voters in Montana as part of an experiment to measure whether voters who are given more information are more likely to vote. The sample size in this experiment was roughly 15% of eligible voters in the state (Willis 2014). Reproduced from Motl (2015).

Stanford and Dartmouth disagreed with Motl's ruling. A Stanford spokeswoman named Lisa Lapin said "Stanford ...does not believe any election laws were violated" and that the mailing "did not contain any advocacy supporting or opposing any candidate." She pointed out that the mailer explicitly stated that it "is nonpartisan and does not endorse any candidate or party" (Richman 2015).

a) Assess this study using the four principles and two frameworks described in this chapter.

b) Assuming that the mailers were sent to a random sample of voters (but more on this in a moment), under what conditions might this mailing have altered the outcome of the Supreme Court Justice election?

c) In fact, the mailers were not sent to a random sample of voters. According to a report by Jeremy Johnson (a political scientists who assisted in the investigation), mailers "were sent to 64,265 voters identified as likely liberal to centrist leaning in Democratic leaning precincts and 39,515 voters identified as conservative to centrist in Republican leaning precincts. The researchers justified the disparity between Democratic and Republican numbers on grounds that they anticipated turnout to be significantly lower among Democratic voters." Does this change your assessment of the research design? If so, how?

Dartmouth   Stanford

October 28, 2014

An open letter to the voters and citizens of Montana

On behalf of Stanford and Dartmouth universities, we sincerely apologize for the confusion and concern caused by an election mailer recently sent as part of an academic research study. It should have been much more clearly presented as the research tool it was intended to be, leaving no ambiguity about its purpose or origin. We recognize that the purpose of elections is to enable our democratic systems to operate, and that no research study should risk disrupting an election. **We genuinely regret that it was sent and we ask Montana voters to ignore the mailer.**

The informational mailer was part of an independent study by political science professors to determine whether voters who are given more information are more likely to vote. The mailer was not affiliated with any political party, candidate or organization, and was not intended to influence any race. The mailer was in no way affiliated with or approved by the State of Montana, and we are very sorry that it created the impression that it was.

The mailer included a graph that ranked judicial candidates in a nonpartisan race on a scale from liberal to conservative. That ranking was <u>not</u> based on the candidates' decisions or public positions, instead it relied upon public information about who had donated to each of the campaigns. Unfortunately, even though the mailer contained a statement that it "is non-partisan and does not endorse any candidate or party," many people felt that the graph appeared to create a partisan alignment of the candidates. That was certainly not the intent.

Both of our campuses are investigating all aspects of the matter, including whether Stanford and Dartmouth research rules and standards have been appropriately followed. We are also fully cooperating with the inquiry being undertaken by election officials in the State of Montana. We do know that the research proposal was not submitted to Stanford's Institutional Review Board for approval, which is a clear violation of university policy.

We are sorry that this mailer has been disconcerting and disruptive to many Montanans. We take very seriously our responsibility to conduct research and provide education that contributes to, but does not hinder, an informed citizenry.

Sincerely,

Philip Hanlon

Philip Hanlon
President
Dartmouth College

John Hennessy

John Hennessy
President
Stanford University

cc: Linda McCulloch, Montana Secretary of State
          Jonathan Motl, Montana Commissioner of Political Practices

Figure 6.11: Apology letter that was sent to the 102,780 registered voters in Montana who had received the mailer shown in figure 6.10. The letter was sent by the Presidents of Dartmouth and Stanford, the universities that employed the researchers who sent the mailer. Reproduced from Motl (2015).

d) In response to the investigation, the researchers said that they picked this election in part because "neither judicial race had been closely contested in the primary. Based on an analysis of the 2014 primary election results in the context of previous Montana judicial elections, the researchers

Table 6.6: Results from the 2014 Montana Supreme Court Justice Elections

Candidates	Votes received	Percentage
Supreme Court Justice #1		
W. David Herbert	65,404	21.59%
Jim Rice	236,963	78.22%
Supreme Court Justice #2		
Lawrence VanDyke	134,904	40.80%
Mike Wheat	195,303	59.06%

Source: Web page of the Montana Secretary of State.

determined that the research study as designed would not change the outcome of either contest" (Motl 2015). Does this change your assessment of the research? If so, how?

e) In fact, the election turned out to be not particularly close (table 6.6). Does this change your assessment of the research? If so, how?

f) It turns out that a study was submitted to the Dartmouth IRB by one of the researchers, but the details differed substantially from those of the actual Montana study. The mailer used in Montana was never submitted to the IRB. The study was never submitted to the Stanford IRB. Does this change your assessment of the research? If so, how?

g) It also turned out that the researchers had sent similar election materials to 143,000 voters in California and 66,000 in New Hampshire. As far as I know, there were no formal complaints triggered by these approximately 200,000 additional mailers. Does this change your assessment of the research? If so, how?

h) What, if anything, would you have done differently if you were the principal investigators? How would you have designed the study if you were interested in exploring whether additional information increases voter turnout in nonpartisan races?

15. [🔒] On May 8, 2016, two researchers—Emil Kirkegaard and Julius Bjerrekaer—scraped information from the online dating site OkCupid and publicly released a dataset of about 70,000 users, including variables such as username, age, gender, location, religion-related opinions, astrology-related opinions, dating interests, number of photos, etc., as well as answers given to the top 2,600 questions on the site. In a draft paper accompanying the released data, the authors stated that "Some may object to the ethics of gathering and releasing this data. However, all the data found in the dataset are or were already publicly available, so releasing this dataset merely presents it in a more useful form."

In response to the data release, one of the authors was asked on Twitter: "This dataset is highly re-identifiable. Even includes usernames? Was any work at all done to anonymize it?" His response was "No. Data is already public." (Zimmer 2016; Resnick 2016)

a) Assess this data release using the principles and ethical frameworks discussed in this chapter.

b) Would you use these data for your own research?

c) What if you scraped them yourself?

16. [🎯] In 2010, an intelligence analyst with the US Army gave 250,000 classified diplomatic cables to the organization WikiLeaks, and they were subsequently posted online. Gill and Spirling (2015) argue that "the WikiLeaks disclosure potentially represents a trove of data that might be tapped to test subtle theories in international relations" and then statistically characterize the sample of leaked documents. For example, the authors estimate that they represent about 5% of all diplomatic cables during that time period, but that this proportion varies from embassy to embassy (see figure 1 of their paper).

a) Read the paper, and then write an ethical appendix to it.

b) The authors did not analyze the content of any of the leaked documents. Is there any project using these cables that you would conduct? Is there any project using these cables that you would not conduct?

17. [🎯] In order to study how companies respond to complaints, a researcher sent fake complaint letters to 240 high-end restaurants in New York City. Here's an excerpt from the fictitious letter.

"I am writing this letter to you because I am outraged about a recent experience I had at your restaurant. Not long ago, my wife and I celebrated our first anniversary. .... The evening became soured when the symptoms began to appear about four hours after eating. Extended nausea, vomiting, diarrhea, and abdominal cramps all pointed to one thing: food poisoning. It makes me furious just thinking that our special romantic evening became reduced to my wife watching me curl up in a fetal position on the tiled floor of our bathroom in between rounds of throwing up.

... Although it is not my intention to file any reports with the Better Business Bureau or the Department of Health, I want you, [name of the restaurateur], to understand what I went through in anticipation that you will respond accordingly."

a) Evaluate this study using the principles and ethical frameworks described in this chapter. Given your assessment, would you do the study?

b) Here's how the restaurants who received the letter reacted (Kifner 2001):

"It was culinary chaos as owners, managers and chefs searched through computers for [name redacted] reservations or credit card records, reviewed menus and produce deliveries for possibly spoiled food, and questioned kitchen workers about possible lapses, all spurred by what both the university and the professor now concede was the business school study from hell."

Does this information change how you assess the study?

c) As far as I know, this study was not reviewed by an IRB or any other third party. Does that change how you assess the study? Why or why not?

18. [⟨icon⟩] Building on the previous question, I'd like you to compare this study with a completely different study that also involved restaurants. In this other study, Neumark and colleagues (1996) sent two male and two female college students with fabricated resumes to apply for jobs as waiters and waitresses at 65 restaurants in Philadelphia, in order to investigate sex discrimination in restaurant hiring. The 130 applications led to 54 interviews and 39 job offers. The study found statistically significant evidence of sex discrimination against women in high-price restaurants.

a) Write an ethical appendix for this study.

b) Do you think this study is ethically different from the one described in the previous question. If so, how?

19. [⟨icon⟩, ♥] Some time around 2010, 6,548 professors in the United States received emails similar to this one.

"Dear Professor Salganik,

I am writing you because I am a prospective Ph.D. student with considerable interest in your research. My plan is to apply to

Ph.D. programs this coming fall, and I am eager to learn as much as I can about research opportunities in the meantime.

I will be on campus today, and although I know it is short notice, I was wondering if you might have 10 minutes when you would be willing to meet with me to briefly talk about your work and any possible opportunities for me to get involved in your research. Any time that would be convenient for you would be fine with me, as meeting with you is my first priority during this campus visit.

Thank you in advance for your consideration.

Sincerely, Carlos Lopez"

These emails were fake; they were part of a field experiment to measure whether professors were more likely to respond to the email depending on (1) the time-frame (today versus next week) and (2) the name of the sender, which was varied to signal ethnicity and gender (Carlos Lopez, Meredith Roberts, Raj Singh, etc.). The researchers found that when the requests were to meet in one week, Caucasian males were granted access to faculty members about 25% more often than were women and minorities. But when the fictitious students requested meetings that same day, these patterns were essentially eliminated (Milkman, Akinola, and Chugh 2012).

a) Assess this experiment according to the principles and frameworks in this chapter.

b) After the study was over, the researchers sent the following debriefing email to all participants.

> "Recently, you received an email from a student asking for 10 minutes of your time to discuss your Ph.D. program (the body of the email appears below). We are emailing you today to debrief you on the actual purpose of that email, as it was part of a research study. We sincerely hope our study did not cause you any disruption and we apologize if you were at all inconvenienced. Our hope is that this letter will provide a sufficient explanation of the purpose and design of our study to alleviate any concerns you may have about your involvement. We want to thank you for your time and for reading further if you are interested in understanding why you received this message. We hope you will see the value of the knowledge we anticipate producing with this large academic study."

After explaining the purpose and design of the study, they further noted that:

> "As soon as the results of our research are available, we will post them on our websites. Please rest assured that no identifiable data will ever be reported from this study, and our between subject design ensures that we will only be able to identify email responsiveness patterns in aggregate—not at the individual level. No individual or university will be identifiable in any of the research or data we publish. Of course, any one individual email response is not meaningful as there are multiple reasons why an individual faculty member might accept or decline a meeting request. All data has already been de-identified and the identifiable email responses have already been deleted from our databases and related server. In addition, during the time when the data was identifiable, it was protected with strong and secure passwords. And as is always the case when academics conduct research involving human subjects, our research protocols were approved by our universities' Institutional Review Boards (the Columbia University Morningside IRB and the University of Pennsylvania IRB).
>
> If you have any questions about your rights as a research subject, you may contact the Columbia University Morningside Institutional Review Board at [redacted] or by email at [redacted] and/or the University of Pennsylvania Institutional Review Board at [redacted].
>
> Thank you again for your time and understanding of the work we are doing."

c) What are the arguments for debriefing in this case? What are the arguments against? Do you think that the researchers should have debriefed the participants in this case?

d) In the supporting online materials, the researchers have a section titled "Human Subjects Protections." Read this section. Is there anything that you would add or remove?

e) What was the cost of this experiment to the researchers? What was the cost of this experiment to participants? Andrew Gelman (2010) has argued that participants in this study could have been compensated for their time after the experiment was over. Do you agree? Try to make your argument using the principles and ethical frameworks in this chapter.

CHAPTER 7
THE FUTURE

7.1 Looking forward

As I said in chapter 1, social researchers are in the process of making a transition like that from photography to cinematography. In this book, we've seen how researchers have started using the capabilities of the digital age to observe behavior (chapter 2), ask questions (chapter 3), run experiments (chapter 4), and collaborate (chapter 5) in ways that were simply impossible in the recent past. Researchers who take advantage of these opportunities will also have to confront difficult, ambiguous ethical decisions (chapter 6). In this last chapter, I'd like to highlight three themes that run through these chapters and that will be important for the future of social research.

7.2 Themes of the future

7.2.1 The blending of readymades and custommades

> Neither a pure readymade strategy nor a pure custommade strategy fully utilizes the capabilities of the digital age. In the future, we are going to create hybrids.

In the introduction, I contrasted the readymade style of Marcel Duchamp with the custommade style of Michelangelo. This contrast also captures a difference between data scientists, who tend to work with readymades, and social scientists, who tend to work with custommades. In the future, however, I expect that we will see more hybrids because each of these pure approaches is limited. Researchers who want to use only readymades are going to struggle because there are not many beautiful readymades in the world. Researchers who want to use only custommades, on the other hand, are going to sacrifice scale. Hybrid approaches, however, can combine the scale that comes with readymades with the tight fit between question and data that comes from custommades.

We saw examples of these hybrids in each of the four empirical chapters. In chapter 2, we saw how Google Flu Trends combined an always-on big data system (search queries) with a probability-based traditional measurement system (the CDC influenza surveillance system) to produce faster estimates (Ginsberg et al. 2009). In chapter 3, we saw how Stephen Ansolabehere and Eitan Hersh (2012) combined custommade survey data with readymade government administrative data in order to learn more about the characteristics of the people who actually vote. In chapter 4, we saw how the Opower experiments combined the readymade electricity measurement infrastructure with a custommade treatment to study the effects of social norms on the behavior of millions of people (Allcott 2015). Finally, in chapter 5, we saw how Kenneth Benoit and colleagues (2016) applied a custommade crowd-coding process to a readymade set of manifestos created by political parties in order to create data that researchers can use to study the dynamics of policy debates.

These four examples all show that a powerful strategy in the future will be to enrich big data sources, which are not created for research, with additional information that makes them more suitable for research (Groves 2011). Whether it starts with the custommade or the readymade, this hybrid style holds great promise for many research problems.

7.2.2 Participant-centered data collection

Data collection approaches of the past, which are researcher-centered, are not going to work as well in the digital age. In the future, we will take a participant-centered approach.

If you want to collect data in the digital age, you need to realize that you are competing for people's time and attention. The time and attention of your participants is incredibly valuable to you; it is the raw material of your research. Many social scientists are accustomed to designing research for relatively captive populations, such as undergraduates in campus labs. In these settings, the needs of the researcher dominate, and the enjoyment of participants is not a high priority. In digital-age research, this approach is not sustainable. Participants are often physically distant from researchers, and the interaction between the two is often mediated by a computer. This setting means that researchers are competing for participants' attention and therefore must create a more enjoyable participant experience. That is why in each chapter that involved interacting with participants, we saw examples of studies that took a participant-centered approach to data collection.

For example, in chapter 3, we saw how Sharad Goel, Winter Mason, and Duncan Watts (2010) created a game called Friendsense that was actually a clever frame around an attitude survey. In chapter 4, we saw how you can create zero variable cost data by designing experiments that people actually want to be in, such as the music downloading experiment that I created with Peter Dodds and Duncan Watts (Salganik, Dodds, and Watts 2006). Finally, in chapter 5, we saw how Kevin Schawinski, Chris Lintott, and the Galaxy Zoo team created a mass collaboration that motivated more than 100,000 people to participate in an astronomical (in both senses of the word) image labeling task (Lintott et al. 2011). In each of these cases, researchers focused on creating a good experience for participants, and in each case, this participant-centered approach enabled new kinds of research.

I expect that in the future, researchers will continue to develop approaches to data collection that strive to create a good user experience. Remember that in the digital age, your participants are one click away from a video of a skateboarding dog.

7.2.3 Ethics in research design

Ethics will move from a peripheral concern to a central concern and therefore will become a topic of research.

In the digital age, ethics will become an increasingly central issue shaping research. That is, in the future, we will struggle less with what can be done and more with what should be done. As that happens, I expect that the rules-based approach of social scientists and the ad hoc approach of data scientists will evolve toward something like the principles-based approached described in chapter 6. I also expect that as ethics becomes increasingly central it will grow as a topic of methodological research. In much the same way that social researchers now devote time and energy to developing new methods that enable cheaper and more accurate estimates, I expect that we will also work to develop methods that are more ethically responsible. This change will happen not just because researchers care about ethics as an end, but also because they care about ethics as a means to conducting social research.

An example of this trend is the research on *differential privacy* (Dwork 2008). Imagine that, for example, a hospital has detailed health records and that researchers want to understand the patterns in these data. Differentially private algorithms enable researchers to learn about aggregate patterns (e.g., people who smoke are more likely to have cancer) while minimizing the risk of learning anything about the characteristics of any particular individual. The development of these privacy-preserving algorithms has become an active area of research; see Dwork and Roth (2014) for a book-length treatment. Differential privacy is an example of the research community taking an ethical challenge, turning it into a research project, and then making progress on it. This is a pattern that I think we will increasingly see in other areas of social research.

As the power of researchers, often in collaboration with companies and governments, continues to grow, it will become increasingly difficult to avoid complex ethical issues. It has been my experience that many social scientists and data scientists view these ethical issues as a swamp to be avoided. But I think that avoidance will become increasingly untenable as a strategy. We, as a community, can address these problems if we jump in and tackle them with the creativity and effort that we apply to other research problems.

7.3 Back to the beginning

> The future of social research will be a combination of social science and data science.

At the end of our journey, let's return to the study described on the very first page of the first chapter of this book. Joshua Blumenstock, Gabriel Cadamuro, and Robert On (2015) combined detailed phone call data from about 1.5 million people with survey data from about 1,000 people in order to estimate the geographic distribution of wealth in Rwanda. Their estimates were similar to those from the Demographic and Health Survey, the gold standard of surveys in developing countries, but their method was about 10 times faster and 50 times cheaper. These dramatically faster and cheaper estimates are not an end in themselves, they are a means to end, creating new possibilities for researchers, governments, and companies. At the beginning of the book, I described this study as a window into the future of social research, and now I hope you see why.

ACKNOWLEDGMENTS

This book has an entire chapter on mass collaboration, but it is itself a mass collaboration. Quite simply, this book would not exist were it not for the generous support of many wonderful people and organizations. For that, I am extremely grateful.

Many people provided feedback about one or more of these chapters or had extended conversations with me about the book. For this valuable feedback, I am grateful to Hunt Allcott, David Baker, Solon Baracas, Chico Bastos, Ken Benoit, Clark Bernier, Michael Bernstein, Megan Blanchard, Josh Blumenstock, Tom Boellstorff, Robert Bond, Moira Burke, Yo-Yo Chen, Dalton Conley, Shelley Correll, Don Dillman, Jennifer Doleac, Ethan Fast, Nick Feamster, Cybelle Fox, Maggie Frye, Alan Gerber, Sharad Goel, Don Green, Eitan Hersh, Jake Hofman, Greg Huber, Joanna Huey, Patrick Ishizuka, Ben Jones, Steve Kelling, Sasha Killewald, Dawn Koffman, Andrés Lajous, Harrissa Lamothe, Andrew Ledford, David Lee, Amy Lerman, Meagan Levinson, Karen Levy, Kevin Lewis, Dai Li, Ian Lundberg, Xiao Ma, Andrew Mao, John Levi Martin, Judie Miller, Arvind Naranyanan, Gina Neff, Cathy O'Neil, Devah Pager, Nicole Pangborn, Ryan Parsons, Arnout van de Rijt, David Rothschild, Bill Salganik, Laura Salganik, Christian Sandvig, Mattias Smångs, Brandon Stewart, Naomi Sugie, Sid Suri, Michael Szell, Sean Taylor, Florencia Torche, Rajan Vaish, Janet Vertesi, Taylor Winfield, Han Zhang, and Simone Zhang. I would also like to thank three anonymous reviewers who provided helpful feedback. Further, I am grateful to the following people for telling me about errors and typos in the hardback edition: Nimrod Priell, David Marker, Giannis Kanellopoulos, Hiroki Takikawa, Jun Tsunematsu, Takuto Sakamoto, Shinya Obayashi, and the hypothesis user named arnaud.

I also received wonderful feedback on a draft manuscript from the participants in the Open Review process: akustov, benzevenbergen, bp3, cailinh, cc23, cfelton, chase171, danivos, DBLarremore, differentgranite, dmerson, dmf, efosse, fasiha, hrthomas, huntr, istewart, janetxu, jboy, jeremycohen, jeschonnek.1, jtorous, judell, jugander, kerrymcc, leohavemann, LMZ,

MMisra, Nick_Adams, nicolemarwell, nir, person, pkrafft, raminasotoudeh, rchew, rkharkar, sculliwag, sjk, Stephen_L_Morgan, sweissman, toz, and vnemana. I would also like to thank the Sloan Foundation and Josh Greenberg for supporting the Open Review Toolkit. If you'd like to put your own book through Open Review, please visit http://www.openreviewtoolkit.org.

I would also like to thank the organizers and participants at the following events where I had a chance to speak about the book: Cornell Tech Connective Media Seminar; Princeton Center for the Study of Democratic Politics Seminar; Stanford HCI Colloquium; Berkeley Sociology Colloquium; Russell Sage Foundation Working Group on Computational Social Science; Princeton DeCamp Bioethics Seminar; Columbia Quantitative Methods in the Social Sciences Visiting Speaker Series; Princeton Center for Information Technology Policy Technology and Society Reading Group; Simons Institute for the Theory of Computing Workshop on New Directions in Computational Social Science & Data Science; Data and Society Research Institute Workshop; University of Chicago, Sociology Colloquium; International Conference on Computational Social Science; Data Science Summer School at Microsoft Research; Society for Industrial and Applied Mathematics (SIAM) Annual Meeting; Indiana University, Karl F. Schuessler Lecture in the Methodologies of Social Research; Oxford Internet Institute; MIT, Sloan School of Management; AT&T Research; Renaissance Technologies; University of Washington, Data Science Seminar; SocInfo 2016; Microsoft Research, Redmond; Johns Hopkins, Population Research Center; New York City Data Science Seminar; and ICWSM 2017.

Many students over the years have shaped the ideas in this book. I would especially like to thank the students in Sociology 503 (Techniques and Methods of Social Science) in Spring 2016 for reading an early version of the manuscript, and the students in Sociology 596 (Computational Social Science) in Fall 2017 for pilot testing a complete draft of this manuscript in a classroom setting.

Another source of wonderful feedback was my book manuscript workshop that was organized by Princeton's Center for the Study of Democratic Politics. I would like to thank Marcus Prior and Michele Epstein for supporting the workshop. And I would like to thank all of the participants who took time from their busy lives to help me improve the book: Elizabeth Bruch, Paul DiMaggio, Filiz Garip, Meagan Levinson, Karen Levy, Mor Naaman, Sean Taylor, Markus Prior, Jess Metcalf, Brandon Stewart, Duncan Watts, and

Han Zhang. It really was a wonderful day—one of the most exciting and rewarding of my entire career—and I hope that I've been able to channel some of wisdom from that room into the final manuscript.

A few other people deserve special thanks. Duncan Watts was my dissertation adviser, and it was my dissertation that got me excited about social research in the digital age; without the experience that I had in graduate school this book would not exist. Paul DiMaggio was the first person to encourage me to write this book. It all happened one afternoon while we were both waiting for the coffee machine in Wallace Hall, and I still remember that, up until that time, the idea of writing a book had never even crossed my mind. I am deeply grateful to him for convincing me that I had something to say. I'd also like to thank Karen Levy for reading nearly all of the chapters in their earliest and messiest forms; she helped me see the big picture when I was stuck in the weeds. I'd like to thank Arvind Narayanan for helping me focus and refine the arguments in the book over many wonderful lunches. Brandon Stewart was always happy to chat or look at chapters, and his insights and encouragement kept me moving forward, even when I was starting to drift sideways. And, finally, I would like to thank Marissa King for helping me come up with the title to this book one sunny afternoon in New Haven.

While writing this book, I benefited from the support of three amazing institutions: Princeton University, Microsoft Research, and Cornell Tech. First, at Princeton University, I'm grateful to my colleagues and students in the Department of Sociology for creating and maintaining a warm and supportive culture. I would also like to thank the Center for Information Technology Policy for providing me with a wonderful intellectual second home where I could learn more about how computer scientists see the world. Portions of this book were written while I was on sabbatical from Princeton, and during those leaves I was lucky enough to spend time in two fantastic intellectual communities. First, I would like to thank Microsoft Research New York City for being my home in 2013–14. Jennifer Chayes, David Pennock, and the entire computational social science group were wonderful hosts and colleagues. Second, I would like to thank Cornell Tech for being my home in 2015–16. Dan Huttenlocher, Mor Naaman, and everyone in the Social Technologies Lab helped make Cornell Tech the ideal environment for me to finish this book. In many ways, this book is about combining ideas from data science and social science, and Microsoft Research and Cornell Tech are models of this kind of intellectual cross-pollination.

While writing this book, I had excellent research assistance. I am grateful to Han Zhang, especially for his help making the graphs in this book. I am also grateful to Yo-Yo Chen, especially for her help drafting the activities in this book. Finally, I am grateful to Judie Miller and Kristen Matlofsky for assistance of all kinds.

The web version of this book was created by Luke Baker, Paul Yuen, and Alan Ritari of the Agathon Group. Working with them on this project was a pleasure, as always. I would especially like to thank Luke for also developing the build process for this book and helping me navigate the dark corners of Git, pandoc, and Make.

I would like to thank the contributors to the following open source projects that we used: Git, pandoc, pandoc-crossref, pandoc-citeproc, pandoc-citeproc-preamble, Hypothesis, Middleman, Bootstrap, Nokogiri, GNU Make, Vagrant, Ansible, LaTeX, and Zotero. All graphs in this book were created in R (R Core Team, 2016) and used the following packages: ggplot2 (Wickham 2009), dplyr (Wickham and Francois 2015), reshape2 (Wickham 2007), stringr (Wickham 2015), car (Fox and Weisberg 2011), cowplot (Wilke 2016), png (Urbanek 2013), grid (R Core Team, 2016), and ggrepel (Slowikowski 2016). I would also like to thank Kieran Healy for his blog post that got me started with pandoc.

I would like to thank Arnout van de Rijt and David Rothschild for providing data used to recreate some of the graphs from their papers and Josh Blumenstock and Raj Chetty for making public replication files for their paper.

At Princeton University Press, I would like to thank Eric Schwartz who believed in this project at the beginning, and Meagan Levinson who helped make it a reality. Meagan was the best editor that a writer could have; she was always there to support this project, in good times and in bad times. I'm particularly grateful for how her support has evolved as the project has changed. Al Bertrand did a great job stepping in during Meagan's leave, and Samantha Nader and Kathleen Cioffi helped turn this manuscript into a real book.

Finally, I would like to thank my friends and family. You have been supportive of this project in so many ways, often in ways that you did not even know. I would especially like to thank my parents, Laura and Bill, and my parents-in-law, Jim and Cheryl, for their understanding while this project went on and on and on. I would also like to thank my kids. Eli and Theo, you have asked me so many times when my book will *finally* be finished. Well, it is finally finished. And, most importantly, I want to thank my wife Amanda. I'm sure that you too have wondered when this book would finally be finished, but you never showed it. Over the years that I've worked on this book, I've been absent too much, both physically and mentally. I am so appreciative of your never-ending support and love.

REFERENCES

Abelson, Hal, Ken Ledeen, and Harry Lewis. 2008. *Blown to Bits: Your Life, Liberty, and Happiness After the Digital Explosion*. Upper Saddle River, NJ: Addison-Wesley.

Acquisti, Alessandro, Laura Brandimarte, and George Loewenstein. 2015. "Privacy and Human Behavior in the Age of Information." *Science* 347 (6221): 509–14. doi:10.1126/science.aaa1465.

Adair, John G. 1984. "The Hawthorne Effect: A Reconsideration of the Methodological Artifact." *Journal of Applied Psychology* 69 (2): 334–45. doi:10.1037/0021-9010.69.2.334.

Adams, Nicholas. 2016. "A Crowd Content Analysis Assembly Line: Annotating Text Units of Analysis." SSRN Scholarly Paper ID 2808731. Rochester, NY: Social Science Research Network. http://papers.ssrn.com/abstract=2808731.

Adams, Tim. 2012. "Galaxy Zoo and the New Dawn of Citizen Science." *Guardian*, March. http://www.guardian.co.uk/science/2012/mar/18/galaxy-zoo-crowdsourcing-citizen-scientists.

Administrative Data Taskforce. 2012. "The UK Administrative Data Research Network: Improving Access for Research and Policy." Economic and Social Research Council. http://www.esrc.ac.uk/files/research/administrative-data-taskforce-adt/improving-access-for-research-and-policy/.

Agarwal, Sameer, Yasutaka Furukawa, Noah Snavely, Ian Simon, Brian Curless, Steven M. Seitz, and Richard Szeliski. 2011. "Building Rome in a Day." *Communications of the ACM* 54 (10): 105–12. doi:10.1145/2001269.2001293.

Ajunwa, Ifeoma, Kate Crawford, and Jason Schultz. 2016. "Limitless Worker Surveillance." SSRN Scholarly Paper ID 2746211. Rochester, NY: Social Science Research Network. https://papers.ssrn.com/abstract=2746211.

Al-Ubaydli, Omar, and John A. List. 2013. "On the Generalizability of Experimental Results in Economics: With a Response to Camerer." Working Paper 19666. National Bureau of Economic Research. http://www.nber.org/papers/w19666.

Alexander, Larry, and Michael Moore. 2015. "Deontological Ethics." In *The Stanford Encyclopedia of Philosophy*, edited by Edward N. Zalta, Spring 2015. http://plato.stanford.edu/archives/spr2015/entries/ethics-deontological/.

Allcott, Hunt. 2011. "Social Norms and Energy Conservation." *Journal of Public Economics*, Special Issue: The Role of Firms in Tax Systems, 95 (910): 1082–95. doi:10.1016/j.jpubeco.2011.03.003.

———. 2015. "Site Selection Bias in Program Evaluation." *Quarterly Journal of Economics* 130 (3): 1117–65. doi:10.1093/qje/qjv015.

Allcott, Hunt, and Todd Rogers. 2014. "The Short-Run and Long-Run Effects of Behavioral Interventions: Experimental Evidence from Energy Conservation." *American Economic Review* 104 (10): 3003–37. doi:10.1257/aer.104.10.3003.

Alsan, Marcella, and Marianne Wanamaker. 2016. "Tuskegee and the Health of Black Men." Working Paper 22323. National Bureau of Economic Research. http://www.nber.org/papers/w22323.

Althouse, Benjamin M., Yih Yng Ng, and Derek A. T. Cummings. 2011. "Prediction of Dengue Incidence Using Search Query Surveillance." *PLoS Neglected Tropical Diseases* 5 (8): e1258. doi:10.1371/journal.pntd.0001258.

Althouse, Benjamin M., Samuel V. Scarpino, Lauren A. Meyers, John W. Ayers, Marisa Bargsten, Joan Baumbach, John S. Brownstein, et al. 2015. "Enhancing Disease Surveillance with Novel Data Streams: Challenges and Opportunities." *EPJ Data Science* 4 (1): 17. doi:10.1140/epjds/s13688-015-0054-0.

American Association of Public Opinion Researchers. 2016. *Standard Definitions: Final Dispositions of Case Codes and Outcome Rates for Surveys*, 9th ed. AAPOR. http://www.aapor.org/AAPOR_Main/media/publications/Standard-Definitions20169theditionfinal.pdf.

Amorín, R., E. Pérez-Montero, J. M. Vílchez, and P. Papaderos. 2012. "The Star Formation History and Metal Content of the Green Peas. New Detailed GTC-OSIRIS Spectrphotometry of Three Galaxies." *Astrophysical Journal* 749 (2): 185. doi:10.1088/0004-637X/749/2/185.

Andersen, Erik, Eleanor O'Rourke, Yun-En Liu, Rich Snider, Jeff Lowdermilk, David Truong, Seth Cooper, and Zoran Popovic. 2012. "The Impact of Tutorials on Games of Varying Complexity." In *Proceedings of the 2012 ACM Annual Conference on Human Factors in Computing Systems*, 59–68. CHI '12. New York: ACM. doi:10.1145/2207676.2207687.

Anderson, Ashton, Sharad Goel, Gregory Huber, Neil Malhotra, and Duncan Watts. 2014. "Political Ideology and Racial Preferences in Online Dating." *Sociological Science*, 28–40. doi:10.15195/v1.a3.

Anderson, Ashton, Sharad Goel, Gregory Huber, Neil Malhotra, and Duncan J. Watts. 2015. "Rejoinder to Lewis." *Sociological Science* 2: 32–35. doi:10/15195/v2.a3.

Anderson, Chris. 2008. "The End of Theory: The Data Deluge Makes the Scientific Method Obsolete." *Wired*, June. http://www.wired.com/2008/06/pb-theory/.

Anderson, Richard G. 2013. "Registration and Replication: A Comment." *Political Analysis* 21 (1): 38–39. doi:10.1093/pan/mps034.

Angiuli, Olivia, Joe Blitzstein, and Jim Waldo. 2015. "How to de-Identify Your Data." *Communications of the ACM* 58 (12): 48–55. doi:10.1145/2814340.

Angotti, Nicole, and Christie Sennott. 2015. "Implementing Insider Ethnography: Lessons from the Public Conversations about HIV/AIDS Project in Rural South Africa." *Qualitative Research* 15 (4): 437–53. doi:10.1177/1468794114543402.

Angotti, Nicole, Margaret Frye, Amy Kaler, Michelle Poulin, Susan Cotts Watkins, and Sara Yeatman. 2014. "Popular Moralities and Institutional Rationalities in Malawi's Struggle Against AIDS." *Population and Development Review* 40 (3): 447–73. doi:10.1111/j.1728-4457.2014.00693.x.

Angrist, Joshua D. 1990. "Lifetime Earnings and the Vietnam Era Draft Lottery: Evidence from Social Security Administrative Records." *American Economic Review* 80 (3): 313–36. http://www.jstor.org/stable/2006669.

Angrist, Joshua D., and Alan B. Krueger. 2001. "Instrumental Variables and the Search for Identification: From Supply and Demand to Natural Experiments." *Journal of Economic Perspectives* 15 (4): 69–85. doi:10.1257/jep.15.4.69.

Angrist, Joshua D., and Jörn-Steffen Pischke. 2009. *Mostly Harmless Econometrics: An Empiricist's Companion*. Princeton, NJ: Princeton University Press.

Angrist, Joshua D., Guido W. Imbens, and Donald B. Rubin. 1996. "Identification of Causal Effects Using Instrumental Variables." *Journal of the American Statistical Association* 91 (434): 444–55. doi:10.2307/2291629.

Ansolabehere, Stephen, and Eitan Hersh. 2012. "Validation: What Big Data Reveal About Survey Misreporting and the Real Electorate." *Political Analysis* 20 (4): 437–59. doi:10.1093/pan/mps023.

Ansolabehere, Stephen, and Douglas Rivers. 2013. "Cooperative Survey Research." *Annual Review of Political Science* 16 (1): 307–29. doi:10.1146/annurev-polisci-022811-160625.

Ansolabehere, Stephen, and Brian F. Schaffner. 2014. "Does Survey Mode Still Matter? Findings from a 2010 Multi-Mode Comparison." *Political Analysis* 22 (3): 285–303. doi:10.1093/pan/mpt025.

Antoun, Christopher, Chan Zhang, Frederick G. Conrad, and Michael F. Schober. 2015. "Comparisons of Online Recruitment Strategies for Convenience Samples Craigslist, Google AdWords, Facebook, and Amazon Mechanical Turk." *Field Methods*, September. doi:10.1177/1525822X15603149.

APA Working Group. 2008. "Reporting Standards for Research in Psychology: Why Do We Need Them? What Might They Be?" *American Psychologist* 63 (9): 839–51. doi:10.1037/0003-066X.63.9.839.

Aral, Sinan, and Dylan Walker. 2011. "Creating Social Contagion through Viral Product Design: A Randomized Trial of Peer Influence in Networks." *Management Science* 57 (9): 1623–39. doi:10.1287/mnsc.1110.1421.

Aral, Sinan, Lev Muchnik, and Arun Sundararajan. 2009. "Distinguishing Influence-Based Contagion from Homophily-Driven Diffusion in Dynamic Networks." *Proceedings of the National Academy of Sciences of the USA* 106 (51): 21544–9. doi:10.1073/pnas.0908800106.

Aral, Sinan and Chirstos Nicolaides. 2017. "Exercise contagion in a global social network." *Nature Communications* 8: Article number 14753. doi:10.1038/ncomms14753.

Arceneaux, Kevin, Alan S. Gerber, and Donald P. Green. 2006. "Comparing Experimental and Matching Methods Using a Large-Scale Voter Mobilization Experiment." *Political Analysis* 14 (1): 37–62. doi:10.1093/pan/mpj001.

———. 2010. "A Cautionary Note on the Use of Matching to Estimate Causal Effects: An Empirical Example Comparing Matching Estimates to an Experimental Benchmark." *Sociological Methods & Research* 39 (2): 256–82. doi:10.1177/0049124110378098.

Aronow, Peter M., and Allison Carnegie. 2013. "Beyond LATE: Estimation of the Average Treatment Effect with an Instrumental Variable." *Political Analysis* 21 (4): 492–506. doi:10.1093/pan/mpt013.

Aronow, Peter M., and Joel A. Middleton. 2013. "A Class of Unbiased Estimators of the Average Treatment Effect in Randomized Experiments." *Journal of Causal Inference* 1 (1): 135–54. doi:10.1515/jci-2012-0009.

Aronson, Elliot, Phoebe C. Ellsworth, J. Merrill Carlsmith, and Marti Hope Gonzales. 1989. *Methods of Research In Social Psychology*, 2nd ed. New York: McGraw-Hill.

Arras, John D. 2008. "The Jewish Chronic Disease Hospital Case." In *The Oxford Textbook of Clinical Research Ethics*, edited by E. J. Emanuel, R. A. Crouch, C. Grady, R. K. Lie, F. G. Miller, and D. Wendler, 73–79. Oxford: Oxford University Press.

Arrow, Kenneth J., Robert Forsythe, Michael Gorham, Robert Hahn, Robin Hanson, John O. Ledyard, Saul Levmore, et al. 2008. "The Promise of Prediction Markets." *Science* 320 (5878): 877–78. doi:10.1126/science.1157679.

Asur, S., and B. A Huberman. 2010. "Predicting the Future with Social Media." In *2010 IEEE/WIC/ACM International Conference on Web Intelligence and Intelligent Agent Technology (WI-IAT)*, 1: 492–99. doi:10.1109/WI-IAT.2010.63.

Athey, Susan, and Guido Imbens. 2016a. "Recursive Partitioning for Heterogeneous Causal Effects." *Proceedings of the National Academy of Sciences of the USA* 113 (27): 7353–60. doi:10.1073/pnas.1510489113.

———. 2016b. "The Econometrics of Randomized Experiments." *ArXiv:1607.00698 [stat.ME]*, July. http://arxiv.org/abs/1607.00698.

Ayres, Ian, Mahzarin Banaji, and Christine Jolls. 2015. "Race Effects on eBay." *RAND Journal of Economics* 46 (4): 891–917. doi:10.1111/1756-2171.12115.

Ayres, Ian, Sophie Raseman, and Alice Shih. 2013. "Evidence from Two Large Field Experiments That Peer Comparison Feedback Can Reduce Residential Energy Usage." *Journal of Law, Economics, and Organization* 29 (5): 992–1022. doi:10.1093/jleo/ews020.

Back, Mitja D., Albrecht C. P. Küfner, and Boris Egloff. 2011. "Automatic or the People?: Anger on September 11, 2001, and Lessons Learned for the Analysis of Large Digital Data Sets." *Psychological Science* 22 (6): 837–38. doi:10.1177/0956797611409592.

Back, Mitja D., Albrecht C.P. Küfner, and Boris Egloff. 2010. "The Emotional Timeline of September 11, 2001." *Psychological Science* 21 (10): 1417–19. doi:10.1177/0956797610382124.

Baele, Stéphane J. 2013. "The Ethics of New Development Economics: Is the Experimental Approach to Development Economics Morally Wrong?" *Journal of Philosophical Economics* 12 (1): 2–42. http://hdl.handle.net/10871/17048.

Bail, Christopher A. 2015. "Taming Big Data Using App Technology to Study Organizational Behavior on Social Media." *Sociological Methods & Research*, May, 0049124115587825. doi:10.1177/0049124115587825.

Bailey, Michael, David Dittrich, and Erin Kenneally. 2013. "Applying Ethical Principles to Information and Communications Technology Research: A Companion to the Menlo Report." Washington, DC: Department of Homeland Security.

Baker, Chris. 2008. "Trying to Design a Truly Entertaining Game Can Defeat Even a Certified Genius." *Wired*, March. http://www.wired.com/gaming/gamingreviews/magazine/16-04/pl_games.

Baker, Reg, J. Michael Brick, Nancy A. Bates, Mike Battaglia, Mick P. Couper, Jill A. Dever, Krista J. Gile, and Roger Tourangeau. 2013. "Summary Report of the AAPOR Task Force on Non-Probability Sampling." *Journal of Survey Statistics and Methodology* 1 (2): 90–143. doi:10.1093/jssam/smt008.

Baker, Scott R., and Constantine Yannelis. 2015. "Income Changes and Consumption: Evidence from the 2013 Federal Government Shutdown." SSRN Scholarly Paper ID 2575461. Rochester, NY: Social Science Research Network. http://papers.ssrn.com/abstract=2575461.

Bakshy, Eytan, and Dean Eckles. 2013. "Uncertainty in Online Experiments with Dependent Data: An Evaluation of Bootstrap Methods." In *Proceedings of the 19th ACM SIGKDD International Conference on Knowledge Discovery and Data Mining*, 1303–11. KDD '13. New York: ACM. doi:10.1145/2487575.2488218.

Bakshy, Eytan, Dean Eckles, Rong Yan, and Itamar Rosenn. 2012. "Social Influence in Social Advertising: Evidence from Field Experiments." In *Proceedings of the 13th ACM Conference on Electronic Commerce*, 146–61. EC '12. New York: ACM. doi:10.1145/2229012.2229027.

Bakshy, Eytan, Itamar Rosenn, Cameron Marlow, and Lada Adamic. 2012. "The Role of Social Networks in Information Diffusion." In *Proceedings of the 21st International Conference on World Wide Web*, 519–28. WWW '12. New York: ACM. doi:10.1145/2187836.2187907.

Bamford, James. 2012. "The NSA Is Building the Country's Biggest Spy Center (Watch What You Say)." *Wired*, March. https://www.wired.com/2012/03/ff_nsadatacenter/all/1/.

Bamford, Steven P, Robert C Nichol, Ivan K Baldry, Kate Land, Chris J Lintott, Kevin Schawinski, Anže Slosar, et al. 2009. "Galaxy Zoo: The Dependence of Morphology and Colour on Environment." *Monthly Notices of the Royal Astronomical Society* 393 (4): 1324–52. doi:10.1111/j.1365-2966.2008.14252.x.

Bamman, David, Brendan O'Connor, and Noah Smith. 2012. "Censorship and Deletion Practices in Chinese Social Media." *First Monday* 17 (3). doi:10.5210/fm.v17i3.3943.

Banerjee, Abhijit V., and Esther Duflo. 2009. "The Experimental Approach to Development Economics." *Annual Review of Economics* 1 (1): 151–78. doi:10.1146/annurev.economics.050708.143235.

Banerji, Manda, Ofer Lahav, Chris J. Lintott, Filipe B. Abdalla, Kevin Schawinski, Steven P. Bamford, Dan Andreescu, et al. 2010. "Galaxy Zoo: Reproducing Galaxy Morphologies via Machine Learning." *Monthly Notices of the Royal Astronomical Society* 406 (1): 342–53. doi:10.1111/j.1365-2966.2010.16713.x.

Banfield, J. K., H. Andernach, A. D. Kapińska, L. Rudnick, M. J. Hardcastle, G. Cotter, S. Vaughan, et al. 2016. "Radio Galaxy Zoo: Discovery of a Poor Cluster Through a Giant Wide-Angle Tail Radio Galaxy." *Monthly Notices of the Royal Astronomical Society* 460 (3): 2376–84. doi:10.1093/mnras/stw1067.

Bankston, Kevin S., and Ashkan Soltani. 2013. "Tiny Constables and the Cost of Surveillance: Making Cents Out of United States v. Jones." *Yale L.J. Online* 123: 335. http://yalelawjournal.org/forum/tiny-constables-and-the-cost-of-surveillance-making-cents-out-of-united-states-v-jones.

Bańbura, Marta, Domenico Giannone, Michele Modugno, and Lucrezia Reichlin. 2013. "Now-Casting and the Real-Time Data Flow." In *Handbook of Economic Forecasting*, edited by Graham Elliott and Allan Timmermann, 2, Part A: 195–237. Handbook of Economic Forecasting. Elsevier. doi:10.1016/B978-0-444-53683-9.00004-9.

Bapna, Ravi, Ramprasad Jui, Galit Shmueli, and Akmed Umyyarov. 2016. "One-Way Mirrors in Online Dating: A Randomized Field Experiment." *Management Science*, February. doi:10.1287/mnsc.2015.2301.

Barbaro, Michael, and Tom Zeller Jr. 2006. "A Face Is Exposed for AOL Searcher No. 4417749." *New York Times*, August. http://select.nytimes.com/gst/abstract.html?res=F10612FC345B0C7A8CDDA10894DE404482.

Bardsley, Nicolas, Robin Cubitt, Graham Loomes, Peter Moffatt, Chris Starmer, and Robert Sugden. 2009. *Experimental Economics: Rethinking the Rules*. Princeton, NJ: Princeton University Press.

Barocas, Solon, and Andrew D. Selbst. 2016. "Big Data's Disparate Impact." *California Law Review* 104: 671–732. doi:10.15779/Z38BG31.

Baron, Reuben M., and David A. Kenny. 1986. "The Moderator–Mediator Variable Distinction in Social Psychological Research: Conceptual, Strategic, and Statistical Considerations." *Journal of Personality and Social Psychology* 51 (6): 1173–82. doi:10.1037/0022-3514.51.6.1173.

Batson, C. Daniel, Shannon Early, and Giovanni Salvarani. 1997. "Perspective Taking: Imagining How Another Feels Versus Imaging How You Would Feel." *Personality and Social Psychology Bulletin* 23 (7): 751–58. doi:10.1177/0146167297237008.

Baumeister, Roy F., Kathleen D. Vohs, and David C. Funder. 2007. "Psychology as the Science of Self-Reports and Finger Movements: Whatever Happened to Actual Behavior?" *Perspectives on Psychological Science* 2 (4): 396–403. doi:10.1111/j.1745-6916.2007.00051.x.

Baumrind, Diana. 1985. "Research Using Intentional Deception: Ethical Issues Revisited." *American Psychologist* 40 (2): 165–74. doi:10.1037/0003-066X.40.2.165.

Bean, Louis H. 1950. "Reviewed Work: The Pre-Election Polls of 1948. by Frederick Mosteller, Herbert Hyman, Philip J. McCarthy, Eli S. Marks, David B. Truman." *Journal of the American Statistical Association* 45 (251): 461–64. doi:10.2307/2280305.

Beasley, Asaf, and Winter Mason. 2015. "Emotional States vs. Emotional Words in Social Media." In *Proceedings of the ACM Web Science Conference*, 31:1–31:10. WebSci '15. New York,: ACM. doi:10.1145/2786451.2786473.

Beauchamp, Tom L. 2011. "The Belmont Report." In *The Oxford Textbook of Clinical Research Ethics*, edited by Ezekiel J. Emanuel, Christine C. Grady, Robert A. Crouch, Reidar K. Lie, Franklin G. Miller, and David D. Wendler. Oxford: Oxford University Press.

Beauchamp, Tom L., and James F. Childress. 2012. *Principles of Biomedical Ethics*, 7th ed. New York: Oxford University Press.

Beauchamp, Tom L., and Yashar Saghai. 2012. "The Historical Foundations of the Research–Practice Distinction in Bioethics." *Theoretical Medicine and Bioethics* 33 (1): 45–56. doi:10.1007/s11017-011-9207-8.

Bederson, Benjamin B., and Alexander J. Quinn. 2011. "Web Workers Unite! Addressing Challenges of Online Laborers." In *CHI '11 Extended Abstracts on Human Factors in Computing Systems*, 97–106. CHI EA '11. New York: ACM. doi:10.1145/1979742.1979606.

Beenen, Gerard, Kimberly Ling, Xiaoqing Wang, Klarissa Chang, Dan Frankowski, Paul Resnick, and Robert E. Kraut. 2004. "Using Social Psychology to Motivate Contributions to Online Communities." In *Proceedings of the 2004 ACM Conference on Computer Supported Cooperative Work*, 212–21. CSCW '04. New York: ACM. doi:10.1145/1031607.1031642.

Bell, Gordon, and Jim Gemmell. 2009. *Total Recall: How the E-Memory Revolution Will Change Everything*. New York: Dutton Adult.

Bell, Robert M., Yehuda Koren, and Chris Volinsky. 2010. "All Together Now: A Perspective on the Netflix Prize." *Chance* 23 (1): 24–24. doi:10.1007/s00144-010-0005-2.

Belli, Robert F., Michael W. Traugott, Margaret Young, and Katherine A. McGonagle. 1999. "Reducing Vote Overreporting in Surveys: Social Desirability, Memory Failure, and Source Monitoring." *Public Opinion Quarterly* 63 (1): 90–108. doi:10.1086/297704.

Bello, G A, J Chipeta, and J Aberle-Grasse. 2006. "Assessment of Trends in Biological and Behavioural Surveillance Data: Is There Any Evidence of Declining HIV Prevalence or Incidence in Malawi?" *Sexually Transmitted Infections* 82 (Suppl 1): i9–i13. doi:10.1136/sti.2005.016030.

Belmont Report. 1979. *The Belmont Report: Ethical Principles and Guidelines for the Protection of Human Subjects of Research*. US Department of Health, Education, and Welfare.

Bengtsson, Linus, Xin Lu, Anna Thorson, Richard Garfield, and Johan von Schreeb. 2011. "Improved Response to Disasters and Outbreaks by Tracking Population Movements with Mobile Phone Network Data: A Post-Earthquake Geospatial Study in Haiti." *PLoS Medicine* 8 (8): e1001083. doi:10.1371/journal.pmed.1001083.

Bennett, James, and Stan Lanning. 2007. "The Netflix Prize." In *Proceedings of KDD Cup and Workshop*, 2007: 35.

Benoit, Kenneth, Drew Conway, Benjamin E. Lauderdale, Michael Laver, and Slava Mikhaylov. 2016. "Crowd-Sourced Text Analysis: Reproducible and Agile Production of Political Data." *American Political Science Review* 110 (2): 278–95. doi:10.1017/S0003055416000058.

Berent, Matthew K., Jon A. Krosnick, and Arthur Lupia. 2016. "Measuring Voter Registration and Turnout in Surveys: Do Official Government Records Yield More Accurate Assessments?" *Public Opinion Quarterly* 80 (3): 597–621. doi:10.1093/poq/nfw021.

Berinsky, Adam J., and Sara Chatfield. 2015. "An Empirical Justification for the Use of Draft Lottery Numbers as a Random Treatment in Political Science Research." *Political Analysis* 23 (3): 449–54. doi:10.1093/pan/mpv015.

Berinsky, Adam J., Gregory A. Huber, and Gabriel S. Lenz. 2012. "Evaluating Online Labor Markets for Experimental Research: Amazon.com's Mechanical Turk." *Political Analysis* 20 (3): 351–68. doi:10.1093/pan/mpr057.

Berinsky, Adam J., Michele F. Margolis, and Michael W. Sances. 2014. "Separating the Shirkers from the Workers? Making Sure Respondents Pay Attention on Self-Administered Surveys." *American Journal of Political Science* 58 (3): 739–53. doi:10.1111/ajps.12081.

———. 2016. "Can We Turn Shirkers into Workers?" *Journal of Experimental Social Psychology* 66: 20–28. doi:10.1016/j.jesp.2015.09.010.

Berk, Richard, Emil Pitkin, Lawrence Brown, Andreas Buja, Edward George, and Linda Zhao. 2013. "Covariance Adjustments for the Analysis of Randomized Field Experiments." *Evaluation Review* 37 (3–4): 170–96. doi:10.1177/0193841X13513025.

Bernedo, María, Paul J. Ferraro, and Michael Price. 2014. "The Persistent Impacts of Norm-Based Messaging and Their Implications for Water Conservation." *Journal of Consumer Policy* 37 (3): 437–52. doi:10.1007/s10603-014-9266-0.

Bertrand, Marianne, and Sendhil Mullainathan. 2004. "Are Emily and Greg More Employable Than Lakisha and Jamal? A Field Experiment on Labor Market Discrimination." *American Economic Review* 94 (4): 991–1013. http://www.jstor.org/stable/3592802.

Beskow, Laura M., Lauren Dame, and E. Jane Costello. 2008. "Certificates of Confidentiality and the Compelled Disclosure of Research Data." *Science* 322 (5904): 1054–55. doi:10.1126/science.1164100.

Beskow, Laura M., Robert S. Sandler, and Morris Weinberger. 2006. "Research Recruitment Through US Central Cancer Registries: Balancing Privacy and Scientific Issues." *American Journal of Public Health* 96 (11): 1920–26. doi:10.2105/AJPH.2004.061556.

Bestor, Daniel R., and Eric Hamp. 2010. "Peer to Patent: A Cure for Our Ailing Patent Examination System." *Northwestern Journal of Technology and Intellectual Property* 9 (2): 16–28. http://scholarlycommons.law.northwestern.edu/njtip/vol9/iss2/1.

Bethlehem, Jelke. 1988. "Reduction of Nonresponse Bias Through Regression Estimation." *Journal of Official Statistics* 4 (3): 251–60. http://www.jos.nu/Articles/abstract.asp?article=43251.

———. 2010. "Selection Bias in Web Surveys." *International Statistical Review* 78 (2): 161–88. doi:10.1111/j.1751-5823.2010.00112.x.

———. 2016. "Solving the Nonresponse Problem With Sample Matching?" *Social Science Computer Review* 34 (1). doi:10.1177/0894439315573926.

Bethlehem, Jelke, Fannie Cobben, and Barry Schouten. 2011. *Handbook of Nonresponse in Household Surveys.* Hoboken, NJ: Wiley.

Bhattacharjee, Yudhijit. 2005. "Citizen Scientists Supplement Work of Cornell Researchers." *Science* 308 (5727): 1402–3. doi:10.1126/science.308.5727.1402.

Blank, Steve. 2013. "Why the Lean Start-Up Changes Everything." *Harvard Business Review*, May. https://hbr.org/2013/05/why-the-lean-start-up-changes-everything.

Bloniarz, Adam, Hanzhong Liu, Cun-Hui Zhang, Jasjeet S. Sekhon, and Bin Yu. 2016. "Lasso Adjustments of Treatment Effect Estimates in Randomized Experiments." *Proceedings of the National Academy of Sciences of the USA* 113 (27): 7383–90. doi:10.1073/pnas.1510506113.

Blumenstock, Joshua E. 2014. "Calling for Better Measurement: Estimating an Individual's Wealth and Well-Being from Mobile Phone Transaction Records." Presented at KDD—Data Science for Social Good 2014, New York. http://escholarship.org/uc/item/8zs63942.

Blumenstock, Joshua E., Gabriel Cadamuro, and Robert On. 2015. "Predicting Poverty and Wealth from Mobile Phone Metadata." *Science* 350 (6264): 1073–6. doi:10.1126/science.aac4420.

Blumenstock, Joshua E., Niall C. Keleher, and Joseph Reisinger. 2016. "The Premise of Local Information: Building Reliable Economic Indicators from a Decentralized Network of Contributors." In *Proceedings of the Eighth International Conference on Information and Communication Technologies and Development*, 61:1–61:5. ICTD '16. New York: ACM. doi:10.1145/2909609.2909646.

Blumenstock, Joshua Evan, Marcel Fafchamps, and Nathan Eagle. 2011. "Risk and Reciprocity Over the Mobile Phone Network: Evidence from Rwanda." *SSRN ELibrary*, October. http://papers.ssrn.com/sol3/papers.cfm?abstract_id=1958042.

Boase, Jeffrey, and Rich Ling. 2013. "Measuring Mobile Phone Use: Self-Report versus Log Data." *Journal of Computer-Mediated Communication* 18 (4): 508–19. doi:10.1111/jcc4.12021.

Boellstorff, Tom, Bonnie Nardi, Celia Pearce, T. L. Taylor, and George E. Marcus. 2012. *Ethnography and Virtual Worlds: A Handbook of Method*. Princeton, NJ: Princeton University Press.

Bohannon, John. 2009. "Gamers Unravel the Secret Life of Protein." *Wired*, April. https://www.wired.com/2009/04/ff-protein/.

———. 2016. "Mechanical Turk Upends Social Sciences." *Science* 352 (6291): 1263–64. doi:10.1126/science.352.6291.1263.

Bollen, Johan, Huina Mao, and Xiaojun Zeng. 2011. "Twitter Mood Predicts the Stock Market." *Journal of Computational Science* 2 (1): 1–8. doi:10.1016/j.jocs.2010.12.007.

Bollen, Kenneth A. 2012. "Instrumental Variables in Sociology and the Social Sciences." *Annual Review of Sociology* 38 (1): 37–72. doi:10.1146/annurev-soc-081309-150141.

Bond, Robert M., Christopher J. Fariss, Jason J. Jones, Adam D. I. Kramer, Cameron Marlow, Jaime E. Settle, and James H. Fowler. 2012. "A 61-Million-Person Experiment in Social Influence and Political Mobilization." *Nature* 489 (7415): 295–98. doi:10.1038/nature11421.

Bonney, Rick, Jennifer L. Shirk, Tina B. Phillips, Andrea Wiggins, Heidi L. Ballard, Abraham J. Miller-Rushing, and Julia K. Parrish. 2014. "Next Steps for Citizen Science." *Science* 343 (6178): 1436–37. doi:10.1126/science.1251554.

Bothwell, Laura E., Jeremy A. Greene, Scott H. Podolsky, and David S. Jones. 2016. "Assessing the Gold Standard Lessons from the History of RCTs." *New England Journal of Medicine* 374 (22): 2175–81. doi:10.1056/NEJMms1604593.

Boudreau, Kevin J., and Karim R. Lakhani. 2013. "Using the Crowd as an Innovation Partner." *Harvard Business Review* 91 (4): 60–69, 140.

Bourdieu, Pierre. 1987. *Distinction: A Social Critique of the Judgement of Taste*, translated by Richard Nice. Cambridge, MA: Harvard University Press.

Bowser, Anne, Andrea Wiggins, Lea Shanley, Jennifer Preece, and Sandra Henderson. 2014. "Sharing Data while Protecting Privacy in Citizen Science." *Interactions* 21 (1): 70–73. doi:10.1145/2540032.

Box, George E. P., J. Stuart Hunter, and William G. Hunter. 2005. *Statistics for Experimenters: Design, Innovation, and Discovery*, 2nd edition. Hoboken, NJ: Wiley-Interscience.

boyd, danah. 2016. "Untangling Research and Practice: What Facebook's Emotional Contagion Study Teaches Us." *Research Ethics* 12 (1): 4–13. doi:10.1177/1747016115583379.

boyd, danah, and Kate Crawford. 2012. "Critical Questions for Big Data." *Information, Communication & Society* 15 (5): 662–79. doi:10.1080/1369118X.2012.678878.

Bradburn, Norman M., Seymour Sudman, and Brian Wansink. 2004. *Asking Questions: The Definitive Guide to Questionnaire Design*, rev. ed. San Francisco: Jossey-Bass.

Brandt, Allan M. 1978. "Racism and Research: The Case of the Tuskegee Syphilis Study." *Hastings Center Report* 8 (6): 21–29. doi:10.2307/3561468.

Brayne, Sarah. 2014. "Surveillance and System Avoidance: Criminal Justice Contact and Institutional Attachment." *American Sociological Review* 79 (3): 367–91. doi:10.1177/0003122414530398.

Breiman, Leo. 2001. "Statistical Modeling: The Two Cultures (with Comments and a Rejoinder by the Author)." *Statistical Science* 16 (3): 199–231. doi:10.1214/ss/1009213726.

Brick, J. Michael. 2013. "Unit Nonresponse and Weighting Adjustments: A Critical Review." *Journal of Official Statistics* 29 (3): 329–53. doi:10.2478/jos-2013-0026.

Brick, J. Michael, and Clyde Tucker. 2007. "Mitofsky–Waksberg: Learning From The Past." *Public Opinion Quarterly* 71 (5): 703–16. doi:10.1093/poq/nfm049.

Brickell, Justin, and Vitaly Shmatikov. 2008. "The Cost of Privacy: Destruction of Data-Mining Utility in Anonymized Data Publishing." In *Proceedings of the 14th ACM SIGKDD International Conference on Knowledge Discovery and Data Mining*, 70–78. KDD '08. doi:10.1145/1401890.1401904.

Brownstein, John S., Christopher A. Cassa, and Kenneth D. Mandl. 2006. "No Place to Hide: Reverse Identification of Patients from Published Maps." *New England Journal of Medicine* 355 (16): 1741–42. doi:10.1056/NEJMc061891.

Bruckman, Amy. 2016a. "Do Researchers Need to Abide by Terms of Service (TOS)? An Answer." *The Next Bison: Social Computing and Culture.* https://nextbison.wordpress.com/2016/02/26/tos/.

———. 2016b. "More on TOS: Maybe Documenting Intent Is Not So Smart." *The Next Bison: Social Computing and Culture.* https://nextbison.wordpress.com/2016/02/29/tos2/.

Bryson, Maurice C. 1976. "The Literary Digest Poll: Making of a Statistical Myth." *American Statistician* 30 (4): 184–85. doi:10.1080/00031305.1976.10479173.

Budak, Ceren, and Duncan Watts. 2015. "Dissecting the Spirit of Gezi: Influence vs. Selection in the Occupy Gezi Movement." *Sociological Science* 2: 370–97. doi:10.15195/v2.a18.

Budak, Ceren, Sharad Goel, and Justin M. Rao. 2016. "Fair and Balanced? Quantifying Media Bias Through Crowdsourced Content Analysis." *Public Opinion Quarterly* 80 (S1): 250–71. doi:10.1093/poq/nfw007.

Buelens, Bart, Piet Daas, Joep Burger, Marco Puts, and Jan van den Brakel. 2014. "Selectivity of Big Data." Discussion paper, Statistics Netherlands. http://www.pietdaas.nl/beta/pubs/pubs/Selectivity_Buelens.pdf.

Bullock, John G., Donald P. Green, and Shang E. Ha. 2010. "Yes, but What's the Mechanism? (Don't Expect an Easy Answer)." *Journal of Personality and Social Psychology* 98 (4): 550–58. doi:10.1037/a0018933.

Burke, Moira, and Robert E. Kraut. 2014. "Growing Closer on Facebook: Changes in Tie Strength Through Social Network Site Use." In *Proceedings of the SIGCHI Conference on Human Factors in Computing Systems*, 4187–96. CHI '14. New York: ACM. doi:10.1145/2556288.2557094.

Burnett, Sam, and Nick Feamster. 2015. "Encore: Lightweight Measurement of Web Censorship with Cross-Origin Requests." In *Proceedings of the 2015 ACM Conference on Special Interest Group on Data Communication*, 653–67. SIGCOMM '15. London: ACM. doi:10.1145/2785956.2787485.

Buttice, Matthew K., and Benjamin Highton. 2013. "How Does Multilevel Regression and Post-stratification Perform with Conventional National Surveys?" *Political Analysis* 21 (4): 449–67. doi:10.1093/pan/mpt017.

Cahalan, Don. 1989. "Comment: The Digest Poll Rides Again!" *Public Opinion Quarterly* 53 (1): 129–33. doi:10.1086/269146.

Callegaro, Mario, Reginald P. Baker, Jelke Bethlehem, Anja S. Göritz, Jon A. Krosnick, and Paul J. Lavrakas, eds. 2014. *Online Panel Research: A Data Quality Perspective.* Chichester, UK: Wiley.

Calo, Ryan. 2011. "The Boundaries of Privacy Harm." *Indiana Law Journal* 86: 1131. http://ilj.law.indiana.edu/articles/86/86_3_Calo.pdf.

———. 2013. "Consumer Subject Review Boards: A Thought Experiment." *Stanford Law Review Online*, 97–102. https://www.stanfordlawreview.org/online/privacy-and-big-data-consumer-subject-review-boards/.

Camerer, Colin. 2011. "The Promise and Success of Lab–Field Generalizability in Experimental Economics: A Critical Reply to Levitt and List." *SSRN ELibrary*, December. http://papers.ssrn.com/sol3/papers.cfm?abstract_id=1977749.

Camerer, Colin, Linda Babcock, George Loewenstein, and Richard Thaler. 1997. "Labor Supply of New York City Cabdrivers: One Day at a Time." *Quarterly Journal of Economics* 112 (2): 407–41. doi:10.1162/003355397555244.

Campbell, Donald T. 1957. "Factors Relevant to the Validity of Experiments in Social Settings." *Psychological Bulletin* 54 (4): 297–312. doi:10.1037/h0040950.

Canfield, Casey, Wändi Bruine de Bruin, and Gabrielle Wong-Parodi. 2016. "Perceptions of Electricity-Use Communications: Effects of Information, Format, and Individual Differences." *Journal of Risk Research*, January: 1–22. doi:10.1080/13669877.2015.1121909.

Card, David, Raj Chetty, Martin S. Feldstein, and Emmanuel Saez. 2010. "Expanding Access to Administrative Data for Research in the United States." SSRN Scholarly Paper ID 1888586. Rochester, NY: Social Science Research Network. http://papers.ssrn.com/abstract=1888586.

Cardamone, Carolin, Kevin Schawinski, Marc Sarzi, Steven P Bamford, Nicola Bennert, C. M Urry, Chris Lintott, et al. 2009. "Galaxy Zoo Green Peas: Discovery of a Class of Compact Extremely Star-Forming Galaxies." *Monthly Notices of the Royal Astronomical Society* 399 (3): 1191–205. doi:10.1111/j.1365-2966.2009.15383.x.

Carneiro, Pedro Manuel, Sokbae Lee, and Daniel Wilhelm. 2016. "Optimal Data Collection for Randomized Control Trials." SSRN Scholarly Paper ID 2776913. Rochester, NY: Social Science Research Network. http://papers.ssrn.com/abstract=2776913.

Carpenter, Kenneth J. 1988. *The History of Scurvy and Vitamin C*. Cambridge: Cambridge University Press.

Carpenter, Patricia A., Marcel A. Just, and Peter Shell. 1990. "What One Intelligence Test Measures: A Theoretical Account of the Processing in the Raven Progressive Matrices Test." *Psychological Review* 97 (3): 404–31. doi:10.1037/0033-295X.97.3.404.

Carter, Stephen L. 1996. *Integrity*. New York: HarperCollins.

Casella, George. 2008. *Statistical Design*. New York: Springer.

Castillo, Carlos. 2016. *Big Crisis Data: Social Media in Disasters and Time-Critical Situations*. New York: Cambridge University Press.

Centola, D. 2010. "The Spread of Behavior in an Online Social Network Experiment." *Science* 329 (5996): 1194–97. doi:10.1126/science.1185231.

Centola, Damon. 2011. "An Experimental Study of Homophily in the Adoption of Health Behavior." *Science* 334 (6060): 1269–72. doi:10.1126/science.1207055.

Cerulo, Karen A. 2014. "Reassessing the Problem: Response to Jerolmack and Khan." *Sociological Methods & Research* 43 (2): 219–26. doi:10.1177/0049124114526378.

Chaabane, Abdelberi, Terence Chen, Mathieu Cunche, Emiliano De Cristofaro, Arik Friedman, and Mohamed Ali Kaafar. 2014. "Censorship in the Wild: Analyzing Internet Filtering in Syria." In *Proceedings of the 2014 Conference on Internet Measurement Conference*, 285–98. IMC '14. New York: ACM. doi:10.1145/2663716.2663720.

Chakraborti, Sayan, Naveen Yadav, Carolin Cardamone, and Alak Ray. 2012. "Radio Detection of Green Peas: Implications for Magnetic Fields in Young Galaxies." *Astrophysical Journal Letters* 746 (1): L6. doi:10.1088/2041-8205/746/1/L6.

Chandler, Jesse, Gabriele Paolacci, and Pam Mueller. 2013. "Risks and Rewards of Crowdsourcing Marketplaces." In *Handbook of Human Computation*, edited by Pietro Michelucci, 377–92. New York: Springer.

Chandler, Jesse, Gabriele Paolacci, Eyal Peer, Pam Mueller, and Kate A. Ratliff. 2015. "Using Nonnaive Participants Can Reduce Effect Sizes." *Psychological Science* 26 (7): 1131–39. doi:10.1177/0956797615585115.

Charness, Gary, Uri Gneezy, and Michael A. Kuhn. 2012. "Experimental Methods: Between-Subject and Within-Subject Design." *Journal of Economic Behavior & Organization* 81 (1): 1–8. doi:10.1016/j.jebo.2011.08.009.

———. 2013. "Experimental Methods: Extra-Laboratory Experiments—Extending the Reach of Experimental Economics." *Journal of Economic Behavior & Organization* 91 (July): 93–100. doi:10.1016/j.jebo.2013.04.002.

Chen, Yan, and Joseph Konstan. 2015. "Online Field Experiments: A Selective Survey of Methods." *Journal of the Economic Science Association* 1 (1): 29–42. doi:10.1007/s40881-015-0005-3.

Chen, Yan, F. Maxwell Harper, Joseph Konstan, and Sherry Xin Li. 2010. "Social Comparisons and Contributions to Online Communities: A Field Experiment on MovieLens." *American Economic Review* 100 (4): 1358–98. doi:10.1257/aer.100.4.1358.

Cheng, Justin, and Michael S. Bernstein. 2015. "Flock: Hybrid Crowd-Machine Learning Classifiers." In *Proceedings of the 18th ACM Conference on Computer Supported Cooperative Work & Social Computing*, 600–611. CSCW '15. New York: ACM. doi:10.1145/2675133.2675214.

Chetty, Raj, Nathaniel Hendren, Patrick Kline, and Emmanuel Saez. 2014. "Where Is the Land of Opportunity? The Geography of Intergenerational Mobility in the United States." *Quarterly Journal of Economics* 129 (4): 1553–1623. doi:10.1093/qje/qju022.

Choi, Hyunyoung, and Hal Varian. 2012. "Predicting the Present with Google Trends." *Economic Record* 88 (June): 2–9. doi:10.1111/j.1475-4932.2012.00809.x.

Chu, Z., S. Gianvecchio, H. Wang, and S. Jajodia. 2012. "Detecting Automation of Twitter Accounts: Are You a Human, Bot, or Cyborg?" *IEEE Transactions on Dependable and Secure Computing* 9 (6): 811–24. doi:10.1109/TDSC.2012.75.

Cialdini, Robert B. 2009. "We Have to Break Up." *Perspectives on Psychological Science* 4 (1): 5–6. doi:10.1111/j.1745-6924.2009.01091.x.

Cialdini, Robert B., Carl A. Kallgren, and Raymond R. Reno. 1991. "A Focus Theory of Normative Conduct: A Theoretical Refinement and Reevaluation of the Role of Norms in Human Behavior." *Advances in Experimental Social Psychology* 24 (20): 201–34.

Clark, Eric M., Chris A. Jones, Jake Ryland Williams, Allison N. Kurti, Mitchell Craig Norotsky, Christopher M. Danforth, and Peter Sheridan Dodds. 2016. "Vaporous Marketing: Uncovering Pervasive Electronic Cigarette Advertisements on Twitter." *PLoS ONE* 11 (7): e0157304. doi:10.1371/journal.pone.0157304.

Clark, William Roberts, and Matt Golder. 2015. "Big Data, Causal Inference, and Formal Theory: Contradictory Trends in Political Science?" *PS: Political Science & Politics* 48 (1): 65–70. doi:10.1017/S1049096514001759.

Clery, Daniel. 2011. "Galaxy Zoo Volunteers Share Pain and Glory of Research." *Science* 333 (6039): 173–75. doi:10.1126/science.333.6039.173.

Cohen, Jacob. 1988. *Statistical Power Analysis for the Behavioral Sciences*, 2nd ed. Hillsdale, NJ: Routledge.
———. 1992. "A Power Primer." *Psychological Bulletin* 112 (1): 155–59. doi:10.1037/0033-2909.112.1.155.

Cohn, Michael A., Matthias R. Mehl, and James W. Pennebaker. 2004. "Linguistic Markers of Psychological Change Surrounding September 11, 2001." *Psychological Science* 15 (10): 687–93. doi:10.1111/j.0956-7976.2004.00741.x.

Connelly, Roxanne, Christopher J. Playford, Vernon Gayle, and Chris Dibben. 2016. "The Role of Administrative Data in the Big Data Revolution in Social Science Research." *Social Science Research*, 59: 1–12. doi:10.1016/j.ssresearch.2016.04.015.

Conrad, Frederick G., and Michael F. Schober, eds. 2008. *Envisioning the Survey Interview of the Future*. Hoboken, NJ: Wiley.

Conrad, Frederick G., Jessica S. Broome, José R. Benkí, Frauke Kreuter, Robert M. Groves, David Vannette, and Colleen McClain. 2013. "Interviewer Speech and the Success of Survey Invitations." *Journal of the Royal Statistical Society: Series A (Statistics in Society)* 176 (1): 191–210. doi:10.1111/j.1467-985X.2012.01064.x.

Converse, Jean M. 1987. *Survey Research in the United States: Roots and Emergence 1890–1960*. Berkeley: University of California Press.

Cook, Samantha, Corrie Conrad, Ashley L. Fowlkes, and Matthew H. Mohebbi. 2011. "Assessing Google Flu Trends Performance in the United States during the 2009 Influenza Virus A (H1N1) Pandemic." *PLoS ONE* 6 (8): e23610. doi:10.1371/journal.pone.0023610.

Cooper, Seth, Firas Khatib, Adrien Treuille, Janos Barbero, Jeehyung Lee, Michael Beenen, Andrew Leaver-Fay, David Baker, Zoran Popovic, and Foldit players. 2010. "Predicting Protein Structures with a Multiplayer Online Game." *Nature* 466 (7307): 756–60. doi:10.1038/nature09304.

Coppock, Alexander, and Donald P. Green. 2015. "Assessing the Correspondence between Experimental Results Obtained in the Lab and Field: A Review of Recent Social Science Research." *Political Science Research and Methods* 3 (1): 113–31. doi:10.1017/psrm.2014.10.

Coppock, Alexander, Andrew Guess, and John Ternovski. 2016. "When Treatments Are Tweets: A Network Mobilization Experiment over Twitter." *Political Behavior* 38 (1): 105–28. doi:10.1007/s11109-015-9308-6.

Cornwell, Erin York. 2010. "Opening and Closing the Jury Room Door: A Sociohistorical Consideration of the 1955 Chicago Jury Project Scandal." *Justice System Journal* 31 (1): 49–73. doi:10.1080/0098261X.2010.10767954.

Correll, Shelley J., Stephen Benard, and In Paik. 2007. "Getting a Job: Is There a Motherhood Penalty?" *American Journal of Sociology* 112 (5): 1297–1339. doi:10.1086/511799.

Cosley, Dan, Dan Frankowski, Sara Kiesler, Loren Terveen, and John Riedl. 2005. "How Oversight Improves Member-Maintained Communities." In *Proceedings of the SIGCHI Conference on Human Factors in Computing Systems*, 11–20. CHI '05. New York: ACM. doi:10.1145/1054972.1054975.

Costa, Dora L., and Matthew E. Kahn. 2013. "Energy Conservation Nudges and Environmentalist Ideology: Evidence from a Randomized Residential Electricity Field Experiment." *Journal of the European Economic Association* 11 (3): 680–702. doi:10.1111/jeea.12011.

Couper, Mick P. 2011. "The Future of Modes of Data Collection." *Public Opinion Quarterly* 75 (5): 889–908. doi:10.1093/poq/nfr046.

Coviello, L., J.H. Fowler, and M. Franceschetti. 2014. "Words on the Web: Noninvasive Detection of Emotional Contagion in Online Social Networks." *Proceedings of the IEEE* 102 (12): 1911–21. doi:10.1109/JPROC.2014.2366052.

Coviello, Lorenzo, Yunkyu Sohn, Adam D. I. Kramer, Cameron Marlow, Massimo Franceschetti, Nicholas A. Christakis, and James H. Fowler. 2014. "Detecting Emotional Contagion in Massive Social Networks." *PLoS ONE* 9 (3): e90315. doi:10.1371/journal.pone.0090315.

Cox, J., E. Y. Oh, B. Simmons, C. Lintott, K. Masters, A. Greenhill, G. Graham, and K. Holmes. 2015. "Defining and Measuring Success in Online Citizen Science: A Case Study of Zooniverse Projects." *Computing in Science & Engineering* 17 (4): 28–41. doi:10.1109/MCSE.2015.65.

Crain, Rhiannon, Caren Cooper, and Janis L. Dickinson. 2014. "Citizen Science: A Tool for Integrating Studies of Human and Natural Systems." *Annual Review of Environment and Resources* 39 (1): 641–65. doi:10.1146/annurev-environ-030713-154609.

Cranshaw, Justin, and Aniket Kittur. 2011. "The Polymath Project: Lessons from a Successful Online Collaboration in Mathematics." In *Proceedings of the 2011 Annual Conference on Human Factors in Computing Systems*, 1865–74. CHI '11. New York: ACM. doi:10.1145/1978942.1979213.

Crawford, Kate. 2014. "The Test We Can and Should Run on Facebook." *Atlantic*, July. http://www.theatlantic.com/technology/archive/2014/07/the-test-we-canand-shouldrun-on-facebook/373819/.

Crawford, Kate and Megan Finn. 2015. "The Limits of Crisis Data: Analytical and Ethical Challenges of Using Social and Mobile Data to Understand Disasters." *GeoJournal* 80 (4): 491–502. doi:10.1007/s10708-014-9597-z.

Cronbach, Lee J., and Paul E. Meehl. 1955. "Construct Validity in Psychological Tests." *Psychological Bulletin* 52 (4): 281–302. doi:10.1037/h0040957.

Currie, Janet. 2013. "Big Data versus Big Brother: On the Appropriate Use of Large-Scale Data Collections in Pediatrics." *Pediatrics* 131 (Suppl. 2): S127–S132. doi:10.1542/peds.2013-0252c.

Dabalen, Andrew, Alvin Etang, Johannes Hoogeveen, Elvis Mushi, Youdi Schipper, and Johannes von Engelhardt. 2016. *Mobile Phone Panel Surveys in Developing Countries: A Practical Guide for Microdata Collection.* Directions in Development–Poverty. Washington, DC: World Bank Publications. http://hdl.handle.net/10986/24595.

Daries, Jon P., Justin Reich, Jim Waldo, Elise M. Young, Jonathan Whittinghill, Daniel Thomas Seaton, Andrew Dean Ho, and Isaac Chuang. 2014. "Privacy, Anonymity, and Big Data in the Social Sciences." *Queue* 12 (7): 30:30–30:41. doi:10.1145/2639988.2661641.

De Choudhury, Munmun, Winter A Mason, Jake M Hofman, and Duncan J Watts. 2010. "Inferring Relevant Social Networks from Interpersonal Communication." In *Proceedings of the 19th International Conference on World Wide Web*, 301–10. WWW '10. Raleigh, NC: ACM. doi:10.1145/1772690.1772722.

De Mauro, Andrea, Marco Greco, Michele Grimaldi, Georgios Giannakopoulos, Damianos P. Sakas, and Daphne Kyriaki-Manessi. 2015. "What Is Big Data? A Consensual Definition and a Review of Key Research Topics." *AIP Conference Proceedings* 1644 (1): 97–104. doi:10.1063/1.4907823.

De Waal, Ton, Marco Puts, and Piet Daas. 2014. "Statistical Data Editing of Big Data." *Paper for the Royal Statistical Society.* https://www.researchgate.net/profile/Ton_De_Waal/publication/268923823_Statistical_Data_Editing_of_Big_Data/links/547b03440cf293e2da2bbe25.pdf.

Dean, J., and S. Ghemawat. 2008. "MapReduce: Simplified Data Processing on Large Clusters." *Communications of the ACM* 51 (1): 107–13.

Dean, Jeffrey, and Sanjay Ghemawat. 2004. "MapReduce: Simplified Data Processing on Large Clusters." In *Proceedings of the 6th Conference on Symposium on Opearting Systems Design & Implementation*, vol. 6. Berkeley, CA: USENIX Association. https://static.googleusercontent.com/media/research.google.com/en//archive/mapreduce-osdi04.pdf.

Deaton, Angus. 2010. "Instruments, Randomization, and Learning About Development." *Journal of Economic Literature* 48 (2): 424–55. doi:10.1257/jel.48.2.424.

Dehejia, Rajeev H. and Sadek Wahba. 1999. "Causal Effects in Nonexperimental Studies: Reevaluating the Evaluation of Training Programs." *Journal of the American Statistical Association* 94 (448): 1053–62. doi:10.1080/01621459.1999.10473858.

Deng, Alex, Ya Xu, Ron Kohavi, and Toby Walker. 2013. "Improving the Sensitivity of Online Controlled Experiments by Utilizing Pre-Experiment Data." In *Proceedings of the Sixth ACM International Conference on Web Search and Data Mining*, 123–32. WSDM '13. New York: ACM. doi:10.1145/2433396.2433413.

Desai, Tanvi, Felix Ritchie, and Richard Welpton. 2016. "Five Safes: Designing Data Access for Research." University of the West of England. http://www1.uwe.ac.uk/bl/research/bristoleconomicanalysis/economicsworkingpapers/economicspapers2016.aspx.

Desposato, Scott. 2016a. "Conclusion and Recommendations." In *Ethics and Experiments: Problems and Solutions for Social Scientists and Policy Professionals*, edited by Scott Desposato 267–89. New York: Routledge.

———, ed. 2016b. *Ethics and Experiments: Problems and Solutions for Social Scientists and Policy Professionals.* New York: Routledge.

Diaz, Fernando, Michael Gamon, Jake M. Hofman, Emre Kiciman, and David Rothschild. 2016. "Online and Social Media Data As an Imperfect Continuous Panel Survey." *PLoS ONE* 11 (1): e0145406. doi:10.1371/journal.pone.0145406.

Dickert, Neal, and Christine Grady. 2008. "Incentives for Research Participants." In *The Oxford Textbook of Clinical Research Ethics*, edited by E. J. Emanuel, R. A. Crouch, C. Grady, R. K. Lie, F. G. Miller, and D. Wendler, 386–97. Oxford: Oxford University Press.

Dickinson, Janis L., Benjamin Zuckerberg, and David N. Bonter. 2010. "Citizen Science as an Ecological Research Tool: Challenges and Benefits." *Annual Review of Ecology, Evolution, and Systematics* 41 (1): 149–72. doi:10.1146/annurev-ecolsys-102209-144636.

Dieleman, Sander, Kyle W. Willett, and Joni Dambre. 2015. "Rotation-Invariant Convolutional Neural Networks for Galaxy Morphology Prediction." *Monthly Notices of the Royal Astronomical Society* 450 (2): 1441–59. doi:10.1093/mnras/stv632.

Dillman, Don A. 2002. "Presidential Address: Navigating the Rapids of Change: Some Observations on Survey Methodology in the Early Twenty-First Century." *Public Opinion Quarterly* 66 (3): 473–94. http://www.jstor.org/stable/3078777.

Dillman, Don A., Jolene D. Smyth, and Leah Melani Christian. 2008. *Internet, Mail, and Mixed-Mode Surveys: The Tailored Design Method*, 3rd ed. Hoboken, NJ: Wiley.

———. 2014. *Internet, Phone, Mail, and Mixed-Mode Surveys: The Tailored Design Method*, 4th ed. Hoboken, NJ: Wiley.

DiMaggio, Paul, John Evans, and Bethany Bryson. 1996. "Have American's Social Attitudes Become More Polarized?" *American Journal of Sociology* 102 (3): 690–755. http://www.jstor.org/stable/2782461.

Dittrich, D., K. Carpenter, and M. Karir. 2015. "The Internet Census 2012 Dataset: An Ethical Examination." *IEEE Technology and Society Magazine* 34 (2): 40–46. doi:10.1109/MTS.2015.2425592.

Dittrich, David, Erin Kenneally, and others. 2011. "The Menlo Report: Ethical Principles Guiding Information and Communication Technology Research." *US Department of Homeland Security*. http://www.caida.org/publications/papers/2012/menlo_report_ethical_principles/.

Doleac, Jennifer L., and Luke C.D. Stein. 2013. "The Visible Hand: Race and Online Market Outcomes." *Economic Journal* 123 (572): F469–F492. doi:10.1111/ecoj.12082.

Doll, Richard, and A. Bradford Hill. 1954. "The Mortality of Doctors in Relation to Their Smoking Habits: A Preliminary Report." *British Medical Journal* 1 (4877): 1451–55. http://www.ncbi.nlm.nih.gov/pmc/articles/PMC2085438/.

Doll, Richard, Richard Peto, Jillian Boreham, and Isabelle Sutherland. 2004. "Mortality in Relation to Smoking: 50 Years' Observations on Male British Doctors." *BMJ* 328 (7455): 1519. doi:10.1136/bmj.38142.554479.AE.

Donoho, David. 2015. "50 Years of Data Science." Based on a presentation at Tukey Centennial Workshop, Princeton NJ, September. http://courses.csail.mit.edu/18.337/2015/docs/50YearsDataScience.pdf.

Dreber, Anna, Thomas Pfeiffer, Johan Almenberg, Siri Isaksson, Brad Wilson, Yiling Chen, Brian A. Nosek, and Magnus Johannesson. 2015. "Using Prediction Markets to Estimate the Reproducibility of Scientific Research." *Proceedings of the National Academy of Sciences of the USA* 112 (50): 15343–47. doi:10.1073/pnas.1516179112.

Drenner, Sara, Max Harper, Dan Frankowski, John Riedl, and Loren Terveen. 2006. "Insert Movie Reference Here: A System to Bridge Conversation and Item-Oriented Web Sites." In *Proceedings of the SIGCHI Conference on Human Factors in Computing Systems*, 951–54. CHI '06. New York: ACM. doi:10.1145/1124772.1124914.

Druckman, James N., and Arthur Lupia. 2012. "Experimenting with Politics." *Science* 335 (6073): 1177–79. doi:10.1126/science.1207808.

Druckman, James N., Donald P. Green, James H. Kuklinski, and Arthur Lupia. 2006. "The Growth and Development of Experimental Research in Political Science." *American Political Science Review* 100 (4): 627–35. doi:10.1017/S0003055406062514.

Dunn, Halbert L. 1946. "Record Linkage." *American Journal of Public Health and the Nations Health* 36 (12): 1412–16. doi:10.2105/AJPH.36.12.1412.

Dunning, Thad. 2012. *Natural Experiments in the Social Sciences: A Design-Based Approach*. Cambridge: Cambridge University Press.

Dwork, Cynthia. 2008. "Differential Privacy: A Survey of Results." In *International Conference on Theory and Applications of Models of Computation*, 1–19. Berlin: Springer. doi:10.1007/978-3-540-79228-4_1.

Dwork, Cynthia, and Aaron Roth. 2014. "The Algorithmic Foundations of Differential Privacy." *Foundations and Trends in Theoretical Computer Science* 9 (34): 211–407. doi:10.1561/0400000042.

Dwork, Cynthia, Adam D. Smith, Thomas Steinke, and Jonathan Ullman. 2017. "Hiding in Plain Sight: A Survey of Attacks on Private Data." *Annual Review of Statistics and Its Application* 4: 61–84. doi:10.1146/annurev-statistics-060116-054123.

Dwyer, Patrick C., Alexander Maki, and Alexander J. Rothman. 2015. "Promoting Energy Conservation Behavior in Public Settings: The Influence of Social Norms and Personal Responsibility." *Journal of Environmental Psychology* 41 (March): 30–34. doi:10.1016/j.jenvp.2014.11.002.

Eckles, Dean, René F. Kizilcec, and Eytan Bakshy. 2016. "Estimating Peer Effects in Networks with Peer Encouragement Designs." *Proceedings of the National Academy of Sciences of the USA* 113 (27): 7316–22. doi:10.1073/pnas.1511201113.

Edelman, Benjamin G., Michael Luca, and Dan Svirsky. 2016. "Racial Discrimination in the Sharing Economy: Evidence from a Field Experiment." SSRN Scholarly Paper ID 2701902. Rochester, NY: Social Science Research Network. http://papers.ssrn.com/abstract=2701902.

Efrati, Amir. 2016. "Facebook Struggles to Stop Decline in Original Sharing." *The Information.* https://www.theinformation.com/facebook-struggles-to-stop-decline-in-original-sharing.

Einav, Liran, and Jonathan Levin. 2014. "Economics in the Age of Big Data." *Science* 346 (6210): 1243089. doi:10.1126/science.1243089.

Einav, Liran, Theresa Kuchler, Jonathan Levin, and Neel Sundaresan. 2015. "Assessing Sale Strategies in Online Markets Using Matched Listings." *American Economic Journal: Microeconomics* 7 (2): 215–47. doi:10.1257/mic.20130046.

Ekstrand, Michael D., Daniel Kluver, F. Maxwell Harper, and Joseph A. Konstan. 2015. "Letting Users Choose Recommender Algorithms: An Experimental Study." In *Proceedings of the 9th ACM Conference on Recommender Systems*, 11–18. RecSys '15. New York, NY, USA: ACM. doi:10.1145/2792838.2800195.

Elmagarmid, Ahmed K., Panagiotis G. Ipeirotis, and Vassilios S. Verykios. 2007. "Duplicate Record Detection: A Survey." *IEEE Transactions on Knowledge and Data Engineering* 19 (1): 1–16. doi:10.1109/TKDE.2007.250581.

Emanuel, Ezekiel J., Christine C. Grady, Robert A. Crouch, Reidar K. Lie, Franklin G. Miller, and David D. Wendler, eds. 2008. *The Oxford Textbook of Clinical Research Ethics.* Oxford: Oxford University Press.

Emanuel, Ezekiel J., David Wendler, and Christine Grady. 2000. "What Makes Clinical Research Ethical?" *Journal of the American Medical Association* 283 (20): 2701–11. doi:10.1001/jama.283.20.2701.

Enserink, Martin, and Gilbert Chin. 2015. "The End of Privacy." *Science* 347 (6221): 490–91. doi:10.1126/science.347.6221.490.

Epstein, Steven. 2009. *Inclusion: The Politics of Difference in Medical Research.* Chicago: University of Chicago Press.

Eriksson, Jakob, Lewis Girod, Bret Hull, Ryan Newton, Samuel Madden, and Hari Balakrishnan. 2008. "The Pothole Patrol: Using a Mobile Sensor Network for Road Surface Monitoring." In *Proceedings of the 6th International Conference on Mobile Systems, Applications, and Services*, 29–39. MobiSys '08. New York: ACM. doi:10.1145/1378600.1378605.

Evans, Barbara J. 2011. "Much Ado About Data Ownership." *Harvard Journal of Law and Technology* 25. http://jolt.law.harvard.edu/articles/pdf/v25/25HarvJLTech69.pdf.

———. 2013. "Why the Common Rule Is Hard to Amend." SSRN Scholarly Paper ID 2183701. Rochester, NY: Social Science Research Network. http://papers.ssrn.com/abstract=2183701.

Eyal, Nir. 2012. "Informed Consent." In *The Stanford Encyclopedia of Philosophy*, edited by Edward N. Zalta, Fall 2012. http://plato.stanford.edu/archives/fall2012/entries/informed-consent/.

Falk, Armin, and James J. Heckman. 2009. "Lab Experiments Are a Major Source of Knowledge in the Social Sciences." *Science* 326 (5952): 535–38. doi:10.1126/science.1168244.

Farber, Henry S. 2015. "Why You Can't Find a Taxi in the Rain and Other Labor Supply Lessons from Cab Drivers." *Quarterly Journal of Economics* 130 (4): 1975–2026. doi:10.1093/qje/qjv026.

Fellegi, Ivan P., and Alan B. Sunter. 1969. "A Theory for Record Linkage." *Journal of the American Statistical Association* 64 (328): 1183–1210. doi:10.2307/2286061.

Felstiner, Alek. 2011. "Working the Crowd: Employment and Labor Law in the Crowdsourcing Industry." *Berkeley Journal of Employment and Labor Law* 32 (1): 143–203. http://www.jstor.org/stable/24052509.

Ferrara, Emilio, Onur Varol, Clayton Davis, Filippo Menczer, and Alessandro Flammini. 2016. "The Rise of Social Bots." *Communications of the ACM* 59 (7): 96–104. doi:10.1145/2818717.

Ferraro, Paul J., Juan Jose Miranda, and Michael K. Price. 2011. "The Persistence of Treatment Effects with Norm-Based Policy Instruments: Evidence from a Randomized Environmental Policy Experiment." *American Economic Review (Papers and Proceedings of the 123rd Annual Meeting of the American Economic Association)* 101 (3): 318–22. http://www.jstor.org/stable/29783762.

Feuerverger, Andrey, Yu He, and Shashi Khatri. 2012. "Statistical Significance of the Netflix Challenge." *Statistical Science* 27 (2): 202–31. http://www.jstor.org/stable/41714795.

Fienberg, Stephen E. 1971. "Randomization and Social Affairs: The 1970 Draft Lottery." *Science* 171 (3968): 255–61. doi:10.1126/science.171.3968.255.

Fink, Daniel, Wesley M. Hochachka, Benjamin Zuckerberg, David W. Winkler, Ben Shaby, M. Arthur Munson, Giles Hooker, Mirek Riedewald, Daniel Sheldon, and Steve Kelling. 2010. "Spatiotemporal Exploratory Models for Broad-Scale Survey Data." *Ecological Applications* 20 (8): 2131–47. doi:10.1890/09-1340.1.

Fink, Günther, Margaret McConnell, and Sebastian Vollmer. 2014. "Testing for Heterogeneous Treatment Effects in Experimental Data: False Discovery Risks and Correction Procedures." *Journal of Development Effectiveness* 6 (1): 44–57. doi:10.1080/19439342.2013.875054.

Finn, P., and M. Jakobsson. 2007. "Designing Ethical Phishing Experiments." *IEEE Technology and Society Magazine* 26 (1): 46–58. doi:10.1109/MTAS.2007.335565.

Fischer, Claude S. 2011. *Still Connected: Family and Friends in America Since 1970*. New York: Russell Sage Foundation.

Fiske, Susan T., and Robert M. Hauser. 2014. "Protecting Human Research Participants in the Age of Big Data." *Proceedings of the National Academy of Sciences of the USA* 111 (38): 13675–76. doi:10.1073/pnas.1414626111.

Fitzpatrick, J. W., F. B. Gill, M. Powers, and K. V. Rosenberg. 2002. "Introducing eBird: The Union of Passion and Purpose." *North American Birds* 56: 11–13.

Flick, Catherine. 2016. "Informed Consent and the Facebook Emotional Manipulation Study." *Research Ethics*12 (1) 14–28. doi:10.1177/1747016115599568.

Fortson, Lucy, Karen Masters, Robert Nichol, Kirk Borne, Edd Edmondson, Chris Lintott, Jordan Raddick, Kevin Schawinski, and John Wallin. 2011. "Galaxy Zoo: Morphological Classification and Citizen Science." *ArXiv:1104.5513 [astro-ph.IM]*, April. http://arxiv.org/abs/1104.5513.

Foucault, Michel. 1995. *Discipline & Punish: The Birth of the Prison*, translated by Alan Sheridan. New York: Vintage Books.

Fox, John, and Sanford Weisberg. 2011. *An R Companion to Applied Regression*, 2nd ed. Thousand Oaks, CA: SAGE. http://socserv.socsci.mcmaster.ca/jfox/Books/Companion.

Frangakis, Constantine E., and Donald B. Rubin. 2002. "Principal Stratification in Causal Inference." *Biometrics* 58 (1): 21–29. doi:10.1111/j.0006-341X.2002.00021.x.

Frank, Robert H. 2016. *Success and Luck: Good Fortune and the Myth of Meritocracy*. Princeton, NJ: Princeton University Press.

Frank, Robert H., and Philip J. Cook. 1996. *The Winner-Take-All Society: Why the Few at the Top Get So Much More Than the Rest of Us*, reprint ed. New York: Penguin Books.

Freedman, David A. 1991. "Statistical Models and Shoe Leather." *Sociological Methodology* 21: 291–313. doi:10.2307/270939.

———. 2008. "On Regression Adjustments to Experimental Data." *Advances in Applied Mathematics* 40 (2): 180–93. doi:10.1016/j.aam.2006.12.003.

Freedman, David, Robert Pisani, and Roger Purves. 2007. *Statistics*, 4th ed. New York: W. W. Norton.

Frison, Lars, and Stuart J. Pocock. 1992. "Repeated Measures in Clinical Trials: Analysis Using Mean Summary Statistics and Its Implications for Design." *Statistics in Medicine* 11 (13): 1685–1704. doi:10.1002/sim.4780111304.

Galaxy Zoo. 2016. "Exclusive Interview with Our Recent Citizen Science Co-Authors." *Galaxy Zoo*. https://blog.galaxyzoo.org/2016/04/18/exclusive-interview-with-our-recent-citizen-science-co-authors/.

Garbarski, Dana, Nora Cate Schaeffer, and Jennifer Dykema. 2016. "Interviewing Practices, Conversational Practices, and Rapport Responsiveness and Engagement in the Standardized Survey Interview." *Sociological Methodology* 46 (1): 1–38. doi:10.1177/0081175016637890.

Gardner, Howard. 2011. *Frames of Mind: The Theory of Multiple Intelligences.* New York: Basic Books.

Gayo-Avello, Daniel. 2011. "Don't Turn Social Media into Another 'Literary Digest' Poll." *Communications of the ACM* 54 (10): 121–28. doi:10.1145/2001269.2001297.

———. 2013. "A Meta-Analysis of State-of-the-Art Electoral Prediction From Twitter Data." *Social Science Computer Review* 31 (6): 649–79. doi:10.1177/0894439313493979.

Gee, Laura K. 2015. "The More You Know: Information Effects in Job Application Rates by Gender in a Large Field Experiment." SSRN Scholarly Paper ID 2612979. Rochester, NY: Social Science Research Network. http://papers.ssrn.com/abstract=2612979.

Geiger, R. Stuart. 2014. "Bots, Bespoke, Code and the Materiality of Software Platforms." *Information, Communication & Society* 17 (3): 342–56. doi:10.1080/1369118X.2013.873069.

Gelman, Andrew. 2007. "Struggles with Survey Weighting and Regression Modeling." *Statistical Science* 22 (2): 153–64. doi:10.1214/088342306000000691.

———. 2010. "63,000 Worth of Abusive Research … or Just a Really Stupid Waste of Time?" *Statistical Modeling, Causal Inference, and Social Science.* http://andrewgelman.com/2010/05/06/63000_worth_of/.

———. 2013. "Preregistration of Studies and Mock Reports." *Political Analysis* 21 (1): 40–41. doi:10.1093/pan/mps032.

Gelman, Andrew, and John Carlin. 2014. "Beyond Power Calculations Assessing Type S (Sign) and Type M (Magnitude) Errors." *Perspectives on Psychological Science* 9 (6): 641–51. doi:10.1177/1745691614551642.

Gelman, Andrew, and John B. Carlin. 2002. "Poststratification and Weighting Adjustments." In *Survey Nonresponse*, edited by Robert M. Groves, Don A. Dillman, John L. Eltinge, and Roderick J.A. Little, 289–302. Hoboken, NJ: Wiley.

Gerber, Alan S., and Donald P. Green. 2000. "The Effects of Canvassing, Telephone Calls, and Direct Mail on Voter Turnout: A Field Experiment." *American Political Science Review* 94 (3): 653–63. doi:10.2307/2585837.

———. 2005. "Correction to Gerber and Green (2000), Replication of Disputed Findings, and Reply to Imai (2005)." *American Political Science Review* 99 (2): 301–13. doi:10.1017/S000305540505166X.

———. 2012. *Field Experiments: Design, Analysis, and Interpretation.* New York: W. W. Norton.

Gerber, Alan S., Kevin Arceneaux, Cheryl Boudreau, Conor Dowling, and D. Sunshine Hillygus. 2015. "Reporting Balance Tables, Response Rates and Manipulation Checks in Experimental Research: A Reply from the Committee That Prepared the Reporting Guidelines." *Journal of Experimental Political Science* 2 (2): 216–29. doi:10.1017/XPS.2015.20.

Gerber, Alan S., Donald P. Green, and Christopher W. Larimer. 2008. "Social Pressure and Voter Turnout: Evidence from a Large-Scale Field Experiment." *American Political Science Review* 102 (1): 33–48. doi:10.1017/S000305540808009X.

Gerber, Alan, Kevin Arceneaux, Cheryl Boudreau, Conor Dowling, Sunshine Hillygus, Thomas Palfrey, Daniel R. Biggers, and David J. Hendry. 2014. "Reporting Guidelines for Experimental Research: A Report from the Experimental Research Section Standards Committee." *Journal of Experimental Political Science* 1 (1): 81–98. doi:10.1017/xps.2014.11.

Gilbert, Sarah. 2015. "Participants in the Crowd: Deliberations on the Ethical Use of Crowdsourcing in Research." In *CSCW 15 Workshop on Ethics at the 2015 Conference on Computer Supported Cooperative Work.* https://cscwethics2015.files.wordpress.com/2015/02/gilbert.pdf.

Gill, Michael, and Arthur Spirling. 2015. "Estimating the Severity of the WikiLeaks U.S. Diplomatic Cables Disclosure." *Political Analysis* 23 (2): 299–305. doi:10.1093/pan/mpv005.

Gillon, Raanan. 2015. "Defending the Four Principles Approach as a Good Basis for Good Medical Practice and Therefore for Good Medical Ethics." *Journal of Medical Ethics* 41 (1): 111–16. doi:10.1136/medethics-2014-102282.

Ginsberg, Jeremy, Matthew H. Mohebbi, Rajan S. Patel, Lynnette Brammer, Mark S. Smolinski, and Larry Brilliant. 2009. "Detecting Influenza Epidemics Using Search Engine Query Data." *Nature* 457 (7232): 1012–14. doi:10.1038/nature07634.

Glaeser, Edward L., Andrew Hillis, Scott Duke Kominers, and Michael Luca. 2016. "Crowdsourcing City Government: Using Tournaments to Improve Inspection Accuracy." Working Paper 22124. National Bureau of Economic Research. http://www.nber.org/papers/w22124.

Glaser, Barney, and Anselm Strauss. 1967. *The Discovery of Grounded Theory: Strategies for Qualitative Research.* New Brunswick, NJ: Aldine Transaction.

Gleick, James. 2011. *The Information: A History, a Theory, a Flood.* New York: Pantheon.

Glennerster, Rachel, and Kudzai Takavarasha. 2013. *Running Randomized Evaluations: A Practical Guide.* Princeton, NJ: Princeton University Press.

Goel, Sharad, Jake M. Hofman, Sébastien Lahaie, David M. Pennock, and Duncan J. Watts. 2010. "Predicting Consumer Behavior with Web Search." *Proceedings of the National Academy of Sciences of the USA* 107 (41): 17486–90. doi:10.1073/pnas.1005962107.

Goel, Sharad, Winter Mason, and Duncan J. Watts. 2010. "Real and Perceived Attitude Agreement in Social Networks." *Journal of Personality and Social Psychology* 99 (4): 611–21. doi:10.1037/a0020697.

Goel, Sharad, Adam Obeng, and David Rothschild. 2016. "Non-Representative Surveys: Fast, Cheap, and Mostly Accurate." *Working Paper.* https://5harad.com/papers/dirtysurveys.pdf.

Goldberg, Amir. 2015. "In Defense of Forensic Social Science." *Big Data & Society* 2 (2): doi:10.1177/2053951715601145.

Golder, Scott A., and Michael W. Macy. 2011. "Diurnal and Seasonal Mood Vary with Work, Sleep, and Daylength across Diverse Cultures." *Science* 333 (6051): 1878–81. doi:10.1126/science.1202775.

———. 2014. "Digital Footprints: Opportunities and Challenges for Online Social Research." *Annual Review of Sociology* 40 (1): 129–52. doi:10.1146/annurev-soc-071913-043145.

Goldman, William. 1989. *Adventures in the Screen Trade: A Personal View of Hollywood and Screenwriting,* reissue ed. New York: Grand Central Publishing.

Goldstein, Daniel G., R. Preston McAfee, and Siddharth Suri. 2013. "The Cost of Annoying Ads." In *Proceedings of the 22nd International Conference on World Wide Web,* 459–70. WWW '13. Republic and Canton of Geneva, Switzerland: International World Wide Web Conferences Steering Committee. doi:10.1145/2488388.2488429.

Goldstein, Daniel G., Siddharth Suri, R. Preston McAfee, Matthew Ekstrand-Abueg, and Fernando Diaz. 2014. "The Economic and Cognitive Costs of Annoying Display Advertisements." *Journal of Marketing Research* 51 (6): 742–52. doi:10.1509/jmr.13.0439.

Goldstone, Robert L., and Gary Lupyan. 2016. "Discovering Psychological Principles by Mining Naturally Occurring Data Sets." *Topics in Cognitive Science* 8 (3): 548–68. doi:10.1111/tops.12212.

Goldthorpe, John H. 1991. "The Uses of History in Sociology: Reflections on Some Recent Tendencies." *British Journal of Sociology* 42 (2): 211–30. doi:10.2307/590368.

Goroff, Daniel L. 2015. "Balancing Privacy Versus Accuracy in Research Protocols." *Science* 347 (6221): 479–80. doi:10.1126/science.aaa3483.

Gowers, Timothy, and Michael Nielsen. 2009. "Massively Collaborative Mathematics." *Nature* 461 (7266): 879–81. doi:10.1038/461879a.

Gray, Mary L., Siddharth Suri, Syed Shoaib Ali, and Deepti Kulkarni. 2016. "The Crowd Is a Collaborative Network." In *Proceedings of the 19th ACM Conference on Computer-Supported Cooperative Work & Social Computing,* 134–47. CSCW '16. New York: ACM. doi:10.1145/2818048.2819942.

Grayson, Richard. 2016. "A Life in the Trenches? The Use of Operation War Diary and Crowdsourcing Methods to Provide an Understanding of the British Army's Day-to-Day Life on the Western Front." *British Journal for Military History* 2 (2). http://bjmh.org.uk/index.php/bjmh/article/view/96.

Green, Donald P., and Alan S. Gerber. 2003. "The Underprovision of Experiments in Political Science." *Annals of the American Academy of Political and Social Science* 589 (1): 94–112. doi:10.1177/0002716203254763.

———. 2015. *Get Out the Vote: How to Increase Voter Turnout*, 3rd ed. Washington, DC: Brookings Institution Press.

Green, Donald P., and Holger L. Kern. 2012. "Modeling Heterogeneous Treatment Effects in Survey Experiments with Bayesian Additive Regression Trees." *Public Opinion Quarterly* 76 (3): 491–511. doi:10.1093/poq/nfs036.

Green, Donald P., Brian R. Calfano, and Peter M. Aronow. 2014. "Field Experimental Designs for the Study of Media Effects." *Political Communication* 31 (1): 168–80. doi:10.1080/10584609.2013. 828142.

Greenwald, Anthony G. 1976. "Within-Subjects Designs: To Use or Not to Use?" *Psychological Bulletin* 83 (2): 314–20. doi:10.1037/0033-2909.83.2.314.

Greenwood, Jeremy J. D. 2007. "Citizens, Science and Bird Conservation." *Journal of Ornithology* 148 (S1): 77–124. doi:10.1007/s10336-007-0239-9.

Grimmelmann, James. 2015. "The Law and Ethics of Experiments on Social Media Users." SSRN Scholarly Paper ID 2604168. Rochester, NY: Social Science Research Network. http://papers. ssrn.com/abstract=2604776.

Grimmer, Justin, and Brandon M. Stewart. 2013. "Text as Data: The Promise and Pitfalls of Automatic Content Analysis Methods for Political Texts." *Political Analysis* 21 (3): 267–97. doi:10.1093/ pan/mps028.

Grimmer, Justin, Solomon Messing, and Sean J. Westwood. 2014. "Estimating Heterogeneous Treatment Effects and the Effects of Heterogeneous Treatments with Ensemble Methods." Working paper, Stanford University. http://stanford.edu/ jgrimmer/het.pdf.

Groen, Jeffrey A. 2012. "Sources of Error in Survey and Administrative Data: The Importance of Reporting Procedures." *Journal of Official Statistics* 28 (2). http://www.jos.nu/Articles/ abstract.asp?article=282173.

Groves, Robert M. 2004. *Survey Errors and Survey Costs*. Hoboken, NJ: Wiley.

———. 2006. "Nonresponse Rates and Nonresponse Bias in Household Surveys." *Public Opinion Quarterly* 70 (5): 646–75. doi:10.1093/poq/nfl033.

———. 2011. "Three Eras of Survey Research." *Public Opinion Quarterly* 75 (5): 861–71. doi:10.1093/ poq/nfr057.

Groves, Robert M., and Robert Louis Kahn. 1979. *Surveys by Telephone: A National Comparison with Personal Interviews*. New York: Academic Press.

Groves, Robert M., and Lars Lyberg. 2010. "Total Survey Error: Past, Present, and Future." *Public Opinion Quarterly* 74 (5): 849–79. doi:10.1093/poq/nfq065.

Groves, Robert M., Floyd J. Fowler Jr., Mick P. Couper, James M. Lepkowski, Eleanor Singer, and Roger Tourangeau. 2009. *Survey Methodology*. Hoboken, NJ: Wiley.

Grusky, David B., Timothy M. Smeeding, and C. Matthew Snipp. 2015. "A New Infrastructure for Monitoring Social Mobility in the United States." *Annals of the American Academy of Political and Social Science* 657 (1): 63–82. doi:10.1177/0002716214549941.

Gueron, Judith M. 2002. "The Politics of Random Assignment: Implementing Studies and Affecting Policy." In *Evidence Matters: Randomized Trials in Education Research*, edited by Frederick F. Mosteller and Robert F. Boruch, 15–49. Washington, DC: Brookings Institution Press.

Hafner, Katie. 2006. "Researchers Yearn to Use AOL Logs, but They Hesitate." *New York Times*, August. http://www.nytimes.com/2006/08/23/technology/23search.html.

Halevy, Alon, Peter Norvig, and Fernando Pereira. 2009. "The Unreasonable Effectiveness of Data." *IEEE Intelligent Systems* 24 (2): 8–12. doi:10.1109/MIS.2009.36.

Halpern, Scott D, Rachel Kohn, Aaron Dornbrand-Lo, Thomas Metkus, David A Asch, and Kevin G Volpp. 2011. "Lottery-Based Versus Fixed Incentives to Increase Clinicians' Response to Surveys." *Health Services Research* 46 (5): 1663–74. doi:10.1111/j.1475-6773.2011.01264.x.

Hand, Eric. 2010. "Citizen Science: People Power." *Nature News* 466 (7307): 685–87. doi:10.1038/466685a.

Hanmer, Michael J., Antoine J. Banks, and Ismail K. White. 2014. "Experiments to Reduce the Over-Reporting of Voting: A Pipeline to the Truth." *Political Analysis* 22 (1): 130–41. doi:10.1093/ pan/mpt027.

Hansen, Ben B., and Jake Bowers. 2008. "Covariate Balance in Simple, Stratified and Clustered Comparative Studies." *Statistical Science* 23 (2): 219–36. doi:10.1214/08-STS254.

Hargittai, Eszter. 2015. "Is Bigger Always Better? Potential Biases of Big Data Derived from Social Network Sites." *Annals of the American Academy of Political and Social Science* 659 (1): 63–76. doi:10.1177/0002716215570866.

Hargittai, Eszter, and Christian Sandvig, eds. 2015. *Digital Research Confidential: The Secrets of Studying Behavior Online*. Cambridge, MA: MIT Press.

Harper, F. Maxwell, and Joseph A. Konstan. 2015. "The MovieLens Datasets: History and Context." *ACM Transactions on Interactive Intelligent Systems* 5 (4): 19:1–19:19. doi:10.1145/2827872.

Harper, F. Maxwell, Shilad Sen, and Dan Frankowski. 2007. "Supporting Social Recommendations with Activity-Balanced Clustering." In *Proceedings of the 2007 ACM Conference on Recommender Systems*, 165–68. RecSys '07. New York: ACM. doi:10.1145/1297231.1297262.

Harrison, G. W, and J. A List. 2004. "Field Experiments." *Journal of Economic Literature* 42 (4): 1009–55.

Hart, Nicky. 1994. "John Goldthorpe and the Relics of Sociology." *British Journal of Sociology* 45 (1): 21–30. doi:10.2307/591522.

Hastie, Trevor, Robert Tibshirani, and Jerome Friedman. 2009. *The Elements of Statistical Learning: Data Mining, Inference, and Prediction*. 2nd ed. New York: Springer.

Hauge, Michelle V., Mark D. Stevenson, D. Kim Rossmo, and Steven C. Le Comber. 2016. "Tagging Banksy: Using Geographic Profiling to Investigate a Modern Art Mystery." *Journal of Spatial Science* 61 (1): 185–90. doi:10.1080/14498596.2016.1138246.

Hauser, David J., and Norbert Schwarz. 2015a. "Attentive Turkers: MTurk Participants Perform Better on Online Attention Checks Than Do Subject Pool Participants." *Behavior Research Methods* 48 (1): 400–7. doi:10.3758/s13428-015-0578-z.

———. 2015b. "Its a Trap! Instructional Manipulation Checks Prompt Systematic Thinking on Tricky Tasks." *SAGE Open* 5 (2): 2158244015584617. doi:10.1177/2158244015584617.

Hausman, Jerry. 2012. "Contingent Valuation: From Dubious to Hopeless." *Journal of Economic Perspectives* 26 (4): 43–56. doi:10.1257/jep.26.4.43.

Hawley, Steven A. 2012. "Abundances in Green Pea Star-Forming Galaxies." *Publications of the Astronomical Society of the Pacific* 124 (911): 21–35. doi:10.1086/663866.

Healy, Andrew, and Neil Malhotra. 2013. "Retrospective Voting Reconsidered." *Annual Review of Political Science* 16 (1): 285–306. doi:10.1146/annurev-polisci-032211-212920.

Healy, Kieran. 2015. "The Performativity of Networks." *European Journal of Sociology/Archives Européennes de Sociologie* 56 (2): 175–205. doi:10.1017/S0003975615000107.

Heckman, James J., and Jeffrey A. Smith. 1995. "Assessing the Case for Social Experiments." *Journal of Economic Perspectives* 9 (2): 85–110. http://www.jstor.org/stable/2138168.

Heckman, James J., and Sergio Urzúa. 2010. "Comparing IV With Structural Models: What Simple IV Can and Cannot Identify." *Journal of Econometrics* 156 (1): 27–37. doi:10.1016/j.jeconom.2009.09.006.

Hedström, Peter. 2006. "Experimental Macro Sociology: Predicting the Next Best Seller." *Science* 311 (5762): 786–87. doi:10.1126/science.1124707.

Hedström, Peter, and Petri Ylikoski. 2010. "Causal Mechanisms in the Social Sciences." *Annual Review of Sociology* 36 (1): 49–67. doi:10.1146/annurev.soc.012809.102632.

Heller, Jean. 1972. "Syphilis Victims in U.S. Study Went Untreated for 40 Years." *New York Times*, July, pp. 1 and 8.

Henrich, Joseph, Steven J. Heine, and Ara Norenzayan. 2010a. "The Weirdest People in the World?" *Behavioral and Brain Sciences* 33 (2–3): 61–83. doi:10.1017/S0140525X0999152X.

———. 2010b. "Most People Are Not WEIRD." *Nature* 466 (7302): 29–29. doi:10.1038/466029a.

Hernandez, Daniela, and Deepa Seetharaman. 2016. "Facebook Offers Details on How It Handles Research." *Wall Street Journal*, June. http://www.wsj.com/articles/facebook-offers-details-how-it-handles-research-1465930152.

Hernán, Miguel A., and James M. Robins. 2016. "Using Big Data to Emulate a Target Trial When a Randomized Trial Is Not Available." *American Journal of Epidemiology* 183 (8): 758–64. doi:10.1093/aje/kwv254.

Hersh, Eitan D. 2013. "Long-Term Effect of September 11 on the Political Behavior of Victims Families and Neighbors." *Proceedings of the National Academy of Sciences of the USA* 110 (52): 20959–63. doi:10.1073/pnas.1315043110.

Higgins, Michael J., Fredrik Sävje, and Jasjeet S. Sekhon. 2016. "Improving Massive Experiments with Threshold Blocking." *Proceedings of the National Academy of Sciences of the USA* 113 (27): 7369–76. doi:10.1073/pnas.1510504113.

Hilbert, Martin, and Priscila López. 2011. "The World's Technological Capacity to Store, Communicate, and Compute Information." *Science* 332 (6025): 60–65. doi:10.1126/science.1200970.

Ho, Daniel E., Kosuke Imai, Gary King, and Elizabeth A. Stuart. 2007. "Matching as Nonparametric Preprocessing for Reducing Model Dependence in Parametric Causal Inference." *Political Analysis* 15 (3): 199–236. doi:10.1093/pan/mpl013.

Hogan, Bernie, and Brent Berry. 2011. "Racial and Ethnic Biases in Rental Housing: An Audit Study of Online Apartment Listings." *City & Community* 10 (4): 351–72. doi:10.1111/j.1540-6040.2011.01376.x.

Holland, Paul W. 1986. "Statistics and Causal Inference." *Journal of the American Statistical Association* 81 (396): 945. doi:10.2307/2289064.

Holm, S. 1995. "Not Just Autonomy–the Principles of American Biomedical Ethics." *Journal of Medical Ethics* 21 (6): 332–38. doi:10.1136/jme.21.6.332.

Holmes, David S. 1976a. "Debriefing After Psychological Experiments: I. Effectiveness of Postdeception Dehoaxing." *American Psychologist* 31 (12): 858–67. doi:10.1037/0003-066X.31.12.858.

———. 1976b. "Debriefing After Psychological Experiments: II. Effectiveness of Postexperimental Desensitizing." *American Psychologist* 31 (12): 868–75. doi:10.1037/0003-066X.31.12.868.

Holt, D., and T. M. F. Smith. 1979. "Post Stratification." *Journal of the Royal Statistical Society. Series A (General)* 142 (1): 33–46. doi:10.2307/2344652.

Hong, Lu, and Scott E. Page. 2004. "Groups of Diverse Problem Solvers Can Outperform Groups of High-Ability Problem Solvers." *Proceedings of the National Academy of Sciences of the USA* 101 (46): 16385–9. doi:10.1073/pnas.0403723101.

Hoonaard, Will C. van den. 2011. *Seduction of Ethics: Transforming the Social Sciences*. Toronto: University of Toronto Press.

Hopkins, Daniel, and Gary King. 2010. "A Method of Automated Nonparametric Content Analysis for Social Science." *American Journal of Political Science* 54 (1): 229–47. doi:10.1111/j.1540-5907.2009.00428.x.

Horton, John J., and Prasanna Tambe. 2015. "Labor Economists Get Their Microscope: Big Data and Labor Market Analysis." *Big Data* 3 (3): 130–37. doi:10.1089/big.2015.0017.

Horton, John J., and Richard J. Zeckhauser. 2016. "The Causes of Peer Effects in Production: Evidence from a Series of Field Experiments." Working Paper 22386. National Bureau of Economic Research. http://www.nber.org/papers/w22386.

Horton, John J., David G. Rand, and Richard J. Zeckhauser. 2011. "The Online Laboratory: Conducting Experiments in a Real Labor Market." *Experimental Economics* 14 (3): 399–425. doi:10.1007/s10683-011-9273-9.

Horvitz, D. G., and D. J. Thompson. 1952. "A Generalization of Sampling Without Replacement from a Finite Universe." *Journal of the American Statistical Association* 47 (260): 663–85. doi:10.1080/01621459.1952.10483446.

Hout, Michael, and Thomas A. DiPrete. 2006. "What We Have Learned: RC28's Contributions to Knowledge About Social Stratification." *Research in Social Stratification and Mobility* 24 (1): 1–20. doi:10.1016/j.rssm.2005.10.001.

Howe, Jeff. 2009. *Crowdsourcing: Why the Power of the Crowd Is Driving the Future of Business*. New York: Crown Business.

Howison, James, Andrea Wiggins, and Kevin Crowston. 2011. "Validity Issues in the Use of Social Network Analysis with Digital Trace Data." *Journal of the Association for Information Systems* 12 (12). http://aisel.aisnet.org/jais/vol12/iss12/2.

Huber, Gregory A., and Celia Paris. 2013. "Assessing the Programmatic Equivalence Assumption in Question Wording Experiments Understanding Why Americans Like Assistance to the Poor More Than Welfare." *Public Opinion Quarterly* 77 (1): 385–97. doi:10.1093/poq/nfs054.

Huber, Gregory A., Seth J. Hill, and Gabriel S. Lenz. 2012. "Sources of Bias in Retrospective Decision Making: Experimental Evidence on Voters Limitations in Controlling Incumbents." *American Political Science Review* 106 (4): 720–41. doi:10.1017/S0003055412000391.

Huberman, Bernardo A. 2012. "Big Data Deserve a Bigger Audience." *Nature* 482 (7385): 308. doi:10.1038/482308d.

Huberty, Mark. 2015. "Can We Vote with Our Tweet? On the Perennial Difficulty of Election Forecasting with Social Media." *International Journal of Forecasting* 31 (3): 992–1007. doi:10.1016/j.ijforecast.2014.08.005.

Hudson, Kathy L., and Francis S. Collins. 2015. "Bringing the Common Rule into the 21st Century." *New England Journal of Medicine* 373 (24): 2293–6. doi:10.1056/NEJMp1512205.

Hulth, Anette, Gustaf Rydevik, and Annika Linde. 2009. "Web Queries as a Source for Syndromic Surveillance." *PLoS ONE* 4 (2): e4378. doi:10.1371/journal.pone.0004378.

Humphreys, Macartan. 2015. "Reflections on the Ethics of Social Experimentation." *Journal of Globalization and Development* 6 (1): 87–112. doi:10.1515/jgd-2014-0016.

Humphreys, Macartan, and Jeremy M. Weinstein. 2009. "Field Experiments and the Political Economy of Development." *Annual Review of Political Science* 12 (1): 367–78. doi:10.1146/annurev.polisci.12.060107.155922.

Humphreys, Macartan, Raul Sanchez de la Sierra, and Peter van der Windt. 2013. "Fishing, Commitment, and Communication: A Proposal for Comprehensive Nonbinding Research Registration." *Political Analysis* 21 (1): 1–20. doi:10.1093/pan/mps021.

Hunter, David, and Nicholas Evans. 2016. "Facebook Emotional Contagion Experiment Controversy." *Research Ethics* 12 (1): 2–3. doi:10.1177/1747016115626341.

Hurlbert, Allen H., and Zhongfei Liang. 2012. "Spatiotemporal Variation in Avian Migration Phenology: Citizen Science Reveals Effects of Climate Change." *PLoS ONE* 7 (2): e31662. doi:10.1371/journal.pone.0031662.

Hutton, Luke, and Tristan Henderson. 2015. "'I Didn't Sign Up for This!': Informed Consent in Social Network Research." In *Ninth International AAAI Conference on Web and Social Media.* http://www.aaai.org/ocs/index.php/ICWSM/ICWSM15/paper/view/10493.

Igo, Sarah E. 2008. *The Averaged American: Surveys, Citizens, and the Making of a Mass Public.* Cambridge, MA: Harvard University Press.

Imai, Kosuke. 2005. "Do Get-Out-the-Vote Calls Reduce Turnout? The Importance of Statistical Methods for Field Experiments." *American Political Science Review* 99 (2): 283–300. doi:10.1017/S0003055405051658.

Imai, Kosuke, and Marc Ratkovic. 2013. "Estimating Treatment Effect Heterogeneity in Randomized Program Evaluation." *Annals of Applied Statistics* 7 (1): 443–70. doi:10.1214/12-AOAS593.

Imai, Kosuke, and Teppei Yamamoto. 2013. "Identification and Sensitivity Analysis for Multiple Causal Mechanisms: Revisiting Evidence from Framing Experiments." *Political Analysis* 21 (2): 141–71. doi:10.1093/pan/mps040.

Imai, Kosuke, Luke Keele, Dustin Tingley, and Teppei Yamamoto. 2011. "Unpacking the Black Box of Causality: Learning About Causal Mechanisms from Experimental and Observational Studies." *American Political Science Review* 105 (4): 765–89. doi:10.1017/S0003055411000414.

Imai, Kosuke, Dustin Tingley, and Teppei Yamamoto. 2013. "Experimental Designs for Identifying Causal Mechanisms." *Journal of the Royal Statistical Society: Series A (Statistics in Society)* 176 (1): 5–51. doi:10.1111/j.1467-985X.2012.01032.x.

Imbens, Guido W. 2010. "Better LATE Than Nothing: Some Comments on Deaton (2009) and Heckman and Urzua (2009)." *Journal of Economic Literature* 48 (2): 399–423. doi:10.1257/jel.48.2.399.

Imbens, Guido W., and Paul R. Rosenbaum. 2005. "Robust, Accurate Confidence Intervals with a Weak Instrument: Quarter of Birth and Education." *Journal of the Royal Statistical Society: Series A (Statistics in Society)* 168 (1): 109–26. doi:10.1111/j.1467-985X.2004.00339.x.

Imbens, Guido W., and Donald B. Rubin. 2015. *Causal Inference in Statistics, Social, and Biomedical Sciences.* Cambridge: Cambridge University Press.

Institute of Medicine and National Academy of Sciences and National Academy of Engineering. 2009. *On Being a Scientist: A Guide to Responsible Conduct in Research,* 3rd ed. Washington, DC: National Academies Press. http://dx.doi.org/10.17226/12192.

Issenberg, Sasha. 2012. *The Victory Lab: The Secret Science of Winning Campaigns.* New York: Broadway Books.

Izotov, Yuri I., Natalia G. Guseva, and Trinh X. Thuan. 2011. "Green Pea Galaxies and Cohorts: Luminous Compact Emission-Line Galaxies in the Sloan Digital Sky Survey." *Astrophysical Journal* 728 (2): 161. doi:10.1088/0004-637X/728/2/161.

Jackman, Molly, and Lauri Kanerva. 2016. "Evolving the IRB: Building Robust Review for Industry Research." *Washington and Lee Law Review Online* 72 (3): 442. http://scholarlycommons.law.wlu.edu/wlulr-online/vol72/iss3/8.

Jackson, Michelle, and D. R. Cox. 2013. "The Principles of Experimental Design and Their Application in Sociology." *Annual Review of Sociology* 39 (1): 27–49. doi:10.1146/annurev-soc-071811-145443.

Jagatic, Tom N., Nathaniel A. Johnson, Markus Jakobsson, and Filippo Menczer. 2007. "Social Phishing." *Communications of the ACM* 50 (10): 94–100. doi:10.1145/1290958.1290968.

Jakobsson, Markus, and Jacob Ratkiewicz. 2006. "Designing Ethical Phishing Experiments: A Study of (ROT13) rOnl Query Features." In *Proceedings of the 15th International Conference on World Wide Web,* 513–22. WWW '06. New York: ACM. doi:10.1145/1135777.1135853.

James, Gareth, Daniela Witten, Trevor Hastie, and Robert Tibshirani. 2013. *An Introduction to Statistical Learning.* New York: Springer.

Japec, Lilli, Frauke Kreuter, Marcus Berg, Paul Biemer, Paul Decker, Cliff Lampe, Julia Lane, Cathy O'Neil, and Abe Usher. 2015. "Big Data in Survey Research AAPOR Task Force Report." *Public Opinion Quarterly* 79 (4): 839–80. doi:10.1093/poq/nfv039.

Jarmin, Ron S., and Amy B. O'Hara. 2016. "Big Data and the Transformation of Public Policy Analysis." *Journal of Policy Analysis and Management* 35 (3): 715–21. doi:10.1002/pam.21925.

Jaschik, Scott. 2017. "New 'Common Rule' for Research." *Inside Higher Ed,* January. https://www.insidehighered.com/news/2017/01/19/us-issues-final-version-common-rule-research-involving-humans.

Jensen, David D., Andrew S. Fast, Brian J. Taylor, and Marc E. Maier. 2008. "Automatic Identification of Quasi-Experimental Designs for Discovering Causal Knowledge." In *Proceedings of the 14th ACM SIGKDD International Conference on Knowledge Discovery and Data Mining,* 372–80. KDD '08. New York: ACM. doi:10.1145/1401890.1401938.

Jensen, Robert. 2007. "The Digital Provide: Information (Technology), Market Performance, and Welfare in the South Indian Fisheries Sector." *Quarterly Journal of Economics* 122 (3): 879–924. doi:10.1162/qjec.122.3.879.

Jerit, Jennifer, Jason Barabas, and Scott Clifford. 2013. "Comparing Contemporaneous Laboratory and Field Experiments on Media Effects." *Public Opinion Quarterly* 77 (1): 256–82. doi:10.1093/poq/nft005.

Jerolmack, Colin, and Shamus Khan. 2014. "Talk Is Cheap: Ethnography and the Attitudinal Fallacy." *Sociological Methods & Research* 43 (2): 178–209. doi:10.1177/0049124114523396.

Jones, Ben, and Nick Feamster. 2015. "Can Censorship Measurements Be Safe(R)?" In *Proceedings of the 14th ACM Workshop on Hot Topics in Networks,* 1:1–1:7. HotNets-XIV. New York: ACM. doi:10.1145/2834050.2834066.

Jones, Damon. 2015. "The Economics of Exclusion Restrictions in IV Models." Working Paper 21391. National Bureau of Economic Research. http://www.nber.org/papers/w21391.

Jones, James H. 1993. *Bad Blood: The Tuskegee Syphilis Experiment, New and Expanded Edition.* New York: Free Press.

———. 2011. "The Tuskegee Syphilis Experiment." In *The Oxford Textbook of Clinical Research Ethics,* edited by Ezekiel J. Emanuel, Christine C. Grady, Robert A. Crouch, Reidar K. Lie, Franklin G. Miller, and David D. Wendler. Oxford: Oxford University Press.

Jones, Jason J., Robert M. Bond, Christopher J. Fariss, Jaime E. Settle, Adam D. I. Kramer, Cameron Marlow, and James H. Fowler. 2013. "Yahtzee: An Anonymized Group Level Matching Procedure." *PLoS ONE* 8 (2): e55760. doi:10.1371/journal.pone.0055760.

Jones, Jason J., Robert M. Bond, Eytan Bakshy, Dean Eckles, and James H. Fowler. 2017. "Social Influence and Political Mobilization: Further Evidence from a Randomized Experiment in the 2012 U.S. Presidential Election." *PLoS ONE* 12 (4): e0173851. doi:10.1371/journal.pone.0173851.

Jordan, Jack. 2010. "Hedge Fund Will Track Twitter to Predict Stock Moves." *Bloomberg.com.* http://www.bloomberg.com/news/articles/2010-12-22/hedge-fund-will-track-twitter-to-predict-stockmarket-movements.

Judson, D. H. 2007. "Information Integration for Constructing Social Statistics: History, Theory and Ideas Towards a Research Programme." *Journal of the Royal Statistical Society: Series A (Statistics in Society)* 170 (2): 483–501. doi:10.1111/j.1467-985X.2007.00472.x.

Jungherr, Andreas. 2013. "Tweets and Votes, a Special Relationship: The 2009 Federal Election in Germany." In *Proceedings of the 2nd Workshop on Politics, Elections and Data,* 5–14. PLEAD '13. New York: ACM. doi:10.1145/2508436.2508437.

———. 2015. *Analyzing Political Communication with Digital Trace Data.* Contributions to Political Science. Cham: Springer.

Jungherr, Andreas, Pascal Jürgens, and Harald Schoen. 2012. "Why the Pirate Party Won the German Election of 2009 or The Trouble With Predictions: A Response to Tumasjan, A., Sprenger, T. O., Sander, P. G., & Welpe, I. M. Predicting Elections with Twitter: What 140 Characters Reveal About Political Sentiment." *Social Science Computer Review* 30 (2): 229–34. doi:10.1177/0894439311404119.

Kahn, Jeffrey P., Effy Vayena, and Anna C. Mastroianni. 2014. "Opinion: Learning as We Go: Lessons from the Publication of Facebook's Social-Computing Research." *Proceedings of the National Academy of Sciences of the USA* 111 (38): 13677–9. doi:10.1073/pnas.1416405111.

Kaler, Amy. 2004. "AIDS-Talk in Everyday Life: The Presence of HIV/AIDS in Men's Informal Conversation in Southern Malawi." *Social Science & Medicine* 59 (2): 285–97. doi:10.1016/j.socscimed.2003.10.023.

Kaler, Amy, Susan Cotts Watkins, and Nicole Angotti. 2015. "Making Meaning in the Time of AIDS: Longitudinal Narratives from the Malawi Journals Project." *African Journal of AIDS Research* 14 (4): 303–14. doi:10.2989/16085906.2015.1084342.

Kalton, Graham, and Ismael Flores-Cervantes. 2003. "Weighting Methods." *Journal of Official Statistics* 19 (2): 81–98. http://www.jos.nu/articles/abstract.asp?article=192081.

Kalton, Graham, and Howard Schuman. 1982. "The Effect of the Question on Survey Responses: A Review." *Journal of the Royal Statistical Society. Series A (General)* 145 (1): 42–73. doi:10.2307/2981421.

Katz, Jay, Alexander Morgan Capron, and Eleanor Swift Glass. 1972. *Experimentation with Human Beings: The Authority of the Investigator, Subject, Professions, and State in the Human Experimentation Process.* Russell Sage Foundation. http://www.jstor.org/stable/10.7758/9781610448345.

Keating, Conrad. 2014. *Smoking Kills: The Revolutionary Life of Richard Doll.* Oxford: Signal Books.

Keeter, Scott, Courtney Kennedy, Michael Dimock, Jonathan Best, and Peyton Craighill. 2006. "Gauging the Impact of Growing Nonresponse on Estimates from a National RDD Telephone Survey." *Public Opinion Quarterly* 70 (5): 759–79. doi:10.1093/poq/nfl035.

Keeter, Scott, Carolyn Miller, Andrew Kohut, Robert M. Groves, and Stanley Presser. 2000. "Consequences of Reducing Nonresponse in a National Telephone Survey." *Public Opinion Quarterly* 64 (2): 125–48. http://www.jstor.org/stable/3078812.

Keiding, Niels, and Thomas A. Louis. 2016. "Perils and Potentials of Self-Selected Entry to Epidemiological Studies and Surveys." *Journal of the Royal Statistical Society: Series A (Statistics in Society)* 179 (2): 319–76. doi:10.1111/rssa.12136.

Kelling, Steve, Daniel Fink, Frank A. La Sorte, Alison Johnston, Nicholas E. Bruns, and Wesley M. Hochachka. 2015. "Taking a Big Data Approach to Data Quality in a Citizen Science Project." *Ambio* 44 (Suppl. 4): 601–11. doi:10.1007/s13280-015-0710-4.

Kelling, Steve, Jeff Gerbracht, Daniel Fink, Carl Lagoze, Weng-Keen Wong, Jun Yu, Theodoros Damoulas, and Carla Gomes. 2012. "eBird: A Human/Computer Learning Network to Improve Biodiversity Conservation and Research." *AI Magazine* 34 (1): 10. http://www.aaai.org/ojs/index.php/aimagazine/article/view/2431.

Kelling, Steve, Alison Johnston, Wesley M. Hochachka, Marshall Iliff, Daniel Fink, Jeff Gerbracht, Carl Lagoze, et al. 2015. "Can Observation Skills of Citizen Scientists Be Estimated Using Species Accumulation Curves?" *PLoS ONE* 10 (10): e0139600. doi:10.1371/journal.pone.0139600.

Kent, DM, and RA Hayward. 2007. "Limitations of Applying Summary Results of Clinical Trials to Individual Patients: The Need for Risk Stratification." *JAMA* 298 (10): 1209–12. doi:10.1001/jama.298.10.1209.

Khan, Shamus, and Dana R. Fisher. 2013. *The Practice of Research: How Social Scientists Answer Their Questions.* New York: Oxford University Press.

Khatib, Firas, Seth Cooper, Michael D. Tyka, Kefan Xu, Ilya Makedon, Zoran Popović, David Baker, and Foldit Players. 2011. "Algorithm Discovery by Protein Folding Game Players." *Proceedings of the National Academy of Sciences of the USA* 108 (47): 18949–53. doi:10.1073/pnas.1115898108.

Kifner, John. 2001. "Scholar Sets Off Gastronomic False Alarm." *New York Times,* September. http://www.nytimes.com/2001/09/08/nyregion/scholar-sets-off-gastronomic-false-alarm.html.

King, Gary, and Ying Lu. 2008. "Verbal Autopsy Methods with Multiple Causes of Death." *Statistical Science* 23 (1): 78–91. doi:10.1214/07-STS247.

King, Gary, and Melissa Sands. 2015. "How Human Subjects Research Rules Mislead You and Your University, and What to Do About It." *Working Paper,* August. http://j.mp/1d2gSQQ.

King, Gary, Robert O. Keohane, and Sidney Verba. 1994. *Designing Social Inquiry: Scientific Inference in Qualitative Research.* Princeton, NJ: Princeton University Press.

King, Gary, Emmanuel Gakidou, Nirmala Ravishankar, Ryan T. Moore, Jason Lakin, Manett Vargas, Martha María Téllez-Rojo, Juan Eugenio Hernández Ávila, Mauricio Hernández Ávila, and Héctor Hernández Llamas. 2007. "A 'Politically Robust' Experimental Design for Public Policy Evaluation, with Application to the Mexican Universal Health Insurance Program." *Journal of Policy Analysis and Management* 26 (3): 479–506. doi:10.1002/pam.20279.

King, Gary, Jennifer Pan, and Margaret E. Roberts. 2013. "How Censorship in China Allows Government Criticism but Silences Collective Expression." *American Political Science Review* 107 (2): 326–43. doi:10.1017/S0003055413000014.

———. 2014. "Reverse-Engineering Censorship in China: Randomized Experimentation and Participant Observation." *Science* 345 (6199): 1251722. doi:10.1126/science.1251722.

———. 2017. "How the Chinese Government Fabricates Social Media Posts for Strategic Distraction, Not Engaged Argument." *American Political Science Review,* in press. http://j.mp/2ovks0q.

Kish, Leslie. 1979. "Samples and Censuses." *International Statistical Review* 47 (2): 99–109. doi:10.2307/1402563.

Kittur, Aniket, Jeffrey V. Nickerson, Michael Bernstein, Elizabeth Gerber, Aaron Shaw, John Zimmerman, Matt Lease, and John Horton. 2013. "The Future of Crowd Work." In *Proceedings of the 2013 Conference on Computer Supported Cooperative Work,* 1301–18. CSCW '13. New York: ACM. doi:10.1145/2441776.2441923.

Kleinberg, Jon, Jens Ludwig, Sendhil Mullainathan, and Ziad Obermeyer. 2015. "Prediction Policy Problems." *American Economic Review* 105 (5): 491–95. doi:10.1257/aer.p20151023.

Kleinsman, John, and Sue Buckley. 2015. "Facebook Study: A Little Bit Unethical But Worth It?" *Journal of Bioethical Inquiry* 12 (2): 179–82. doi:10.1007/s11673-015-9621-0.

Klitzman, Robert. 2015. *The Ethics Police? The Struggle to Make Human Research Safe.* Oxford: Oxford University Press.

Kloumann, Isabel Mette, Chenhao Tan, Jon Kleinberg, and Lillian Lee. 2016. "Internet Collaboration on Extremely Difficult Problems: Research versus Olympiad Questions on the Polymath Site." In *Proceedings of the 25th International Conference on World Wide Web*, 1283–92. WWW '16. International World Wide Web Conferences Steering Committee. doi:10.1145/2872427.2883023.

Kohavi, Ron, Alex Deng, Brian Frasca, Roger Longbotham, Toby Walker, and Ya Xu. 2012. "Trustworthy Online Controlled Experiments: Five Puzzling Outcomes Explained." In *Proceedings of the 18th ACM SIGKDD International Conference on Knowledge Discovery and Data Mining*, 786–94. KDD '12. New York: ACM. doi:10.1145/2339530.2339653.

Kohavi, Ron, Alex Deng, Brian Frasca, Toby Walker, Ya Xu, and Nils Pohlmann. 2013. "Online Controlled Experiments at Large Scale." In *Proceedings of the 19th ACM SIGKDD International Conference on Knowledge Discovery and Data Mining*, 1168–76. KDD '13. New York: ACM. doi:10.1145/2487575.2488217.

Kohli, Pushmeet, Michael Kearns, Yoram Bachrach, Ralf Herbrich, David Stillwell, and Thore Graepel. 2012. "Colonel Blotto on Facebook: The Effect of Social Relations on Strategic Interaction." In *Proceedings of the 4th Annual ACM Web Science Conference*, 141–50. WebSci '12. New York: ACM. doi:10.1145/2380718.2380738.

Kohut, Andrew, Scott Keeter, Carroll Doherty, Michael Dimock, and Leah Christian. 2012. "Assessing the Representativeness of Public Opinion Surveys." *Pew Research Center, Washington, DC.* http://www.people-press.org/files/legacy-pdf/Assessing%20the%20Representativeness%20of%20Public%20Opinion%20Surveys.pdf.

Konstan, Joseph A., and Yan Chen. 2007. "Online Field Experiments: Lessons from CommunityLab." In *Proceedings of Third International Conference on E-Social Science.* Citeseer. http://citeseerx.ist.psu.edu/viewdoc/download?doi=10.1.1.100.3925&rep=rep1&type=pdf.

Kosinski, Michal, Sandra C. Matz, Samuel D. Gosling, Vesselin Popov, and David Stillwell. 2015. "Facebook as a Research Tool for the Social Sciences: Opportunities, Challenges, Ethical Considerations, and Practical Guidelines." *American Psychologist* 70 (6): 543–56. doi:10.1037/a0039210.

Kosinski, Michal, David Stillwell, and Thore Graepel. 2013. "Private Traits and Attributes Are Predictable from Digital Records of Human Behavior." *Proceedings of the National Academy of Sciences of the USA*, March. doi:10.1073/pnas.1218772110.

Kossinets, Gueorgi, and Duncan J. Watts. 2006. "Empirical Analysis of an Evolving Social Network." *Science* 311 (5757): 88–90.

———. 2009. "Origins of Homophily in an Evolving Social Network." *American Journal of Sociology* 115 (2): 405–50. http://www.jstor.org/stable/10.1086/599247.

Krafft, Peter M., Michael Macy, and Alex "Sandy" Pentland. 2017. "Bots as Virtual Confederates: Design and Ethics." In *Proceedings of the 2017 ACM Conference on Computer Supported Cooperative Work and Social Computing*, 1831–190. CSCW '17. New York: ACM. doi:10.1145/2998181.2998354.

Kramer, Adam D. I., Jamie E. Guillory, and Jeffrey T. Hancock. 2014. "Experimental Evidence of Massive-Scale Emotional Contagion Through Social Networks." *Proceedings of the National Academy of Sciences of the USA* 111 (24): 8788–90. doi:10.1073/pnas.1320040111.

Kramer, Adam D.I. 2012. "The Spread of Emotion via Facebook." In *Proceedings of the SIGCHI Conference on Human Factors in Computing Systems*, 767–70. CHI '12. New York: ACM. doi:10.1145/2207676.2207787.

Kraut, Robert E., Paul Resnick, Sara Kiesler, Moira Burke, Yan Chen, Niki Kittur, Joseph Konstan, Yuqing Ren, and John Riedl. 2012. *Building Successful Online Communities: Evidence-Based Social Design.* Cambridge, MA: MIT Press.

Kravitz, Richard L., Naihua Duan, and Joel Braslow. 2004. "Evidence-Based Medicine, Heterogeneity of Treatment Effects, and the Trouble with Averages." *Milbank Quarterly* 82 (4): 661–87. doi:10.1111/j.0887-378X.2004.00327.x.

Kreuter, Frauke, Stanley Presser, and Roger Tourangeau. 2008. "Social Desirability Bias in CATI, IVR, and Web Surveys The Effects of Mode and Question Sensitivity." *Public Opinion Quarterly* 72 (5): 847–65. doi:10.1093/poq/nfn063.

Krosnick, Jon A. 2011. "Experiments for Evaluating Survey Questions." In *Question Evaluation Methods*, edited by Jennifer Madans, Kristen Miller, Aaron Maitland, and Gordon Willis, 213–38. Hoboken, NJ: Wiley. http://dx.doi.org/10.1002/9781118037003.ch14.

Kruskal, William, and Frederick Mosteller. 1979a. "Representative Sampling, I: Non-Scientific Literature." *International Statistical Review/Revue Internationale de Statistique* 47 (1): 13–24. doi:10.2307/1403202.

———. 1979b. "Representative Sampling, II: Scientific Literature, Excluding Statistics." *International Statistical Review/Revue Internationale de Statistique* 47 (2): 111–27. doi:10.2307/1402564.

———. 1979c. "Representative Sampling, III: The Current Statistical Literature." *International Statistical Review/Revue Internationale de Statistique* 47 (3): 245–65. doi:10.2307/1402647.

———. 1980. "Representative Sampling, IV: The History of the Concept in Statistics, 1895-1939." *International Statistical Review/Revue Internationale de Statistique* 48 (2): 169–95. doi:10.2307/1403151.

Kuminski, Evan, Joe George, John Wallin, and Lior Shamir. 2014. "Combining Human and Machine Learning for Morphological Analysis of Galaxy Images." *Publications of the Astronomical Society of the Pacific* 126 (944): 959–67. doi:10.1086/678977.

Kwak, Haewoon, Changhyun Lee, Hosung Park, and Sue Moon. 2010. "What Is Twitter, a Social Network or a News Media?" In *Proceedings of the 19th International Conference on World Wide Web*, 591–600. WWW '10. New York: ACM. doi:10.1145/1772690.1772751.

Laitin, David D. 2013. "Fisheries Management." *Political Analysis* 21 (1): 42–47. doi:10.1093/pan/mps033.

Lakhani, Karim R., Kevin J. Boudreau, Po-Ru Loh, Lars Backstrom, Carliss Baldwin, Eric Lonstein, Mike Lydon, Alan MacCormack, Ramy A. Arnaout, and Eva C. Guinan. 2013. "Prize-Based Contests Can Provide Solutions to Computational Biology Problems." *Nature Biotechnology* 31 (2): 108–11. doi:10.1038/nbt.2495.

Lamb, Anne, Jascha Smilack, Andrew Ho, and Justin Reich. 2015. "Addressing Common Analytic Challenges to Randomized Experiments in MOOCs: Attrition and Zero-Inflation." In *Proceedings of the Second (2015) ACM Conference on Learning @ Scale*, 21–30. L@S '15. New York: ACM. doi:10.1145/2724660.2724669.

Landau, Susan. 2016. "Transactional Information Is Remarkably Revelatory." *Proceedings of the National Academy of Sciences of the USA* 113 (20): 5467–69. doi:10.1073/pnas.1605356113.

Lane, Jeffrey. 2016. "The Digital Street An Ethnographic Study of Networked Street Life in Harlem." *American Behavioral Scientist* 60 (1): 43–58. doi:10.1177/0002764215601711.

Lanier, Jaron. 2014. *Who Owns the Future?*, reprint ed. New York: Simon & Schuster.

Larsen, Michael, and William E. Winkler. 2014. *Handbook of Record Linkage Methods*. Hobolen, NJ: Wiley.

Law, Edith, and Luis von Ahn. 2011. *Human Computation*. Synthesis Lectures on Artificial Intelligence and Machine Learning. Morgan & Claypool. doi:10.2200/S00371ED1V01Y201107AIM013.

Lax, Jeffrey R., and Justin H. Phillips. 2009. "How Should We Estimate Public Opinion in The States?" *American Journal of Political Science* 53 (1): 107–21. doi:10.1111/j.1540-5907.2008.00360.x.

Lazer, David. 2015. "Issues of Construct Validity and Reliability in Massive, Passive Data Collections." *The City Papers: An Essay Collection from The Decent City Initiative*. http://citiespapers.ssrc.org/issues-of-construct-validity-and-reliability-in-massive-passive-data-collections/.

Lazer, David, Ryan Kennedy, Gary King, and Alessandro Vespignani. 2014. "The Parable of Google Flu: Traps in Big Data Analysis." *Science* 343 (6176): 1203–5. doi:10.1126/science.1248506.

Lazer, David, Alex Pentland, Lada Adamic, Sinan Aral, Albert-László Barabási, Devon Brewer, Nicholas Christakis, et al. 2009. "Computational Social Science." *Science* 323 (5915): 721–23. doi:10.1126/science.1167742.

Ledford, Heidi. 2007. "Patent Examiners Call in the Jury." *Nature* 448 (7151): 239. doi:10.1038/448239a.

Lee, Sunghee. 2006. "Propensity Score Adjustment as a Weighting Scheme for Volunteer Panel Web Surveys." *Journal of Official Statistics* 22 (2): 329–49. http://www.jos.nu/Articles/abstract.asp?article=222329.

Lee, Sunghee, and Richard Valliant. 2009. "Estimation for Volunteer Panel Web Surveys Using Propensity Score Adjustment and Calibration Adjustment." *Sociological Methods & Research* 37 (3): 319–43. doi:10.1177/0049124108329643.

Lee, Young Jack, Jonas H. Ellenberg, Deborah G. Hirtz, and Karin B. Nelson. 1991. "Analysis of Clinical Trials by Treatment Actually Received: Is It Really an Option?" *Statistics in Medicine* 10 (10): 1595–1605. doi:10.1002/sim.4780101011.

Legewie, Joscha. 2015. "The Promise and Perils of Big Data for Social Science Research." *The Cities Papers*. http://citiespapers.ssrc.org/the-promise-and-perils-of-big-data-for-social-science-research/.

———. 2016. "Racial Profiling and Use of Force in Police Stops: How Local Events Trigger Periods of Increased Discrimination." *American Journal of Sociology* 122 (2): 379–424. doi:10.1086/687518.

Lerner, Barron H. 2004. "Sins of Omission: Cancer Research Without Informed Consent." *New England Journal of Medicine* 351 (7): 628–30. doi:10.1056/NEJMp048108.

Levitt, Steven D., and John A. List. 2007a. "What Do Laboratory Experiments Measuring Social Preferences Reveal about the Real World?" *Journal of Economic Perspectives* 21 (2): 153–74. http://www.jstor.org/stable/30033722.

———. 2007b. "Viewpoint: On the Generalizability of Lab Behaviour to the Field." *Canadian Journal of Economics/Revue Canadienne d'économique* 40 (2): 347–70. doi:10.1111/j.1365-2966.2007.00412.x.

———. 2009. "Field Experiments in Economics: The Past, the Present, and the Future." *European Economic Review* 53 (1): 1–18. doi:10.1016/j.euroecorev.2008.12.001.

———. 2011. "Was There Really a Hawthorne Effect at the Hawthorne Plant? An Analysis of the Original Illumination Experiments." *American Economic Journal: Applied Economics* 3 (1): 224–38. doi:10.1257/app.3.1.224.

Levy, Karen E. C. and Solon Baracas. 2017. "Refractive Surveillance: Monitoring Customers to Manage Workers." *International Journal of Communications.* In press.

Lewis, Kevin. 2015a. "Studying Online Behavior: Comment on Anderson et al. 2014." *Sociological Science* 2 (January): 20–31. doi:10.15195/v2.a2.

———. 2015b. "Three Fallacies of Digital Footprints." *Big Data & Society* 2 (2): 2053951715602496. doi:10.1177/2053951715602496.

Lewis, Kevin, Marco Gonzalez, and Jason Kaufman. 2012. "Social Selection and Peer Influence in an Online Social Network." *Proceedings of the National Academy of Sciences of the USA* 109 (1): 68–72. doi:10.1073/pnas.1109739109.

Lewis, Kevin, Jason Kaufman, Marco Gonzalez, Andreas Wimmer, and Nicholas Christakis. 2008. "Tastes, Ties, and Time: A New Social Network Dataset Using Facebook.com." *Social Networks* 30 (4): 330–42. doi:10.1016/j.socnet.2008.07.002.

Lewis, Randall A., and Justin M. Rao. 2015. "The Unfavorable Economics of Measuring the Returns to Advertising." *The Quarterly Journal of Economics* 130 (4): 1941–73. doi:10.1093/qje/qjv023.

Lin, Mingfeng, Henry C. Lucas, and Galit Shmueli. 2013. "Research Commentary—Too Big to Fail: Large Samples and the p-Value Problem." *Information Systems Research* 24 (4): 906–17. doi:10.1287/isre.2013.0480.

Lin, Winston. 2013. "Agnostic Notes on Regression Adjustments to Experimental Data: Reexamining Freedman's Critique." *Annals of Applied Statistics* 7 (1): 295–318. doi:10.1214/12-AOAS583.

Lin, Winston, and Donald P. Green. 2016. "Standard Operating Procedures: A Safety Net for Pre-Analysis Plans." *PS: Political Science & Politics* 49 (3): 495–500. doi:10.1017/S1049096516000810.

Lind, Laura H., Michael F. Schober, Frederick G. Conrad, and Heidi Reichert. 2013. "Why Do Survey Respondents Disclose More When Computers Ask the Questions?" *Public Opinion Quarterly* 77 (4): 888–935. doi:10.1093/poq/nft038.

Link, Michael W. 2015. "Presidential Address AAPOR2025 and the Opportunities in the Decade Before Us." *Public Opinion Quarterly* 79 (3): 828–36. doi:10.1093/poq/nfv028.

Lintott, Chris J., Kevin Schawinski, Anže Slosar, Kate Land, Steven Bamford, Daniel Thomas, M. Jordan Raddick, et al. 2008. "Galaxy Zoo: Morphologies Derived from Visual Inspection of Galaxies from the Sloan Digital Sky Survey." *Monthly Notices of the Royal Astronomical Society* 389 (3): 1179–89. doi:10.1111/j.1365-2966.2008.13689.x.

Lintott, Chris, Kevin Schawinski, Steven Bamford, Anže Slosar, Kate Land, Daniel Thomas, Edd Edmondson, et al. 2011. "Galaxy Zoo 1: Data Release of Morphological Classifications for Nearly 900 000 Galaxies." *Monthly Notices of the Royal Astronomical Society* 410 (1): 166–78. doi:10.1111/j.1365-2966.2010.17432.x.

List, John A. 2011. "Why Economists Should Conduct Field Experiments and 14 Tips for Pulling One Off." *Journal of Economic Perspectives* 25 (3): 3–16. doi:10.1257/jep.25.3.3.

List, John A., Sally Sadoff, and Mathis Wagner. 2011. "So You Want to Run an Experiment, Now What? Some Simple Rules of Thumb for Optimal Experimental Design." *Experimental Economics* 14 (4): 439. doi:10.1007/s10683-011-9275-7.

List, John A., Azeem M. Shaikh, and Yang Xu. 2016. "Multiple Hypothesis Testing in Experimental Economics." Working Paper 21875. National Bureau of Economic Research. http://www.nber.org/papers/w21875.

Little, R. J. A. 1993. "Post-Stratification: A Modeler's Perspective." *Journal of the American Statistical Association* 88 (423): 1001–12. doi:10.2307/2290792.

Little, Roderick J. A., and Donald B. Rubin. 2002. *Statistical Analysis with Missing Data*, 2nd ed. Hoboken, NJ: Wiley-Interscience.

Liu, Yabing, Chloe Kliman-Silver, and Alan Mislove. 2014. "The Tweets They Are a-Changin: Evolution of Twitter Users and Behavior." In *ICWSM*, 30:5–314. https://www.aaai.org/ocs/index.php/ICWSM/ICWSM14/paper/viewFile/8043/8131/.

Loewen, Peter John, Daniel Rubenson, and Leonard Wantchekon. 2010. "Help Me Help You: Conducting Field Experiments with Political Elites." *Annals of the American Academy of Political and Social Science* 628 (1): 165–75. doi:10.1177/0002716209351522.

Lohr, Sharon L. 2009. *Sampling: Design and Analysis*, 2nd ed. Boston, MA: Cengage Learning.

Longford, Nicholas T. 1999. "Selection Bias and Treatment Heterogeneity in Clinical Trials." *Statistics in Medicine* 18 (12): 1467–74. doi:10.1002/(SICI)1097-0258(19990630)18:12<1467::AID-SIM149>3.0.CO;2-H.

Lowrance, William W. 2012. *Privacy, Confidentiality, and Health Research*. Cambridge: Cambridge University Press.

Lu, Xin, Linus Bengtsson, and Petter Holme. 2012. "Predictability of Population Displacement after the 2010 Haiti Earthquake." *Proceedings of the National Academy of Sciences of the USA* 109 (29): 11576–81. doi:10.1073/pnas.1203882109.

Lucking-Reiley, David. 1999. "Using Field Experiments to Test Equivalence between Auction Formats: Magic on the Internet." *American Economic Review* 89 (5): 1063–80. http://www.jstor.org/stable/117047.

Ludwig, Jens, Jeffrey R. Kling, and Sendhil Mullainathan. 2011. "Mechanism Experiments and Policy Evaluations." *Journal of Economic Perspectives* 25 (3): 17–38. doi:10.1257/jep.25.3.17.

Lung, J. 2012. "Ethical and Legal Considerations of reCAPTCHA." In *2012 Tenth Annual International Conference on Privacy, Security and Trust (PST)*, 211–16. doi:10.1109/PST.2012.6297942.

Lusinchi, Dominic. 2012. "President Landon and the 1936 Literary Digest Poll." *Social Science History* 36 (1): 23–54. http://www.jstor.org/stable/41407095.

MacCarthy, Mark. 2015. "Privacy Restrictions and Contextual Harm." *Working Paper.* http://moritzlaw.osu.edu/students/groups/is/files/2016/07/Privacy-Policy-and-Contextual-Harm-June-2016-Final-.pdf.

Mackenzie, Donald. 2008. *An Engine, Not a Camera: How Financial Models Shape Markets*. Cambridge, MA: MIT Press.

Maddock, Jim, Robert Mason, and Kate Starbird. 2015. "Using Historical Twitter Data for Research: Ethical Challenges of Tweet Deletions." In *CSCW 15 Workshop on Ethics at the 2015 Conference on Computer Supported Cooperative Work, Vancouver, Canada.* https://cscwethics2015.files. wordpress.com/2015/02/maddock.pdf.

Magdy, Walid, Kareem Darwish, and Ingmar Weber. 2016. "#FailedRevolutions: Using Twitter to Study the Antecedents of ISIS Support." *First Monday* 21 (2). doi:10.5210/fm.v21i2.6372.

Malhotra, Neil, and Jon A. Krosnick. 2007. "The Effect of Survey Mode and Sampling on Inferences About Political Attitudes and Behavior: Comparing the 2000 and 2004 ANES to Internet Surveys with Nonprobability Samples." *Political Analysis* 15 (3): 286–323. doi:10.1093/pan/mpm003.

Malone, Thomas W., and Michael S. Bernstein. 2015. *Handbook of Collective Intelligence.* Cambridge, MA: MIT Press.

Manson, Neil C., and Onora O'Neill. 2007. *Rethinking Informed Consent in Bioethics.* Cambridge: Cambridge University Press.

Manzi, Jim. 2012. *Uncontrolled: The Surprising Payoff of Trial-and-Error for Business, Politics, and Society.* New York: Basic Books.

Mao, Andrew, Winter Mason, Siddharth Suri, and Duncan J. Watts. 2016. "An Experimental Study of Team Size and Performance on a Complex Task." *PLoS ONE* 11 (4): e0153048. doi:10.1371/ journal.pone.0153048.

Mao, Huina, Scott Counts, Johan Bollen, and others. 2015. "Quantifying the Effects of On-line Bullishness on International Financial Markets." In *ECB Workshop on Using Big Data for Forecasting and Statistics, Frankfurt, Germany.* http://www.busman.qmul.ac.uk/newsandevents/ events/eventdownloads/bfwgconference2013acceptedpapers/114925.pdf.

Margetts, Helen, Peter John, Tobias Escher, and Stéphane Reissfelder. 2011. "Social Information and Political Participation on the Internet: An Experiment." *European Political Science Review* 3 (3): 321–44. doi:10.1017/S1755773911000129.

Markham, Annette, and Elizabeth Buchanan. 2012. "Ethical Decision-Making and Internet Research: Recommendations from the AoIR Ethics Working Committee." Version 2.0. Association of Internet Researchers. https://cms.bsu.edu/sitecore/shell/-/media/WWW/DepartmentalContent/ ResearchIntegrity/Files/Education/Active/AoIR%20Social%20Media%20Working%20Committee. pdf.

Marshall, Philip J., Chris J. Lintott, and Leigh N. Fletcher. 2015. "Ideas for Citizen Science in Astronomy." *Annual Review of Astronomy and Astrophysics* 53 (1): 247–78. doi:10.1146/annurev-astro-081913-035959.

Martinez-Ebers, Valerie. 2016. "Introduction." *PS: Political Science & Politics* 49 (2): 287–88. doi:10.1017/S1049096516000214.

Marx, Gary T. 2016. *Windows Into the Soul: Surveillance and Society in an Age of High Technology.* Chicago: University of Chicago Press.

Mas, Alexandre, and Enrico Moretti. 2009. "Peers at Work." *American Economic Review* 99 (1): 112–45. doi:10.1257/aer.99.1.112.

Mason, Winter, and Siddharth Suri. 2012. "Conducting Behavioral Research on Amazon's Mechanical Turk." *Behavior Research Methods* 44 (1): 1–23. doi:10.3758/s13428-011-0124-6.

Mason, Winter, and Duncan J Watts. 2009. "Financial Incentives and the 'Performance of Crowds'." *Proceedings of the Human Computation (HCOMP) Workshop: Knowledge Discovery and Data Mining Conference* 11: 100–108. doi:10.1145/1809400.1809422.

Masters, Karen L. 2009. "She's an Astronomer: Aida Berges." *Galaxy Zoo.* https://blog.galaxyzoo.org/ 2009/10/01/shes-an-astronomer-aida-berges/.

Masters, Karen L, Robert C Nichol, Ben Hoyle, Chris Lintott, Steven P Bamford, Edward M Edmondson, Lucy Fortson, et al. 2011. "Galaxy Zoo: Bars in Disc Galaxies." *Monthly Notices of the Royal Astronomical Society* 411 (3): 2026–34. doi:10.1111/j.1365-2966.2010.17834.x.

Masters, Karen L. 2012. "A Zoo of Galaxies." *Proceedings of the International Astronomical Union* 10 (H16): 1–15. doi:10.1017/S1743921314004608.

Mastroianni, Anna, and Jeffrey Kahn. 2001. "Swinging on the Pendulum: Shifting Views of Justice in Human Subjects Research." *Hastings Center Report* 31 (3): 21–28. doi:10.2307/3527551.

Mauboussin, Michael J. 2012. *The Success Equation: Untangling Skill and Luck in Business, Sports, and Investing.* Boston, MA: Harvard Business Review Press.

Mayer, Jonathan, Patrick Mutchler, and John C. Mitchell. 2016. "Evaluating the Privacy Properties of Telephone Metadata." *Proceedings of the National Academy of Sciences of the USA* 113 (20): 5536–41. doi:10.1073/pnas.1508081113.

Mayer-Schönberger, Viktor. 2009. *Delete: The Virtue of Forgetting in the Digital Age.* Princeton, NJ: Princeton University Press.

Mayer-Schönberger, Viktor, and Kenneth Cukier. 2013. *Big Data: A Revolution That Will Transform How We Live, Work, and Think.* Boston: Eamon Dolan/Houghton Mifflin Harcourt.

Maynard, Douglas W. 2014. "News From Somewhere, News From Nowhere On the Study of Interaction in Ethnographic Inquiry." *Sociological Methods & Research* 43 (2): 210–18. doi:10.1177/0049124114527249.

Maynard, Douglas W., and Nora Cate Schaeffer. 1997. "Keeping the Gate: Declinations of the Request to Participate in a Telephone Survey Interview." *Sociological Methods & Research* 26 (1): 34–79. doi:10.1177/0049124197026001002.

Maynard, Douglas W., Jeremy Freese, and Nora Cate Schaeffer. 2010. "Calling for Participation Requests, Blocking Moves, and Rational (Inter)action in Survey Introductions." *American Sociological Review* 75 (5): 791–814. doi:10.1177/0003122410379582.

Mayo-Wilson, Evan, Paul Montgomery, Sally Hopewell, Geraldine Macdonald, David Moher, and Sean Grant. 2013. "Developing a Reporting Guideline for Social and Psychological Intervention Trials." *British Journal of Psychiatry* 203 (4): 250–54. doi:10.1192/bjp.bp.112.123745.

McDonald, Sean. 2016. "Ebola: A Big Data Disaster." CIS Papers 2016.01. The Centre for Internet & Society. http://cis-india.org/papers/ebola-a-big-data-disaster.

McFarland, Daniel A., and H. Richard McFarland. 2015. "Big Data and the Danger of Being Precisely Inaccurate." *Big Data & Society* 2 (2). doi:10.1177/2053951715602495.

McKenzie, David. 2012. "Beyond Baseline and Follow-up: The Case for More T in Experiments." *Journal of Development Economics* 99 (2): 210–21. doi:10.1016/j.jdeveco.2012.01.002.

Meissner, Peter, and R Core Team. 2016. "Wikipediatrend: Public Subject Attention via Wikipedia Page View Statistics." https://CRAN.R-project.org/package=wikipediatrend.

Mervis, Jeffrey. 2014. "How Two Economists Got Direct Access to IRS Tax Records." http://www.sciencemag.org/news/2014/05/how-two-economists-got-direct-access-irs-tax-records.

Merz, Nicolas, Sven Regel, and Jirka Lewandowski. 2016. "The Manifesto Corpus: A New Resource for Research on Political Parties and Quantitative Text Analysis." *Research & Politics* 3 (2): 2053168016643346. doi:10.1177/2053168016643346.

Metcalf, Jacob. 2016. "Big Data Analytics and Revision of the Common Rule." *Communications of the ACM* 59 (7): 31–33. doi:10.1145/2935882.

Metcalf, Jacob, and Kate Crawford. 2016. "Where Are Human Subjects in Big Data Research? The Emerging Ethics Divide." *Big Data & Society* 3 (1): 1–14. doi:10.1177/2053951716650211.

Meyer, Bruce D., Wallace K. C. Mok, and James X. Sullivan. 2015. "Household Surveys in Crisis." *Journal of Economic Perspectives* 29 (4): 199–226. doi:10.1257/jep.29.4.199.

Meyer, Michelle N. 2014. "Misjudgements Will Drive Social Trials Underground." *Nature* 511 (7509): 265–65. doi:10.1038/511265a.

———. 2015. "Two Cheers for Corporate Experimentation: The A/B Illusion and the Virtues of Data-Driven Innovation." *Colorado Technology Law Review* 13 (2): 273–332. ctlj.colorado.edu/wp-content/uploads/2015/08/Meyer-final.pdf.

Michel, Jean-Baptiste, Yuan Kui Shen, Aviva P. Aiden, Adrian Veres, Matthew K. Gray, the Google Books Team, Joseph P. Pickett, et al. 2011. "Quantitative Analysis of Culture Using Millions of Digitized Books." *Science* 331 (6014): 176–82. doi:10.1126/science.1199644.

Middlemist, R. D., E. S. Knowles, and C. F. Matter. 1976. "Personal Space Invasions in the Lavatory: Suggestive Evidence for Arousal." *Journal of Personality and Social Psychology* 33 (5): 541–46.

Milkman, Katherine L., Modupe Akinola, and Dolly Chugh. 2012. "Temporal Distance and Discrimination An Audit Study in Academia." *Psychological Science* 23 (7): 710–17. doi:10.1177/0956797611434539.

Miller, Franklin G. 2014. "Clinical Research Before Informed Consent." *Kennedy Institute of Ethics Journal* 24 (2): 141–57. doi:10.1353/ken.2014.0009.

Mills, Judson. 1976. "A Procedure for Explaining Experiments Involving Deception." *Personality and Social Psychology Bulletin* 2 (1): 3–13. doi:10.1177/014616727600200102.

Mitchell, Gregory. 2012. "Revisiting Truth or Triviality: The External Validity of Research in the Psychological Laboratory." *Perspectives on Psychological Science* 7 (2): 109–17. doi:10.1177/1745691611432343.

Mitofsky, Warren J. 1989. "Presidential Address: Methods and Standards: A Challenge for Change." *Public Opinion Quarterly* 53 (3): 446–53. doi:10.1093/poq/53.3.446.

Molloy, Jennifer C. 2011. "The Open Knowledge Foundation: Open Data Means Better Science." *PLoS Biology* 9 (12): e1001195. doi:10.1371/journal.pbio.1001195.

Monogan, James E. 2013. "A Case for Registering Studies of Political Outcomes: An Application in the 2010 House Elections." *Political Analysis* 21 (1): 21–37. doi:10.1093/pan/mps022.

Montjoye, Yves-Alexandre de, Laura Radaelli, Vivek Kumar Singh, and Alex Sandy Pentland. 2015. "Unique in the Shopping Mall: On the Reidentifiability of Credit Card Metadata." *Science* 347 (6221): 536–39. doi:10.1126/science.1256297.

Moore, David W. 2002. "Measuring New Types of Question-Order Effects: Additive and Subtractive." *Public Opinion Quarterly* 66 (1): 80–91. doi:10.1086/338631.

Morens, David M., and Anthony S. Fauci. 2007. "The 1918 Influenza Pandemic: Insights for the 21st Century." *Journal of Infectious Diseases* 195 (7): 1018–28. doi:10.1086/511989.

Morgan, Stephen L., and Christopher Winship. 2014. *Counterfactuals and Causal Inference: Methods and Principles for Social Research*, 2nd ed. New York: Cambridge University Press.

Morton, Rebecca B., and Kenneth C. Williams. 2010. *Experimental Political Science and the Study of Causality: From Nature to the Lab*. Cambridge: Cambridge University Press.

Mosteller, Frederick. 1949. *The Pre-Election Polls of 1948: The Report to the Committee on Analysis of Pre-Election Polls and Forecasts*. Vol. 60. Social Science Research Council.

Motl, Jonathan R. 2015. "McCulloch V. Stanford and Dartmouth." COPP 2014-CFP-046. Helena, MT: Commissioner of Political Practices of the State of Montana. http://politicalpractices.mt.gov/content/2recentdecisions/McCullochvStanfordandDartmouthFinalDecision.

Muchnik, Lev, Sinan Aral, and Sean J. Taylor. 2013. "Social Influence Bias: A Randomized Experiment." *Science* 341 (6146): 647–51. doi:10.1126/science.1240466.

Munger, Kevin. 2016. "Tweetment Effects on the Tweeted: Experimentally Reducing Racist Harassment." *Working Paper*. http://kmunger.github.io/pdfs/Twitter_harassment_final.pdf.

Murphy, Kevin P. 2012. *Machine Learning: A Probabilistic Perspective*. Cambridge, MA: MIT Press.

Murray, Michael P. 2006. "Avoiding Invalid Instruments and Coping with Weak Instruments." *Journal of Economic Perspectives* 20 (4): 111–32. http://www.jstor.org/stable/30033686.

Mutz, Diana C. 2011. *Population-Based Survey Experiments*. Princeton, NJ: Princeton University Press.

Mutz, Diana C., and Robin Pemantle. 2015. "Standards for Experimental Research: Encouraging a Better Understanding of Experimental Methods." *Journal of Experimental Political Science* 2 (2): 192–215. doi:10.1017/XPS.2015.4.

Narayanan, Arvind, and Vitaly Shmatikov. 2008. "Robust De-Anonymization of Large Sparse Datasets." In *Proceedings of the 2008 IEEE Symposium on Security and Privacy*, 111–25. Washington, DC: IEEE Computer Society. doi:10.1109/SP.2008.33.

———. 2010. "Myths and Fallacies of 'Personally Identifiable Information'." *Communications of the ACM* 53 (6): 24–26. doi:10.1145/1743546.1743558.

Narayanan, Arvind, and Bendert Zevenbergen. 2015. "No Encore for Encore? Ethical Questions for Web-Based Censorship Measurement." *Technology Science*, December. http://techscience.org/a/2015121501/.

Narayanan, Arvind, Joseph Bonneau, Edward Felten, Andrew Miller, and Steven Goldfeder. 2016. *Bitcoin and Cryptocurrency Technologies: A Comprehensive Introduction.* Princeton, NJ: Princeton University Press.

Narayanan, Arvind, Joanna Huey, and Edward W. Felten. 2016. "A Precautionary Approach to Big Data Privacy." In *Data Protection on the Move,* edited by Serge Gutwirth, Ronald Leenes, and Paul De Hert, 357–85. Law, Governance and Technology Series 24. Dordrecht: Springer Netherlands. http://link.springer.com/chapter/10.1007/978-94-017-7376-8_13.

Nardo, Michela, Marco Petracco-Giudici, and Minás Naltsidis. 2016. "Walking down Wall Street with a Tablet: A Survey of Stock Market Predictions Using the Web." *Journal of Economic Surveys* 30 (2): 356–69. doi:10.1111/joes.12102.

National Research Council. 2013. *Nonresponse in Social Science Surveys: A Research Agenda.* Edited by Roger Tourangeau and Thomas J. Plewe. Panel on a Research Agenda for the Future of Social Science Data Collection, Committee on National Statistics. Division of Behavioral and Social Sciences and Education. Washington, DC: National Academies Press. http://www.nap.edu/catalog/18293.

———. 2014. *Proposed Revisions to the Common Rule for the Protection of Human Subjects in the Behavioral and Social Sciences.* Committee on Revisions to the Common Rule for the Protection of Human Subjects in Research in the Behavioral and Social Sciences. Board on Behavioral, Cognitive, and Sensory Sciences, Committee on National Statistics, Division of Behavioral and Social Sciences and Education. Washington, DC: National Academies Press.

Netflix. 2009. "Netflix Prize: View Leaderboard." http://www.netflixprize.com/leaderboard.

Neuhaus, Fabian and Timothy Webmoor. 2012. "Agile Ethics for Massified Research and Visualization." *Information, Communication & Society* 15 (1): 43–65. doi:10.1080/1369118X.2011.616519.

Neumark, David, Roy J. Bank, and Kyle D. Van Nort. 1996. "Sex Discrimination in Restaurant Hiring: An Audit Study." *Quarterly Journal of Economics* 111 (3): 915–41. doi:10.2307/2946676.

Newman, Mark W., Debra Lauterbach, Sean A. Munson, Paul Resnick, and Margaret E. Morris. 2011. "It's Not That I Don't Have Problems, I'm Just Not Putting Them on Facebook: Challenges and Opportunities in Using Online Social Networks for Health." In *Proceedings of the ACM 2011 Conference on Computer Supported Cooperative Work,* 341–50. CSCW '11. New York,: ACM. doi:10.1145/1958824.1958876.

Newport, Frank. 2011. "Presidential Address: Taking AAPOR's Mission To Heart." *Public Opinion Quarterly* 75 (3): 593–604. doi:10.1093/poq/nfr027.

Nickerson, David W., and Susan D. Hyde. 2016. "Conducting Research with NGOs: Relevant Counterfactuals from the Perspective of Subjects." In *Ethics and Experiments: Problems and Solutions for Social Scientists and Policy Professionals,* edited by Scott Desposato, 198–216. New York: Routledge.

Nielsen, Michael. 2012. *Reinventing Discovery: The New Era of Networked Science.* Princeton, NJ: Princeton University Press.

Nisbett, Richard E., and Timothy D. Wilson. 1977. "Telling More Than We Can Know: Verbal Reports on Mental Processes." *Psychological Review* 84 (3): 231–59. doi:10.1037/0033-295X.84.3.231.

Nissenbaum, Helen. 2010. *Privacy in Context: Technology, Policy, and the Integrity of Social Life.* Stanford, CA: Stanford Law Books.

———. 2011. "A Contextual Approach to Privacy Online." *Daedalus* 140 (4): 32–48. doi:10.1162/DAED_a_00113.

———. 2015. "Respecting Context to Protect Privacy: Why Meaning Matters." *Science and Engineering Ethics,* July. doi:10.1007/s11948-015-9674-9.

Nosek, Brian A., and Daniël Lakens. 2014. "Registered Reports: A Method to Increase the Credibility of Published Results." *Social Psychology* 45 (3): 137–41. doi:10.1027/1864-9335/a000192.

Nov, Oded, Ofer Arazy, and David Anderson. 2011. "Dusting for Science: Motivation and Participation of Digital Citizen Science Volunteers." In *Proceedings of the 2011 iConference,* 68–74. iConference '11. New York: ACM. doi:10.1145/1940761.1940771.

Noveck, Beth Simone. 2006. "Peer to Patent: Collective Intelligence, Open Review, and Patent Reform." *Harvard Journal of Law and Technology* 20 (1): 123–62.

———. 2009. *Wiki Government: How Technology Can Make Government Better, Democracy Stronger, and Citizens More Powerful*. Washington, DC: Brookings Institution Press.

Oczak, Malgorzata, and Agnieszka Niedźwieńska. 2007. "Debriefing in Deceptive Research: A Proposed New Procedure." *Journal of Empirical Research on Human Research Ethics* 2 (3): 49–59. doi:10.1525/jer.2007.2.3.49.

Ohm, Paul. 2010. "Broken Promises of Privacy: Responding to the Surprising Failure of Anonymization." *UCLA Law Review* 57: 1701–77. http://papers.ssrn.com/sol3/papers.cfm?abstract_id=1450006.

———. 2015. "Sensitive Information." *Southern California Law Review* 88: 1125–96.

Ohmer, Susan. 2006. *George Gallup in Hollywood*. New York: Columbia University Press.

Olken, Benjamin A. 2015. "Promises and Perils of Pre-Analysis Plans." *Journal of Economic Perspectives* 29 (3): 61–80. http://www.jstor.org/stable/43550121.

Olson, Donald R., Kevin J. Konty, Marc Paladini, Cecile Viboud, and Lone Simonsen. 2013. "Reassessing Google Flu Trends Data for Detection of Seasonal and Pandemic Influenza: A Comparative Epidemiological Study at Three Geographic Scales." *PLoS Computational Biology* 9 (10): e1003256. doi:10.1371/journal.pcbi.1003256.

Olson, Janice A. 1996. "The Health and Retirement Study: The New Retirement Survey." *Social Security Bulletin* 59: 85. http://heinonline.org/HOL/Page?handle=hein.journals/ssbul59&id=87&div=13&collection=journals.

———. 1999. "Linkages with Data from Social Security Administrative Records in the Health and Retirement Study." *Social Security Bulletin* 62: 73. http://heinonline.org/HOL/Page?handle=hein.journals/ssbul62&id=207&div=25&collection=journals.

Orne, Martin T. 1962. "On the Social Psychology of the Psychological Experiment: With Particular Reference to Demand Characteristics and Their Implications." *American Psychologist* 17 (11): 776–83. doi:10.1037/h0043424.

Orr, Larry L. 1998. *Social Experiments: Evaluating Public Programs With Experimental Methods*. Thousand Oaks, CA: SAGE.

Overton, W. Scott, and Stephen V. Stehman. 1995. "The Horvitz–Thompson Theorem as a Unifying Perspective for Probability Sampling: With Examples from Natural Resource Sampling." *American Statistician* 49 (3): 261–68. doi:10.2307/2684196.

O'Connor, Dan. 2013. "The Apomediated World: Regulating Research when Social Media Has Changed Research." *Journal of Law, Medicine & Ethics* 41 (2): 470–83. doi:10.1111/jlme.12056.

O'Doherty, Kieran C., Emily Christofides, Jeffery Yen, Heidi Beate Bentzen, Wylie Burke, Nina Hallowell, Barbara A. Koenig, and Donald J. Willison. 2016. "If You Build It, They Will Come: Unintended Future Uses of Organised Health Data Collections." *BMC Medical Ethics* 17: 54. doi:10.1186/s12910-016-0137-x.

O'Neil, Cathy. 2016. *Weapons of Math Destruction: How Big Data Increases Inequality and Threatens Democracy*. New York: Crown.

Pacheco, Julianna. 2011. "Using National Surveys to Measure Dynamic U.S. State Public Opinion A Guideline for Scholars and an Application." *State Politics & Policy Quarterly* 11 (4): 415–39. doi:10.1177/1532440011419287.

Packard, Vance. 1964. *The Naked Society*. New York: D. McKay.

Page, Lindsay C., Avi Feller, Todd Grindal, Luke Miratrix, and Marie-Andree Somers. 2015. "Principal Stratification: A Tool for Understanding Variation in Program Effects Across Endogenous Subgroups." *American Journal of Evaluation* 36 (4): 514–31. doi:10.1177/1098214015594419.

Page, Scott E. 2008. *The Difference: How the Power of Diversity Creates Better Groups, Firms, Schools, and Societies*. Princeton, NJ: Princeton University Press.

Pager, Devah. 2007. "The Use of Field Experiments for Studies of Employment Discrimination: Contributions, Critiques, and Directions for the Future." *Annals of the American Academy of Political and Social Science* 609: 104–33. http://www.jstor.org/stable/25097877.

Paluck, Elizabeth Levy, and Donald P. Green. 2009. "Deference, Dissent, and Dispute Resolution: An Experimental Intervention Using Mass Media to Change Norms and Behavior in Rwanda." *American Political Science Review* 103 (4): 622–44. doi:10.1017/S0003055409990128.

Panagopoulos, Costas. 2010. "Affect, Social Pressure and Prosocial Motivation: Field Experimental Evidence of the Mobilizing Effects of Pride, Shame and Publicizing Voting Behavior." *Political Behavior* 32 (3): 369–86. doi:10.1007/s11109-010-9114-0.

Panger, Galen. 2016. "Reassessing the Facebook Experiment: Critical Thinking About the Validity of Big Data Research." *Information, Communication & Society* 19 (8): 1108–26. doi:10.1080/1369118X.2015.1093525.

Paolacci, G., J. Chandler, and P. G Ipeirotis. 2010. "Running Experiments on Amazon Mechanical Turk." *Judgment and Decision Making* 5 (5): 411–19. http://journal.sjdm.org/10/10630a/jdm10630a.html.

Parigi, Paolo, Jessica J. Santana, and Karen S. Cook. 2017. "Online Field Experiments Studying Social Interactions in Context." *Social Psychology Quarterly* 80 (1): 1–19 doi:10.1177/0190272516680842.

Park, David K., Andrew Gelman, and Joseph Bafumi. 2004. "Bayesian Multilevel Estimation with Poststratification: State-Level Estimates from National Polls." *Political Analysis* 12 (4): 375–85. doi:10.1093/pan/mph024.

Parry, Marc. 2011. "Harvard Researchers Accused of Breaching Students' Privacy." *Chronicle of Higher Education*, July. http://chronicle.com/article/Harvards-Privacy-Meltdown/128166/.

Partridge, Craig and Mark Allman. 2016. "Ethical considerations in network measurement papers." *Communications of the ACM* 59 (10): 58–64. doi:10.1145/2896816.

Pasek, Josh, S. Mo Jang, Curtiss L. Cobb, J. Michael Dennis, and Charles Disogra. 2014. "Can Marketing Data Aid Survey Research? Examining Accuracy and Completeness in Consumer-File Data." *Public Opinion Quarterly* 78 (4): 889–916. doi:10.1093/poq/nfu043.

Pe-Than, Ei Pa Pa, Dion Hoe-Lian Goh, and Chei Sian Lee. 2015. "A Typology of Human Computation Games: An Analysis and a Review of Current Games." *Behaviour & Information Technology* 34 (8): 809–24. doi:10.1080/0144929X.2013.862304.

Pearl, Judea. 2009. *Causality: Models, Reasoning and Inference*, 2nd ed. Cambridge: Cambridge University Press.

———. 2015. "Generalizing Experimental Findings." *Journal of Causal Inference* 3 (2): 259–66. doi:10.1515/jci-2015-0025.

Pearl, Judea, and Elias Bareinboim. 2014. "External Validity: From Do-Calculus to Transportability across Populations." *Statistical Science* 29 (4): 579–95. doi:10.1214/14-STS486.

Pearl, Judea, Madelyn Glymour, and Nicholas P. Jewell. 2016. *Causal Inference in Statistics: A Primer*. Chichester, UK: Wiley.

Penney, Jonathon. 2016. "Chilling Effects: Online Surveillance and Wikipedia Use." *Berkeley Technology Law Journal* 31 (1): 117. doi:10.15779/Z38SS13.

Pepe, Margaret Sullivan. 1992. "Inference Using Surrogate Outcome Data and a Validation Sample." *Biometrika* 79 (2): 355–65. doi:10.2307/2336846.

Phan, Tuan Q., and Edoardo M. Airoldi. 2015. "A Natural Experiment of Social Network Formation and Dynamics." *Proceedings of the National Academy of Sciences of the USA* 112 (21): 6595–6600. doi:10.1073/pnas.1404770112.

Phelan, Chanda, Cliff Lampe, and Paul Resnick. 2016. "It's Creepy, But It Doesn't Bother Me." In *Proceedings of the 2016 CHI Conference on Human Factors in Computing Systems*, 5240–51. CHI '16. New York: ACM. doi:10.1145/2858036.2858381.

Piatetsky, Gregory. 2007. "Interview with Simon Funk." *SIGKDD Explorations Newsletter* 9 (1): 38–40. doi:10.1145/1294301.1294311.

Pickard, Galen, Wei Pan, Iyad Rahwan, Manuel Cebrian, Riley Crane, Anmol Madan, and Alex Pentland. 2011. "Time-Critical Social Mobilization." *Science* 334 (6055): 509–12. doi:10.1126/science.1205869.

Pink, Sarah, Heather Horst, John Postill, Larissa Hjorth, Tania Lewis, and Jo Tacchi. 2015. *Digital Ethnography: Principles and Practice*. Los Angeles: SAGE.

Pirlott, Angela G., and David P. MacKinnon. 2016. "Design Approaches to Experimental Mediation." *Journal of Experimental Social Psychology* 66: 29–38 doi:10.1016/j.jesp.2015.09.012.

Polgreen, Philip M., Yiling Chen, David M. Pennock, and Forrest D. Nelson. 2008. "Using Internet Searches for Influenza Surveillance." *Clinical Infectious Diseases* 47 (11): 1443–8. doi:10.1086/593098.

Polonetsky, Jules, Omer Tene, and Joseph Jerome. 2015. "Beyond the Common Rule: Ethical Structures for Data Research in Non-Academic Settings." SSRN Scholarly Paper ID 2621559. Rochester, NY: Social Science Research Network. http://papers.ssrn.com/abstract=2621559.

Porter, Joan P., and Greg Koski. 2008. "Regulations for the Protection of Humans in Research in the United States: The Common Rule." In *The Oxford Textbook of Clinical Research Ethics*. Oxford: Oxford University Press.

Porter, Nathaniel D., Ashton M. Verdery, and S. Michael Gaddis. 2016. "Big Data's Little Brother: Enhancing Big Data in the Social Sciences with Micro-Task Marketplaces." *ArXiv:1609.08437 [cs.CY]*, September. http://arxiv.org/abs/1609.08437.

Preist, Chris, Elaine Massung, and David Coyle. 2014. "Competing or Aiming to Be Average?: Normification As a Means of Engaging Digital Volunteers." In *Proceedings of the 17th ACM Conference on Computer Supported Cooperative Work & Social Computing*, 1222–33. CSCW '14. New York: ACM. doi:10.1145/2531602.2531615.

Prentice, Deborah A., and Dale T. Miller. 1992. "When Small Effects Are Impressive." *Psychological Bulletin* 112 (1): 160–64. doi:10.1037/0033-2909.112.1.160.

Presser, Stanley, and Johnny Blair. 1994. "Survey Pretesting: Do Different Methods Produce Different Results?" *Sociological Methodology* 24: 73–104. doi:10.2307/270979.

Presser, Stanley, Mick P. Couper, Judith T. Lessler, Elizabeth Martin, Jean Martin, Jennifer M. Rothgeb, and Eleanor Singer. 2004. "Methods for Testing and Evaluating Survey Questions." *Public Opinion Quarterly* 68 (1): 109–30. doi:10.1093/poq/nfh008.

Provost, Foster, and Tom Fawcett. 2013. "Data Science and Its Relationship to Big Data and Data-Driven Decision Making." *Big Data* 1 (1): 51–59. doi:10.1089/big.2013.1508.

Purdam, Kingsley. 2014. "Citizen Social Science and Citizen Data? Methodological and Ethical Challenges for Social Research." *Current Sociology* 62 (3): 374–92. doi:10.1177/001139211452 7997.

Pury, Cynthia L. S. 2011. "Automation Can Lead to Confounds in Text Analysis." *Psychological Science* 22 (6): 835–36. doi:10.1177/0956797611408735.

Puschmann, Cornelius, and Engin Bozdag. 2014. "Staking Out the Unclear Ethical Terrain of Online Social Experiments." *Internet Policy Review* 3 (4). doi:10.14763/2014.4.338.

Puts, Marco, Piet Daas, and Ton de Waal. 2015. "Finding Errors in Big Data." *Significance* 12 (3): 26–29. doi:10.1111/j.1740-9713.2015.00826.x.

Quinn, Alexander J., and Benjamin B. Bederson. 2011. "Human Computation: A Survey and Taxonomy of a Growing Field." In *Proceedings of the 2011 Annual Conference on Human Factors in Computing Systems*, 1403–12. CHI '11. New York: ACM. doi:10.1145/1978942.1979148.

Raddick, M. Jordan, Georgia Bracey, Pamela L. Gay, Chris J. Lintott, Carie Cardamone, Phil Murray, Kevin Schawinski, Alexander S. Szalay, and Jan Vandenberg. 2013. "Galaxy Zoo: Motivations of Citizen Scientists." *Astronomy Education Review* 12 (1). doi:10.3847/AER2011021.

Raftery, Adrian E., Nan Li, Hana Ševčíková, Patrick Gerland, and Gerhard K. Heilig. 2012. "Bayesian Probabilistic Population Projections for All Countries." *Proceedings of the National Academy of Sciences of the USA* 109 (35): 13915–21. doi:10.1073/pnas.1211452109.

Rand, David G. 2012. "The Promise of Mechanical Turk: How Online Labor Markets Can Help Theorists Run Behavioral Experiments." *Journal of Theoretical Biology*, Evolution of Cooperation, 299 (April): 172–79. doi:10.1016/j.jtbi.2011.03.004.

Rao, J.N.K, and Isabel Molina. 2015. *Small Area Estimation*, 2nd edi. Hoboken, NJ: Wiley.

Rashid, Al Mamunur, Istvan Albert, Dan Cosley, Shyong K. Lam, Sean M. McNee, Joseph A. Konstan, and John Riedl. 2002. "Getting to Know You: Learning New User Preferences in Recommender Systems." In *Proceedings of the 7th International Conference on Intelligent User Interfaces*, 127–34. IUI '02. New York: ACM. doi:10.1145/502716.502737.

Rasinski, Kenneth A. 1989. "The Effect of Question Wording on Public Support for Government Spending." *Public Opinion Quarterly* 53 (3): 388–94. doi:10.1086/269158.

Ratkiewicz, Jacob, Michael D. Conover, Mark Meiss, Bruno Goncalves, Alessandro Flammini, and Filippo Menczer Menczer. 2011. "Detecting and Tracking Political Abuse in Social Media." In *Fifth*

International AAAI Conference on Weblogs and Social Media. http://www.aaai.org/ocs/index.php/ICWSM/ICWSM11/paper/view/2850.

R Core Team. 2016. "R: A Language and Environment for Statistical Computing." Vienna: R Foundation for Statistical Computing.

Reichman, Nancy E., Julien O. Teitler, Irwin Garfinkel, and Sara S. McLanahan. 2001. "Fragile Families: Sample and Design." *Children and Youth Services Review* 23 (45): 303–26. doi:10.1016/S0190-7409(01)00141-4.

Reiter, Jerome P. 2012. "Statistical Approaches to Protecting Confidentiality for Microdata and Their Effects on the Quality of Statistical Inferences." *Public Opinion Quarterly* 76 (1): 163–81. doi:10.1093/poq/nfr058.

Reiter, Jerome P., and Satkartar K. Kinney. 2011. "Sharing Confidential Data for Research Purposes: A Primer." *Epidemiology* 22 (5): 632–35. doi:10.1097/EDE.0b013e318225c44b.

Ren, Yuqing, F. Maxwell Harper, Sara Drenner, Loren Terveen, Sara Kiesler, John Riedl, and Robert E. Kraut. 2012. "Building Member Attachment in Online Communities: Applying Theories of Group Identity and Interpersonal Bonds." *MIS Quarterly* 36 (3): 841–64. http://dl.acm.org/citation.cfm?id=2481655.2481665.

Reno, Raymond R., Robert B. Cialdini, and Carl A. Kallgren. 1993. "The Transsituational Influence of Social Norms." *Journal of Personality and Social Psychology* 64 (1): 104–12. doi:10.1037/0022-3514.64.1.104.

Resnick, Brian. 2016. "Researchers Just Released Profile Data on 70,000 OkCupid Users without Permission." *Vox.* http://www.vox.com/2016/5/12/11666116/70000-okcupid-users-data-release.

Resnick, Paul, Richard Zeckhauser, John Swanson, and Kate Lockwood. 2006. "The Value of Reputation on eBay: A Controlled Experiment." *Experimental Economics* 9 (2): 79–101. doi:10.1007/s10683-006-4309-2.

Resnik, David B., Kevin C. Elliott, and Aubrey K. Miller. 2015. "A Framework for Addressing Ethical Issues in Citizen Science." *Environmental Science & Policy* 54 (December): 475–81. doi:10.1016/j.envsci.2015.05.008.

Restivo, Michael, and Arnout van de Rijt. 2012. "Experimental Study of Informal Rewards in Peer Production." *PLoS ONE* 7 (3): e34358. doi:10.1371/journal.pone.0034358.

———. 2014. "No Praise without Effort: Experimental Evidence on How Rewards Affect Wikipedia's Contributor Community." *Information, Communication & Society* 17 (4): 451–62. doi:10.1080/1369118X.2014.888459.

Riach, P. A, and J. Rich. 2002. "Field Experiments of Discrimination in the Market Place." *Economic Journal* 112 (483): F480–F518. doi:10.1111/1468-0297.00080.

Riach, Peter A., and Judith Rich. 2004. "Deceptive Field Experiments of Discrimination: Are They Ethical?" *Kyklos* 57 (3): 457–70. doi:10.1111/j.0023-5962.2004.00262.x.

Rich, Judith. 2014. "What Do Field Experiments of Discrimination in Markets Tell Us? A Meta Analysis of Studies Conducted Since 2000." SSRN Scholarly Paper ID 2517887. Rochester, NY: Social Science Research Network. http://papers.ssrn.com/abstract=2517887.

Richman, Josh. 2015. "Stanford and Dartmouth Researchers Broke Law with Election Mailer, Montana Official Says." *San Jose Mercury News*, May. http://www.mercurynews.com/nation-world/ci_28100916/stanford-and-dartmouth-researchers-broke-law-election-mailer.

Robbins, Jim. 2013. "Crowdsourcing, for the Birds." *New York Times*, August. http://www.nytimes.com/2013/08/20/science/earth/crowdsourcing-for-the-birds.html.

Robinson, Walter M., and Brandon T. Unruh. 2008. "The Hepatitis Experiments at the Willowbrook State School." In *The Oxford Textbook of Clinical Research Ethics*, edited by E. J. Emanuel, R. A. Crouch, C. Grady, R. K. Lie, F. G. Miller, and D. Wendler, 386–97. Oxford: Oxford University Press.

Rosenbaum, Paul R. 2002. *Observational Studies.* 2nd edition. New York: Springer.

———. 2010. *Design of Observational Studies.* New York: Springer.

———. 2015. "How to See More in Observational Studies: Some New Quasi-Experimental Devices." *Annual Review of Statistics and Its Application* 2 (1): 21–48. doi:10.1146/annurev-statistics-010814-020201.

Rosenzweig, Mark R., and Kenneth I. Wolpin. 2000. "Natural 'Natural Experiments' in Economics." *Journal of Economic Literature* 38 (4): 827–74. doi:10.1257/jel.38.4.827.

Rothman, Kenneth J., John EJ Gallacher, and Elizabeth E. Hatch. 2013. "Why Representativeness Should Be Avoided." *International Journal of Epidemiology* 42 (4): 1012–14. doi:10.1093/ije/dys223.

Rubin, Donald B. 2004. *Multiple Imputation for Nonresponse in Surveys.* Hoboken, NJ: Wiley-Interscience.

Russell, William Moy Stratton, and Rex Leonard Burch. 1959. *The Principles of Humane Experimental Technique.* http://altweb.jhsph.edu/pubs/books/humane_exp/addendum.

Rust, John and Susan Golombok. 2009. *Modern Psychometrics: The Science of Psychological Assessment*, 3rd ed. Hove, UK: Routledge.

Rutherford, Alex, Manuel Cebrian, Sohan Dsouza, Esteban Moro, Alex Pentland, and Iyad Rahwan. 2013. "Limits of Social Mobilization." *Proceedings of the National Academy of Sciences of the USA* 110 (16): 6281–86. doi:10.1073/pnas.1216338110.

Ruths, Derek, and Jürgen Pfeffer. 2014. "Social Media for Large Studies of Behavior." *Science* 346 (6213): 1063–64. doi:10.1126/science.346.6213.1063.

Saez-Rodriguez, Julio, James C. Costello, Stephen H. Friend, Michael R. Kellen, Lara Mangravite, Pablo Meyer, Thea Norman, and Gustavo Stolovitzky. 2016. "Crowdsourcing Biomedical Research: Leveraging Communities as Innovation Engines." *Nature Reviews Genetics* 17 (8): 470–86. doi:10.1038/nrg.2016.69.

Sakshaug, Joseph W., and Frauke Kreuter. 2012. "Assessing the Magnitude of Non-Consent Biases in Linked Survey and Administrative Data." *Survey Research Methods* 6 (2): 113–22.

Sakshaug, Joseph W., Mick P. Couper, Mary Beth Ofstedal, and David R. Weir. 2012. "Linking Survey and Administrative Records Mechanisms of Consent." *Sociological Methods & Research* 41 (4): 535–69. doi:10.1177/0049124112460381.

Salehi, Niloufar, Lilly C. Irani, Michael S. Bernstein, Ali Alkhatib, Eva Ogbe, Kristy Milland, and Clickhappier. 2015. "We Are Dynamo: Overcoming Stalling and Friction in Collective Action for Crowd Workers." In *Proceedings of the 33rd Annual ACM Conference on Human Factors in Computing Systems*, 1621–30. CHI '15. New York: ACM. doi:10.1145/2702123.2702508.

Salganik, Matthew J. 2007. "Success and Failure in Cultural Markets." PhD Thesis, Columbia University.

Salganik, Matthew J., and Karen E. C. Levy. 2015. "Wiki Surveys: Open and Quantifiable Social Data Collection." *PLoS ONE* 10 (5): e0123483. doi:10.1371/journal.pone.0123483.

Salganik, Matthew J., and Duncan J. Watts. 2008. "Leading the Herd Astray: An Experimental Study of Self-Fulfilling Prophecies in an Artificial Cultural Market." *Social Psychology Quarterly* 71 (4): 338–55. doi:10.1177/019027250807100404.

———. 2009a. "Social Influence: The Puzzling Nature of Success in Cultural Markets." In *The Oxford Handbook of Analytical Sociology*, edited by Peter Hedström and Peter Bearman, 315–41. Oxford: Oxford University Press.

———. 2009b. "Web-Based Experiments for the Study of Collective Social Dynamics in Cultural Markets." *Topics in Cognitive Science* 1 (3): 439–68. doi:10.1111/j.1756-8765.2009.01030.x.

Salganik, Matthew J., Peter Sheridan Dodds, and Duncan J. Watts. 2006. "Experimental Study of Inequality and Unpredictability in an Artificial Cultural Market." *Science* 311 (5762): 854–56. doi:10.1126/science.1121066.

Sampson, Robert J., and Mario Luis Small. 2015. "Bringing Social Science Back In: The Big Data Revolution and Urban Theory." *The Cities Papers.* http://citiespapers.ssrc.org/bringing-social-science-back-in-the-big-data-revolution-and-urban-theory/.

Sandvig, Christian, and Eszter Hargittai. 2015. "How to Think About Digital Research." In *Digital Research Confidential: The Secrets of Studying Behavior Online*, edited by Eszter Hargittai and Christian Sandvig. Cambridge, MA: MIT Press.

Sandvig, Christian, and Karrie Karahalios. 2016. "Most of What You Do Online Is Illegal. Let's End the Absurdity," *Guardian*, June. https://www.theguardian.com/commentisfree/2016/jun/30/cfaa-online-law-illegal-discrimination.

Santos, Robert L. 2014. "Presidential Address Borne of a Renaissance—A Metamorphosis for Our Future." *Public Opinion Quarterly* 78 (3): 769–77. doi:10.1093/poq/nfu034.

Saris, Willem E., and Irmtraud N. Gallhofer. 2014. *Design, Evaluation, and Analysis of Questionnaires for Survey Research*, 2nd ed. Hoboken, NJ: Wiley. http://dx.doi.org/10.1002/9781118634646.

Sauermann, Henry, and Chiara Franzoni. 2015. "Crowd Science User Contribution Patterns and Their Implications." *Proceedings of the National Academy of Sciences of the USA* 112 (3): 679–84. doi:10.1073/pnas.1408907112.

Sauver, Jennifer L. St, Brandon R. Grossardt, Barbara P. Yawn, L. Joseph Melton, and Walter A. Rocca. 2011. "Use of a Medical Records Linkage System to Enumerate a Dynamic Population Over Time: The Rochester Epidemiology Project." *American Journal of Epidemiology* 173 (9): 1059–68. doi:10.1093/aje/kwq482.

Särndal, Carl-Erik, and Sixten Lundström. 2005. *Estimation in Surveys with Nonresponse*. Hoboken, NJ: Wiley.

Särndal, Carl-Erik, Bengt Swensson, and Jan Wretman. 2003. *Model Assisted Survey Sampling*. New York: Springer.

Schaeffer, Nora Cate, Dana Garbarski, Jeremy Freese, and Douglas W. Maynard. 2013. "An Interactional Model of the Call for Survey Participation Actions and Reactions in the Survey Recruitment Call." *Public Opinion Quarterly* 77 (1): 323–51. doi:10.1093/poq/nft006.

Schauer, Frederick. 1978. "Fear, Risk and the First Amendment: Unraveling the Chilling Effect." *Boston University Law Review* 58: 685. http://heinonline.org/HOL/Page?handle=hein.journals/bulr58&id=695&div=&collection=.

Schechter, Stuart, and Cristian Bravo-Lillo. 2014. "Using Ethical-Response Surveys to Identify Sources of Disapproval and Concern with Facebook's Emotional Contagion Experiment and Other Controversial Studies." *Microsoft Research Technical Report* MSR-TR-2014-97 (October). http://research.microsoft.com/pubs/220718/CURRENT%20DRAFT%20-%20Ethical-Response%20Survey.pdf.

Schmidt, F. A. 2013. "The Good, The Bad and the Ugly: Why Crowdsourcing Needs Ethics." In *2013 Third International Conference on Cloud and Green Computing (CGC)*, 531–35. doi:10.1109/CGC.2013.89.

Schneider, Carl E. 2015. *The Censor's Hand: The Misregulation of Human-Subject Research*. Cambridge, MA: MIT Press.

Schnell, Rainer. 2013. "Linking Surveys and Administrative Data." *German Record Linkage Center, Working Paper Series*. http://www.record-linkage.de/-download=wp-grlc-2013-03.pdf.

Schober, Michael F., and Frederick G. Conrad. 2015. "Improving Social Measurement by Understanding Interaction in Survey Interviews." *Policy Insights from the Behavioral and Brain Sciences* 2 (1): 211–19. doi:10.1177/2372732215601112.

Schober, Michael F., Frederick G. Conrad, Christopher Antoun, Patrick Ehlen, Stefanie Fail, Andrew L. Hupp, Michael Johnston, Lucas Vickers, H. Yanna Yan, and Chan Zhang. 2015. "Precision and Disclosure in Text and Voice Interviews on Smartphones." *PLoS ONE* 10 (6): e0128337. doi:10.1371/journal.pone.0128337.

Schober, Michael F., Josh Pasek, Lauren Guggenheim, Cliff Lampe, and Frederick G. Conrad. 2016. "Social Media Analyses for Social Measurement." *Public Opinion Quarterly* 80 (1): 180–211. doi:10.1093/poq/nfv048.

Schonlau, Matthias, Arthur van Soest, Arie Kapteyn, and Mick Couper. 2009. "Selection Bias in Web Surveys and the Use of Propensity Scores." *Sociological Methods & Research* 37 (3): 291–318. doi:10.1177/0049124108327128.

Schrag, Zachary M. 2010. *Ethical Imperialism: Institutional Review Boards and the Social Sciences, 1965-2009*. Baltimore: Johns Hopkins University Press.

———. 2011. "The Case Against Ethics Review in the Social Sciences." *Research Ethics* 7 (4): 120–31. doi:10.1177/174701611100700402.

Schrage, Michael. 2011. "Q and A: The Experimenter." *MIT Technology Review*. http://www.technologyreview.com/news/422784/qa-the-experimenter/.

Schultz, P. Wesley, Azar M. Khazian, and Adam C. Zaleski. 2008. "Using Normative Social Influence to Promote Conservation Among Hotel Guests." *Social Influence* 3 (1): 4–23. doi:10.1080/15534510701755614.

Schultz, P. Wesley, Jessica M. Nolan, Robert B. Cialdini, Noah J. Goldstein, and Vladas Griskevicius. 2007. "The Constructive, Destructive, and Reconstructive Power of Social Norms." *Psychological Science* 18 (5): 429–34. doi:10.1111/j.1467-9280.2007.01917.x.

Schultze, Ulrike, and Richard O. Mason. 2012. "Studying Cyborgs: Re-Examining Internet Studies as Human Subjects Research." *Journal of Information Technology* 27 (4): 301–12. doi:10.1057/jit.2012.30.

Schulz, Kenneth F., Douglas G. Altman, David Moher, and for the CONSORT Group. 2010. "CONSORT 2010 Statement: Updated Guidelines for Reporting Parallel Group Randomised Trials." *PLoS Medicine* 7 (3): e1000251. doi:10.1371/journal.pmed.1000251.

Schuman, Howard, and Stanley Presser. 1979. "The Open and Closed Question." *American Sociological Review* 44 (5): 692–712. doi:10.2307/2094521.

———. 1996. *Questions and Answers in Attitude Surveys: Experiments on Question Form, Wording, and Context.* Thousand Oaks, CA: SAGE.

Schwartz, Paul M., and Daniel J. Solove. 2011. "The PII Problem: Privacy and a New Concept of Personally Identifiable Information." SSRN Scholarly Paper ID 1909366. Rochester, NY: Social Science Research Network. http://papers.ssrn.com/abstract=1909366.

Sears, David O. 1986. "College Sophomores in the Laboratory: Influences of a Narrow Data Base on Social Psychology's View of Human Nature." *Journal of Personality and Social Psychology* 51 (3): 515–30. doi:10.1037/0022-3514.51.3.515.

Sekhon, Jasjeet S. 2009. "Opiates for the Matches: Matching Methods for Causal Inference." *Annual Review of Political Science* 12 (1): 487–508. doi:10.1146/annurev.polisci.11.060606.135444.

Sekhon, Jasjeet S., and Rocío Titiunik. 2012. "When Natural Experiments Are Neither Natural nor Experiments." *American Political Science Review* 106 (1): 35–57. doi:10.1017/S0003055411000542.

Selinger, Evan, and Woodrow Hartzog. 2016. "Facebook's Emotional Contagion Study and the Ethical Problem of Co-Opted Identity in Mediated Environments Where Users Lack Control." *Research Ethics* 12 (1): 35–43. doi:10.1177/1747016115579531.

Seltzer, William, and Margo Anderson. 2008. "Using Population Data Systems to Target Vulnerable Population Subgroups and Individuals: Issues and Incidents." In *Statistical Methods for Human Rights*, edited by Jana Asher, David Banks, and Fritz J. Scheuren, 273–328. New York: Springer. http://link.springer.com/chapter/10.1007/978-0-387-72837-7_13.

Shadish, William R. 2002. "Revisiting Field Experimentation: Field Notes for the Future." *Psychological Methods* 7 (1): 3–18. doi:10.1037/1082-989X.7.1.3.

Shadish, William R., and Thomas D. Cook. 2009. "The Renaissance of Field Experimentation in Evaluating Interventions." *Annual Review of Psychology* 60 (1): 607–29. doi:10.1146/annurev.psych.60.110707.163544.

Shadish, William R., Thomas D. Cook, and Donald T. Campbell. 2001. *Experimental and Quasi-Experimental Designs for Generalized Causal Inference*, 2nd ed. Boston: Cengage Learning.

Shamir, Lior, Carol Yerby, Robert Simpson, Alexander M. von Benda-Beckmann, Peter Tyack, Filipa Samarra, Patrick Miller, and John Wallin. 2014. "Classification of Large Acoustic Datasets Using Machine Learning and Crowdsourcing: Application to Whale Calls." *Journal of the Acoustical Society of America* 135 (2): 953–62. doi:10.1121/1.4861348.

Sharma, Amit, Jake M. Hofman, and Duncan J. Watts. 2015. "Estimating the Causal Impact of Recommendation Systems from Observational Data." In *Proceedings of the Sixteenth ACM Conference on Economics and Computation*, 453–70. EC '15. New York: ACM. doi:10.1145/2764468.2764488.

———. 2016. "Split-Door Criterion for Causal Identification: Automatic Search for Natural Experiments." *ArXiv:1611.09414 [stat.ME]*, November. http://arxiv.org/abs/1611.09414.

Shaw, David. 2015. "Facebooks Flawed Emotion Experiment: Antisocial Research on Social Network Users." *Research Ethics*, May, 1747016115579535. doi:10.1177/1747016115579535.

Sheehan, Mark. 2011. "Can Broad Consent Be Informed Consent?" *Public Health Ethics* 4 (3): 226–35. doi:10.1093/phe/phr020.

Shiffrin, Richard M. 2016. "Drawing Causal Inference from Big Data." *Proceedings of the National Academy of Sciences of the USA* 113 (27): 7308–9. doi:10.1073/pnas.1608845113.

Shmueli, Galit. 2010. "To Explain or to Predict?" *Statistical Science* 25 (3): 289–310. doi:10.1214/10-STS330.

Simester, Duncan, Yu (Jeffrey) Hu, Erik Brynjolfsson, and Eric T Anderson. 2009. "Dynamics of Retail Advertising: Evidence from a Field Experiment." *Economic Inquiry* 47 (3): 482–99. doi:10.1111/j.1465-7295.2008.00161.x.

Simmons, Joseph P., Leif D. Nelson, and Uri Simonsohn. 2011. "False-Positive Psychology Undisclosed Flexibility in Data Collection and Analysis Allows Presenting Anything as Significant." *Psychological Science* 22 (11): 1359–66. doi:10.1177/0956797611417632.

Singal, Amit G., Peter D. R. Higgins, and Akbar K. Waljee. 2014. "A Primer on Effectiveness and Efficacy Trials." *Clinical and Translational Gastroenterology* 5 (1): e45. doi:10.1038/ctg.2013.13.

Singel, Ryan. 2009. "Netflix Spilled Your Brokeback Mountain Secret, Lawsuit Claims." *Wired*. http://www.wired.com/2009/12/netflix-privacy-lawsuit/.

Singleton Jr, Royce A., and Bruce C. Straits. 2009. *Approaches to Social Research*, 5th ed. New York: Oxford University Press.

Sinnott-Armstrong, Walter. 2014. "Consequentialism." In *The Stanford Encyclopedia of Philosophy*, edited by Edward N. Zalta, Spring 2014. http://plato.stanford.edu/archives/spr2014/entries/consequentialism/.

Slowikowski, Kamil. 2016. "Ggrepel: Repulsive Text and Label Geoms for 'Ggplot2'." https://CRAN.R-project.org/package=ggrepel.

Small, Mario Luis. 2009. "How Many Cases Do I Need? On Science and the Logic of Case Selection in Field-Based Research." *Ethnography* 10 (1): 5–38. doi:10.1177/1466138108099586.

Smith, Gordon C. S., and Jill P. Pell. 2003. "Parachute Use to Prevent Death and Major Trauma Related to Gravitational Challenge: Systematic Review of Randomised Controlled Trials." *BMJ* 327 (7429): 1459–61. doi:10.1136/bmj.327.7429.1459.

Smith, T. M. F. 1976. "The Foundations of Survey Sampling: A Review." *Journal of the Royal Statistical Society. Series A (General)* 139 (2): 183–204. doi:10.2307/2345174.

———. 1991. "Post-Stratification." *Journal of the Royal Statistical Society. Series D (The Statistician)* 40 (3): 315–23. doi:10.2307/2348284.

Smith, Tom W. 1987. "That Which We Call Welfare by Any Other Name Would Smell Sweeter: An Analysis of the Impact of Question Wording on Response Patterns." *Public Opinion Quarterly* 51 (1): 75–83. doi:10.1086/269015.

———. 2011. "The Report of the International Workshop on Using Multi-Level Data from Sample Frames, Auxiliary Databases, Paradata and Related Sources to Detect and Adjust for Nonresponse Bias in Surveys." *International Journal of Public Opinion Research* 23 (3): 389–402. doi:10.1093/ijpor/edr035.

Sobel, Dava. 1996. *Longitude: The True Story of a Lone Genius Who Solved the Greatest Scientific Problem of His Time*. Harmondsworth, UK: Penguin.

Soeller, Gary, Karrie Karahalios, Christian Sandvig, and Christo Wilson. 2016. "MapWatch: Detecting and Monitoring International Border Personalization on Online Maps." In *Proceedings of the 25th International Conference on World Wide Web*, 867–78. WWW '16. Republic and Canton of Geneva, Switzerland: International World Wide Web Conferences Steering Committee. doi:10.1145/2872427.2883016.

Solove, Daniel J. 2010. *Understanding Privacy*. Cambridge, MA: Harvard University Press.

Sommer, Robert. 1969. *Personal Space: The Behavioral Basis of Design*. Englewood Cliffs, NJ.: Prentice Hall.

Sommers, Roseanna, and Franklin G. Miller. 2013. "Forgoing Debriefing in Deceptive Research: Is It Ever Ethical?" *Ethics & Behavior* 23 (2): 98–116. doi:10.1080/10508422.2012.732505.

Sovey, Allison J., and Donald P. Green. 2011. "Instrumental Variables Estimation in Political Science: A Readers Guide." *American Journal of Political Science* 55 (1): 188–200. doi:10.1111/j.1540-5907.2010.00477.x.

Spector, Alfred, Peter Norvig, and Slav Petrov. 2012. "Google's Hybrid Approach to Research." *Communications of the ACM* 55 (7): 34–37. doi:10.1145/2209249.2209262.

Spitz, Vivien. 2005. *Doctors from Hell: The Horrific Account of Nazi Experiments on Humans.* Boulder, CO: Sentient.

Squire, Peverill. 1988. "Why the 1936 Literary Digest Poll Failed." *Public Opinion Quarterly* 52 (1): 125–33. doi:10.1086/269085.

Srivastava, Sameer B., Amir Goldberg, V. Govind Manian, and Christopher Potts. 2017. "Enculturation Trajectories: Language, Cultural Adaptation, and Individual Outcomes in Organizations." *Management Science* in press. doi:10.1287/mnsc.2016.2671.

Stark, Laura. 2012. *Behind Closed Doors: IRBs and the Making of Ethical Research.* Chicago: University Of Chicago Press.

Stephens-Davidowitz, Seth. 2014. "The Cost of Racial Animus on a Black Candidate: Evidence Using Google Search Data." *Journal of Public Economics* 118: 26–40. doi:10.1016/j.jpubeco.2014.04.010.

Stewart, Neil, Christoph Ungemach, Adam J. L. Harris, Daniel M. Bartels, Ben R. Newell, Gabriele Paolacci, and Jesse Chandler. 2015. "The Average Laboratory Samples a Population of 7,300 Amazon Mechanical Turk Workers." *Judgment and Decision Making* 10 (5): 479–91. http://journal.sjdm.org/14/14725/h2.html.

Stokes, Donald E. 1997. *Pasteur's Quadrant: Basic Science and Technological Innovation.* Washington, DC: Brookings Institution Press.

Stone, Arthur A., and Saul Shiffman. 1994. "Ecological Momentary Assessment (EMA) in Behavioral Medicine." *Annals of Behavioral Medicine* 16 (3): 199–202.

Stone, Arthur, Saul Shiffman, Audie Atienza, and Linda Nebeling, eds. 2007. *The Science of Real-Time Data Capture: Self-Reports in Health Research.* New York: Oxford University Press.

Stuart, Elizabeth A. 2010. "Matching Methods for Causal Inference: A Review and a Look Forward." *Statistical Science* 25 (1): 1–21. doi:10.1214/09-STS313.

Su, Jessica, Aneesh Sharma, and Sharad Goel. 2016. "The Effect of Recommendations on Network Structure." In *Proceedings of the 25th International Conference on World Wide Web*, 1157–67. WWW '16. Republic and Canton of Geneva, Switzerland: International World Wide Web Conferences Steering Committee. doi:10.1145/2872427.2883040.

Subrahmanian, V. S., Amos Azaria, Skylar Durst, Vadim Kagan, Aram Galstyan, Kristina Lerman, Linhong Zhu, et al. 2016. "The DARPA Twitter Bot Challenge." *ArXiv:1601.05140 [cs.SI]*, January. http://arxiv.org/abs/1601.05140.

Sugie, Naomi F. 2014. "Finding Work: A Smartphone Study of Job Searching, Social Contacts, and Wellbeing After Prison." PhD Thesis, Princeton University. http://dataspace.princeton.edu/jspui/handle/88435/dsp011544br32k.

———. 2016. "Utilizing Smartphones to Study Disadvantaged and Hard-to-Reach Groups." *Sociological Methods & Research*, January. doi:10.1177/0049124115626176.

Sunstein, Cass R. 2002. "Probability Neglect: Emotions, Worst Cases, and Law." *Yale Law Journal* 112 (1): 61–107. http://www.yalelawjournal.org/essay/probability-neglect-emotions-worst-cases-and-law.

———. 2005. *Laws of Fear: Beyond the Precautionary Principle.* Cambridge: Cambridge University Press.

Swanson, Alexandra, Margaret Kosmala, Chris Lintott, and Craig Packer. 2016. "A Generalized Approach for Producing, Quantifying, and Validating Citizen Science Data from Wildlife Images." *Conservation Biology* 30 (3): 520–31. doi:10.1111/cobi.12695.

Sweeney, Latanya 2002. "K-Anonymity: A Model for Protecting Privacy." *International Journal on Uncertainty Fuzziness and Knowledge-Based Systems* 10 (5): 557–70. doi:10.1142/S0218488502001648.

Sweeney, Latanya, Mercè Crosas, and and Michael Bar-Sinai. 2015. "Sharing Sensitive Data with Confidence: The Datatags System." *Technology Science*, October. http://techscience.org/a/2015101601/.

Taddy, Matt, Matt Gardner, Liyun Chen, and David Draper. 2016. "A Nonparametric Bayesian Analysis of Heterogeneous Treatment Effects in Digital Experimentation." *Journal of Business & Economic Statistics*, 34 (4): 661–72. doi:10.1080/07350015.2016.1172013.

Tang, John C., Manuel Cebrian, Nicklaus A. Giacobe, Hyun-Woo Kim, Taemie Kim, and Douglas "Beaker" Wickert. 2011. "Reflecting on the DARPA Red Balloon Challenge." *Communications of the ACM* 54 (4): 78–85. doi:10.1145/1924421.1924441.

Tavory, Iddo, and Ann Swidler. 2009. "Condom Semiotics: Meaning and Condom Use in Rural Malawi." *American Sociological Review* 74 (2): 171–89. doi:10.1177/000312240907400201.

Taylor, Sean J. 2013. "Real Scientists Make Their Own Data." http://seanjtaylor.com/post/41463778912/real-scientists-make-their-own-data.

Taylor, Sean J., Eytan Bakshy, and Sinan Aral. 2013. "Selection Effects in Online Sharing: Consequences for Peer Adoption." In *Proceedings of the Fourteenth ACM Conference on Electronic Commerce*, 821–36. EC '13. New York: ACM. doi:10.1145/2482540.2482604.

Tene, Omer, and Jules Polonetsky. 2016. "Beyond IRBs: Ethical Guidelines for Data Research." *Washington and Lee Law Review Online* 72 (3): 458. http://scholarlycommons.law.wlu.edu/wlulr-online/vol72/iss3/7.

Thompson, Clive. 2008. "If You Liked This, You're Sure to Love That." *New York Times Magazine*, November. http://www.nytimes.com/2008/11/23/magazine/23Netflix-t.html.

Thomsen, Ib. 1973. "A Note on the Efficiency of Weighting Subclass Means to Reduce the Effects of Nonresponse When Analyzing Survey Data." *Statistisk Tidskrift* 4: 278–83. https://statistics.no/a/histstat/ano/ano_io73_02.pdf.

Tilston, Natasha L., Ken T. D. Eames, Daniela Paolotti, Toby Ealden, and W. John Edmunds. 2010. "Internet-Based Surveillance of Influenza-Like-Illness in the UK During the 2009 H1N1 Influenza Pandemic." *BMC Public Health* 10: 650. doi:10.1186/1471-2458-10-650.

Tockar, Anthony. 2014. "Riding with the Stars: Passenger Privacy in the NYC Taxicab Dataset." *Neustar Research*. https://research.neustar.biz/2014/09/15/riding-with-the-stars-passenger-privacy-in-the-nyc-taxicab-dataset/.

Toole, Jameson L., Yu-Ru Lin, Erich Muehlegger, Daniel Shoag, Marta C. González, and David Lazer. 2015. "Tracking Employment Shocks Using Mobile Phone Data." *Journal of the Royal Society Interface* 12 (107): 20150185. doi:10.1098/rsif.2015.0185.

Toomim, Michael, Travis Kriplean, Claus Pörtner, and James Landay. 2011. "Utility of Human–Computer Interactions: Toward a Science of Preference Measurement." In *Proceedings of the 2011 Annual Conference on Human Factors in Computing Systems*, 2275–84. CHI '11. New York: ACM. doi:10.1145/1978942.1979277.

Torche, Florencia, and Uri Shwed. 2015. "The Hidden Costs of War: Exposure to Armed Conflict and Birth Outcomes." *Sociological Science* 2: 558–81. doi:10.15195/v2.a27.

Toshkov, Dimiter. 2015. "Exploring the Performance of Multilevel Modeling and Poststratification with Eurobarometer Data." *Political Analysis* 23 (3): 455–60. doi:10.1093/pan/mpv009.

Tourangeau, Roger. 2004. "Survey Research and Societal Change." *Annual Review of Psychology* 55 (1): 775–801. doi:10.1146/annurev.psych.55.090902.142040.

Tourangeau, Roger, and Ting Yan. 2007. "Sensitive Questions in Surveys." *Psychological Bulletin* 133 (5): 859–83. doi:10.1037/0033-2909.133.5.859.

Tufekci, Zeynep. 2014. "Big Questions for Social Media Big Data: Representativeness, Validity and Other Methodological Pitfalls." In *Proceedings of the Eighth International AAAI Conference on Weblogs and Social Media*, 505–14. http://www.aaai.org/ocs/index.php/ICWSM/ICWSM14/paper/view/8062.

Tuite, Kathleen, Noah Snavely, Dun-yu Hsiao, Nadine Tabing, and Zoran Popovic. 2011. "PhotoCity: Training Experts at Large-Scale Image Acquisition Through a Competitive Game." In *Proceedings of the 2011 Annual Conference on Human Factors in Computing Systems*, 1383–92. CHI '11. New York: ACM. doi:10.1145/1978942.1979146.

Tumasjan, Andranik, Timm O. Sprenger, Philipp G. Sandner, and Isabell M. Welpe. 2010. "Predicting Elections with Twitter: What 140 Characters Reveal About Political Sentiment." In *Proceedings of the Fourth International AAAI Conference on Weblogs and Social Media*, 178–85. http://www.aaai.org/ocs/index.php/ICWSM/ICWSM10/paper/view/1441.

———. 2012. "Where There is a Sea There are Pirates: Response to Jungherr, Jürgens, and Schoen." *Social Science Computer Review* 30 (2): 235–9. doi:10.1177/0894439311404123.

Tversky, Amos, and Daniel Kahneman. 1981. "The Framing of Decisions and the Psychology of Choice." *Science* 211 (4481): 453–58. http://www.jstor.org/stable/1685855.

Ugander, Johan, Brian Karrer, Lars Backstrom, and Cameron Marlow. 2011. "The Anatomy of the Facebook Social Graph." *ArXiv:1111.4503 [cs.SI]*, November. http://arxiv.org/abs/1111.4503.

Urbanek, Simon. 2013. "Png: Read and Write PNG Images." https://CRAN.R-project.org/package=png.

Vaccaro, K., K. Karahalios, C. Sandvig, K. Hamilton, and C. Langbort. 2015. "Agree or Cancel? Research and Terms of Service Compliance." In *ACM CSCW Ethics Workshop: Ethics for Studying Sociotechnical Systems in a Big Data World.* http://social.cs.uiuc.edu/papers/pdfs/Vaccaro-CSCW-Ethics-2015.pdf.

Vaillant, Gabriela Gonzalez, Juhi Tyagi, Idil Afife Akin, Fernanda Page Poma, Michael Schwartz, and Arnout van de Rijt. 2015. "A Field-Experimental Study of Emergent Mobilization in Online Collective Action." *Mobilization: An International Quarterly* 20 (3): 281–303. doi:10.17813/1086-671X-20-3-281.

Vaisey, Stephen. 2014. "The Attitudinal Fallacy Is a Fallacy: Why We Need Many Methods to Study Culture." *Sociological Methods & Research* 43 (2): 227–31. doi:10.1177/0049124114523395.

Valliant, Richard, and Jill A. Dever. 2011. "Estimating Propensity Adjustments for Volunteer Web Surveys." *Sociological Methods & Research* 40 (1): 105–37. doi:10.1177/0049124110392533.

van de Rijt, Arnout, Idil Akin, Robb Willer, and Matthew Feinberg. 2016. "Success-Breeds-Success in Collective Political Behavior: Evidence from a Field Experiment." *Sociological Science* 3: 940–50. doi:10.15195/v3.a41.

van de Rijt, Arnout, Soong Moon Kang, Michael Restivo, and Akshay Patil. 2014. "Field Experiments of Success-Breeds-Success Dynamics." *Proceedings of the National Academy of Sciences of the USA* 111 (19): 6934–9. doi:10.1073/pnas.1316836111.

VanderWeele, T. J., and S. Vansteelandt. 2014. "Mediation Analysis with Multiple Mediators." *Epidemiologic Methods* 2 (1): 95–115. doi:10.1515/em-2012-0010.

VanderWeele, Tyler. 2015. *Explanation in Causal Inference: Methods for Mediation and Interaction.* New York: Oxford University Press.

VanderWeele, Tyler J. 2009. "Mediation and Mechanism." *European Journal of Epidemiology* 24 (5): 217–24. doi:10.1007/s10654-009-9331-1.

VanderWeele, Tyler J., and Ilya Shpitser. 2013. "On the Definition of a Confounder." *Annals of Statistics* 41 (1): 196–220. doi:10.1214/12-AOS1058.

van Noort, Sander P., Cláudia T. Codeço, Carl E. Koppeschaar, Marc van Ranst, Daniela Paolotti, and M. Gabriela M. Gomes. 2015. "Ten-Year Performance of Influenzanet: ILI Time Series, Risks, Vaccine Effects, and Care-Seeking Behaviour." *Epidemics* 13 (December): 28–36. doi:10.1016/j.epidem.2015.05.001.

Vaughan, Ted R. 1967. "Governmental Intervention in Social Research: Political and Ethical Dimensions in the Wichita Jury Recordings." In *Ethics, Politics, and Social Research*, edited by Gideon Sjoberg, 50–77. Cambridge, MA: Schenkman.

Verma, Inder M. 2014. "Editorial Expression of Concern: Experimental Evidence of Massive-scale Emotional Contagion Through Social Networks." *Proceedings of the National Academy of Sciences of the USA* 111 (29): 10779. doi:10.1073/pnas.1412469111.

Vo, Huy, and Claudio Silvia. 2016. "Programming with Big Data." In *Big Data and Social Science: A Practical Guide to Methods and Tools*, edited by Ian Foster, Rayid Ghani, Ron S. Jarmin, Frauke Kreuter, and Julia Lane, 125–43. Boca Raton, FL: CRC Press.

von Ahn, Luis. 2005. "Human Computation." PhD Thesis, Carnegie Mellon University.

von Ahn, Luis, and Laura Dabbish. 2004. "Labeling Images with a Computer Game." In *Proceedings of the SIGCHI Conference on Human Factors in Computing Systems*, 319–26. CHI '04. New York. doi:10.1145/985692.985733.

———. 2008. "Designing Games with a Purpose." *Communications of the ACM* 51 (8): 58–67. doi:10.1145/1378704.1378719.

von Ahn, Luis, Benjamin Maurer, Colin McMillen, David Abraham, and Manuel Blum. 2008. "re-CAPTCHA: Human-Based Character Recognition via Web Security Measures." *Science* 321 (5895): 1465–8. doi:10.1126/science.1160379.

Wakefield, Sara, and Christopher Uggen. 2010. "Incarceration and Stratification." *Annual Review of Sociology* 36 (1): 387–406. doi:10.1146/annurev.soc.012809.102551.

Waksberg, Joseph. 1978. "Sampling Methods for Random Digit Dialing." *Journal of the American Statistical Association* 73 (361): 40–46. doi:10.1080/01621459.1978.10479995.

Waldrop, M. Mitchell. 2016. "The Chips Are down for Moore's Law." *Nature* 530 (7589): 144–47. doi:10.1038/530144a.

Wallgren, Anders, and Britt Wallgren. 2007. *Register-Based Statistics: Administrative Data for Statistical Purposes.* Chichester, UK: Wiley.

Walton, Gregory M. 2014. "The New Science of Wise Psychological Interventions." *Current Directions in Psychological Science* 23 (1): 73–82. doi:10.1177/0963721413512856.

Wang, Jing, Panagiotis G. Ipeirotis, and Foster Provost. 2015. "Cost-Effective Quality Assurance in Crowd Labeling." SSRN Scholarly Paper ID 2479845. Rochester, NY: Social Science Research Network. http://papers.ssrn.com/abstract=2479845.

Wang, Wei, David Rothschild, Sharad Goel, and Andrew Gelman. 2015. "Forecasting Elections with Non-Representative Polls." *International Journal of Forecasting* 31 (3): 980–91. doi:10.1016/j.ijforecast.2014.06.001.

Warren, Samuel D., and Louis D. Brandeis. 1890. "The Right to Privacy." *Harvard Law Review* 4 (5): 193–220. doi:10.2307/1321160.

Watkins, Susan Cotts, and Ann Swidler. 2009. "Hearsay Ethnography: Conversational Journals as a Method for Studying Culture in Action." *Poetics* 37 (2): 162–84. doi:10.1016/j.poetic.2009.03.002.

Watts, Duncan J. 2012. *Everything Is Obvious: How Common Sense Fails Us.* New York: Crown Business.

———. 2014. "Common Sense and Sociological Explanations." *American Journal of Sociology* 120 (2): 313–51. doi:10.1086/678271.

Webb, Eugene J., Donald T. Campbell, Richard D. Schwartz, and Lee Sechrest. 1966. *Unobtrusive Measures.* Chicago: Rand McNally.

Weisberg, Herbert F. 2005. *The Total Survey Error Approach: A Guide to the New Science of Survey Research.* Chicago: University of Chicago Press.

Wendler, David, Leah Belsky, Kimberly M. Thompson, and Ezekiel J. Emanuel. 2005. "Quantifying the Federal Minimal Risk Standard: Implications for Pediatric Research Without a Prospect of Direct Benefit." *JAMA* 294 (7): 826–32. doi:10.1001/jama.294.7.826.

Wesolowski, Amy, Caroline O. Buckee, Linus Bengtsson, Erik Wetter, Xin Lu, and Andrew J. Tatem. 2014. "Commentary: Containing the Ebola Outbreak—The Potential and Challenge of Mobile Network Data." *PLoS Currents.* doi:10.1371/currents.outbreaks.0177e7fcf52217b8b634376e2f3efc5e.

West, Brady T., and Annelies G. Blom. 2016. "Explaining Interviewer Effects: A Research Synthesis." *Journal of Survey Statistics and Methodology*, November. doi:10.1093/jssam/smw024.

Westen, Drew, and Robert Rosenthal. 2003. "Quantifying Construct Validity: Two Simple Measures." *Journal of Personality and Social Psychology* 84 (3): 608–18. doi:10.1037/0022-3514.84.3.608.

Wickham, H. 2011. "The Split–Apply–Combine Strategy for Data Analysis." *Journal of Statistical Software* 40 (1): 1–29.

Wickham, Hadley. 2007. "Reshaping Data with the Reshape Package." *Journal of Statistical Software* 21 (12): 1–20. http://www.jstatsoft.org/v21/i12/.

———. 2009. *Ggplot2: Elegant Graphics for Data Analysis.* New York: Springer.

———. 2015. "Stringr: Simple, Consistent Wrappers for Common String Operations." https://CRAN.R-project.org/package=stringr.

Wickham, Hadley, and Romain Francois. 2015. "Dplyr: A Grammar of Data Manipulation." https://CRAN.R-project.org/package=dplyr.

Wiggins, Andrea. 2011. "eBirding: Technology Adoption and the Transformation of Leisure into Science." In *Proceedings of the 2011 iConference*, 798–99. iConference '11. New York: ACM. doi:10.1145/1940761.1940910.

Wilke, Claus O. 2016. "Cowplot: Streamlined Plot Theme and Plot Annotations for 'ggplot2'." https://CRAN.R-project.org/package=cowplot.

Willer, David, and Henry Walker. 2007. *Building Experiments: Testing Social Theory*. Stanford, CA: Stanford Social Sciences.

Williamson, Vanessa. 2016. "On the Ethics of Crowdsourced Research." *PS: Political Science & Politics* 49 (1): 77–81. doi:10.1017/S104909651500116X.

Willis, Derek. 2014. "Professors' Research Project Stirs Political Outrage in Montana," *New York Times*, October. https://www.nytimes.com/2014/10/29/upshot/professors-research-project-stirs-political-outrage-in-montana.html.

Wilson, Timothy D., Elliot Aronson, and Kevin Carlsmith. 2010. "The Art of Laboratory Experimentation." In *Handbook of Social Psychology*. Hoboken, NJ: Wiley. http://onlinelibrary.wiley.com/doi/10.1002/9780470561119.socpsy001002/abstract.

Wimmer, Andreas, and Kevin Lewis. 2010. "Beyond and Below Racial Homophily: ERG Models of a Friendship Network Documented on Facebook." *American Journal of Sociology* 116 (2): 583–642. http://www.jstor.org/stable/10.1086/653658.

Windt, Peter Van der, and Macartan Humphreys. 2016. "Crowdseeding in Eastern Congo Using Cell Phones to Collect Conflict Events Data in Real Time." *Journal of Conflict Resolution* 60 (4): 748–81. doi:10.1177/0022002714553104.

Wolfers, Justin, and Eric Zitzewitz. 2004. "Prediction Markets." *Journal of Economic Perspectives* 18 (2): 107–26. http://www.jstor.org/stable/3216893.

Wood, Chris, Brian Sullivan, Marshall Iliff, Daniel Fink, and Steve Kelling. 2011. "eBird: Engaging Birders in Science and Conservation." *PLoS Biology* 9 (12): e1001220. doi:10.1371/journal.pbio.1001220.

Wu, Felix T. 2013. "Defining Privacy and Utility in Data Sets." *University of Colorado Law Review* 84: 1117–77. http://lawreview.colorado.edu/wp-content/uploads/2013/11/13.-Wu_710_s.pdf.

Xie, Huizhi, and Juliette Aurisset. 2016. "Improving the Sensitivity of Online Controlled Experiments: Case Studies at Netflix." In *Proceedings of the 22nd ACM SIGKDD International Conference on Knowledge Discovery and Data Mining*, 645–654. doi:10.1145/2939672.2939733.

Yakowitz, Jane. 2011. "Tragedy of the Data Commons." *Harvard Journal of Law & Technology* 25: 1–67. http://jolt.law.harvard.edu/articles/pdf/v25/25HarvJLTech1.pdf.

Yang, Shihao, Mauricio Santillana, and S. C. Kou. 2015. "Accurate Estimation of Influenza Epidemics Using Google Search Data via ARGO." *Proceedings of the National Academy of Sciences of the USA* 112 (47): 14473–8. doi:10.1073/pnas.1515373112.

Yeager, David S., Jon A. Krosnick, LinChiat Chang, Harold S. Javitz, Matthew S. Levendusky, Alberto Simpser, and Rui Wang. 2011. "Comparing the Accuracy of RDD Telephone Surveys and Internet Surveys Conducted with Probability and Non-Probability Samples." *Public Opinion Quarterly* 75 (4): 709–47. doi:10.1093/poq/nfr020.

Yoon, Carol Kaesuk. 1997. "Families Emerge as Silent Victims Of Tuskegee Syphilis Experiment." *New York Times*, May. http://www.nytimes.com/1997/05/12/us/families-emerge-as-silent-victims-of-tuskegee-syphilis-experiment.html.

Youyou, Wu, Michal Kosinski, and David Stillwell. 2015. "Computer-Based Personality Judgments Are More Accurate Than Those Made by Humans." *Proceedings of the National Academy of Sciences of the USA* 112 (4): 1036–40. doi:10.1073/pnas.1418680112.

Yu, Guangchuang. 2016. "Emojifont: Emoji Fonts for Using in R." https://CRAN.R-project.org/package=emojifont.

Zevenbergen, Bendert, Brent Mittelstadt, Carissa Véliz, Christian Detweiler, Corinne Cath, Julian Savulescu, and Meredith Whittaker. 2015. "Philosophy Meets Internet Engineering: Ethics in

Networked Systems Research. (GTC Workshop Outcomes Paper)." SSRN Scholarly Paper ID 2666934. Rochester, NY: Social Science Research Network. http://papers.ssrn.com/abstract=2666934.

Zhang, Han. 2016. "Causal Effect of Witnessing Political Protest on Civic Engagement." SSRN Scholarly Paper ID 2647222. Rochester, NY: Social Science Research Network. http://papers.ssrn.com/abstract=2647222.

Zhang, Li-Chun. 2000. "Post-Stratification and Calibration: A Synthesis." *American Statistician* 54 (3): 178–84. doi:10.1080/00031305.2000.10474542.

Zhou, Haotian, and Ayelet Fishbach. 2016. "The Pitfall of Experimenting on the Web: How Unattended Selective Attrition Leads to Surprising (Yet False) Research Conclusions." *Journal of Personality and Social Psychology* 111 (4): 493–504. doi:10.1037/pspa0000056.

Zignani, Matteo, Sabrina Gaito, Gian Paolo Rossi, Xiaohan Zhao, Haitao Zheng, and Ben Y. Zhao. 2014. "Link and Triadic Closure Delay: Temporal Metrics for Social Network Dynamics." In *Eighth International AAAI Conference on Weblogs and Social Media*. http://www.aaai.org/ocs/index.php/ICWSM/ICWSM14/paper/view/8042.

Zimmer, Michael. 2010. "But the Data Is Already Public: On the Ethics of Research in Facebook." *Ethics and Information Technology* 12 (4): 313–25. doi:10.1007/s10676-010-9227-5.

———. 2016. "OkCupid Study Reveals the Perils of Big-Data Science." *Wired*. https://www.wired.com/2016/05/okcupid-study-reveals-perils-big-data-science/.

Zimmerman, Birgitte. 2016. "Information and Power: Ethical Considerations of Political Information Experiments." In *Ethics and Experiments: Problems and Solutions for Social Scientists and Policy Professionals*, edited by Scott Desposato, 183–97. New York: Routledge.

Zittrain, Jonathan. 2008. "Ubiquitous Human Computing." *Philosophical Transactions of the Royal Society A: Mathematical, Physical and Engineering Sciences* 366 (1881): 3813–21. doi:10.1098/rsta.2008.0116.

Zizzo, Daniel John. 2010. "Experimenter Demand Effects in Economic Experiments." *Experimental Economics* 13 (1): 75–98. doi:10.1007/s10683-009-9230-z.

Zook, Matthew, Solon Barocas, Kate Crawford, Emily Keller, Seeta Peña Gangadharan, Alyssa Goodman, Rachelle Hollander, et al. 2017. "Ten Simple Rules for Responsible Big Data Research." *PLoS Computational Biology* 13 (3): e1005399. doi:10.1371/journal.pcbi.1005399.

INDEX

Abelson, Hal, 11

A/B tests, 185

administrative records, 82–83; data linkage for, 140–41

advertising, 186–87; return on investment tied to, 226–27

Affluent Worker Project, 82

African Americans: in Tuskegee Syphilis Study, 294, 325–28; *See also* race

Agarwal, Sameer, 259

AIDS and HIV, 262–63, 269

Ai Weiwei, 44

algorithmic confounding, 24, 34–36, 74; in Google Flu Trends, 49

Allcott, Hunt, 164–68, 170–71, 212

always-on data, 21–22, 71; in natural experiments, 53; pre-treatment information in, 157

Amazon Mechanical Turk. *See* MTurk

American Association of Public Opinion Research (AAPOR), 136

amplified asking, 122–30, 141

analog data, 2–3

analog experiments, 152, 154–57, 210–11; costs of, 190

ANCOVA (Analysis of Covariance), 209

Anderson, Ashton, 74

Anderson, Margo, 290

Angrist, Joshua, 51, 53, 62–63

animals, ethical issues in experiments using, 196–97

anonymization of data, 8, 12, 28; to manage informational risks, 307–12, 336–37; of Netflix movie ratings, 39–40, 269

Ansolabehere, Stephen, 119–21, 140, 356

Antoun, Christopher, 144

AOL (firm), 28, 72

armada strategy, 189–90, 216

asking questions, observing versus, 87–89, 137

astronomy. *See* Galaxy Zoo

auction behavior, 55–60

Aurisset, Juliette, 201

autonomy of people, 295

auxiliary information: in non-probability sampling, 136; for nonresponse problem, 135; in stratified sampling, 132–33

Back, Mitja D., 37, 38

Bafumi, Joseph, 139

Baker, David, 250, 270

balance checks, 212

Bamford, James, 27

Banerji, Manda, 238, 239

Banksy, 343–45

Baracas, Solon, 11

barnstars (Wikipedia awards), 150

bathrooms, privacy in, 340–41

Beauchamp, Tom L., 333

behavior: ethical issues in observation of, 288; observational data on, 13; reported, 137

behavioral drift, 34

Belmont Report, 294–95, 301, 331; on assessment of risks and benefits, 318; on Beneficence, 296; Common Rule compared with, 329; history of, 328; on Justice, 298–99; on Respect for Persons, 295, 333

Benard, Stephen, 153–54

Beneficence, 296–98, 302, 317, 334

Bengtsson, Linus, 83

Benoit, Kenneth, 241–44, 278, 356

Bentham, Jeremy, 288, 302

Berges, Aida, 270

Berinsky, Adam J., 77, 214

Bernedo, María, 223

Bethlehem, Jelke, 135, 136

between-subjects designs, 160–61

biases, 89; coverage bias, 93; in human computation mass collaborations, 237; nonresponse bias, 93, 135; social desirability bias, 108; trade-off between variance and, 138

big data, 3, 60–62, 71; algorithmic confounded data in, 34–36; always-on characteristic of, 21–22; characteristics of, 17; definitions of, 13,

14, 70; dirty data in, 36–39; drifting of, 33–34; inaccessibility of, 27–29; incompleteness of, 24–27; nonreactivity of, 23–24; nonrepresentativeness of, 29–33; nowcasting using, 46–50; purposes and scale of, 17–21; repurposing of, 14–17; sensitive data in, 39–41; surveys linked to, 117–30, 140–41

biology, protein folding in, 249–51

bird data, eBird for, 257–59

Bitcoin, 306

Bjerrekaer, Julius, 350–51

blacks: in Tuskegee Syphilis Study, 294, 325–28; *See also* race

blocked experimental designs (stratified experimental designs), 218–19

Blumenstock, Joshua E.: amplified asking used by, 122–30; machine learning model used by, 145; mixed research design used by, 5, 8, 332; Rwanda telephone study by, 1–2, 358–59

Boellstorff, Tom, 70

bogus data, in mass collaborations, 236–37

Bond, Robert M., 208, 216, 217

boomerang effects, 159, 160, 168

Bradburn, Norman, 94

Brandeis, Louis D., 337

Bravo-Lillo, Cristian, 320

Brexit, 144–45

Brick, J. Michael, 137

British Doctors Study, 30

British Election Study (BES), 144–45

broad consent, 336

Bruine de Bruin, Wändi, 223

Buckley, Sue, 339

Budak, Ceren, 21

Burch, Rex Leonard, 196–97, 217

Burke, Moira, 88, 118–19

Burnett, Sam, 286

business. *See* corporations

Buxtun, Robert, 327

Cadamuro, Gabriel, 125, 358–59

call detail records (CDRs), 146

Camerer, Colin, 74

Campbell, Donald T., 211

cancer: ethical issues in research into, 345–47; smoking and, 30–31

Canfield, Casey, 223

Cardamone, Carolin, 268

Carter, Stephen L., 322

casinos, 36, 224

Castronova, Edward, 215, 270

causality, 209; fundamental problem of causal inference, 64, 204–5; making causal inferences from non-experimental approaches, 62

cause-and-effect questions, 147–48

cell phones. *See* mobile phones

censorship of Internet, 43–46, 74–75; Encore study of, 286, 297–98; *See also* Encore

Census Bureau, US, 70

census data, 122–23; secondary uses of, 290

Centers for Disease Control and Prevention, US (CDC), 46–49

Centola, Damon, 181–82

Chatfield, Sara, 77

Chetty, Raj, 18–20, 71, 72

Chicago Jury Project, 334

Childress, James F., 333

China, censorship of Internet in, 43–46, 74–75

cholera, 29–30

Chowdhury, Abdur, 28

Cialdini, Robert, 220

Cinematch, 246–47

citizen science, 10, 272

Clark, Eric M., 78

closed questions, 111–13

collective intelligence, 272

Common Rule, 328–29; attempts to modernize, 293; based on Belmont Report, 294; Encore research not covered by, 286; updating of, 332

compensation for participants, 217, 334; Belmont Report on, 299; in mass collaborations, 265–66, 268–69

compliance with laws, 300

complier average causal effect (CACE), 68–69, 76

computer-administered surveys, 108

computer-assisted human computation system, 239, 241, 274

Computer Fraud and Abuse Act (US), 300

computers, 3; humans compared with, 273

computer science, ethical issues in, 329–30

conditional average treatment effect (CATE), 206

confidential data, 39–41; in study of ex-offenders, 111

confounders, 147–48

Conrad, Frederick G., 139

consensus, in mass collaborations, 236–37

consent. *See* informed consent

consequentialism, 302–3

CONSORT (Consolidated Standard Reporting of Trials) guidelines, 216

construct validity, 25–26, 163, 199, 212

consumer studies, 55–60

context-relative informational norms, 315–17

contextual integrity, 315–16

control groups, 150, 197–98, 224

Cooperative Congressional Election Study (CCES), 99

Coppock, Alexander, 188

corporations: administrative records of, 82–83; ethical issues in experiments with data from, 290–93; experimentation in, 222; inaccessibility of data held by, 27–29; nowcasting useful for, 46; partnering with, 184–88; sensitive data of, 39–41

Correll, Shelley J., 153–54

Costa, Dora L., 168

costs: in building your own experiments, 182; of experiments, 190–96, 216–17; of human interviewers, 108; of survey research, 98–99, 138, 141; of working with powerful partners, 184

counting, 41–46, 74–75

coverage bias, 93

coverage errors, 92–93, 100

Coviello, Lorenzo, 200, 218

credit for work, in mass collaborations, 269, 277

crowdsourcing, 10, 272

Cukier, Kenneth, 11

cultural products, 192–96

cumulative advantage, 176

custommades, 7–8, 355–56

data augmentation, 274

database of ruin, 27, 289, 290

data collection: distributed, 256–64; participant-centered, 356–57

data protection plans, 312

data scientists, 6, 355; ethical concerns of, 281–82; on repurposing data, 16

Deaton, Angus, 76

debriefing participants, 306, 335–36, 353–54

Defense Advanced Research Projects Agency (DARPA) Network Challenge, 272

deferred consent, 336

demand effects, 210

Demographic and Health Surveys, 2, 128–29, 358

demographic forecasting, 75

Deng, Alex, 201

deontology, 302–3

Desposato, Scott, 334

difference-in-differences estimators, 201, 203, 208, 219; difference-in-mean estimators compared with, 224

difference-of-means estimators, 205, 208–9; difference-in-differences estimators compared with, 224

differential privacy, 358

digital experiments. *See* experiments, digital

digital fingerprints, 71

digital footprints, 71

digital traces, 13, 71

dirty data, 36–39, 74

distributed data collection mass collaborations, 232, 256–57, 262–64, 271, 274; eBird, 257–59; ethical issues in, 269; PhotoCity, 259–62

Dodds, Peter, 192, 357

Doleac, Jennifer, 175

Doll, Richard, 30, 72

Donoho, David, 12

draft lottery (conscription), 51, 53–55, 63, 66–69, 76–77

drift, 33–34, 49, 73

Duchamp, Marcel, 6–7, 355

Duncan, Otis Dudley, 33

Dunn, Halbert L., 26

Dunning, Thad, 76

Dwyer, Patrick C., 221–22

eBay auctions, 55–60

eBird (ornithology data), 257–59, 274

Ebola virus, 281, 316

e-cigarettes, 78

ecological momentary assessments (EMA), 108–11

The Economist (magazine), 277–78

Efrati, Amir, 81

Egloff, Boris, 38

Einav, Liran, 28, 55–60

elections, 82; on Brexit, 144–45; Cooperative Congressional Election Study of, 99; errors in predicting results of, 100; experiment to simulate, 180–81; Facebook study of, 185–88; German parliamentary elections, 31–32; *Literary Digest* poll on, 91–94; non-probability samples for, 102–6; political manifestos crowd coded during, 241–44; problems in studying, 179–80; representation errors in samples predicting, 91–94; Twitter for data on, 33, 73; *See also* voting

Emotional Contagion experiment, 197–201, 218, 221; ethical issues in, 284–85, 290–93, 319, 324, 331–32, 339; principle of Beneficence applied to, 297; principle of Justice applied to, 299; principle of Respect for Law and Public Interest applied to, 300, 301; worst-case scenarios in, 323

empirically driven theorizing, 61–62

employment discrimination, 304–5, 352

Encore, 286–87; ethical issues in, 297–99, 318, 319; informed consent issue for, 305; not under Common Rule, 330; principle of Respect for Law and Public Interest applied to, 301

encouragement designs, 66, 228

energy usage, 158–68, 170–71

enriched asking, 118–22, 140

ensemble solutions, 275

environments for experiments: building new, 179–82; using existing, 174–79

epidemiology, 46–49

errors: in measurement, 94–98; in representation, 91–94; systematic, 20–21; total survey error framework, 89–91

ESP Game, 273–74

ethical issues, 8–11, 281–83, 324–25, 331–32, 357–58; in amplified asking, 141; in design of experiments, 196–202; in digital research, 288–93; ethical frameworks for, 301–3, 335; ethics as continuous, 324; in experiments in existing environments, 178–79; in Facebook study of Emotional Contagion, 284–85; of field experiments, 211; history of, 325–30; in inaccessible data, 27–29; informed consent, 303–7; institutional review boards and, 321–22; management of informational risk as, 307–14, 336–37; in mass collaborations, 268–69, 273, 277–78; nonreactivity as, 24; principles of, 294–301, 333; privacy as, 314–17, 337–38; in studies of ex-offenders, 110–11; in Tastes, Ties, and Time research project, 285; uncertainty and decisions on, 317–21, 338; in use of sensitive data, 40; worst-case scenarios in, 323–24

ethical-response surveys, 320

ethnography, 136

exclusion restrictions, 54–55, 68

existing environments, experiments within, 174–79

ex-offenders, 109–11

experiments, 147–49, 210; advice on design of, 188–90, 216; approximating, 50–60, 76–77; within businesses, 222; digital, 152, 154–57, 173–88, 210–11; digital, building, 179–82, 214–15; digital, building your own products for, 182–83, 215; digital, costs of, 190–96; digital, ethical issues in, 196–202, 288–93; digital, with powerful partners, 184–88, 215–16; digital,

using existing environments, 174–79; elements of, 149–51; ethical issues in design of, 196–202; explanatory mechanisms (intervening variables) in, 169–73, 213–14; heterogeneity of treatment effects in, 167–69; lab versus field and analog versus digital, 151–57, 210–11; non-experimental data distinguished from, 209; potential outcomes framework for, 202–7; precision in, 207–9; survey experiments, 97; validity of, 161–67, 211–12

external validity, 163–64

Eyal, Nir, 305

Facebook, 34; algorithmic confounding of data from, 35–36; data from merged with student data, 285; decline in sharing on, 81; in election study, 185–88; Emotional Contagion experiment using, 197–201, 218; Emotional Contagion experiment using, ethical issues in, 284–85, 290–93, 297; Friendsense survey on, 115–17; impact on friendships of, 88; predictions made by, 145; Tastes, Ties, and Time research project used data from, 285, 290, 297; on voting behavior, 72; voting behavior linked to, 140; See also Emotional Contagion experiment

Farber, Henry, 42–43, 74, 311

Feamster, Nick, 286

feature engineering, 238–39

Ferraro, Paul J., 171–73, 223

field experiments, 151–54, 210–11; digital, 156–57; informed consent in, 304–5; simulating, 181–82

Fisher, Dana R., 11

"fishing," 213, 219

Fitzpatrick, J. W., 257

fixed costs, 141, 190; in MusicLab, 194, 196

Foldit, 249–51, 273, 275; credit for participants in, 269, 277; participants in, 270

forecasting, 46–50, 75–76

found data, 82–83

Fragile Families and Child Wellbeing Study, 255–56

frame populations, 92–93

Friendsense (survey), 115–17, 357

fundamental problem of causal inference, 64, 204–5

Funk, Simon, 248–49

Gaddis, S. Michael, 274

Galaxy Zoo, 232–41, 245, 274, 357; credit for participants in, 269; new discoveries from,

267–68; participants in, 270
Gallacher, John E. J., 72–73
Gallup, George, 138
games, 273–74
gamification, 115–17
Gardner, Howard, 25
Gelman, Andrew, 102–4, 139, 354
gender: employment discrimination based on, 352; post-stratification techniques for, 104
generalizing from samples to populations, 31
General Social Survey (GSS), 70, 116, 142; data collection for, 256–57; Twitter compared with, 14–15
Gerber, Alan S., 207, 342, 343
Gill, Michael, 351
Ginsberg, Jeremy, 47
Glaeser, Edward, 255
Glaser, Barney, 61
Gleick, James, 11
Goel, Sharad, 102–6, 115, 117, 142, 357
Goldman, William, 192
Goldthorpe, John H., 82
Google: Flu Trends reports of, 36, 47–49, 75, 77, 356; Google Books, 18; Google NGrams dataset, 79–80
government administrative records, 15–16; data linkage to, 140
governments: administrative records of, 82–83; ethical issues in experiments with data from, 290–93; inaccessibility of data held by, 27–29; nowcasting useful for, 46; sensitive data of, 39–41; as source of big data, 15–16, 70; voting records kept by, 119
Graepel, Thore, 12, 145
Grebner, Mark, 342, 343
Green, Donald P., 207, 341–42
Grimmelmann, James, 300
grounded theory, 61–62
Group Insurance Commission (GIC; Massachusetts), 308–9
Groves, Robert M., 12, 137, 138
Guess, Andrew, 188
Guillory, Jamie, 197–201, 221

Hancock, Jeffrey, 197–201, 221
Hargittai, Eszter, 11, 12, 83
Harper, F. Maxwell, 215
Harrison, John, 274–75
Hart, Nicky, 82
hashtags, 34
Hatch, Elizabeth E., 72–73

Hauge, Michelle, 344
Hausel, Peter, 196
Hawthorne effects, 210
Heckman, James J., 76
Heller, Jean, 327
Hersh, Eitan, 119–21, 140, 356
heterogeneity: in mass collaborations, 266–67; of treatment effects, 167–69, 212–13
Hill, A. Bradford, 30, 72
Hill, Seth, 179–81
history, sociology compared with, 82
Holland, Paul W., 64, 204
Home Energy Reports, 164–68, 170–71
Homeland Security, US Department of: on ethical guidelines for information and communications technology, 330; Menlo Report of, 294; tracking and monitoring of social media by, 80
homogeneous-response-propensities-within-groups assumption, 104–5
Horvitz–Thompson estimator, 131–33
Huber, Gregory A., 179–81, 214, 215
Huberty, Mark, 73
human computation mass collaborations, 231–34, 244–46, 271, 273–75; crowd-coding of political manifestos, 241–44; Galaxy Zoo project, 234–41; open call projects compared with, 254–55
human interviewers, 108
human rights abuses, 290
Humphreys, Macartan, 278, 336, 339–40, 347

Imbens, Guido W., 76
imputation (user-attribute inference), 26; See also amplified asking
inaccessibility of data, 27–29, 72
inattentive participants, 215
incarceration rates, 109
incompleteness, 24–27, 72
in-depth interviews, 85
inferred consent, 336
influenza (flu), 46–49, 75
InfluenzaNet project, 277
informational risk, management of, 307–14, 336–37
informed consent, 295, 303–7, 333–36, 343; Belmont Report and Common Rule on, 329; for data linkage, 140; ethical frameworks on, 302; lacking in Encore research, 286–87; in mass collaborations, 269; in study of ex-offenders,

111; in Tuskegee Syphilis Study, 327

injunctive norms, 159–60

institutional review boards (IRBs), 281–82, 321–22; attempts to avoid, 332; Common Rule on, 329; on informed consent, 304; Montana voting study and, 350; nonresearchers on, 297

instrumental variables, 66, 76

intelligence, 25

Intelligence Community Comprehensive National Cybersecurity Initiative Data Center (Utah Data Center), 27

intergenerational social mobility, 19–20

internal states, 88

internal validity, 163, 212

Internet: advertising on, 186–87, 226–27; Chinese censorship of, 43–46, 74–75; Encore study of censorship of, 286–87, 297–98; mass collaborations using, 231, 270; online courses on, 225–26; online dating sites on, 350–51; of things, 3; See also Encore; social media

interrupted time series design, 80

Inter-university Consortium for Political and Social Research, 314

intervening variables (mechanisms), 169–73, 213–14

interviewer effects, 108

interviews, 85; by humans versus computer-administered, 108; new techniques versus, 107

Issenberg, Sasha, 209, 343

item nonresponse, 133

Jensen, Robert, 83

Jewish Chronic Disease Hospital, 345–47

Johnson, Jeremy, 348

Jones, Jason J., 216

Judson, D. H., 140

jury deliberations, 334

Justice, 298–99, 334

Kahn, Matthew E., 168

Kahn, Robert Louis, 137

Kant, Immanuel, 302

Kauffman, Jason, 343

Keeter, Scott, 98

Keohane, Robert O., 11

Khan, Shamus, 11

King, Gary, 11, 43–46, 74

Kirkegaard, Emil, 350–51

Kleinberg, Jon, 74, 76

Kleinsman, John, 339

Kohavi, Ron, 212

Konstan, Joseph A., 215

Kosinski, Michal, 12, 145, 332

Koun S. C., 49

Kramer, Adam D. I., 197–201, 218, 221

Kraut, Robert E., 88, 118–19

Küfner, Albrecht C.P., 38

lab experiments, 151–54, 210–11; building, 179–82, 214–15; costs of, 190; digital, 155

Labour Party (United Kingdom), 241

Lakhani, Karim, 278–79

Landon, Alf, 92

language, Google Books data on, 18

Lapin, Lisa, 348

Larimer, Christopher, 342

Lazer, David, 49

League of Conservation Voters, 188

Le Comber, Steven C., 344

Ledeen, Ken, 11

Lenz, Gabriel S., 179–81, 214

Levy, Karen E. C., 11, 113

Lewis, Harry, 11

Lewis, Randall A., 227

Lintott, Chris, 235, 237, 245, 270, 357

Literary Digest, 91–94, 100, 138

local average treatment effect (LATE), 68, 76

Longford, Nicholas T., 210

Longitude Prize, 274–75

longitudinal studies, big data for, 21

lotteries: draft lottery, 51, 53–55, 63, 66–69, 76–77; for research subjects, 217

Loveman, Gary, 224

Lowrance, William W., 314–15

lung cancer, 30–31

Maddock, Jim, 339

Maki, Alexander, 221–22

Malawi Journals Project, 262–63, 269, 274

Malchow, Hal, 341–42

Manifesto Project, 241–44, 278

Manzi, Jim, 11, 209, 222, 224

Maryland, 300–301

Mas, Alexandre, 52–53, 55

Mason, Robert, 339

Mason, Winter, 115, 357

Massachusetts, 308–9

mass collaborations, 10, 231–33, 271–77; crowd-coding of political manifestos, 241–44; designing your own, 265–71; distributed data collection, 256–57, 262–64; eBird, 257–59;

Rao, Justin M., 227
rare events, 18
reactivity, 23–24
readymades, 7–8, 355–56
real-time estimates, 22
record linkage, 26–27, 119, 140–41
recruiting participants, 179–81, 210; MTurk for, 214–15
reduction in number of participants, 197, 217–19
redundancy, in mass collaborations, 236
refining the treatment, 197, 217, 218
re-identification of data. *See* anonymization of data
replacement, 197, 217–18
representation, 91–94, 99–107, 138; errors in, 90; representative data, 29–30
repurposing data, 219
research design, 5; counting in, 41–46; encouragement designs for, 66; ethical issues in, 357–58; experiments approximated in, 50–60; forecasting and nowcasting, 46–50
Respect for Law and Public Interest, 299–301, 335; Menlo Report on, 330
Respect for Persons, 295, 317, 333–34; based on deontology, 302; informed consent and, 306–7
respondents, 93; nonresponse problem and, 133–35; viral recruitment of, 116, 144
restaurants, 351–52
Restivo, Michael: ethical issues in work of, 296–97; participants conscripted by, 217; Wikipedia experiment by, 150–51, 155, 157, 190–91, 203–4, 206–9
retrospective data, 22, 37
return on investment (ROI), 226–27
retweets (Twitter), 78
risk/benefit analysis, 296–97
Roberts, Molly, 43–44
Rogers, Todd, 171
Rome (Italy), 259–62
Romney, Mitt, 103
Roosevelt, Franklin, 92
Rossmo, D. Kim, 344
Rothman, Alexander J., 221–22
Rothman, Kenneth J., 72–73
Rothschild, David, 102–6
Rubin, Donald, 62
Russell, William Moy Stratton, 196–97, 217
Rwanda, 1–2, 123–32, 332, 358–59

sample populations, 93
samples: errors in, 90–91; generalizing to populations from, 31
sampling, 99–107; errors in, 93; non-probability sampling methods, 99–107, 136; probability sampling, 131–33; probability sampling, with nonresponse, 133–35; representation in, 91–94; representativeness of, 29
sampling frames, 92
Sandvig, Christian, 11, 12, 83
Santillana, Mauricio, 49
Schawinski, Kevin, 234–35, 237, 245, 270, 357
Schechter, Stuart, 320
Schober, Michael F., 107, 139
Schultz, P. Wesley, 223; costs of research by, 190; energy conservation experiment by, 158–68, 171, 211, 219
Schuman, Howard, 112, 143
scurvy (disease), 170
self-report measures, 143
Seltzer, William, 290
sensitive data, 39–41, 74; Chinese censorship of social media on, 44; mobile phone metadata as, 123; re-identification of, 309–11; in study of ex-offenders, 111
September eleventh terrorist attacks, 20–21, 37–38
sharing data, 312–14
Shmatikov, Vitaly, 39–40, 269, 310
SIGCOMM (computer science conference), 287
simple experiments, 158
Singel, Ryan, 311
Singleton, Royce A., Jr., 11
smartphones, 107; for digital experiments, 155; ecological momentary assessments using, 109; *See also* mobile phones
Smith, Gordon C. S., 224
smoking, 30–31
Snapshot Serengeti, 274
Snow, John, 29–30
social bots, 74
social desirability bias, 108
social experiments, 211
social media: algorithmic confounding of data from, 35–36; in China, censorship of, 43–46; for elections data, 73; for real-time data, 22; as source of big data, 15; tracking and monitoring of, 80–81; viral recruitment of respondents using, 116; *See also* Facebook; Twitter
social mobility, 18–20
social networks, 181–82; Tastes, Ties, and Time research project on, 285
social scientists, 6, 355; ethical concerns of, 281–82; on repurposing data, 16

Utah Data Center (Intelligence Community Comprehensive National Cybersecurity Initiative Data Center), 27

validity, 161–67, 211–12
van Arkel, Hanny, 268
van de Rijt, Arnout: ethical issues in work of, 296–97; low costs of research by, 190–91; random rewards experiment by, 176–77, 220; Wikipedia experiment by, 150–51, 155, 157, 203–4, 206–9, 217
van der Windt, Peter, 278, 347
variable costs, 190
variables: instrumental variables, 66, 76; intervening variables (mechanisms), 169–73
variance, 89; trade-off between bias and, 138
Verba, Sidney, 11
Verdery, Ashton M., 274
viral recruitment, 116
vitamin C, 170
von Ahn , Luis, 273
voting: Affluent Worker Project study of, 82; on Brexit, 144–45; Facebook study of, 185–88; get-out-the-vote experiments, 216, 347–50; privacy and, 315, 341–43; research into, 119–21

Waksberg, Joseph, 87
walled garden approach, 313–14
Wang, Wei, 102–6, 136, 138–39
Wansink, Brian, 94
Warren, Samuel D., 337

Watkins, Susan, 262–63
Watts, Duncan: Friendsense survey by, 115, 357; MusicLab website by, 192, 196; Twitter data used by, 21
Webb, Eugene J., 71
Weld, William, 308–9
Wichita Jury Study, 334
Wickham, Hadley, 273
WikiLeaks, 351
Wikipedia, 113; bot-created edits to, 39; ethical issues in study of, 296–97; as mass collaboration, 231; privacy concerns in using, 80–81; rewards in, 150–51, 191, 202–4, 206–9
wiki surveys, 111–15
winner-take-all markets, 192, 194, 217
within-sample comparisons, 30, 33
within-subjects designs, 160
women: employment discrimination against, 352; motherhood penalty for, 153–54; study of voting by, 82
Wong-Parodi, Gabrielle, 223
wording effects, 95–96

Xbox users, 102–6, 136, 138–39
Xie, Huizhi, 201

Yang, Shihao, 49
YouGov (firm), 144–45

Zaccanelli, Scott "Boots," 270
Zevenbergen, Ben, 286–87